NASSER

NASSER

Anthony Nutting

NEW YORK
E. P. DUTTON & CO., INC.
1972

Contents

Acknowledgements

In writing this account of the life of President Nasser I have drawn almost entirely on the opinions and recollections of his principal colleagues and associates and on my own knowledge of the man from personal acquaintance from 1954 onwards. Among those of his Egyptian associates who have helped me are such men as Zacharia Mohieddin, Mahmoud Fawzi, Mohammed Hassanein Heikal and Mahmoud Riad. I have also been able to profit from the views of a number of Nasser's Arab contemporaries, whom I have known over the years, including the late King Saud, King Hussein of Jordan, Salah Bitar, former Prime Minister of Syria, President Chamoun of Lebanon, Colonel Sarraj, former head of Syria's Deuxième Bureau, Saeb Salam, Prime Minister of Lebanon, and President Bourguiba of Tunisia. In addition I have drawn on the recollections of the late President Kassem of Iraq, Israel's former Prime Minister, David Ben Gurion, Mr Eugene Black, one time President of the World Bank, the British and American Ambassadors in Egypt from 1952 onwards, and Mr Tom Little, former head of the Arab News Agency in Cairo, who kindly lent me certain personal notes and papers.

To them, and to the scores of other associates of Nasser's who helped me and whose names space does not permit me to list, I should like to express my most grateful thanks for their cooperation and assistance. To the reader I should also like to explain that, in many cases, my sources specifically asked that the views and statements which they expressed should not be attributed to them. To comply with their wishes I have therefore been obliged to refrain from either quoting them directly or adding explanatory footnotes.

Finally I must express my thanks to Lord Trevelyan and Sir Harold Beeley, former British Ambassadors in Egypt for an

ACKNOWLEDGEMENTS

important part of Nasser's reign, for their kindness in vetting the manuscript of this work and for their unfailing help and advice.

There are of course a large number of Arab personalities mentioned in the ensuing pages, some of whom may be unfamiliar to the reader. For this reason I have thought it helpful to include an abbreviated 'Who's Who' of the principal figures.

ANTHONY NUTTING

Abboud, General Ibrahim (Sudan)
b. 1900; Commander-in-Chief 1956–64; Prime Minister and Defence Minister 1958–64.

Aflaq, Michel (Syria)
b. 1910; founder 1941 and Secretary-General of the Baath party until 1965; arrested and expelled in February 1966 after Atassi/Jadid coup in Syria.

Amer, Field-Marshal Abdel Hakim (Egypt)
b. 1919; fought in Palestine War 1948; Member of Revolutionary Command Council (RCC) 1952–56; Commander-in-Chief 1953; appointed first Vice-President and Deputy Supreme Commander 1964; arrested for treason after the war with Israel June 1967; committed suicide September 1967.

Amin, Ali (Egypt)
b. 1914; senior civil servant 1936–44; founded *Akhbar al-Yom* with his brother Mustapha; exiled in London since 1966.

Amin, Mustapha (Egypt)
b. 1914; Associate Editor of *Al-Ahram* 1940–44; founded *Akhbar al-Yom* with brother Ali, 1944; arrested and sentenced to life imprisonment 1966.

Amri, General Hasan (Yemen)
Took part in rebellion against Imamate 1962; Vice-President 1963–66; Commander-in-Chief since 1967 and Prime Minister 1967–69 and August–September, 1971.

Arafat, Yasser (Palestine)
b. 1929; President of League of Palestinian students at Cairo University 1952–56; formed Al-Fatah with others 1956; launched armed resistance 1965; President of Palestine Liberation Organisa-

tion 1969; currently President and Commander-in-Chief of Palestinian Resistance Movement.

Aref, General Abdel Rahman (Iraq)
b. 1916; active in July revolution 1958; Chief of General Staff armoured corps 1958–61; assisted in overthrow of General Kassem 1963; Chief of Staff 1964 and President 1966–68 after brother, President Abdel Salam Aref, killed in air-crash; deposed by Bakr in coup 1968.

Aref, General Abdel Salam (Iraq)
b. 1921; fought in Palestine War 1948; played leading role in Kassem's coup against monarchy in 1958; Deputy Premier, until he fell out of favour with Kassem; sentenced to death for conspiracy 1959; led coup with Baath support to overthrow Kassem 1963; President 1963–66 when he was killed in an air-crash.

Assali, Sabri (Syria)
b. 1903; active in revolt against French 1925–27; Prime Minister 1945; Secretary-General of National Bloc party from 1947; Prime Minister 1954, 1955 and 1956–58; Vice-President of UAR 1958.

Atassi, Dr Nur ed-Din (Syria)
b. 1929; Interior Minister 1963; Deputy Premier 1964; President of Syria and Secretary-General of Baath party 1966–70.

Azhari, Ismail (Sudan)
b. 1900; President of National Unionist party 1952; Prime Minister 1954–56; died 1969.

Azm, Khaled (Syria)
Syrian millionaire and businessman; Prime Minister December 1948–March 1949 and December 1949–May 1950; Foreign Minister 1956–58 and instrumental in developing relations between Syria and USSR; Prime Minister 1962–63.

Badr, Imam Saif (Yemen)
b. 1920; succeeded to throne 1962 and was deposed after a few days by Sallal's rebellion; leader of royalist counter-rebellion based in Saudi-Arabia until 1970.

Badran, Shams (Egypt)
Defence Minister 1966–67; sentenced to life imprisonment for conspiracy after war with Israel June 1967.

Bagdash, Khaled (Syria)
b. 1912; joined Communist party 1935; member of parliament 1954–58; Secretary-General of Syrian Communist party 1958–66.

Bakr, General Ahmed Hassan (Iraq)
b. 1914; arrested by Kassem in 1958; Prime Minister under Aref 1963; deposed Aref's brother in coup in July 1968; President, Prime Minister and Commander-in-Chief since 1968.

Banna, Hassan (Egypt)
b. 1906; founded and led the Moslem Brotherhood 1929; assassinated in February 1949 probably on orders of King Farouk's Government.

Baydani, Dr Abdel Rahman (Yemen)
Married to sister of Anwar Sadat; Vice-President in Republican regime until he fell out of favour with Sallal in 1963; rehabilitated in 1966 and appointed Ambassador to Lebanon.

Ben Bella, Ahmed (Algeria)
b. 1919; head of secret rebel military group 1947; imprisoned by French 1949–52; escaped and directed resistance against French 1952–56 from Libya; arrested and held in France from 1956; Prime Minister 1962–65 also President from 1963; overthrown by Boumedienne and imprisoned 1965.

Bitar, Salah (Syria)
b. 1912; co-founder with Michel Aflaq of Baath party 1941; Foreign Minister 1956; Minister of State and of National Guidance of UAR 1958–59; Prime Minister of Syrian Republic several times between 1963 and 1966; expelled to Lebanon October 1966.

Boghdady, Abdel Latif (Egypt)

b. 1917; Commander of Air Force in war with Israel both 1948 and 1956; Member of RCC 1952–56; War Minister 1953–54; Vice-President and Planning Minister of UAR 1958–62 and also Minister of Treasury from 1961; member of Presidency Council 1962–64.

Boumedienne, Colonel Houari (Algeria)

b. 1927; joined resistance against French 1954; Commander of FLN based in Tunisia 1960–62; Defence Minister 1962; First Vice-President 1963–65; deposed Ben Bella in coup in 1965.

Bourguiba, Habib (Tunisia)

b. 1902; founded Neo-Destour party 1934; imprisoned by French 1934–36 and 1952–54; Prime Minister from 1955–59; President since 1957.

Chamoun, Camille (Lebanon)

b. 1900; Interior Minister 1943–44; President 1952–58; leader of National Liberal party from 1958.

Chehab, General Fuad (Lebanon)

b. 1902; Commander of Lebanese Army in 1948 Palestine War; Minister of Defence and Commander-in-Chief 1956; President 1958–64.

Farouk, King (Egypt)

b. 1920; succeeded to throne 1936 a few months before treaty was signed for British withdrawal; abdicated in favour of infant son after revolution in 1952.

Fawzi, Dr Mahmoud (Egypt)

b. 1900; career diplomat 1926–52; Foreign Minister 1952–58; Deputy Premier for Foreign Affairs 1964–67; Vice-President 1967–68; Prime Minister 1970–72; Vice-President 1972.

Feisal, King (Saudi Arabia)

b. circa 1904; brother of former King Saud; took effective control of Government 1958–60; Prime Minister and Foreign Minister 1961–64; proclaimed King 1964.

Habbash, Dr George (Palestine)
b. 1926; one of the founders of the Arab Nationalist Movement in 1948; formed Popular Front for the Liberation of Palestine guerrilla movement after the June 1967 war.

Hafiz, Major-General Amin (Syria)
b. 1911; fought in 1948 Palestine War; took part in coup of March 1963 and became Military Governor of Syria; Commander-in-Chief July 1963–64; President 1964–66; February 1966 ousted by coup led by Atassi and Jadid.

Hassouna, Abdel Khalek (Egypt)
b. 1898; career diplomat 1926–42; held various ministerial posts 1942–52; Secretary-General of Arab League since 1952.

Hatem, Abdel Kader (Egypt)
Minister of State 1961–62; Deputy Prime Minister and Minister of Culture and National Guidance 1964–66; Secretary-General of ASU since 1966; Deputy Premier for Information May 1971.

Heikal, Mohammed Hassanein (Egypt)
b. 1923; Editor in Chief of *Al-Ahram* since 1957, and considered spokesman of official Government policy; Minister of National Guidance April to October 1970; on Central Committee of ASU since 1968.

Hourani, Akram (Syria)
b. 1914; founded Arab Socialist party 1947; Minister of Defence and Agriculture 1949–50; merged with Baath party 1953; Vice-President of UAR and Minister of Justice 1958–59; resigned 1959; under house arrest 1963–65; and expelled to Lebanon 1965.

Hussein, Ahmed (Egypt)
b. 1902; Minister of Social Affairs 1948–52; Ambassador to USA 1952–54.

Hussein, Kemal ed-Din (Egypt)
b. 1921; artillery officer 1939–53; Member of RCC 1952–56; Minister of Social Affairs 1954; Minister of Education 1954–58 and

for UAR 1958–61; Minister of Local Administration and Housing 1961–64; Member of Presidency Council 1962–64.

Hussein, Ibn Talal, King (Jordan)
b. 1934; proclaimed King 1953; grandson of King Abdullah of Transjordan and great grandson of Sherif Hussein of Mecca, initiator of the Arab Revolt against the Ottoman Empire in 1916.

Ibrahim, Wing-Commander Hassan (Egypt)
b. 1917; air force officer 1939–52; Member of RCC 1952–56; Minister for Presidency and Production 1954–56; headed Economic Agency 1957–62; Vice-President 1962–64; business executive from 1966.

Jadid, Major-General Salah (Syria)
b. 1926; Chief of Staff 1963–65; member of Presidency Council 1964–65; led coup against Hafiz regime February 1966; strong man of Atassi regime and leader of left-wing faction of party 1966–70.

Jumblatt, Kemal (Lebanon)
b. 1919; founder 1949 and President of Progressive Socialist party; one of major opponents of Chamoun in 1958 civil war; Minister of Interior 1966–67 and April–June 1970.

Karami, Rashid (Lebanon)
b. 1921; opposed Chamoun in 1958; Prime Minister 1955–56, 1958–60 and 1961–64.

Kassem, General Abdel Karim (Iraq)
b. 1914; Assistant Adjutant General 1948; led revolution against monarchy 1958; Commander-in-Chief and Prime Minister 1958–63; killed 1963 during Baathist coup led by Aref.

Kouni, Mohammed Awad (Egypt)
b. 1906; career diplomat; Ambassador to USSR 1955–61; to U.K. 1961–64; to U.N. 1964–69; Minister of Tourism 1969–70.

Maher, Ali (Egypt)
b. 1883; held various ministries 1924–32; Chief of Royal Cabinet 1935–37; Prime Minister 1939–40; Prime Minister and Foreign Minister June–September 1952.

Mahgoub, Mohammed (Sudan)
b. 1908; lawyer; Umma party opposition leader 1954–56; Minister of Foreign Affairs 1956–58 and 1964–65; Prime Minister 1965–66 and 1967–69.

Malik, Charles (Lebanon)
b. 1906; Academic career 1927–45; Ambassador to USA 1953–55; Foreign Minister 1956–58.

Marei, Said (Egypt)
b. 1913; Minister of Agriculture and Agrarian Reform 1954–58 and for UAR 1958–61; Minister of Agriculture 1967–70.

Mohieddin, Khaled (Egypt)
b. 1923; cavalry officer; Member of RCC 1952–54; exiled for opposing Nasser in 1954 struggle for power; rehabilitated 1956; sometime editor of *Al-Masa* and *Akhbar el-Yom*; brother of Zacharia.

Mohieddin, Zacharia (Egypt)
b. 1918; Former director of Military Intelligence; Member of RCC 1952–56; Minister of Interior 1953–62; Vice-President 1961–68; Member of Presidency Council 1962–64; Prime Minister 1965–66; brother of Khaled.

Nabulsi, Suleimen (Jordan)
b. 1910; founder of National Socialist Bloc 1953; Prime Minister and Foreign Minister 1956–57.

Nahas, Mustapha (Egypt)
b. 1876; Chairman of Wafd party 1927–52; Prime Minister 1928, 1930, 1936–37; Prime Minister and Foreign Minister 1942–44 and 1950–January 1952; died 1965.

Neguib, General Mohammed (Egypt)
b. 1901; brigade commander in 1948 Palestine War; Chairman of RCC 1952–54; Commander-in-Chief 1952–53; Prime Minister 1952–54; President 1953 until placed under house arrest in November 1954.

Numan, Ahmed Mohammed (Yemen)
b. 1901; Leader of Free Yemen Movement; Prime Minister 1965; member of Presidency Council from 1967.

Okasha, Sarwat (Egypt)
b. 1921; fought in Palestine War 1948; Minister of National Guidance and Culture 1958–62; Chairman of National Bank 1962; Minister of Culture 1964–68 and 1970–71.

Quwaitly, Shukri (Syria)
b. 1891; founder of National Bloc party 1931; 1945 first President of Syrian Republic; deposed by coup and exiled to Egypt 1949; President of Syria 1955–58 until union with Egypt.

Riad, Mahmoud (Egypt)
b. 1917; Director of Department of Arab Affairs at Foreign Ministry; Ambassador to Syria 1954–58; Foreign Minister 1964–71.

Sabry, Ali (Egypt)
b. 1920; fought in Palestine War 1948; Minister of Presidential Affairs 1957–58 for Egypt and 1958–62 for UAR; Prime Minister 1964–65; Vice-President 1965–67; Chairman of ASU 1965–67 and 1968–69; Vice-President 1970–71.

Sadat, Anwar (Egypt)
b. 1918; infantry officer 1938–53; Member of RCC 1952–56; President of National Union 1957–61; speaker of National Assembly 1961–69; Member of Presidency Council 1962–64; Vice-President 1964–67 and 1969–70; October 1970 President on Nasser's death.

Said, Nuri (Iraq)
b. 1888; fought in Arab Revolt 1916–18; Commander-in-Chief and Defence Minister for periods from 1922–34; Prime Minister 1930–32, 1939–40, 1950–52 and 1954–57; killed in 1958 in Kassem's coup.

Salam, Saeb (Lebanon)
b. 1905; Foreign Minister 1946; Prime Minister 1952, 1953 and 1960–61 and since 1970.

Salem, Gamal (Egypt)
Air force officer; Member of RCC 1952–56; Deputy Prime Minister 1954–56; brother of Salah; d. 1968.

Salem, Salah (Egypt)
Artillery officer; Member of RCC 1952–55; Minister of National Guidance and Sudanese Affairs 1954–55; brother of Gamal; d. 1962.

Sallal, Field Marshal Abdullah (Yemen)
b. 1917; army officer; imprisoned by Imam Ahmed 1948–55; President of Revolutionary Command Council and Commander-in-Chief 1962–67.

Sarraj, Colonel Abdel Hamid (Syria)
Head of Military Intelligence 1955–58; Minister of Interior for Syrian Region of UAR 1958; Vice-President of UAR 1961; detained in October 1961 after Syria seceded from union; in exile in Egypt from May 1962.

Saud, King
b. 1901; proclaimed King 1953; deposed in favour of his brother Feisal 1964.

Shafei, Hussein (Egypt)
b. 1918; cavalry officer fought in Palestine War 1948; Member of RCC 1952–56; Minister of War and Marine 1954; Minister of Social Affairs 1954–61; Vice-President 1961–62 and 1964–67.

Shaker, Amin (Egypt)
Military career; Chef de Cabinet to President Nasser 1952–60; Minister of Tourism 1967.

Shukhairy, Ahmed (Palestine)
b. 1908; diplomat and lawyer, representative for Syria and Saudi Arabia at U.N. between 1953 and 1963; Chairman of Palestine Liberation Organisation 1964–67.

Zaghloul, Saad (Egypt)
b. circa 1860; Minister of Education 1906–10; Minister of Justice 1910–13; founded 1919 Wafd party seeking independence from British rule; 1923 Prime Minister; died 1927.

Chapter 1

The Years of Subservience

On July 23, 1952 a group of young army officers seized power in Egypt. Three days later King Farouk abdicated his throne; within eleven months the world's oldest kingdom was proclaimed its youngest republic; and Lt. Col. Gamal Abdel Nasser became the first true Egyptian to rule Egypt since the Persian conquest nearly two thousand five hundred years before. The first recorded nation-state in human history, which had come into existence around 3000 B.C., some five hundred years before even the Great Pyramids were built, now recovered its pristine national identity. The Turkish dynasty of Mohammed Ali, which had ruled Egypt since the beginning of the nineteenth century under Turkish and British tutelage, was replaced by an Egyptian army regime calling itself the Revolutionary Command Council and directed by the son of an Egyptian postman. And after two and a half thousand years of taking orders successively from Persian, Greek, Roman, Byzantine, Arab, Kurdish, Turkish, French and British pro-consuls, the people of Egypt were at long last to regain their national statehood.

Yet – as Nasser was the first to recognise in his *Philosophy of the Revolution* – the very length of this epoch of subservience had so sapped Egyptian resistance that, at the time of the revolution, the nationalist spirit was little more than a tiny ember in a heap of cold ashes. Subjected for so many centuries to foreign rule, the ordinary Egyptian had come, not only to feel, but also to accept that his country did not belong to him and that fate had relegated him in perpetuity to the status at best of a tenant, at worst of a slave, to the foreigner who occupied the throne, owned the land and ordered the life of Egypt. What is more, just as the Egyptians of old had deified their Pharaohs, so their descendants had continued down the centuries to revere and glorify their rulers irrespective of their origins or their attributes.

Nor was this spiritual degeneration entirely the result of foreign occupation and repression. Even before Egypt fell under the heel of the Persian conqueror in the sixth century B.C., such was the flaccid nature of the Egyptian people that the last great fighting Pharaoh, Rameses III, was driven to rely on foreign mercenaries to conduct his campaigns against his covetous neighbours. True, there was a moment of national resurgence in the fifth century A.D. when the Copts staged a doctrinal rebellion against the dictates of Byzantium and murdered the Byzantine patriarch on his arrival in Alexandria. But this opposition was short-lived and the Copts paid for their insubordination with another two hundred years of Byzantine repression until the birth of Islam brought a fresh conquest down upon them. And as with earlier invasions, so with the Arab armies of the Caliph pouring in from the east, the Egyptians offered little resistance as their new conquerors settled down to make Egypt part of the Arab Empire and implanted Islam as the established religion of the state and Arabic as its language.

The Egyptian people had already abdicated control over their own destiny. And it was as much against their nature to oppose the Caliph of Islam at the peak of an imperial progression, which was to spread its writ as far west as France and eastwards to the borders of China, as it was to withstand the absorption of Egypt by the Ottoman Turks at the beginning of the sixteenth century after the Arab Empire and Caliphate had finally withered and died. In all these years the descendants of Pharaonic Egypt had been little more than the spectators of change and the sufferers of its consequences. The Crusaders and the Mongols had come and seen and been finally conquered by armies advancing from Egyptian territory; but their conquerors, far from being Egyptian, were not even Arabs. Salah ed-Din, the great Saladin of the history books, who took Jerusalem from the Crusaders, was a Kurd from northern Iraq; and the Sultan Baybars, who finally drove the Crusaders out and then turned back the advancing Mongol hordes, was a Circassian, a former slave who rose to prominence by service in the army and founded the Mameluke Sultanate in Egypt which lasted until the Ottoman conquest in 1517.

From Baybars' day until Napoleon tried to cut his British enemy's links with India and the Far East, Egypt became a backwater in the stream of world politics, ruled first by independent Mameluke Sultans, succeeding one another with bewildering rapidity, at intervals frequently as brief as a few months, and from the beginning of the sixteenth century by Mameluke viceroys acting on the orders of the Ottoman Sultan in Constantinople. These six hundred years were probably Egypt's darkest age. Culture and learning came to a standstill; education was confined to memorising the Koran; irrigation canals silted up and vast areas of formerly fertile lands reverted to desert; plague and famine carried off hundreds of thousands. And along the perilously narrow green line of the Nile, which from time immemorial had been the sole artery of Egypt's existence, the fellah fought or worked with his neighbour to keep his family alive and to satisfy the extortionate demands of the tax-collector and the money-lender.

Now and then a rebellion would break out against the repressions of the regime. But each such manifestation of popular discontent was quickly and ruthlessly crushed by the prevailing Mameluke authority and the people relapsed once more into apathy and destitution. Indeed for more than three hundred and fifty years the only serious threats to the Turkish imperium in Egypt stemmed, not from any Egyptian source, but rather from among the Ottoman Sultan's own appointed henchmen. The first was staged by a Mameluke General, Ali Bey, who in the latter part of the eighteenth century proclaimed himself the autonomous ruler of Egypt. The second, and more enduring, was the work of Mohammed Ali – great-great-grandfather of King Farouk – a Turkish officer, who from commanding the Sultan's Albanian garrison proclaimed himself Pasha of Egypt and was only prevented by Britain's intervention on behalf of her Turkish ally from overthrowing the Ottoman Sultan himself and seizing his entire empire.

But among the Egyptian people there was no real sign of a national reawakening until, in the last quarter of the nineteenth century, Ahmed Arabi, an Egyptian army officer, led a revolt against the authority of the Turkish Sultan, at a time when the Ottoman Empire had begun to crumble under the onslaughts of its Balkan subjects and when its viceroy in Egypt, by recklessly overspending his resources, had mortgaged the country to his European creditors. But Arabi reckoned without the British, who were as determined to uphold the reigning Khedive as the symbol of Ottoman authority as they were to frustrate the earlier designs of his ancestor, Mohammed Ali, to establish Egypt's independence. Even before de Lesseps built the Suez Canal, Egypt provided an important 'overland' route to British India and Britain had looked to her Ottoman ally to protect this vital line of communication. Having intervened to safeguard the overland route against the menace which she saw in Mohammed Ali's ambitions, Britain could scarcely have failed to react to a nationalist revolt now that the Suez Canal had made Egypt strategically one of the most important countries in the world.

So Arabi was crushed and the British army began its seventy-year occupation of Egyptian territory. From then on London succeeded Constantinople as the source of paramount power in Egypt. Although for appearance's sake Britain still officially recognised the ultimate sovereignty of the Ottoman Sultan, when in 1914 the Turks entered World War I on Germany's side, even this pretence was swept aside and Egypt was declared to be a British Protectorate. But while Ottoman rule now effectively gave way to British, the Egyptian people were still subject to powerful Turkish influences. The dynasty of Mohammed Ali continued to occupy the throne by rights agreed in a treaty signed by Lord Palmerston in 1841, on condition that they did as their British rulers told them. The ruling class and landed aristocracy, from which the army and the civil service drew their senior staffs, were still predominantly Turkish, while the Egyptians were mostly confined to the roles of workers, peasants and small traders.

Inevitably, too, the material progress which had been introduced by Mohammed Ali and certain of his successors was largely of foreign origin, for the 'founder' of modern Egypt drew heavily on European skills and products for his modernisation programme. His great-grandson, the Khedive Ismail, proudly proclaimed that Egypt was more a part of Europe than of Africa. And the Turkish aristocracy preferred to send their sons abroad to learn French rather than the common Arabic of the Egyptian proletariat whom they despised. Even the handful of Egyptian nationalists, who were emboldened by Arabi's defiance to speak against the British occupation, had been educated in Europe or at foreign schools in Egypt and, having no contact with the Egyptian army, offered no effective challenge to the old feudal authority of the Turk or to the political and military dominion of their British overseers. Their leader, Mustapha Kamel, published his protests in an English and French language newspaper and, while he came to be revered by later generations as a founder of modern nationalism in Egypt, in his day his impact was essentially confined to the tiny minority of literate Egyptians, and was treated with contempt by the prevailing Anglo-Turkish Establishment.

It is true that British rule brought many reforms of the Ottoman system and curbed the worst excesses practised by Mohammed Ali and his descendants. At the time of the British occupation in 1882 a Liberal Government presided in London to whom it was repellent that the Egyptian fellah should have his taxes flogged out of him. But because that same Liberal Government, inspired by a deep-seated aversion to imperialist acquisitions of territory, had from the outset declared that Britain's occupation of Egypt was only a temporary matter, Lord Cromer and his proconsular successors in Cairo deliberately refrained from initiating any programme of long-term development, except where Britain's strategic interests were involved. Consequently, education and agrarian reform were neglected: learning and land ownership remained the privilege of the predominantly Turkish upper classes.

At the same time, since Cromer was soon to persuade himself that, without British occupation and direction, Egypt would dissolve into anarchy and chaos, so the administration became ever more dissociated from the people. A whole new cadre of British officers settled in to govern the country and, heedless of

London's continued assertions that the occupation was not a permanency, began to regard themselves as an established institution. For the rest, the Ministry consisted largely of Turks who did as British officialdom required of them. One of the very few Egyptians who managed to rise to political prominence at that time was Boutros Ghali, a Copt who was detested by the nationalists for his services to the British occupiers, which included signing the agreement of 1899 by which Britain imposed herself as Egypt's senior partner in the Condominium of the Sudan which had been acknowledged as Egyptian territory since the days of Mohammed Ali. In 1908 Boutros Ghali was appointed Prime Minister and, to the nationalists' fury, he shortly afterwards agreed to a British demand that, in return for certain cash benefits to the Egyptian exchequer, the Anglo-French Suez Canal Company's concession be extended for forty years beyond its terminal date in 1968.

Boutros Ghali paid for this servile deed at the hands of an assassin and the British Government thereafter prudently let the matter lapse. Encouraged by the success of the Young Turks in deposing the Ottoman Sultan Abdel Hamid a while earlier, the nationalists in Egypt had won their first victory. Yet it was only a pinprick in the armour of their overlords and, while the greatest existing imperial power continued to occupy the country, with its officers and officials commanding the army and directing the administration, the subservience of the Egyptian people seemed to be confirmed for yet another epoch. Even the constitutional reforms of Lord Kitchener which gave Egypt some semblance of representative institutions in 1913 were to be overtaken almost immediately by the restrictions demanded by the exigencies of war. In the very next year, Britain, confronted by Germany and Turkey in mortal conflict, formally declared Egypt to be a British Protectorate, deposed the reigning Khedive and appointed his more amenable and pro-British uncle to take his place. A strict censorship was introduced, the nationalists were driven underground and the Egyptian people were assigned the role of supplying the needs of their British masters in the campaign which now unfolded against Germany's Turkish ally. After twenty-four

centuries of alien rule the ordinary Egyptian was as much as ev
before a second-class citizen in his own country.

Such was the Egypt into which Gamal Abdel Nasser was born at
Alexandria on January 15, 1918, the eldest son of a post-office
worker from Assiut. His mother was a northerner from the Nile
Delta, but his father hailed from Upper Egypt, a member of the
Saidi clan who are generally taller, darker, prouder and more
prickly than their easy-going compatriots in the north.

The young Nasser had scarcely finished his primary schooling
when he began to show that it was the Saidi side of his parentage
which was going to predominate both in his physical stature and
in the formation of his character. Long before he had passed his
teens he was to become a fervent nationalist; and by copious
reading of such philosophers and writers as Voltaire, Rousseau,
and Dickens and the lives of Alexander the Great, Julius Caesar,
Napoleon and Mahatma Ghandi, he developed a remarkable
maturity of expression. In a letter to a friend written at the age of
seventeen, he said,

> Egypt ... is in a state of hopeless despair. Who can remove this
> feeling? The Egyptian Government is based on corruption and
> favours.... Who can cry halt to the imperialists? There are men in
> Egypt with dignity who do not want to be allowed to die like dogs.
> But where is ... the man to rebuild the country so that the weak and
> humiliated Egyptian people can rise again and live as free and inde-
> pendent men? Where is dignity? Where is nationalism? ... the
> nation sleeps like men in a cave. Who can awaken these miserable
> creatures who do not even know who they are?

If this was the first time Nasser dwelt on dignity as a central
theme of his nationalist thinking, it was certainly not the last. For
in almost every speech and interview which he gave after he came
to rule Egypt, he was to reiterate it as the very first principle of
Egyptian and Arab nationalism. Dignity required independence
and independence required the final and total elimination of all
foreign occupation and interference. And because it was a British
army which occupied Egyptian territory and a British High

7

Commissioner who told the so-called Government of Egypt what to do, Britain was for Nasser the principal target if not the main enemy. But, as his teenage outburst showed, he equally knew that, if the British were to be evicted, it would require new leaders to shake the Egyptian people out of their lethargy and make them want to govern themselves instead of letting somebody else do it for them as they had done since the last of the Pharaohs.

Nasser was not exaggerating the need for a new dynamic to arouse his fellow countrymen. For although the small band of nationalists who took up the torch of Mustapha Kamel had genuinely tried to bring the British Government to recognise Egypt's right to independence, they had met with little effective response from a demoralised populace. The British had refused to relax their rule in an area of such crucial importance to their imperial communications, and had been supported by the reigning Turkish monarch who was equally afraid of being swept from his throne as an alien interloper, if Egyptian nationalism ever gained control of the country. And in order to survive against these insurmountable obstacles, the nationalists had had to compromise and go on compromising until, in the middle thirties, they had become almost indistinguishable from the servile toadies of the palace clique, offering neither challenge to the occupiers of the land nor animation to the shiftless submissive masses who toiled for their alien masters.

Immediately after World War I, Saad Zaghloul, an Egyptian politician who, after serving in the Government under Cromer's tutelage, had become a leading nationalist, headed a delegation of like-minded Egyptians who requested through the British High Commissioner the right to state the case for Egypt's independence in London. But the British Government rebuffed him and when Zaghloul went on to launch a campaign of agitation in Egypt, he and his leading supporters were promptly deported to Malta. And it was not until Zaghloul accepted Britain's continued right to station troops in the country and to control legislation through British 'advisers', that the British Government were prepared, in 1922, to concede Egypt a nominal independence and to revoke the system of martial law, which had been enforced since 1914, in favour of some semblance of constitutional government. This was far from realising the real aims of the Wafd (delegation) party which took its name from the delegation who had waited on the British High Commissioner at the end of 1918. But it was enough to secure the nomination of Zaghloul as Prime Minister after the Wafd had won a decisive victory in the elections which followed in 1924.

Yet within a few months Egypt's first elected Government were to find themselves treated as the merest vassals when, following the murder in Cairo of the British General commanding the Egyptian army, Lord Allenby as the reigning High Commissioner delivered to them a humiliating ultimatum. Not only were they to render an apology and to punish the criminals, but they had also to agree within twenty-four hours to allow Britain to assume virtually sole control of the so-called Anglo-Egyptian Sudan, as well as absolute responsibility for all foreigners on Egyptian soil. Admittedly, London had telegraphed contrary instructions to the High Commissioner. But Allenby did not open the telegram until after he had delivered his ultimatum and, when Zaghloul resigned rather than accept such punitive demands, a successor was quickly found who gave way on every point.

Three years later, in 1927, Zaghloul died and was replaced as leader of the Wafd by his closest lieutenant, Mustapha Nahas, who marked his succession by boldly telling the British High Commissioner that he would not agree to the continuation of any British military presence in Egypt. But by this time the Wafd, although still the greatest vote-puller among the political parties, had lost much of its initial impetus. From the modicum of independence granted by Britain in 1922 the reigning sovereign, Fuad, now proclaimed King of Egypt, had greatly strengthened his position. By acquiring the power to dissolve Parliament and appoint Ministers by right of Egypt's new constitution, he became a factor with whom any ambitious politician had to reckon to satisfy his ambitions. Thus the nationalists were driven constantly to fight, or to compromise, on two fronts; and so long as the King and the British remained united in their resistance to nationalist aims, it mattered little that the Wafd enjoyed the support of the impotent Egyptian masses. The electors might give Zaghloul or Nahas their votes, but the King, aided and abetted by the British, could and frequently did choose others to head his Governments. Between 1922 and Nasser's revolution thirty years later, the Wafd were in office for only seven years. And in one of the rare intervals when Nahas was called upon to head the Government, he had to eat his first bold words to the British High Commissioner by signing in London in 1936 a treaty of alliance which gave Britain the right to station forces in the Suez Canal Zone for another twenty years, with an option to renew the alliance at the end of that period. Yet because the treaty officially recognised Egypt as a sovereign state and allowed Egyptian troops to return to the Sudan and because the British Government undertook to sponsor Egypt's membership of the League of Nations, the gullible Egyptian public were easily led to regard it as the dawn of a new independence. The small print by which their subservience was to be prolonged was ignored. Nahas returned home to a hero's welcome and the British garrisons in Egypt found themselves acclaimed with cheers of friendship.

Against such a reaction from the public what remained of the Wafd as a nationalist force degenerated rapidly. Its more uncompromising supporters drifted away in disgust. Others decided to come to terms with the regime. A breakaway faction, styling itself the Saadists, after the party's original founder, advocated collaboration with the new King, the sixteen-year-old Farouk who had succeeded on his father Fuad's death a few months before the 1936 treaty was signed. Nahas refused to go this far. Having had to compromise with the British over Egypt's independence, he wanted at least to be able to curb the power of the palace to override the choice of the electorate. He believed that, far from relaxing pressure on Farouk, now was the time to intensify the nationalist challenge to the young King's royal prerogative. But all that he did was to embitter relations with his royal master and bring about his own dismissal after only eighteen months in power. And as the Egyptian nationalist movement disintegrated into rival groups of ambitious office-seekers, as lacking in ideas for reform as they were in resistance to the King and the British, a new faction arose calling itself the Moslem Brotherhood and demanding in the name of Islam that Egypt and the Nile Valley be purified of all foreign occupation.

Founded in 1928 by Hassan el-Banna, a Sheikh of Al-Azhar, Cairo's thousand-year-old Islamic university, the Moslem Brotherhood had begun as a largely religious body which believed that the Islamic Caliphate should be restored with Cairo as its centre. But in the late thirties it developed into an overtly political movement preaching the inflammatory gospel of a holy war to evict the British occupation army. And when, in 1939, Egypt became once more a battleground in a war in which she had neither part nor interest, the only active and vocal nationalist resistance, apart from a handful of Communists, was to be found in this quarter. This the Brotherhood showed in 1945, when one of their number shot and killed the Saadist Prime Minister, Ahmed Maher, after he had announced that the Government intended to declare war on Germany in order to guarantee Egypt the seat at the post-war Peace Conference which she had been denied after World War I. To the Moslem Brotherhood Maher's decision was an unpardonable act of subservience. But it had not been the only one of its kind in the previous six years in which Britain had once more used Egyptian territory to wage war on her enemies and forced her will upon Egypt's King and Government. For, three years before, a far more humiliating surrender of sovereignty had been wrung from the young King and had sown the seed of nationalist revolt within the officer corps of Egypt which was to put an end to the monarchy and to Britain's occupation, and to project Gamal Abdel Nasser onto the world stage.

Chapter 2

The Free Officers' Conspiracy

Like many Egyptian students at the time, the young Nasser regarded the 1936 treaty with Britain as a betrayal of Egyptian nationalism. In the previous year he had taken part in street demonstrations demanding the evacuation of British forces and the restoration of the 1923 constitution, then undergoing one of its periods of suspension at the arbitrary dictates of the King. On one occasion British troops had fired on a group of young demonstrators, killing one of them. Whereupon Nasser, as President of the Secondary Students' Association, organised a mass protest in the square alongside the British army barracks and a march through the streets of Cairo, in the course of which two more students were killed and Nasser himself was wounded by a bullet which grazed his forehead.

In response to these and other political demonstrations, the King agreed to restore the constitution and to allow elections which duly returned Nahas and the Wafd to office after eight years of political exile. But this gain for the nationalist cause was to prove more apparent than real, when Nahas was led to sign away Egypt's independence and to accept a continued British military presence for at least another twenty years. Nasser and his fellow demonstrators were deeply shocked. The Wafd had seemed the best if not the only hope of throwing off the British yoke and introducing democracy to Egypt. But the initial defiance and dedication of the Wafd had died with Zaghloul and his successor had shown more aptitude for compromise than for challenge. Where indeed were dignity and nationalism now and where the man who could awaken the apathetic masses, 'these miserable creatures who do not even know who they are'?

Yet there was one aspect of the 1936 treaty which was to redound to Nasser's advantage and that of many other young

Egyptians of his generation. By the terms of the treaty Egypt was to be an 'ally' of Britain and, whereas formerly it had been established British policy to keep the Egyptian army as a relatively small 'police force', lest it should ever turn against Britain, it now became necessary to expand and improve it as a military machine.

Consequently, the Military Academy was thrown open to young men from the middle and lower middle classes and was no longer restricted to the sons of the landed aristocracy who, with few exceptions, had since time immemorial kept the officer corps as their own private preserve.

With the growth of industry which the needs of the British army in World War I had brought about, the Egyptian bourgeoisie had grown from a few relatively rich peasants to a class of not inconsiderable proportions. But as long as the predominantly Turkish aristocracy maintained its monopoly of the civil service and the officer corps, there had been few outlets for the sons of the middle classes, however clever they might happen to be. This had inevitably created a deep resentment and the Wafd Government were quick to seize the opportunity provided by the 1936 treaty to expand the officer corps and so to quell this element of discontent. As a result, many hundreds of young Egyptians, including Nasser's associates in the 1952 revolution who were for the most part sons of the bourgeoisie, were given a chance to enter the Military Academy which they would never have had in earlier days.

In his early youth Nasser had shown no great inclination towards a military career. From the time of his first brush with the police when he was injured after taking part in a demonstration in Alexandria at the age of fifteen, he had seemed more likely to end up in a life, or perhaps a life sentence, as a political agitator. But as he delved into his history books, reading about the bygone glories of the Arab Empire and the great statesmen of modern history, such as Bismarck, Kemal Ataturk and Winston Churchill, and comparing these men with the self-styled Egyptian nationalists who vied with each other for preferment at the hands of alien rulers, he began to believe that the army was the only force in the life of Egypt capable of liberating the country and emancipating its people.

From then on Nasser vowed to get into the Military Academy. But his first attempt ended in failure. For one thing, he was the son of a fellah and, although the officer corps might now be open to those below the aristocracy in the social scale, nobody had said that the sons of peasants, or postmen, could join. Besides, by reason of his nationalist activities, he was also on the police black list.

Bitterly disillusioned, Nasser tried the Police College. But the police did not consider him the kind of poacher who would turn gamekeeper and, when this attempt likewise ended in failure, he occupied himself for the next six months by reading law at Cairo University. Then, in March 1937, hearing that the Ministry of War were to examine a further batch of candidates for the Military Academy, he resolved to make another attempt. Before doing so, he decided, with that element of gall with which the world was soon to become familiar, to visit the Under-Secretary of State at the Ministry, General Khairi, at his house and to explain, or complain, that he had failed his first interview because, with his humble background, he did not have the right connections. It was a great gamble and Nasser could all too easily have been thrown out on his ear. But like some of the gambles he was subsequently to make, this one came off. The General turned out to be more interested in character than breeding and something about this serious and apparently dedicated young student suggested that, regardless of his background, here was a potential officer of remarkable quality. General Khairi therefore agreed to support Nasser's candidature, the black list was ignored and, at the age of nineteen, he became an officer cadet.

As at his secondary school in Cairo, Nasser spent much of his time at the Military Academy devouring the contents of the library. Not only did he continue to read volumes of military and political history, he also showed an avid interest in the problems of the Arab world outside Egypt. At the same time he studied English as a second language, if only to be able to read still more books on world history many of which were only available in

English editions. And, typically of one to whom detail was to be a life-long fetish, he would toil at the language with the aid of a dictionary and write down the meaning of every word that he had to look up.

Apart from his copious reading and study, Nasser soon proved to possess a natural talent for leadership. Towards the end of his first year at the Academy, therefore, he was put in charge of the new draft of recruits, among whom was Abdel Hakim Amer, a tall, thin young man whose uncle, General Mohammed Haidar, later became the last Commander-in-Chief before the 1952 revolution. Despite the wide difference in their social backgrounds, Amer and Nasser very soon developed a mutual friendship which was to last for nearly thirty years until it was finally severed by Amer's treachery and death. And in 1939, a year after Nasser received his first posting as an infantry subaltern at Mankabad, a few miles from his father's birthplace, he and Amer together volunteered for service in the Sudan.

Nasser was partly seeking an escape from the disagreeable atmosphere of a large army depot where he felt that his superior officers were as arrogant in their attitude towards him as they were obsequious in their treatment of the resident British Military Mission. But he also wanted to see for himself the country which Mohammed Ali and his immediate successors had annexed as part of Egypt, but which Britain, ever since the Condominium agreement of 1899, had seemingly tried to make an exclusively British sphere of influence. He had read the story of the Mahdi's rebellion in the 1880s and of Gordon's martyrdom at Khartoum. As an Egyptian nationalist, he felt no little sympathy for the Mahdists in what had been essentially a nationalist revolt against the repressions of the Khedive of Egypt – who was after all not an Egyptian but a Turk. Yet he could not but feel slighted by the continued British rejection of Egypt's claim to sole sovereignty in the Sudan which had been voiced by the first prophet of modern Egyptian nationalism, Mustapha Kamel, in protest against the Condominium and was later reaffirmed by King Fuad in the 1920s. Besides, had not Winston Churchill himself in his book *The River War*, recounting his experiences in the British conquest of the Sudan, described the Nile river system as resembling a palm-tree, with the Delta symbolising the foliage at the top and the tributaries which join the main stream on Sudanese territory representing the roots? From this graphic description had not Churchill then gone on to assert that the Sudan was 'naturally and geographically an integral part of Egypt'?

Churchill was, of course, explaining why Britain decided that the security of her position in Egypt required the conquest of the Mahdists in the Sudan. But if in the past the British had not felt secure sitting amid the branches of the palm-tree while hostile Mahdists were in possession of its roots, it was even more essential for the Egyptians to ensure in the future that the life-blood of their country, which was the Nile, would not be interfered with by a Government in Khartoum inimical to Egypt. It had, after all, been the need for some central authority to regulate the Nile flow, so as to reduce flood damage and provide for irrigation and drainage, which had brought about the union of Upper and Lower Egypt in one kingdom five thousand years ago and so created the first unified state in recorded history. And with the population now rising at ten times the rate of expansion of the fertile acreage, the need to assure a regular supply of water from behind the Sudanese border was becoming ever greater.

Egypt's claim to the Sudan was, therefore, not solely a question of kingly or national prestige. Rather was it, as many Egyptians saw things, a matter of life and death. And when Britain not only persisted in denying this claim, but also implied, by her policy of 'separate development' for the African and Nilotic peoples of the southern Sudan, that she intended to detach the country's most fertile provinces through which flowed the uppermost reaches of the Nile, Egyptian opinion became understandably alarmed. Thus to Cairo, Britain's evident desire to exclude Egyptian influence from the Sudan suggested more of a design to keep Egypt in bondage than a desire to uphold the right of the Sudan to eventual self-determination. Hence, in the minds of most Egyptian politicians, the question of Britain's withdrawal from Egypt became inseparably linked with the claim to sovereignty in the Sudan. For to their way of thinking, there was little use in evicting the occupier of Egyptian territory, while leaving him free to sever the very artery of Egypt's existence.

Meanwhile, with the outbreak of World War II, Britain was digging herself in and strengthening her hold in Egypt, principally through the agency of Sir Miles Lampson who, since the signature of the 1936 treaty, had changed his title from High Commissioner to Ambassador, yet who still conducted himself as the effective ruler of Egypt. But unlike the pliable pro-British monarch who had been installed by Britain in 1914, the new young King, only nineteen years old when the war began, wanted to be master in his own house. Just as he resisted the attempts of Nahas to curtail his prerogatives, so he resented being dictated to by the British Ambassador. Egypt might be Britain's ally under the 1936 treaty, but it was an alliance which had been largely imposed upon her. And although he broke off relations with Germany, Farouk refused to be told to declare war at least until he could be more certain that Britain would ultimately win.

Lampson's first clash with the King had come in 1937 when he had advised against the peremptory dismissal of Nahas' Government. The next and more serious dispute came in 1940 after Italy joined forces with the Germans. Lampson had long been dissatisfied with the then Prime Minister, a royal favourite called Ali Maher who was by no means a supporter of the British war effort and was suspected of pro-Italian, if not pro-German, sympathies. And when Maher jibbed at the ambassador's demand that the Italian community, including certain employees of the palace, should be expelled or interned, and Italian firms confiscated as enemy property, Lampson peremptorily told the King that he must be sacked. Prompted by the knowledge that Lampson's own wife was Italian and by protests from the palace clique that, if their Italians had to go, so should the ambassador's, Farouk objected angrily. But in due course he gave way, appointed a successor satisfactory to Britain and, when the successor died a few months later, nominated his uncle by marriage, Hussein Sirry, who was even more pro-British than his predecessor.

For the next year relations between the King and the ambassador, sullen though they remained, were unmarked by any further crisis. But during this interval Britain's situation in the Middle East came under severe threat. The earlier victories against the Italians in Libya had turned into defeat and Germany's Marshal Rommel was advancing eastwards into Egypt. Moreover, as if to trap Britain's Middle East forces in a pincer movement, a pro-German coup d'état took place in Iraq and, with France defeated and unable to resist the encroachments of the enemy at home or in her overseas territories, German air forces were taking over French airfields in Syria.

As a gesture of solidarity at this time of crisis for their British ally, Hussein Sirry's Government elected in January 1942, without consulting the King who was currently out of Cairo, to break off diplomatic relations with the puppet Government of Vichy France. Farouk was incensed and demanded the resignation of his Foreign Minister. Sirry, supported by Lampson, at first refused. But rather than continue in office without the King's support, he resigned on February 1. Lampson, having made up his mind that the next Prime Minister should be Nahas, co-author of the 1936 treaty and an arch-enemy of Farouk, hastened to the palace to make his 'recommendation'. Somewhat surprisingly, the King promptly replied that he had himself decided to summon Nahas, though as head of an all-party and not a purely Wafdist Government. But when Nahas, supported by the ambassador, told the King on February 3 that a coalition would not work, Lampson sent a message to the palace saying that the Wafd leader should be asked to form his own Government. Then, when no reply had been received on the following morning, after a meeting with the British Commanders-in-Chief, an ultimatum was sent to Farouk saying that, unless Nahas had been asked to form a Government by six o'clock that evening, he would have either to abdicate his throne or be deposed. Meanwhile an Act of Abdication was drawn up by Lampson's staff in readiness for a negative response.

A few hours later the reply came stating that, on the advice of the Egyptian political leaders, including Nahas himself, the King could not agree to these demands which were an infringement of the 1936 treaty. Whereupon Lampson drove to the palace with an escort of British tanks and, storming into the royal apartments while the tanks lingered ominously in the court-yard, handed to Farouk the Act of Abdication and repeated the terms of his ultimatum. The King's immediate reaction was to sign the Act rather than submit to the ambassador's demands. But, on the urgings of his closest advisers, he capitulated and agreed to summon Nahas without further delay. What is more, in the following year, when Farouk wanted to dismiss the Wafd leader after charges of corruption had been made against him, the ambassador threatened a similar show-down, although this time against the advice of his Commanders-in-Chief. And it was not until the autumn of 1944, when Lampson briefly absented himself on leave in South Africa, that the King was finally able to divest himself of the Prime Minister who had been so high-handedly thrust upon him.

Desperate situations frequently call for desperate measures and there was no doubt that in the winter of 1941-2 the British in Egypt were facing a desperate situation, with the Germans advancing in the western desert and threatening to encircle them through Syria and Iraq. But Lampson's arrogant display, while it served the needs of the moment, was to have the most damaging repercussions imaginable for all concerned. Not only did it create in Farouk an implacable hostility towards Britain; it also served greatly to alienate him from his own people who had hitherto revered him as their anointed King, but who now held him in contempt for having bought his throne at the price of an abject surrender. Also, Lampson's action gravely undermined the Wafd, who were regarded as puppets of the British and whose more militant members henceforth threw in their lot with the Moslem Brotherhood. Most significant of all, it provoked a group of young army officers, led by Nasser, to band together in a conspiracy aimed at ridding Egypt of British occupation and of all the servile elements that kept the country in a state of subservience.

General Mohammed Neguib, who was to be the figure-head leader of the 1952 revolution, immediately sent a letter to the King saying 'I am ashamed to wear my uniform . . . and request permission to resign.' But for Nasser this ultimate insult called for a more positive reaction. All the pent-up indignation of his adolescent nationalism now congealed in a relentless determination to rid Egypt of her British masters. Writing from the Sudan to a friend, he described how the news of Lampson's ultimatum and Farouk's submission had struck him and his fellow officers. 'When your letter first arrived,' he said, 'I almost exploded with rage. . . . As for the army, it has been thoroughly shaken. Until now the officers only talked of how to enjoy themselves; now they are speaking of sacrificing their lives for their honour. . . . It has taught them that there is something called dignity which has to be defended.' And when, in September 1942, he returned to Egypt on promotion to captain, he began to plan for the defence of that national dignity by which he set such store.

Nasser's movement was not the first attempt to organise underground activities within the army during this period of time. For the first three years of World War II, an Egyptian General, Aziz al-Masry, had been actively engaged in disseminating propaganda among his fellow officers on behalf of the Germans, not so much out of any particular fondness for Germany as from a belief that only the kind of power that Hitler represented could drive the British out of Egypt. As the old Arab axiom says, 'the enemy of my enemy is my friend'; and Britain was 'my enemy' for every Egyptian nationalist from the Moslem Brotherhood to the university students who proclaimed in the streets of Cairo, 'We are Rommel's soldiers.' Moreover, General Masry's claim that Germany had promised to grant Egypt independence if the British were defeated made her seem doubly the friend of those Egyptians who yearned for an end to alien domination. And when Marshal Rommel from his headquarters in Libya secretly suggested that Masry too should join him with a view to broadcasting to the Egyptian army to sabotage the British war effort, the General was more than ready to respond. But the British intelligence services were informed of his plans and when he tried to fly to Libya he was arrested and interned by the security authorities. Within the year, Field Marshal Montgomery not only stemmed Rommel's advance, but was chasing him back to Libya whence he had come. And when in May 1943 the British and allied forces drove the Germans out of North Africa altogether, Masry's underground movement abandoned its activities.

Also involved in the conspiracy with the German army was a young officer called Anwar Sadat who, like Nasser, hailed from peasant stock and who was to become one of the leaders of the 1952 revolution and, when Nasser died eighteen years afterwards, succeeded him as President of Egypt. In the early years of World War II, Sadat had taken upon himself the task of organising a nationalist movement among the younger members of the Egyptian officer corps and it was he who had established the initial contacts between General Masry and Marshal Rommel. But, like his ill-fated superior, Sadat had been apprehended and interned and, although he finally managed to escape from his prison camp some two years later, he was obliged to go into hiding, disguising himself as a garage mechanic. Nor was he able to return to the army until the necessary amnesty was proclaimed following the conclusion of the war.

Thus, when Captain Nasser returned from the Sudan in 1942, he found the nationalist movement within the army in a ferment of indignation over the British Ambassador's high-handed treatment of the King, but largely lacking in leadership or sense of pirection. And when, a few months later, he was posted as an instructor at the Military Academy, he quickly began to make contacts with like-minded young officers and to take over the leadership, vacated by Masry and Sadat, of what came to be called the Free Officers' movement.

In due course, this movement was to develop into a revolutionary conspiracy, aimed at the overthrow of Farouk and all his confederates. But at the outset, Nasser's aims and ambitions were strictly limited to the eviction of the British. Far from being directed against the throne, his initial object was, so he subsequently told me, to try to put some stuffing into the King and, by creating a militant opposition to British imperialism within the army, to strengthen Farouk's resistance to further encroachments on Egypt's sovereignty. Neither Nasser nor any of his fellow conspirators had any love for the King as a man, still less for the corrupt palace clique which, as his relations deteriorated with the

British and the Wafd, had come to exercise an increasingly malign influence on their patron. But Farouk was, for better or worse, the symbol of Egypt's nationhood, even though not himself an Egyptian; and if he could be prodded into working for the liberation of the country from foreign occupation and interference, then it was the army's duty to support him. Besides, such tactics would, it was hoped, narrow the front on which the Free Officers would have to fight and gain adherents from those monarchist elements in the army and outside it who actively favoured the King and wanted him to be the real master of Egypt and not a mere vassal of the British.

With these limited objectives in mind, Nasser began the long, laborious process of building up the Free Officers' movement, while Farouk, after getting rid of Nahas and the Wafd, turned to the more malleable Saadists to run his Government. But while Nasser worked quietly behind the scenes, other groups, notably the Moslem Brotherhood, began openly to challenge the regime. Nahas and his henchmen also took up the nationalist cry, if only to refute the accusations of subservience to imperialism which had been levelled at them for their service to the British war effort. After the murder of Ahmed Maher in 1945, the Wafd presented to the British Ambassador a memorandum demanding the evacuation of British forces and recognition of Egypt's claim to sovereignty in the Sudan. And as anti-British riots occurred with increasing frequency and violence, the new Saadist Prime Minister, Fahmy Nokrashy, bowed to popular clamour, endorsed the Wafd's demands as Government policy and asked Britain to negotiate accordingly a revision of the 1936 treaty.

But Nokrashy was not destined to see this matter through. For following violent demonstrations in Alexandria in 1946, Lampson told Farouk in a farewell audience that his Prime Minister was clearly unable to keep order and should be replaced. Whereupon the King promptly summoned Ismail Sidky, a so-called 'strong man' who, though he had shared in Zaghloul's banishment to Malta in 1919, had later served King Fuad during those lengthy intervals when the constitution had been suspended to exclude the popular choice of the electorate. But while the new Government managed to restore some semblance of order, there was no way of quelling the nationalists' demands for Britain's withdrawal.

Sidky was therefore obliged to follow up his predecessor's initiative with a visit to London where, accompanied by his Foreign Minister, Ibrahim Abdel Hadi, he negotiated with Ernest Bevin, Britain's Foreign Secretary, a draft treaty designed to resolve Anglo-Egyptian differences. This document, known thereafter as the Bevin-Sidky Protocol, provided for the withdrawal by September 1949 of all British forces, then numbering as a legacy of the war some 80,000 men, or eight times the number permitted by the 1936 treaty. In return, the Egyptian Government agreed to a joint Defence Board to furnish consultation between Britain and Egypt in the event of an attack on Egypt or any neighbouring country.

Had Sidky been able or willing to negotiate solely about Britain's withdrawal from Egypt, all might have been well and much of the bitterness which was to poison Anglo-Egyptian relations for almost all of the next eight years could have been avoided. But from Farouk downwards the demand was as the Wafd had framed it – evacuation plus recognition of Egyptian sovereignty in the Sudan. Sidky could not, therefore, rest content with an agreement on the withdrawal of British forces alone. But although he extracted from Bevin a formula on the Sudan which, in its opening passage, stated that the two Governments would act 'within the framework of the unity of Sudan and Egypt under the common crown of Egypt', he equally had to concede that the 1899 Condominium should continue in force until both Britain and Egypt agreed on self-determination for the Sudanese people. Yet when he returned to Cairo, Sidky glossed over this crucial concession and proudly informed his eager listeners that, in addition to securing Britain's evacuation by 1949, he had won her agreement, for the first time ever, that the unity of the Nile Valley should be under the Egyptian crown. Rioting immediately broke out in Khartoum and Britain, to reassure her Sudanese charges, felt obliged to issue indignant rebuttals. The draft treaty was torn up, Sidky resigned and Nokrashy resumed the premiership.

Deprived of the fruits of Sidky's negotiations, Egypt now appealed to the United Nations Security Council. But her request that British forces should evacuate both Egyptian and Sudanese territory found little support among the powers. President Truman was unsympathetic to Egypt because of her opposition to the creation of a Jewish state in Palestine; Russia had no use for an Egyptian monarchy seeking to impose its rule upon the Sudan; France was smarting over the loss of Syria and Lebanon to the forces of Arab nationalism; and Britain was bound to favour the Sudan against Egypt. The Moslem Brotherhood, the Wafd, the students and trades unionists might protest. But all that the Egyptian plaintiffs could achieve was to have their request 'left on the agenda' of the Security Council.

Aside from the fact that Britain meanwhile deemed it politic to remove her forces from Cairo and the Nile Delta and to concentrate them in the Canal Zone, nothing had changed and, more than two years after the end of World War II, Egypt seemed no nearer to achieving real independence. Then in May 1948 came the explosion in Palestine that was to transform the situation in the Middle East, to turn the Free Officers' movement irrevocably against the King and to add a new dimension of pan-Arabism to the thinking of Nasser and his fellow nationalists.

Unlike such Middle Eastern countries as Syria, which had housed the Caliph's capital in the heyday of the Arab Empire and, in the nineteenth century, experienced that reawakening of Arab concepts which became crystallised in the Arab Revolt against the Turks in 1916, Egypt had up to this point in time held herself aloof from the Arab world as such. Indeed, Egypt's reawakening at the hands of Mohammed Ali, far from seeking its inspiration from Arab sources, had been essentially a drive to import and imitate European methods. Instead of reviving Arab culture and the Arabic language from the anaesthesia of three centuries of Ottoman rule, as the Syrians and Lebanese did from 1850 onwards, the educated Egyptian had taken a pride in a knowledge of European languages and customs. While he regarded the Arabs' contribution to Egyptian history with less resentment than that of any other conqueror of his native soil, the fact that the language of the people was Arabic, and the established religion Islam, kindled in him little sense of affinity with the Arab world beyond Egypt's borders. After all, the Turks were Moslems, but he had not felt any more liking for Turkish rule on that account.

Thus when, after the defeat of the Ottoman Empire in World War I, Britain broke her pledges of independence to the Arabs who had fought with her and divided up the Arab world between herself and France as so many spoils of war, Egypt was largely deaf to the cries for help and sympathy which went out from Iraq, Syria, Lebanon and Palestine. The Egyptians had their own problems to solve and if the Arabs now found that they too had exchanged Turkish for British or French rule, there was nothing that Egypt could do to help. When the Palestinians came to Cairo to enlist support against the immigration of large numbers of European Jews into their homeland, which the British mandatory authorities were encouraging in fulfilment of the Balfour Declaration's pledge to make Palestine a 'national home' for the Jews, Zaghloul bluntly told them to go back and make their own peace with the new Jewish settlers. Had not the British Government assured them that the Jewish national home would not become a national state and that the civil and religious rights of the 92 per cent Arab majority would be safeguarded? Were not Jew and Arab after all descended from the same Semitic stock and had Arabs not lived for centuries in harmony with Jews, whether native-born or seeking refuge from the Spanish Inquisition and the pogroms of Tsarist Russia?

The fact that such comparisons could not be applied in Palestine soon became evident when, following the rise of Hitler in Nazi Germany, the Jewish proportion of the population rose from 8 to 30 per cent. And with the British Government seemingly unable to resist the determination of the World Zionist movement to create a Jewish state in Palestine, the Arabs, led by the Grand Mufti of Jerusalem, resorted to armed rebellion against the British mandatory power and the Jewish usurpers of their homeland. But still the Egyptians looked the other way, too involved with their own conflicts to spare any real concern for the injustice that was being perpetrated upon the Palestinians. True, at the end of

World War II, Farouk and his Government helped to inaugurate the League of Arab States with its centre in Cairo and an Egyptian as its Secretary-General. But their purpose in so doing was more to prevent a rival design for an Arab Fertile Crescent, comprising Iraq, Syria, Lebanon and Palestine, which would have shifted the centre of gravity in the Middle East from Cairo to Baghdad, than it was to acknowledge any Egyptian obligation to the Arabs in Palestine or anywhere else.

Yet, in fact the days of Egypt's isolation were already numbered, regardless of how the Egyptians might feel towards the Arab world. For, with the end of World War II, the survivors of the Nazi gas chambers in Europe had turned the flow of Jewish migrants into Palestine into a flood totally beyond the capacity of a war-exhausted Britain to control. The Zionists seized their chance to realise their ambitions for a Jewish state. The Jewish underground army, together with the more militant Stern Gang, turned on the British authorities in an all-out effort to enforce their compliance. Britain handed back her League of Nations mandate to the United Nations as the League's successor. And in November 1947, the U.N. General Assembly, by a majority of thirty-three votes to thirteen, agreed to partition Palestine into separate Jewish and Arab states.

This betrayal of the promises made to the Palestinians at the time of the Balfour Declaration was hard enough for the Arabs to swallow. The Arab League protested vigorously both in and outside the United Nations, and throughout the Arab world the Moslem Brotherhood inveighed against the decision to establish an infidel sectarian state in Palestine. But then, on top of this, as the Israeli leader Ygal Allon put it in his book *Ha Sepher Ha Palmach*, the Zionist authorities set to work to 'cleanse' of their Arab inhabitants those areas which the U.N. had awarded to the Jewish state. Aided by the Stern Gang, they not only told the Arabs to leave such areas and threatened dire retribution to any who stayed behind, but in one particular case they gave substance to their warnings by massacring the entire population of the Arab village of Deir Yassin.

Many Israelis recoiled in horror at this atrocity. But the damage was done. As 300,000 terror-stricken Arabs left their homes in what was to become the state of Israel to seek safety in neighbouring Arab territory, the Arab League vowed vengeance for the evicted Palestinians. And on May 15, 1948, when with the departure of the last British soldier from Palestine the Israeli state formally came into being, the armies of Egypt, Transjordan, Iraq, Syria and Lebanon marched across their frontiers to restore the land which had been taken from the Arab population.

Nokrashy was opposed to Egypt taking part in the fighting, believing with a number of senior officers that the army was not properly trained or equipped for the task. All that Egypt could put in the field was a division of about 10,000 men. But by this time there was no holding the Moslem Brotherhood; and the King, seeking to retrieve some of his lost prestige and popularity by a display of heroics, overruled his more cautious Prime Minister and joined the holy war.

In the early stages the battle went well for the Arab armies. The Egyptian forces quickly made contact with the Arab Legion of Transjordan under its British commander, General John Glubb, and advanced to within twenty miles of the Israeli capital at Tel Aviv. But their progress was not adequately consolidated, Israeli forces in their rear were not rounded up, much of their equipment proved obsolete and defective and, apart from the Arab Legion, there was little, if any, coordination with the other Arab armies. After a few weeks of fighting, a truce was called by the U.N. Security Council which helped Israel to stock up with arms from Czechoslovakia, while the Arabs' western suppliers felt obliged by the terms of the cease-fire to deny such aid to their clients. And so, when the fighting was resumed in July, the Israelis regained the initiative never to lose it again. By the beginning of 1949 the Arab armies had been driven, not only from all Israeli territory, but also from much of the area awarded to the Arab state under the U.N. partition plan. More tragic still, as the Israelis extended their 'cleansing' operations into these conquered territories, the numbers of the evicted Palestinians swelled to nearly three quarters of a million. And when Egypt and her allies finally decided to seek an armistice, only a few pockets of resistance stood between the victorious Israelis and the conquest of all of Palestine. One of these was in the Old City of Jerusalem which was held by the Arab Legion, another was at Falluja in the south where an Egyptian brigade was refusing to surrender although surrounded by enemy forces and with no hope of relief.

Nasser was among the resisters at Falluja and, as he later wrote in his *Philosophy of the Revolution*, his experience in this valiant but forlorn stand had a profound influence on his thinking. From the outset he had been in two minds about Egypt joining in the war. The soldier in him said that the army was not prepared for it. Yet from his contacts with the Moslem Brotherhood he equally felt that Egypt could not honourably stand aloof while others fought to resist this alien invasion of the Arab heartland. So he flung himself into the battle and, although wounded early in the campaign by a bullet splinter in the stomach, he insisted on returning to the front after a brief spell in hospital in Cairo. By October 1948 he was shut up in the Falluja pocket with his brigade in danger of being completely overrun. And it was largely thanks to a fierce counter-attack led by him that the enemy's pressure was relaxed sufficiently to enable the defenders to hold out until the armistice between Egypt and Israel was signed in the following February.

Nasser returned to Egypt to be greeted as one of the heroes of the campaign. But to him the compliments were at best bitter-sweet. For while he in no way blamed the Egyptian soldier for the defeat which had been inflicted on him, the talk of heroism at Falluja seemed little more than an attempt to gloss over the humiliations which had been heaped upon Egypt. Like the communiques which spoke of advances in areas where he knew that the army was in full retreat, such deceptions disgusted him. But most of all, he was sickened by the evidence which the Palestine war had revealed of incompetence in the High Command and corruption in those departments responsible for supplying medical equipment, which was hopelessly inadequate, and weapons, such as Mauser rifles made in 1912 or grenades, which were frequently more dangerous to the user than to the enemy. And as he brooded on the rottenness of Egyptian authority, he came to the irrevocable decision that, in addition to evicting the British, the Free Officers had to dedicate themselves to overthrowing, or at least radically reforming, the entire system of government in Egypt. How else could they change a regime which had, as he put it, 'thrust us treacherously into a battle for which we were not ready, our lives the playthings of greed, conspiracy and lust, which left us weaponless under fire'?

Nor was this revolutionary conversion the only change which the Palestine war wrought on Nasser's thinking. For as he pondered in the slit-trenches of Falluja upon the lack of coordination between the armies of the Arab alliance, he began to realise that what had happened in Palestine could not be divorced from what was happening in Egypt and that only by uniting their efforts would the Arabs ever be able to defend themselves. So long as they remained a collection of uncoordinated individual nations, so long would they play into the hands of the 'imperialists' and be picked off one by one by any power seeking to impose its will upon them. However few Egyptians might regard themselves as Arabs, the fact remained that, ever since the Arab conquest, Egypt had been associated and assimilated more with the East than with the West; and as the advent of Israel had shown, she now had no alternative but to link arms with those with whom she shared a common language in mutual defence against this and every other alien incursion. From now on, therefore, Nasser became a pan-Arabist, dedicated to the proposition that Arab unity alone could give Egypt and the other Arab states the strength necessary to assure their security in a threatening world.

Meanwhile the Moslem Brotherhood were exploiting the humiliation of the Palestine débâcle to the full in pursuance of their campaign against the established order in Egypt. Violence erupted once again in Cairo and other cities and, when Nokrashy tried to suppress the movement by official decree, he was speedily assassinated. Vengeance followed a few weeks later when the Brotherhood's own leader, Hassan el-Banna, was also murdered, almost certainly on the orders of Ibrahim Abdel Hadi who succeeded Nokrashy as Prime Minister and who put away literally thousands of Moslem Brothers in detention camps. But while the movement was undoubtedly damaged by these repressions, its influence could not be so easily broken. Farouk, now more disliked than ever for having divorced his popular Queen Farida, sensed the way opinion was running and decided to lead the nationalist hunt himself. Abdel Hadi was summarily dismissed and elections were held in January 1950 which brought Nahas and the now vociferously nationalist Wafdists back into office, as everybody including the King knew would happen.

But neither Farouk nor Nahas were equipped for the role they were to play. Both had a vested interest in keeping things as they were. The palace clique, a polyglot collection of scoundrels who even down to the royal chauffeur swaggered under the titles of Pasha and Bey, had become a byword for corruption and, protected by Farouk's patronage, had amassed huge fortunes by every kind of dishonest and unpatriotic dealing, as had the King himself. True, Nahas, in response to demands from the army, went through the motions of ordering an investigation into the supply of faulty and obsolete weapons in the Palestine war. But the inquiries were discontinued directly they began to show that Farouk, his relatives and his advisers had all helped themselves to government funds which had been allocated for the purchase of more modern equipment. As for the Wafd, they were scarcely less tainted with corruption. One example was Nahas' own young wife, who was involved in rigging the Alexandria Cotton Exchange with the help of her husband's colleagues, one of whom – Fuad Serag ed-Din – was her close friend. Besides, the Wafd was the party of the land-owners and had nothing to gain and much to lose by any changes such as land reform, which could only reduce their revenues and emancipate their tenants who had for so long voted subserviently for Wafdist candidates for fear of eviction if they did otherwise.

Nor was Farouk any more effective as the self-appointed champion of Egyptian nationalism, being more concerned to keep his own throne than to get rid of the British occupation. Nevertheless, on his return to the premiership, Nahas renewed the demand for the total withdrawal of British forces and for recognition of Egypt's claims to the Sudan. Then, as the economic situation began to deteriorate when the artificial cotton boom caused by the Korean war came to an end, he tried to win popularity by releasing the Moslem Brotherhood and setting them to work under their new leader, Hassan el-Hodeiby, to mount a guerrilla campaign against the British bases in the Canal Zone. And in October 1951, after intermittent discussions with London had failed to achieve any progress towards a British withdrawal, he announced in Parliament the abrogation of the 1936 treaty and the 1899 Condominium agreement and the proclamation of Farouk as King of Egypt and the Sudan.

Britain inevitably refused to recognise Egypt's right unilaterally to abrogate these two treaties while they were still in force. Moreover, five days after Nahas' pronouncement, as if nothing had happened, she and her NATO allies, the United States, France and Turkey, presented in Cairo a proposal for a Middle East defence organisation which made it plain that British evacuation would depend on Egypt's acceptance of this new multilateral alliance. Nahas, equally inevitably, rejected the proposal and mustered his forces for the siege which now began against Britain's Canal Zone bases with the withdrawal of Egyptian labour and supplies.

But the British forces were not to be so easily removed, especially with Winston Churchill back in power as Britain's Prime Minister. In December they hit back at their attackers by destroying a village from which saboteurs were operating against their water supplies. The Egyptian Ambassador was recalled from London as a mark of protest. But in January 1952 British forces struck again, this time taking prisoner the auxiliary police at Tel el-Kebir who, on orders from Serag ed-Din, the Minister of the Interior, were supporting the guerrilla campaign. Then a few days later, they tried to do the same thing in Ismailia. But this time the police refused to surrender their post and fought their attackers until, with forty-three dead, seventy-two wounded and their ammunition exhausted, they were forced to give in.

Immediately the Government promised a rupture with Britain and, for good measure, even talked of concluding a treaty of friendship with Russia. But the Government were no longer in control of the people's emotions. The wind sown by Farouk and Nahas now blew itself into a hurricane of popular fury. Not only was every Egyptian incensed against the British; there was also a widespread feeling that once again Egypt was being led unprepared into battle against superior forces by leaders whose patriotism was a mere pretence to hide their selfish search for preferment. Fired by the Moslem Brotherhood and by left-wing militants proclaiming that the time for diplomatic gestures was long past, the Cairo populace exploded when the news of the Ismailia incident was broadcast. Beginning with the burning of such haunts of British officialdom as the Turf Club and Shepheards Hotel, the riots finally ended that same evening with some seventy deaths, including nine Britishers, and the destruction of almost every bar, cinema and restaurant in the centre of Cairo, as places where the hated Pashas and their ilk foregathered with their British patrons.

Whether or not the Moslem Brotherhood and their associates enjoyed any official connivance in starting the riots may never be known. There are those who believe that Farouk, having once again tired of the Wafd and having formed a particular dislike for Serag ed-Din, deliberately encouraged the burning of Cairo in order to discredit the Government, and in particular the Minister of the Interior, and so to dismiss them from office. Others have held that Serag ed-Din instigated the riots to discredit the King. But, whoever was responsible, Farouk had the last word. No sooner had Nahas declared martial law with himself as Military Governor than he was sacked and Ali Maher appointed in his place.

Nasser, now a lieutenant-colonel and since 1950 the elected President of the Free Officers' Executive Committee, was serving in Cairo at the time of what came to be called the 'Black Saturday' riots and was in charge of one of the infantry units which helped to restore order. In some ways he was encouraged to see how the docile Egyptian could be stirred to militant action. Yet what he saw also made him afraid that a revolution started by leftist and Brotherhood extremists might all too easily get out of hand. And although at this point the Free Officers were not planning to strike for another two to three years, he sent an emissary to Serag ed-Din, after the Wafd Government had been dismissed, to say that, if Nahas would cooperate, he and his army associates were prepared to stage a military coup d'état to bring him and the Wafd back to power. Serag ed-Din promptly conveyed Nasser's message to his leader. But Nahas was too afraid to involve himself in such a risky operation and told Serag ed-Din that he did not even wish to know of the possibility of a coup on his behalf.

Yet, while this momentary notion had to be abandoned for lack of Wafdist cooperation, Black Saturday had brought home to Nasser and his Free Officers that the country was more ripe for revolt and the regime less well entrenched than they had thought. Besides, the existence of an underground movement within the army was well known to Farouk's secret police. Although by now he had been careful to use his code-name, Zaghloul, in all his secret activities, Nasser had himself been suspected for some time of being one of the ring-leaders. And in May 1949 he had narrowly escaped arrest by pointing out to his interrogators that he had been too busy fighting in Palestine to conduct any conspiracies. Also the Free Officers had begun to print and circulate leaflets, hand-written to start with until they could afford to buy a typewriter, indicting the regime for corruption. A particular target of this campaign was General Sirri Amer, a royal favourite and drug trafficker whom they went so far as to try, unsuccessfully, to assassinate for a long list of crimes, including personally profiting from the sale of obsolete weapons to the army in Palestine. Thus when, early in January 1952, it was reported that Farouk was about to appoint Sirri Amer to succeed General Haidar as Commander-in-Chief, the Free Officers decided to test their strength among the officer corps. Their chosen method was to nominate General Neguib as President of the Officers Club in opposition to the King's candidate. Neguib was duly elected by an overwhelming majority, no doubt in recognition of his courageous service as a brigadier in the Palestine War. The King, incensed by this defeat, immediately declared the election null and void. But the Free Officers had made their point and had shown that within the army they could command more support than Farouk.

Nor was the army's challenge the only resistance now offered to the King and his clique. As the Free Officers' propaganda began to spread, Farouk was obliged to replace Ali Maher with Neguib el-Hilali, a former Wafdist known for his particular repugnance for corruption. Hilali promptly reopened the arms enquiry, started proceedings against those suspected of graft and resumed talks with Britain about evacuation. He also tried to make General Neguib Minister of War and although this was rejected by the King, he equally refused to bow to Farouk's wish to appoint Sirri Amer to the post.

But Hilali's zeal was too much for Farouk. Afraid that he and his entourage would be all too quickly implicated in the Government's enquiries, the King lent a ready ear to those powerful interests in politics and business who shared his fears of exposure. In June, therefore, Hilali was sacked and a Government of royal favourites was formed under Hussein Sirry. But to allay the mounting disaffection of the army Sirry too suggested that Neguib be appointed as Minister of War. And after less than three weeks in office, he quarrelled bitterly with his royal patron and received his dismissal in a note written by the King's butler. Farouk was thus compelled to send again for Hilali, although this time he insisted on nominating his own choice as Minister of War.

But whoever might be appointed Prime Minister at this stage, it was too late to save the monarchy. Encouraged by the evidence of ever-increasing support within the army, Nasser and his associates had set the date of their projected coup for August 1952 and had drawn up a six-point manifesto proclaiming their aims. These were the destruction of colonialism, the elimination of feudalism, the eradication of monopolies and capitalist exploitation, the establishment of social justice, the strengthening of the army, and the institution of a stable democratic life. What is more, the Free Officers were no longer in any doubt that the achievement of these aims required the abdication of the King. Nor was this only on account of his record of corruption. For it had also become clear that Farouk's real reason for insisting that the question of Egypt's sovereignty in the Sudan be linked with Britain's evacuation was largely to prevent a successful conclusion of any negotiations with London and so to keep British troops in Egypt in the hope that they would come to his aid in the event of a revolution. His Ministers might genuinely believe that Egypt's vital interest depended on her controlling the whole of the Nile Valley. But the King was using his claim to the Sudan to maintain himself by the agency of a foreign occupation force; and this was treason.

But as the Free Officers advanced their plans for the coup, they realised that one important element was lacking. Since they themselves were totally unknown to the public, they needed a figure-head with popular appeal, who would give the revolution, when it came, an air of respectability both at home and abroad. Nasser had toyed with the idea of nominating General Sadek, an officer of character and distinction, who had commanded the Egyptian forces in Palestine. But Sadek had declined and, at the suggestion of Abdel Hakim Amer, Nasser's friend from the Military Academy, who had shared in the work of creating the Free Officers' group, it was decided that General Neguib should be chosen to fill the role of figure-head. Neguib agreed and in June he was introduced to the group of nine young officers who were to direct the coup and was elected President of the Free Officers' Executive, while Nasser stepped down to become Vice-President and Chief of Staff.

By mid-July the preparations for an August coup had been completed. Two plans were agreed. The first provided for the seizure of power and had been worked out largely by Nasser, Amer and Kemal ed-Din Hussein, an artillery major who had been a member of the Moslem Brotherhood. The second plan, which was to be put into operation only if the first should fail and which had been adopted by a majority of the Executive against Nasser's opposition, involved the assassination of Egypt's existing leaders. To ensure coordination of movement when the time came to put the first plan into operation, Nasser had included in his Executive at least two representatives of each element of the armed forces – cavalry, infantry, artillery and air force. But to protect security, the plans were known only to the Committee of Nine who were to direct the coup and a handful of other Free Officers who had been allotted key roles. Not even Nasser's wife knew what he was up to and, when the coup took place, was greatly relieved to know that his earlier nightly absences had not signified any infidelity on his part! Indeed, such had been the security precautions throughout the build-up of Nasser's movement that at no time did the actual Free Officers' membership exceed one hundred.

However, on the day that Hilali returned to office as Prime Minister, the High Command somehow got wind that an army coup was being prepared. Ahmed Abul Fath, the editor of the newspaper *Al-Misri* and a nationalist with connections in high places, told his brother-in-law, who happened to be a Free Officer named Sarwat Okasha, that the King and the authorities, having for so long and with typical Turkish disdain for all Egyptians refused to regard the Free Officers as a threat, were now about to pounce on Nasser and his associates. Nasser's reaction was immediate. The date of the coup was advanced to the very next day, July 23. And proclaiming in their last underground leaflet that 'the army's task is to win the country's independence', the Free Officers made their final dispositions for revolution.

A force was despatched to block the road from the Canal Zone in case the British troops there should try to intervene on behalf of the King. Salah Salem, an artillery major who had been in charge of underground propaganda, was sent with his brother, Gamal, an air force officer, to take care of the units in Sinai. And in Cairo, the rest of the Committee of Nine and their associates took up their appointed positions – Abdel Latif Boghdady and Hassan Ibrahim with the air force, Khaled Mohieddin and Hussein Shafei with the cavalry, Kemal ed-Din Hussein with the artillery, while Nasser and Amer looked after the infantry. Only Sadat was absent from the roll, having been out of Cairo on the night when the date of the coup was changed and having disappeared to the cinema on his return – a not inconsiderable loss since he was supposed to be in charge of signals.

But neither this nor the far more ominous fact that long after nightfall the army headquarters, the first target of the revolutionaries, was ablaze with light in evident expectation of trouble, seemed to cause Nasser the least concern. As he made his final rounds he appeared completely calm and confident. Indeed, when he found Okasha in a state of some emotion over the momentous step which they were to take together, he took him aside and said in English 'Tonight there is no room for sentiment, we must be ready for the unexpected.' And when Okasha asked why he had spoken in English, Nasser replied with a laugh that Arabic was not a suitable language to express the need for calm.

Fortunately for the Free Officers the unexpected did not happen. Although, as Nasser had been warned, the High Command did attempt a few hours before the coup to arrest the plotters, the force which they sent to do so was commanded only by a captain who promptly joined the Free Officers. As for army headquarters, the resistance was token only and by 1 a.m. the armed forces, enthusiastically backing the revolution, had taken over the radio station, the telegraph offices, police posts and Government buildings. Cairo was in the hands of Nasser and the Free Officers. The British embassy was informed that the coup was an internal matter, that the lives and property of British residents would be protected, and that there was therefore no need or justification for British military intervention. And at 7 a.m. Sadat broadcast to the Egyptian people in the name of General Neguib, the titular leader of the revolution, saying that the army had seized power in order to purge itself and the country of the 'traitors and weaklings' who had brought dishonour upon Egypt.

Chapter 3

Revolution and Reform

At this point in time Nasser and his Free Officers had no intention whatever of governing Egypt themselves. For one thing, they had neither experience nor qualifications for the task, having spent their adult years exclusively in the armed forces. For another, as Nasser freely and frequently admitted, they had no political programme other than the broad aims outlined in their six-point manifesto, from which revolutionary policy was subsequently evolved on a pragmatic day-to-day basis. Indeed, throughout the years of preparation for the revolution, they had kept themselves as a body aloof from all political associations. True, many of them, including Nasser himself for a brief while, had had individual ties with the Moslem Brotherhood and a few were connected with the Communist party. But when Hassan el-Banna had suggested that the Free Officers should merge with the Moslem Brotherhood, which would have meant vowing allegiance to him as Supreme Guide, Nasser had adamantly refused. Not only did he object to his movement being subservient to any outside body, however pure or patriotic; he positively insisted, to quote his own words, that the army's sole 'role was to be the commando vanguard' which would awaken the docile Egyptian masses and liberate them from their age-old servitude. And once the revolution had taken place, he intended that the Free Officers would hand over the Government within 'a few hours' to the 'serried ranks' of Egyptian nationalism and confine themselves to a purely super-visory role, while the necessary reforms were carried out by politicians of sound experience and patriotic dedication.

It was this conception which lay behind Nasser's idea, at the time of the Black Saturday riots, of bringing Nahas back to power by an army coup. Although he was not entirely certain that the Wafd, having become such a pale imitation of Zaghloul's once great and vigorous movement, would be able to give Egypt the new deal that was needed, there was really no one else to whom he could turn. Thus, at the moment of the revolution itself, Nasser and his associates favoured the recall of Parliament, which had been suspended by Hilali, and the establishment of a Government with Wafdist participation. But, as it happened, Nahas was currently away on a visit to Europe. And since delay was impossible, Ali Maher was invited to take over the premiership. Whereupon the Free Officers' Executive Committee became the Revolutionary Command Council, with supervisory powers and with Neguib as chairman, Nasser as vice-chairman and a membership composed of Abdel Latif Boghdady, Abdel Hakim Amer, Gamal and Salah Salem, Zacharia and Khaled Mohieddin, Anwar Sadat, Hussein Shafei, Hassan Ibrahim and Kemal ed-Din Hussein.

Although originally known as a King's man, Maher had felt badly betrayed when, less than two months after he had taken office in the wake of the Black Saturday upheaval, Farouk had brought about his downfall through a devious private intrigue with certain dissidents in the Cabinet who were opposed to Maher as Prime Minister. But apart from his disillusionment with Farouk, Maher was a consummate political manipulator, at his best when walking a political tight-rope; and his efforts to thwart Lampson in the early months of World War II marked him as an apt choice to head a Government, whose most immediately challenging task was to get rid of the British. Certainly he raised no objections to the RCC's first list of requirements, which included the restoration of the 1923 constitution, the abolition of martial law and censorship, the disbanding of the political police and release of political prisoners and, most important of all, the deposition of the King. Thus when Neguib, as titular leader of the revolution, called to inform him that the RCC wished him to take over as Prime Minister and Minister of War, Interior and Foreign Affairs, Maher readily agreed.

Meanwhile the King, who according to custom was spending the summer months in Alexandria with his Government, was using every device to save his throne. Directly word reached him that the army headquarters were surrounded by Hussein Shafei's armoured squadrons, he sent word to Neguib begging him to call off the revolt lest the British should intervene as they had done against Arabi's rebellion in 1882. When this warning, although repeated in a further telephone call from Alexandria, elicited no response, he summoned the American Ambassador, Jefferson Caffery, and asked him to tell the British Government that he urgently needed their help. And when this request was refused, after urgent consultations between London and Washington, Farouk tried to buy off Neguib with the offer of the Ministry of War and a field marshal's baton.

But, wriggle as he might, the King could not escape the inevitable. As an armoured regiment with artillery and infantry support moved into Alexandria under the command of Zacharia Mohieddin, an infantry officer who had been one of the key associates of the Committee of Nine, he bowed to the Free Officers' wishes and agreed to accept their nominee as Prime Minister. Hilali was dismissed and Maher promptly left Cairo to present the RCC's demand for Farouk's abdication. On the following day, July 25, Neguib also flew to Alexandria with half the members of the RCC to supervise arrangements, while Nasser and the rest of the Council stayed behind to keep control of the situation in Cairo. With Zacharia Mohieddin's troops surrounding the Ras el Tin palace, Ali Maher then delivered to the King an ultimatum which accused him of corruption and treachery and demanded in the name of the army, as representing the will of the people, that he abdicate in favour of his son, Prince Ahmed Fuad, and leave Egypt that same evening.

Farouk duly agreed and signed the Act of Abdication, on condition that he be allowed to leave in the royal yacht and receive a twenty-one gun royal salute and that Neguib should attend his departure. The RCC accepted the conditions, subject only to an undertaking that the yacht, which they claimed was the property of the Egyptian people, should be returned once the King had reached his destination at Naples. And on the evening of July 26 Farouk accompanied by his new wife and son and the three daughters of his first marriage, together with dozens of trunks and packing cases, left Egypt for the last time. As he took his final farewell, Neguib reminded him of his attempt to resign from the army after the Lampson incident ten years before. 'We were loyal to the throne in 1942,' he said, 'but many things have changed since then. It was you who forced us to do what we have done.' To which Farouk, greatly to Neguib's astonishment, replied 'I know; you have done what I always intended to do myself.' And with a final warning that the new regime would not find it easy to govern Egypt, the King returned Neguib's salute and gave the order to sail.

Perhaps in his early days Farouk wanted to bring about an element of dignity and reform in Egypt. But it was not to be. Instead he had allowed himself to be influenced by men steeped in corruption and treachery and had become at best a worthless playboy, at worst a traitor to the country which he misruled. So bitter were some of the Free Officers about the enormities of his reign that, when Neguib was in Alexandria, they wanted to put the King on trial for treason, if only to avenge those lives which had been lost in the Palestine war for lack of modern arms and ammunition. Gamal Salem, for instance, would have none of Neguib's plea that to kill Farouk for his crimes would not advance the aim of the revolution which should be liberation and not vengeance. And when the argument among Neguib's RCC colleagues in Alexandria reached deadlock, Salem was sent to Cairo to consult Nasser. But Nasser had had a revulsion for killing, ever since the abortive attempt to assassinate Sirri Amer when, haunted throughout the night by the agonised cries of the General's wounded chauffeur, he prayed that nobody had died. Whether done by assassination or by judicial process he believed that violence could only breed more violence. And now when confronted by Gamal Salem and others crying for vengeance, he persuaded his colleagues that they should send the King out of the country as quickly as possible and get down to the work of eradicating the corruption which he would leave behind him. 'Let us spare Farouk and send him into exile,' he told Neguib. 'History will sentence him to death.'

So the King sailed quietly away in the yacht which coincidentally bore the same name as the ship which had conveyed his grandfather, the Khedive Ismail, into an exile imposed upon him by his unsatisfied British creditors. At the last minute it was discovered that Farouk had taken with him a hoard of gold from the Bank of Egypt which some RCC members demanded should be prevented from leaving the country, if necessary by threats to bomb the yacht. But in the event he was allowed this final act of theft and continued on his way into exile without a hand being lifted in his defence or a tear being shed, except among his palace cronies.

With the King out of the way, the RCC moved swiftly to abolish such trappings of royal patronage as the titles of Pasha and Bey which, as survivals of the system of Ottoman rule, had no place in the new Egypt. The palace clique were rounded up, together with a number of other prominent figures at whom the earlier intermittent investigations into graft had pointed an accusing finger. The political parties were told to rid themselves of corrupt leaders. A purge of the armed forces was set in motion, senior officers were placed under arrest and General Haidar was dismissed as Commander-in-Chief and succeeded by Neguib. A Regency Council was established which was to exercise the prerogatives of the infant King and which consisted of Prince Abdel Moneim, a cousin of Farouk, and twenty years his senior, Colonel Rashad Mehanna, a Free Officer closely connected with the Moslem Brotherhood, who had himself organised an abortive conspiracy against the regime in 1947, and Bahieddin Barakat, a former President of the Senate. Most of the members of the RCC, including Nasser, had wanted to declare a republic upon the abdication of Farouk. But in one of the rare instances where he made his view prevail over his young colleagues, Neguib persuaded them that to preserve for a while the appearances of kingship could do no harm and would help to disarm their monarchist opponents. Moreover, with the new King not only an infant but absent from the country with his parents, the people would have time to get used to having no sovereign in their midst and so would in due course come to accept the inevitable republic.

All in all, it had been an astonishingly quiet revolution. In fact, history can have few examples of so important a coup d'état being accomplished with so much speed and so little bother or blood-shed. The total casualties were two killed and eight wounded. Far from intervening to save the King, the British army stayed put, as if rooted to their bases in the Canal Zone. And although Anthony Eden, as Britain's Foreign Secretary, deemed it neces-sary to send a senior embassy official to remind Neguib of his responsibility for British lives and property, no foreigners were molested and no anti-British demonstrations took place. Ali Maher formed a competent Cabinet, appointing as Minister of Finance Abdel Gelil el-Emary, a highly capable former Under-Secretary at the Ministry, whose promotion was widely acclaimed by all who knew how serious was Egypt's current economic situation. And the RCC settled into the routine of their super-visory role, holding joint sessions with the Cabinet to discuss political strategy and leaving, for the time being at least, the execution of policy to Maher and his men.

But this early period of quiet did not last very long. In the middle of August, a group of textile workers at Kafr el-Dawar near Alexandria seized their employer's factory. The police and army were called in to restore order and in the ensuing riot nine people, including a policeman and two soldiers, were killed and twenty-three others seriously injured. The reaction of the RCC was as swift as it was severe. The ringleaders were summarily tried, convicted and sentenced, two of them to death and twelve others to long terms of imprisonment.

Because of his aversion to capital punishment, Nasser, supported by Khaled Mohieddin, wanted the death sentences commuted. But his colleagues adamantly insisted on exemplary treatment of the rioters who, it was said, probably correctly, were Communist agitators and who had, moreover, refused to name those on whose orders they had acted. Apart from Khaled Mohieddin who had close connections with the Communist party, the RCC – includ-ing Nasser – were resolutely opposed to Communism as an alien ideology, imported and directed by alien influences and dedicated to destroying the Islamic religion and the middle classes from which, with a few exceptions such as Nasser himself, the Free

Officers' movement had been drawn. They felt that leniency towards Communist law-breakers especially at this early stage of their proceedings could only encourage tendencies to mob rule and new forms of alien intervention which would defeat the whole purpose of the army's revolution.

So, in accordance with their established procedure of majority voting, the RCC overruled their effective leader. And although on future occasions it was agreed that the rule of unanimity be applied to the review of all capital sentences, the two Kafr el-Dawar ringleaders were duly hanged. The first 'victims' of the revolution were thus not former oppressors of the people but two simple members of the proletariat who had been misled into thinking that Nasser's revolution presaged a repetition of the events of November 1917 in Russia.

But if Egypt's former Pashas and Beys drew any great comfort from the fact that, in contrast to the severity shown to these Communist agitators, they had so far only lost their titles, they were soon to find that they had underestimated the zeal with which Nasser was to pursue the initial aims of his revolution – land reform, coupled with the eviction of British troops. To Nasser these two aims were inseparably linked. For, as he saw it, the task of restoring to the ordinary Egyptian that sense of belonging to his own country, which had been crushed by so many centuries of foreign rule and occupation, could not be accomplished simply by removing British forces from Egyptian soil. That same soil had to be given to the people to work for themselves and not for greedy landlords, many of whom were not even of Egyptian stock. At this point 6 per cent of the total landowners in the country owned 65 per cent of the land. And the revolution would not be able to guarantee Egypt's future independence from foreign interference if, having forced the British to withdraw, it should leave the landlord class to thrive as before. For it was that class which had for the past hundred years been the principal supporter and agent of British tutelage, ever since the loss of raw cotton imports during the American Civil War had brought about the commercial alliance between the textile manufacturers of Britain and the plantation owners of Egypt. In years to come, a similar fear that the revolution might be threatened by the industrialist class led Nasser to embark upon a programme of nationalisation of Egyptian industries and services at first selective and later wholesale. But for the moment his attentions were centred on the first two items of the Free Officers' manifesto, the repulse of imperialism and the destruction of feudalism which to him went hand in hand.

Ali Maher was therefore requested to set in motion the necessary programme of land reform, while Nasser and his colleagues devoted themselves to the problem of procuring Britain's evacuation. Here their first thought was to obtain American support. From the days of World War II when President Roosevelt had shown a sympathy for the efforts of the Indian people to gain their independence, Nasser had nursed great hopes that the Americans would warmly support the kind of revolution which he planned for Egypt. And although, for security reasons, he had been careful not to reveal his conspiracy to any foreign embassy, he had allowed Ali Sabry, a Free Officer serving with the air intelligence department, to use his routine contacts with the American assistant Air Attaché to express the hope that, if a revolution should take place, the United States would use their good offices to prevent any intervention by British forces on behalf of the King. Moreover, through these same contacts he had learned that, early in 1952, the American Government had tried to persuade Farouk to get rid of his corrupt advisers and introduce democratic rule, which they naively hoped would help to bring about stability in the Middle East and peace between the Arabs and Israel.

Therefore, after the revolution had taken place, it came as no surprise to Nasser when Caffery, the American Ambassador, went out of his way to show his friendship with barely disguised hints that he would do his utmost to help in evicting the British, for whom he personally had little love. Moreover the Americans soon showed that they knew who was the real power behind the revolution when, in October 1952, they despatched the most experienced of the Central Intelligence Agency's men in the Middle East, Kermit Roosevelt, to Cairo to establish personal contact with

Nasser, while Caffery continued to deal with Neguib in accordance with the requirements of protocol. Nasser liked the early informality of this relationship – he and Roosevelt were soon on first-name terms – and he greatly appreciated the opportunity it gave him to maintain informal contacts with Washington through the influential head of the CIA, Allen Dulles.

As a professional soldier he could not but feel concerned by the weakness of the Egyptian army. Quite apart from the possibilities of enlisting American aid to get the British out of the Canal Zone, he therefore hoped that the United States would help Egypt by supplying modern weapons. To begin with, the signs from Washington augured well on this count. In September 1952 Nasser had an informal talk with Caffery to whom he explained the purposes of the revolution and the importance he attached to the army being provided with modern arms and equipment. He also assured the ambassador that Washington need have no fears that Egypt would use American arms to attack Israel for, as he put it, 'I do not believe in war as an instrument of policy.' Then, in the very next month, as if in response to this approach, the American Assistant Secretary for Defence, William Foster, turned up in Cairo and, after discussions with Nasser over dinner at Caffery's residence, agreed to recommend that Washington accept a list of Egypt's requirements to a total value of some $100 million dollars.

Nor was this the only encouragement for the revolution which came from across the Atlantic. In a more general sense, there were signs that the American press too welcomed the new regime in Egypt. The idea of land reform was hailed as a necessary and sensible method of countering Communist influence and propaganda, and venerable commentators such as Walter Lippman were writing in praise of the new Egypt's plans to create a system of social justice.

Equally in the RCC's initial contacts with the British there was no detectable hostility. Although more reserved in their attitude than the Americans, which in turn made for a certain aloofness on the Egyptian side, the British did not seem in the least concerned that Farouk had been kicked out. Their only comment on this score, expressed through their Chargé d'Affaires, Michael Creswell, was that they hoped that the deposition of the King would not leave a dangerous vacuum in Egypt. And, far from showing any antipathy or suggesting that they might intervene on behalf of the monarchy, the British seemed, albeit with traditional caution, to welcome the new regime as holding out a hope of settling the two issues, the Canal Zone bases and the Sudan, on which Farouk for his own special reasons had proved so intractable.

To get things moving Nasser decided that the linking of the issues, which had frustrated all negotiations since the abortive Sidky – Bevin agreement of 1947, must be abandoned and each question settled separately. More than this, he told his RCC colleagues that the claim to the unity of Egypt and the Sudan under the Egyptian crown should also be dropped. Apart from the fact that, after a decent interval had elapsed, there would anyhow be no crown of Egypt, it simply was not practical politics to expect Britain to agree to hand over the Sudanese to be governed by Cairo. Besides, the British themselves seemed likely to clear out of the Sudan in the near future. Eden had announced in Parliament that the Governor-General in Khartoum would shortly bring a self-government statute into effect. Therefore Nasser suggested that, instead of appearing more imperialist than the British by pursuing outdated claims to sovereignty, the Egyptians should recognise the right of the Sudanese people to self-government and self-determination and then work on them through their elected representatives to secure whatever influence they required in Khartoum. To insist on sovereignty was a dead-end policy, suitable only to Farouk and others who wanted no settlement involving the departure of British troops. But by coming to terms with the inevitable and conceding the Sudan's right to independence, Egypt might gain some credit and perhaps pave the way for an agreement on British evacuation.

Neguib was somewhat dismayed by this new doctrine. The son of an Egyptian who had fought under Kitchener in the conquest of the Sudan in the 1890s and the grandson of another who had fallen with Gordon when the Mahdi captured Khartoum in 1885, he had spent much of his life in the Sudan. He had been educated at Gordon College, Khartoum, and had served there as a soldier for a number of years. In his early youth he had been told by the son of that pioneer of Egyptian nationalism, Ahmed Arabi, that, as an Egyptian in the Sudan, he would never be anything more than an 'overseer for the British'. And for him it had always been a point of personal honour to see that the overseer of today should become the overlord of tomorrow. But Neguib was outvoted in the RCC and within days of Egypt declaring in favour of the Sudan's independence, the Sudanese political leaders descended on Cairo late in October 1952 to clinch an agreement whereby Egypt recognised the Sudan's right of self-determination and withdrew all previous objections to Sudanese self-government. In return, the Sudanese agreed to support an Egyptian proposal for international commissions to advise the Governor-General during the transition to independence and to supervise elections for a Sudanese Parliament, which the Egyptians deemed essential to guard against any British gerrymandering. More important still, with the exception of the staunchly independent Umma, or People's, party led by the Mahdi's son, Sayed Abdel Rahman, the Sudanese leaders agreed to combine in a single National Union party and to work for the closest possible relations with Egypt.

The British Government, knowing that they had been out-manoeuvred, raised a few irritated eyebrows and there were mutterings from right-wing Conservatives in the House of Commons that the Sudanese had shown themselves too simple and trusting of the devious Egyptians to be allowed their independence. But these clouds soon passed and, in February 1953, Britain signed with Egypt an agreement which conceded the Egyptian proposal for supervisory commissions and gave Egypt, for the first time since the Condominium of 1899, an equal say in the surveillance of Sudanese development. Shortly afterwards a statement by the British Government that the right of self-determination should allow the Sudanese to join the Common-wealth after independence gave Neguib a pretext to protest that Britain was plotting to hold onto the Sudan. And his suspicions received a further boost when he visited Khartoum a year after the agreement and found himself besieged in the Governor-

General's palace by an angry mob of Ansaris – the sectarian descendants of the Mahdi's followers who maintained an ancestral antipathy towards Egypt and who Neguib believed were in the pay of the British. But when elections were held later in the year, the Egyptian gamble seemed to have paid off. The National Unionists won an absolute majority in both Houses of Parliament and the pro-Egyptian Ismail el-Azhari became the first Prime Minister of the Sudan.

Yet while Nasser's new approach seemed to be paying immediate dividends so far as the Sudan was concerned, it was to take some time before there was any comparable progress on the issue of British evacuation. For one thing Britain, with Churchill at the helm of state, clearly wanted to retain military control in the Canal Zone. Admittedly, in response to an Egyptian offer to permit British technicians to continue to perform any essential maintenance duties in the bases, the British negotiators agreed in principle to withdraw the bulk of the 80,000 strong garrisons. But they equally insisted that the technicians who were to replace the troops should wear army uniform. Also, they maintained that any agreement should provide for Egyptian participation in a Middle East defence pact with the West, and for the reactivation of the bases and the return of British troops in the event of an attack, not only on Egypt or any other Arab state, but on Turkey and Iran as well. Nasser and his RCC colleagues resolutely rejected these terms as a demand for the continuance of a veiled occupation and a military alliance linking Egypt with NATO, such as Nahas had previously rejected in the autumn of 1951. So, once again, the negotiations reached deadlock.

Nor was this Nasser's only disappointment in the matter of the new Egypt's relations with the West. For in the autumn of 1952 it became clear that Caffery's sweet words and Foster's prompt acceptance of Egypt's arms requirements did not reflect the real intentions of the United States Government. On the contrary, it transpired that Britain, having herself refused to deliver the jet aircraft which the Egyptians needed to strengthen their puny air force, was busily intervening to stop the Americans sending arms to Egypt, while the issue of the British bases remained unresolved.

And when Ali Sabry was sent to Washington to follow up Foster's talks in Cairo, he spent some two months being shunted from one government department to another, finally to return home empty-handed, save for an offer of some small arms for internal security. Nasser was not amused when Caffery laughingly observed that Foster must have exceeded his authority after having dined too well at his house.

Still further disappointment was to follow when, in May 1953, John Foster Dulles, newly appointed Secretary of State in President Eisenhower's Cabinet, visited Cairo and, in a series of talks with Neguib, Nasser and other leading Egyptians, made it crystal clear that he expected Egypt to join the West's anti-Russian alliance. Nasser retorted that Egypt did not want to get involved in the Cold War, that she would base her own defence arrangements on the Arab League's collective security treaty and would not join any other blocs or pacts, at least until she had won her complete independence by the removal of British forces from her soil. 'How can I tell my people,' he asked, 'that I am going into a military pact in collaboration with those who are still occupying our country? For the purpose of defending our country? And against what?' He did not believe that Egypt was in danger of an attack from Russia. If there were any danger, it came from the threat of internal subversion by Communists in Egypt and that could not be prevented by signing pacts or alliances. On the contrary, such policies would only stimulate it.

But Dulles was, as nearly always, completely inelastic. From start to finish of this encounter he and Nasser never came anywhere near speaking the same language. And although on his return home Dulles did, in fact, tell all concerned that Egypt could not be expected to join any Western alliance until the British had withdrawn, it seemed to Nasser at the time that Washington had no understanding whatever of Egyptian problems. Worse still, the Americans had tamely accepted Britain's veto on supplying arms to Egypt and, with Dulles' mania for military pacts, it seemed unlikely that they would try very hard to induce Britain to modify her terms for withdrawal.

Bitterly reflecting, therefore, that the American talk about helping the underdeveloped nations was so much 'opium' to drug them into subservience, Nasser decided to abandon diplomacy in favour of more direct methods to evict the British occupation. The campaign of attrition in the Canal Zone, which had been started by the Wafd Government in 1951, was resumed. British installations were sabotaged and British soldiers shot by commando volunteers, known as 'fedayeen' from the Arabic word for sacrifice. More brutally still, an Egyptian who had worked for the British troops for many years was hanged as a traitor.

But the British only dug their toes in more firmly. And after a few months, at the beginning of 1954, Nasser had to adopt new tactics. Resorting to the carrot-and-stick method of dealing, he conceded in the interests of an early agreement that the bases could be reactivated if Turkey were attacked, while at the same time warning Sir Ralph Stevenson, Britain's Ambassador, that there would be no relaxation of the siege in the Canal Zone so long as British troops remained. But with no matching concession coming from the British side, the siege continued and Anglo-Egyptian relations remained in a state of bitter deadlock for another five months.

Frustration in these early stages was not, however, confined to the issue of Britain's withdrawal. On the home front too Nasser was to find his plans confounded as early as September 1952. Ali Maher was dragging his feet over land reform and the political parties to whom the RCC had looked for a new spirit of revolutionary dedication had proved a sad disappointment. As Nasser related in his *Philosophy of the Revolution*,

> The vanguard performed its task . . . threw out Farouk . . . and then paused, waiting for the serried ranks to come up in their sacred advance toward the great objective . . . but the masses that came were disunited. . . . Every man we questioned had nothing to recommend except to kill someone else. Every idea we listened to was nothing but an attack on some other idea. . . . We were deluged with petitions and complaints . . . (mostly) no more or less than demands for revenge, as though the revolution had taken place in order to become a weapon in the hands of hatred and vindictiveness. If anyone had

asked me in those days what I wanted most, I would have answered promptly – to hear an Egyptian speak fairly about another Egyptian.

One of the biggest disappointments was the Wafd. Nahas had returned to Egypt a few days after the coup in the belief, fostered by Nasser's offer to reinstate him after the Black Saturday riots, that the revolution had been designed to put him in power. And although Ali Maher had meanwhile been installed as Prime Minister, Nasser and Neguib spent much time discussing with Nahas and his associates the possibility of recalling Parliament with a Wafdist Government which would enable the RCC 'vanguard' to return to their barracks and concentrate on the task of building up a new army. At the same time they insisted, as a precondition of any such arrangement, that the Wafd should agree to carry out the programme of the Free Officers' six-point manifesto. But Nahas and his colleagues, contemptuously declaring that the RCC were completely ignorant of such matters, steadfastly refused to abolish feudalism for fear of undermining the whole basis of their electoral support – the landowning class and their bonded tenants. Added to this, the Wafd took no steps to purge themselves as they had been ordered to do. And to make matters worse, the RCC were to learn from tape recordings of telephone conversations between Madame Nahas, and her friend, Serag ed-Din, that she, rather than her aging husband, was now the real power in the Wafd's leadership. Petticoat government was bad enough to these young Egyptian officers, but libertine petticoat government was quite intolerable. In utter disgust therefore at the entire party system, Nasser promptly dismissed the Wafd and the other parties from his calculations, feeling as he put it, 'with sorrow and bitterness that the task of the vanguard, far from being completed, had only begun'. From now on, the belief that corruption was endemic in all political parties became an obsession with him and, as his disillusionment grew, he came to accept that the time was fast approaching when the RCC would have to take over and run the Government themselves.

The first move in this direction came in September 1952, when

Ali Maher was dismissed for insisting that under the agrarian reforms the upper limit of land-ownership should be 500, and not 200 acres, as the RCC had decided. Neguib then became Prime Minister, presiding over a non-party Cabinet consisting largely of senior civil servants, and a decree was announced which limited individual land-holdings to 200 acres, families being permitted an extra 100. The owners were to be compensated with Government bonds, bearing interest at 3 per cent and calculated at a figure ten times the rental value of the land taken, which was to be distributed to the peasants in five-acre lots and paid for by them over a thirty-year period. For the moment no attempt was to be made to attack such citadels of Egyptian capitalism as the great industrial complex ruled by the Misr companies, or the commercial empire of Ahmed Abboud, whose influence with Farouk had forestalled Hilali's efforts to expose corruption early in 1952. Thus the dispossessed landowners were free to invest in city real estate and amass new fortunes from the current boom in the construction industry. But by emancipating the fellah, the land reforms did what they were intended to do. So much so that the Wafd, seeing the very basis of their power being undermined by the liberation of the peasants from their enforced political allegiance, promptly staged a counter-offensive, attacking the RCC as a power-hungry junta who represented nobody but themselves. But a dramatic drop in the circulation of the Wafdist press soon showed that it was they who lacked popular support and, in due course, the attack petered out, leaving the Wafd to lick their wounds in angry impotence.

A few months later, in January 1953, the RCC moved to apply the coup de grâce to the old party system. Although still sitting on the sidelines and taking no formal part in the new Government, Nasser and his RCC colleagues prevailed upon Neguib to issue decrees disbanding all political parties, abolishing the 1923 constitution and declaring a three-year 'transitional' period of military government. This was followed by a proclamation that a single political congress would be formed, in place of the disbanded parties. Its name was to be the 'Liberation Rally' and among its functions it would supervise the fulfilment of the six-point manifesto, the creation of a welfare state and the strengthening of inter-Arab relations as well as cooperation with all friendly states. In the same month Nasser announced that a drive had begun to suppress the Communists and to punish those among the former party leaders who were guilty of corrupt dealings. Serag ed-Din was arrested on charges of graft, together with Prince Abbas Halim, a cousin of Farouk who was accused of misappropriating Government funds earmarked for the purchase of arms for the Palestine War. And when, nine months later, a special Revolutionary Tribunal was established under the presidency of Abdel Latif Boghdady to try all such cases, the list of those arrested was to include Nahas and his wife, Sirri Amer, Ibrahim Abdel Hadi, the former Saadist Prime Minister, and such palace lackeys as the egregious press adviser, Karim Thabet, who, so Neguib claimed, had gone so far in sycophancy as to encourage Farouk to declare himself to be a descendant of the Prophet Mohammed.

Exemplary punishments were decreed for many of these and other creatures of the Farouk era, although in most cases justice was later tempered with mercy and the offenders released on medical grounds after a few years in prison. Ibrahim Abdel Hadi received the death sentence, later commuted to life imprisonment, for his part in instigating the murder of the Moslem Brotherhood leader, Hassan el-Banna. Serag ed-Din was sentenced to fifteen years imprisonment, Sirri Amer and Karim Thabet to life and other former palace advisers received long sentences. Madame Nahas paid a heavy fine for her manipulations of the Alexandria Cotton Market and her husband was censured for condoning corruption among his party colleagues. Prince Abbas Halim received a suspended sentence, after evidence had shown that the defective arms supplied to the Egyptian forces in Palestine had, in fact, arrived too late to have materially assisted the Israelis in winning the war. About a thousand officers and officials of the armed forces and civil service were also dismissed. And when Rashad Mehanna of the Regency Council denounced the land reform as a Communist device and accused the RCC of seeking to turn Egypt into a godless republic in violation of Islamic principles, he too was arrested.

Mehanna, as a devout supporter of the Moslem Brotherhood, believed that the purpose of the revolution should have been to create a theocracy in Egypt. But, while at this stage they allowed the Brotherhood a license which was firmly denied to all other political groups, the RCC were in no mood to tolerate such deviations, especially when they were accompanied by attacks on the very fundamentals of their policy, such as agrarian reform, which Mehanna branded as pure Communism. Mehanna was therefore put on trial for plotting to overthrow the revolutionary regime. He was given the exemplary sentence of twenty-five years' imprisonment although this was very soon remitted to a mere fraction of its length on production of the customary doctor's certificate.

The defection of Mehanna as the RCC's nominee on the Regency Council brought the constitutional question to a head. This time the pressure for declaring a republic without further delay was not to be denied. On June 18, 1953, therefore, the Regency Council was disbanded, the dynasty founded by Mohammed Ali was brought to an end and the world's oldest kingdom was formally proclaimed a republic, with Neguib as President and Prime Minister. Nasser and three of his RCC associates – Abdel Hakim Amer, Abdel Latif Boghdady and Salah Salem – now decided to come off the sidelines and join the Government. Nasser was made Deputy Prime Minister. Amer, promoted to general, took over from Neguib as Commander-in-Chief of the armed forces, thus succeeding at one remove his own uncle, General Haidar. Boghdady and Salah Salem became respectively Minister of War and Minister of National Guidance and Sudanese Affairs. The 'vanguard' had abandoned the supervisory role which Nasser had originally envisaged as its sole purpose: the conduct of the revolution and what came after had passed into the hands of a dozen young officers whose inexperience in their allotted task was only equalled by their determination somehow to accomplish it.

Chapter 4

The Struggle for Power

After the Suez episode in 1956 when he had triumphed over the combined attempt of Britain and France to humiliate and destroy him, Nasser became the idol not only of Egypt, but of every Arab nationalist from Morocco to the Persian Gulf. And with the uplift which this popularity gave him, he rapidly developed into a relaxed and self-assured ruler, with paramount authority over his colleagues and popularly nicknamed the 'Rais', or ship's captain. But in the early stages of his revolution he was anything but self-assured. And although he always possessed a lively sense of humour in private conversation, by contrast with the avuncular, pipe-smoking image of his titular leader, he presented in public an austere countenance and an air of intent zealotry which did little to endear him to the leisurely Egyptian populace. He was a poor orator who bored his audiences with long speeches unrelieved by the lighter touches which the Egyptian people had come to enjoy and to expect from their political leaders. He was also easily put off by heckling, at least until the day when, confronted by a Communist who kept on interrupting him with parrot cries of 'What about Point IV', he invited his tormentor onto the platform to explain himself to the audience. Much to everyone's delight the heckler was then forced to admit that he did not know what Point IV was, because his party organisation had never told him.

In short, a year after the revolution, its real leader possessed nothing like the popularity of the man who had been selected to be the figure-head. And nobody knew this better than the figure-head himself. Moreover, Neguib was thoroughly enjoying the trappings of high political office. Although he had so far been obliged to bow to the majority decisions of the RCC on most important policy issues, he had formed his own ideas as to how the revolution should be conducted and he was determined to exploit the general approbation which he had won from the public to put these ideas into effect. For one thing, he saw himself as a constitutional ruler of Egypt and he wanted to bring about a return to parliamentary life at the earliest possible opportunity. For another, he disliked even the limited participation of the RCC in the Government which followed the proclamation of the republic. He thought that Nasser and his young colleagues were too impatient and headstrong. And while he agreed with some of their policies, such as land reform, he felt that they had been altogether too hasty and intolerant in deciding that all the old political parties, including the Wafd, were a wash-out. 'Nasser,' he wrote in a subsequent book of memoirs, 'believed with all the bravado of a man of thirty-six that we could afford to alienate every segment of Egyptian public opinion ... to achieve our goals'; whereas what was needed was for the new regime to cultivate friends from every quarter.

Indeed, as was later revealed from tape recordings of telephone conversations of leading Wafdists, Neguib was in frequent contact with Nahas prior to his arrest. And although Nahas arrogantly claimed that he was the leader of twenty million people, whereas the General was only the leader of a hundred thousand soldiers, Neguib had been only too keen to discuss with him the possibility of holding elections well before the end of the three-year transition period and to allow the Wafd full freedom of political activity meanwhile. Neguib, of course, fully shared the RCC's distrust of the Communists and kept the pre-revolution laws against Communism in force. But he disapproved of Nasser's equally implacable hostility to the Moslem Brotherhood and his sweeping condemnation of that body as a bunch of reactionaries dedicated to substituting theocracy for social justice. Although not himself a 'Brother', he prevailed upon those in the RCC who had former close ties with the Moslem Brotherhood to support him in admitting two of its members to his Cabinet.

Inevitably, such dealings created in Nasser's mind a deep suspicion that Neguib's aim was to defeat the whole purpose of the revolution by diluting and slowing it down to a point where it would finally expire for lack of momentum. Whether or not the

ptian people were ready for the revolution, the fact was that
army had created it for them. What was more, Nasser was
not satisfied with one revolution. In his view there had to be two,
a political upheaval to overthrow the tyranny of the King and
evict the foreigner who occupied the soil of Egypt, and a social
revolution to bring about justice, equality and freedom from
exploitation. Saad Zaghloul had failed in his objective because he
had concentrated only on the political revolution, and had
allowed his gains to be dissipated and finally lost in strife and
conflict between the classes which domestic tyranny and foreign
domination had then exploited in order to tighten their grip. If
Neguib got his way, these mistakes would be repeated. And as
Nasser put it, 'It was not within our power to stand on the road of
history like a traffic policeman and hold up the passage of one
revolution until the other had passed by in order to prevent a
collision. It was inevitable that we go through the two revolutions
at the same time.' There could be no use in throwing out Farouk
and a few courtiers if the politicians who had served him were left
free to reintroduce a similar system of corruption and injustice
under their own aegis. Having decided that, to insure against this,
the 'vanguard' must now govern instead of supervising government by others, Nasser was not going to let Neguib divert him
from his aim. Neither was he to be deflected by the General's
facile suggestion that 'I should run things for a few years until he
had acquired the experience necessary to succeed me.'

Indeed, even before he became Deputy Prime Minister in June
1953, Nasser had begun to intervene in administrative matters and
to deal with Ministers over Neguib's head. With his passion for
detail which had led him in pre-revolution times to count every
piastre subscribed by the Free Officers for printing leaflets and
other such activities, he could never bring himself to delegate
effectively. And as he grew to suspect that Neguib and his civilian
Ministers were actively working to frustrate the purposes of the
revolution, he became more and more convinced that he and the
RCC alone could instigate the social and economic reforms that
the Egyptian people needed so desperately.

As early as October 1952, when Kermit Roosevelt first visited him in his house, Nasser had gone out of his way to make it clear that he and not Neguib was the real leader of the revolution, and had contemptuously dismissed or completely ignored the General's every contribution to the discussions with his American guest. Nor was this attitude dictated by mere personal jealousy and ambition on his part. Neguib's nature was simply not the stuff of which revolutionaries were made. Unable to share the radical fervour of his younger colleagues, he felt more at home with the ultra-conservative Wafdists and Moslem Brothers who for their part sensed in him a friend at court and sought his support for their ploys and plots. He even told his RCC colleagues that there was no great urgency in getting the British to withdraw their troops and that setting the economy to rights was of prior importance.

Such talk was, of course, anathema to the RCC. And as the months went by and the disagreements escalated, Nasser and his associates came to overrule Neguib with increasing frequency, while the latter for his part sought to marshal the Government, where the majority was with him, against the RCC. Then, early in 1954, Nasser acting as Minister of the Interior seized upon a clash between some Liberation Rally members and a group of Moslem Brothers to disband the Brotherhood and clap Hodeiby and many other leaders of the organisation into gaol.

Such treatment might seem harsh punishment for a relatively minor affray. But the clash had come as the culmination of a long campaign of pressure by the Brotherhood to obtain a more decisive voice in government, which had on occasion included acts of violence against the army and threats against their former associates in the RCC. Nasser had become convinced that Hodeiby and his followers were out to use the revolution to further their own theocratic aims. They had even suggested that the RCC should accept their supervision for a period of ten years and they had bitterly resented the creation of the Liberation Rally as a threat to supplant them as the collective voice of the people. Not for the first or last time therefore, Nasser reacted violently against coercion and blackmail. But his action brought his differences with Neguib to a crisis and, as the Brotherhood appealed to the General for a reprieve, relations between the two men reached breaking point.

Nasser's first impulse was to urge his RCC colleagues to resign with him en bloc, rather than force Neguib into a resignation which might all too easily make him appear a martyr and the victim of an over-ambitious military junta. But on this occasion, he was overruled on the grounds that the RCC were not sufficiently popular to risk a course of action which might simply result in their returning to their barracks with the public crying 'good riddance'. Consequently it was Neguib who was forced to make the first move. And on February 23 he wrote in a letter of resignation that 'for reasons which you will excuse me for not mentioning here, I can no longer carry out my duties in the manner that I consider best calculated to serve the national interests. I must therefore ask you to accept my resignation from all the posts that I presently occupy . . .'

Only two members of the RCC were opposed to accepting Neguib's offer to resign. One was Gamal Salem who had never got on too well with Nasser. The other was Khaled Mohieddin who, as events were to show, was playing a highly individual game of political chess, designed to diminish the influence of the army in the councils of the nation in favour of the Left. The rest were only too ready to put an end to the mounting differences between Neguib and Nasser which were threatening to disrupt the revolution. Joyfully they proclaimed Nasser as Prime Minister and Chairman of the RCC, while holding the title of President temporarily in abeyance. And on February 25 Salah Salem, as Minister of National Guidance, explained the changes by announcing that Neguib had demanded, and been refused, 'absolute autocratic authority'.

Not only was this statement a distortion of the facts; it was also a bad error of presentation. For to the ordinary Egyptian, it was the earnest and angry young Nasser who evoked the image of the absolute autocrat rather than the comfortable smiling figure of Neguib. But, not content with this unconvincing effort in public relations, the RCC appeared to go out of their way to antagonise Neguib's supporters by placing him under house arrest.

Demonstrations in favour of the General were staged by Cairo University students who protested against army rule and called for elections and a constitutional democracy. Salah Salem was roughly manhandled at one such demonstration and, in a state of great agitation, now told his colleagues that they had overstepped the mark and that there was no way of resisting the popular clamour for Neguib. Also there were repercussions in the Sudan where the National Unionist majority, whose pro-Egyptian attitude was largely based on their trust and respect for Neguib personally, regarded his departure as a threat to their political ascendancy and despatched a deputation to Cairo to express their alarm. And outside the General's house numbers of angry officers gathered to protest and assure him of their support.

Meanwhile, Khaled Mohieddin had told the RCC that he could not accept any responsibility for inducing the army to accept the changes. His fellow cavalrymen were, he said, very disturbed by what had happened. (He should have known since he had done much to disturb them himself.) And on the night of February 25 the cavalry officers invited Nasser to meet them at their Abbassia barracks where, in a noisy, hostile encounter lasting until 1.30 a.m., they bluntly told him that they would not accept Neguib's dismissal, that they wanted elections to be held as soon as possible and that they wished the General to continue as President, but of a parliamentary republic and not of a military autocracy. Finally, they said that they would accept Nasser as Prime Minister, but they insisted that a time-limit be set to the work of preparing a new constitution which had been entrusted to Ali Maher and a committee of experts.

Nasser was greatly taken aback by the vehemence of this protest. The cavalry had been the most important and influential element in the army from the start of the Free Officers' movement, due to the power and mobility of its armoured units, and their opposition seemed to have effectively checkmated his plans. For the moment, therefore, but only for the moment, there was nothing that Nasser could do except concede victory to Neguib. So, at the RCC meeting which followed his encounter at Abbassia, he reported his failure to convince the cavalry. Khaled Mohieddin then delivered an impassioned appeal for elections and parliamentary democracy. Whereupon, with great solemnity and deliberation, Nasser replied, saying that he considered the time was not ripe for such a step but that, if this was his colleagues' view, he would step down from the premiership and hand over to Khaled Mohieddin.

The meeting ended indecisively. But, taking Nasser at his word, Khaled Mohieddin hastened to Neguib's house to tell the General that Nasser had given in and that the two of them were to become respectively President and Prime Minister of a parliamentary republic. However, within a few hours, a further dramatic change was to occur. For one thing, the leading Cairo newspaper, *Al-Akhbar,* proclaimed in an editorial that Nasser was and should remain the real leader of the revolution, despite the fact that Nasser had himself told the editors, the brothers Mustapha and Ali Amin, that he had lost his battle with Neguib and that they had no further obligation or even interest in supporting him. On top of this, the infantry, artillery and air force who had on balance supported Nasser against Neguib, decided to make a fight of it on Nasser's behalf. By daybreak therefore Neguib's cavalry supporters found themselves surrounded by hostile forces with a squadron of aircraft circling menacingly overhead. And to complete the turnabout, a couple of over-zealous supporters of Nasser abducted Neguib and drove him to some hideaway in the desert.

Nasser, however, prudently decided that matters had gone far enough. The Alexandria garrison having meanwhile proclaimed their support for Neguib in a flood of messages to GHQ, he called off his partisans for fear of causing an irreparable split in the army and possibly even a civil war, for which he was unprepared and which he could all too easily have lost. A compromise was then agreed. Neguib returned to office as 'President of the Egyptian Parliamentary Republic', proclaiming that a Constituent Assembly would be elected in time to hold its first meeting on July 23, 1954, the second anniversary of the revolution. Meanwhile Nasser remained Prime Minister in the hope of at least preventing Neguib from allowing the old political parties to resume their activities. Khaled Mohieddin resumed his seat as an ordinary member of the RCC.

But the apparent harmony created by this compromise was not to last for more than a few days. For while Neguib was away in Khartoum attending the inauguration of the Sudanese Parliament, Nasser rounded up several hundreds of those who had taken part in the demonstrations in protest against the General's resignation and charged them with plotting a counter-revolution. Neguib was furious and, on March 9 after he had returned to Cairo, he demanded to be reinstated as Prime Minister. Rather than risk further dissension, the RCC concurred and Nasser stepped down to the deputy premiership once again.

For the next two weeks a sullen quiet reigned in the relations between the General and his military colleagues. But at every joint session of the RCC and the Government it became increasingly clear that a further and decisive clash was inevitable. As it now seemed to Nasser, all his plans for maintaining the revolution were to be set to naught. Elections were to be held, which meant that the disbanded political parties would be allowed to function again. And, since land reform had not yet been in operation long enough to emancipate the fellah and the RCC had had no time to organise a revolutionary party other than the amorphous, uncoordinated Liberation Rally, the Wafd would therefore be free to bribe and bully the electors into returning them to power. Even the three-year transition period of military rule, which would have allowed time to sap the strength of these citadels of reaction, was to be revoked; and within a few months, Egypt was to return to what had euphemistically been called parliamentary and constitutional government, but which, in fact, would be largely a repetition of the old regime with all its corruption and oppression.

It was a depressing prospect. But, in spite of his disgust and disillusionment with the turn of events, Nasser was not finished yet. He had not led his Free Officer associates through a decade of underground activity without learning something about conspiracy. Nor, if he could find a way to fight Neguib and the reactionaries which would avoid a civil war, was he going to surrender without further resistance all that the revolution was struggling to achieve. Therefore on March 25, two weeks after he stepped down from the premiership, Nasser brought matters once again to a head. The position, he told his colleagues, had become intolerable and the RCC could not continue any longer to operate an unworkable compromise. There were therefore only two possible courses open to his colleagues and himself. Either they should return to their barracks and declare that the revolution was at an end and that in the forthcoming elections the press and the political parties would enjoy complete freedom of activity; or they should annul the election proclamation, revert to military rule and intensify the campaign to eradicate reaction in the army and the civil service.

Khaled Mohieddin immediately suggested that there was a third alternative. This would be to hold elections as planned, but to declare all the former political leaders as ineligible to participate. He even proposed that, if necessary, no political parties should take part as such, but that the candidates should submit themselves as individuals and that parties should only be formed from the new Parliament when its members had all been elected. Only Neguib supported these ideas and the RCC themselves voted on Nasser's two alternatives. And when the votes were counted, it was found that, by a majority of eight to four, they had decided in favour of a free-for-all election.

This was precisely what Nasser had planned. Indeed, he had himself organised the ballot so as to ensure this result. Meanwhile he had been busily mobilising support among the Trades Unions and, as he subsequently admitted to Khaled Mohieddin, he had also hired at great expense a large claque of demonstrators, locally known as the 'ten-piastre boys', to turn out and demonstrate for him when he gave the signal. Then, within a few hours of the RCC's vote, an announcement was made confirming that elections were to be held in the immediate future and declaring that the RCC would be dissolved when the newly elected Parliament met in July. The public were told that the disbanded political parties would be able to resume their activities in absolute freedom; the RCC would themselves not form a party or contest the elections;

and the new Parliament would consist entirely of electe
bers. On the same day a further announcement stated
token of the Government's desire to restore freedom or p..
expression, Nahas had been released from custody, together with
Hodeiby, the Moslem Brotherhood leader, and Rashad Mehanna.

There could be no mistaking the meaning of these announcements. Reaction was back in business; the revolution was finished.
And exactly as Nasser had planned, no sooner had the truth
dawned upon the populace than the Trades Unions issued a call
for a general strike in protest against the Government's plans. The
Cairo Transport Workers Union demanded a boycott of the
elections and Nasser's claque staged massive demonstrations
calling for the ban on the old political parties to be maintained
and the purge of the army and civil service extended. A mob
invaded the premises of the State Council, declaiming against the
restoration of reaction. Simultaneously, at Nasser's instigation, the
Amin brothers published the taped records of further telephone
conversations between Neguib and Nahas, which suggested that
the General was actively promoting the Wafd's return to power.
And with the powerful *Al-Akhbar* proclaiming for Nasser and the
revolution, other newspapers took up the cry.

Emboldened by this massive support, Nasser now openly
attacked Neguib. Amin Shaker, his Chef de Cabinet, publicly
accused the President of becoming a tool of dishonest politicians
of the old regime. And Nasser's supporters among the infantry
and artillery voiced their opposition to the General by staying in
their barracks when called upon to turn out and halt the demonstrations. Thus, within a few days of the March 25 announcements,
Neguib came to realise that, as he put it, he had been 'out-
manœuvred by Abdel Nasser and my junior colleagues'. King
Saud, who was currently visiting Cairo at the time, tried to intervene on his behalf with an offer to mediate between the rival
parties. But nothing could now stop Nasser's bandwagon and on
March 29, Salah Salem announced to the Egyptian public that the
RCC, bowing to popular pressures, had reversed their earlier
decision and would remain in office until the three-year transitional period expired in January 1956.

Too late Neguib's university partisans came out to demonstrate, with Communist and Moslem Brotherhood support, against the continuation of military rule. With his bigger battalions among the Trades Unions Nasser had won the second and decisive round in his struggle to assert his own rule. Although Neguib held on as Prime Minister for another nineteen days, the RCC were back in complete control and the General was reduced to a mere cypher. On April 17, therefore, he bowed to the inevitable and resigned the premiership. Nasser took over again as Prime Minister and Chairman of the RCC and, by way of consolidating the army's grip on the administrative machine, the remaining RCC members, except for Khaled Mohieddin, joined the Government, holding every important portfolio save those of foreign affairs and finance which were still retained by civilians. Neguib remained President for another seven months. But in all that time he was little more than a prisoner of the military regime without power, influence or outside contacts, save those which his erstwhile colleagues permitted. Which fact was brought home to me in October of that year when, after I had completed the negotiations for the withdrawal of the British forces, I suggested in a letter to the President that I should pay a courtesy call upon him. The reply in the form of an unsigned third-person note, which bore all the marks of having been written by the RCC, was a classic of its kind. 'His Excellency the President', it said, 'thanks Mr. Nutting for his letter, but regrets that he is indisposed and he has a very full list of engagements'!

Fundamentally a simple soldier with more vanity than judgement, Neguib allowed himself to appear as the instrument of the old-guard politicians and, at the same time, of extremists of the Right and Left such as the Moslem Brothers and even the Communists, who found themselves united in a common bond of suspicion and hostility towards the young zealots of the RCC. At least this was how it seemed to Nasser and those who felt as he did that there could be no compromise about the principles for which the revolution had been fought. Yet, for all the strange bed-fellows with whom he became associated in his efforts to temper the autocratic aspirations of his officer colleagues, Neguib was neither as reactionary nor as guileful as his opponents claimed him to be. As events had shown, he was no match for Nasser as a conspirator. Deceived by his own undoubted popularity into believing that the public would never prefer Nasser's rule to his own relaxed form of government, he underestimated his rival's capacity for intrigue and made no allowance for the Egyptian people's age-old inclination to bow to force majeure, such as the RCC were able to mobilise on their own behalf. So for a few more months he was relegated to the position of figurehead for which Nasser, if not nature itself, had always intended him.

Neguib was not, of course, the only major casualty in the struggle for power. Khaled Mohieddin had also guessed wrong and, in doing so, had made himself an outcast among his RCC colleagues. But here Nasser was to manifest another and more kindly aspect of his character. Khaled, at thirty-one, was one of the youngest of his associates and he had a great affection for this talented officer, with whom he had shared the long hard climb to success. Moreover, as he was to show throughout the early stages of his reign, he was reluctant to break openly with his old comrades of pre-revolution days, and would frequently lean over backwards to pardon their errors and indiscretions. At the same time Khaled had not only opposed him in the struggle with Neguib and incited the cavalry to revolt against the RCC, but he was also a self-confessed adherent of Communism which Nasser had anathematised as an alien ideology, inspired and directed by aliens against the interests of the Egyptian people and the teaching of Islam. In the circumstances, he could not possibly continue in office, even if he still wished to do so. Nasser, therefore, sent for his errant lieutenant and, telling him that, if he stayed in Egypt, he would have to be arrested, suggested that he should go into voluntary exile in Europe, which proposal Khaled accepted with due gratitude.

The RCC were now in supreme control both of policy and of administration. Less than three years hence, the day was to come when Nasser's personal stature was enhanced to such a peak that he alone would exercise this absolute authority. But, for the moment, he was content to share it with his officer colleagues. For, while he might have defeated Neguib largely by superior skill in the art of conspiracy, nobody knew better than he that he could never have won without the loyalty and support of the RCC throughout the contest. And as I was to find later that same year in the course of our negotiations over Britain's withdrawal, he scarcely went anywhere without at least one or two of his RCC associates accompanying him and never took an important decision without consulting them as a body.

Another mark left on Nasser by the struggle with Neguib was a noticeable apprehension about student opinion which was all the more remarkable when contrasted with his uninhibited onslaughts upon much more formidable opponents such as the Wafd or the Moslem Brothers. This was largely a legacy from his own student days when he and his fellows had helped to cause the disturbances which induced King Fuad to restore the 1923 constitution. And, as he confessed to me several times in our early encounters, he had never forgotten that the Cairo University campus had been solidly for Neguib. Remembering the by no means contemptible influence of Egypt's students in the past, he was thus at pains to win them over or, at least, not to antagonise them still further.

Finally, the events of the last few months had shown the importance of having in the RCC at least two representatives of each element of the armed forces. True, this precaution had not prevented the cavalry from supporting Neguib. But Nasser was convinced that, had he not had the support of Hussein Shafei to counterbalance Khaled Mohieddin's intrigues, the opposition at Abbassia would have been even less restrained than it had been and he might well have ended up in a prison cell or with a bullet in his brain. Certainly one of his first moves following Neguib's defeat was to appoint Shafei as Minister of War, who lost no time in changing every regimental commander in the cavalry corps.

With his leadership assured Nasser now turned to the business of getting Britain out of her Egyptian bases. In January 1954 he had agreed to include Turkey in the 'reactivation' clause over the opposition of several of his RCC colleagues. (The Turks, having been among Egypt's former rulers, were still not exactly popular.) But this gesture had elicited no corresponding concession from the British and so the campaign of attrition in the Canal Zone had continued over the next few months. At the outset these harassing tactics had proved counter-productive; the attacks on British troops and installations by fedayeen commandos had only stiffened British resistance. But as time wore on, Whitehall had come to realise the sheer absurdity of trying to maintain bases for the protection of the Middle East which were under constant attack from the very territory which they were supposed to defend. Thus when in May Nasser, taking a gamble with his militant fringe, called off the fedayeen and suggested a resumption of negotiations, there was a ready response from London.

Britain dropped her requirement that military uniforms had to be worn by the technicians who were to take over in the areas retained for British use. As a further sweetener the Treasury announced the release of a further £10 million of the sterling balances earned by Egypt in World War II which were being held in London. Then, as Whitehall readied themselves to send the Secretary of State for War, Antony Head, to clinch the negotiations in Cairo, President Eisenhower sent a letter to Neguib as President of Egypt, saying that the Egyptians could expect from the United States 'firm commitments' to supply large-scale economic and military aid once they had reached agreement with the British.

So different in text and tone was this statement from the attitude struck by Dulles when he visited Cairo in the previous year and from the treatment meted out to Ali Sabry in Washington that, if Nasser had had any remaining doubts about the need to conclude an early agreement with Britain, they were now finally swept away. Twelve days later, on July 27, Head and Nasser signed a document which laid down the heads of agreement for the withdrawal of British forces and the subsequent joint use of the bases. In August Britain lifted the embargo on the sale of arms to Egypt which she had enforced since 1951 when Nahas first raised the wind against her Canal Zone garrisons. In the following month an Egyptian military mission left for Washington. And on October 19, I myself completed in Cairo the negotiations of the Anglo-Egyptian treaty which spelled out the earlier heads of agreement. All British troops were to be withdrawn by June 18, 1956; the 1936 treaty was abrogated; and for the next seven years the Canal Zone bases were to be shared by Britain and Egypt, with British civilian technicians operating in the ordnance depots and army workshops retained for Britain's use. If during the seven-year period Egypt, any other Arab state, or Turkey were attacked by an outside power, the base could be reactivated and British troops return to help repel the aggressor; but it was specifically agreed that the term 'outside power' did not include Israel. Finally, Egypt undertook to uphold the 1888 Constantinople Convention governing freedom of navigation through the Suez Canal.

In spite of the fact that we were bound by the agreement on principles which had been signed in July, the negotiation of the detailed treaty took several weeks of tough bargaining and argument which taught me much about Nasser's character and methods. All the financial and many of the political issues were handled by his Foreign Minister, Mahmoud Fawzi, a most gifted career diplomat and negotiator; such matters were only discussed with Nasser if Fawzi and I could not come to an agreement. But when any question arose affecting arrangements for the bases, it was handled by Nasser personally, however detailed it might be. Even the allocation of housing between the British technicians and senior Egyptian officers in the main base at Moascar outside Ismailia had to be settled with him.

These discussions frequently brought out his nice sense of humour. On one occasion, after he had demanded that all the houses then occupied by British generals should be reserved for Egyptian senior officers, I asked rather testily where our technicians were expected to live. Nasser, kneeling on the floor beside me and poring over a map of the base, pointed to a vacant lot. 'Thank you for nothing,' I said, 'that happens to be the football field.' He then tried again indicating an area with a building on it. 'And that,' I said, 'is the Methodist Church.' Nasser collapsed with laughter and it was some time before we got back to serious discussions. What's more he never forgot our silly joke and would afterwards say what a pity it was that our technicians had not been housed in this holy atmosphere.

Nasser, of course, warmly welcomed the new treaty. 'A dark page in Anglo-Egyptian relations has been turned,' he proclaimed. 'Another page is now being written. Great Britain's prestige and position in the Middle East have been reinforced and now there remains virtually no reason why Great Britain and Egypt cannot work together in a constructive fashion.' And so indeed it could have been, had the tragic chain of events not supervened which began with the Baghdad Pact and ended at Suez. For the treaty was an eminently satisfactory arrangement for both parties. Egypt obtained the withdrawal of British troops; Britain obtained what she needed in the way of base facilities in the Canal Zone. Egypt had not been obliged to join any Western defence organisation; but Nasser had conceded in the 'reactivation' clause that, if the area were involved in war with Russia or some other 'outside power', Britain and Egypt would become and behave as allies one to another.

This was a major concession which Nasser had offered largely to smooth the path of negotiation and to demonstrate that he was willing to accept a constructive alternative to Britain's earlier demands that Egypt should take part in a Middle East extension of NATO. Also, as a soldier, he knew well enough that, if Egypt should ever become involved in a third world war, she would need Britain's help as much as Britain would need hers. But far more important than such hypothetical arrangements was the fact that the treaty achieved Nasser's most precious dream. With the withdrawal of foreign troops Egypt would gain that sense of 'dignity' for which he had striven first as a student, then as a conspirator and now finally as the ruler of his country. For the first time in two and a half thousand years the Egyptian people would know what it was to be independent and not to be ruled or occupied or told what to do by some foreign power.

Not surprisingly Nasser was deeply affected by the significance of this achievement and, when we met for the signing ceremonies, he gripped my hand and held it for several moments as he struggled to control his emotions. But, even in this sentient atmosphere, his sense of humour did not desert him. As his aide, Ali Sabry, put the treaty in front of me for signature, I discovered that my fountain pen had run out of ink and I had to borrow Nasser's. Then, having signed my name, as an automatic reflex I put the pen in my breast-pocket. Nasser held out his hand and with a broad grin said, 'I think you have already got enough out of me in this treaty. Please can I have my pen back.'

But if Nasser was delighted with the new treaty there were others who were not. These included the Moslem Brotherhood who protested that it amounted to another alliance with Britain and the West and was therefore a betrayal of the people. Hodeiby called Nasser a 'traitor to the national cause'. The British, he declared, should have been simply hounded out of Egypt and the Government had no right to submit to any conditions for their withdrawal. Indeed it had at one time been rumoured that the Brothers were plotting to assassinate all those involved in the negotiations in a desperate attempt to get the issue settled by force instead of agreement.

Despite his close confinement in the former royal palace, Neguib got to hear of the Brotherhood's attitude and, in a final desperate move to win the chauvinists to his side against the RCC, he let it be known that he supported their stand. Nasser told me of this during the course of a general discussion which I had with him and a number of his colleagues at the Nile Barrage rest-house after we had signed the treaty. Neguib, he said, was bidding for Moslem Brotherhood support and protesting that he would not ratify our agreement. With remarkable frankness he went on to say that he was fed up with the Brothers who had gone altogether too far in their vendetta against him and his colleagues and he gave me the broadest of hints that it would not be very long before a final show-down took place with Neguib and his fanatical bed-fellows.

In fact, the show-down came within less than a week. On October 26, as Nasser was speaking at a public meeting in Alexandria, a gunman, later identified as a member of the

Brotherhood, fired several shots at him from the audience. The would-be assassin's aim was poor for he managed to hit nothing except an electric light bulb above the platform before he was dragged away by the police. Nasser meanwhile shouted to his hearers, 'Let them kill Nasser. He is one among many and whether he lives or dies the revolution will go on.'

This was the opportunity which Nasser had been awaiting. Before dawn several of the Brotherhood's leaders were back in gaol and, within the next few weeks, Hodeiby and five hundred more members of the fraternity were arrested and sent to varying terms of imprisonment. Death sentences were passed on the assailant, together with Hodeiby and three other leading Brothers, of whom two were 'notables' of the Islamic Establishment. And though Hodeiby's sentence was commuted to life imprisonment, the other condemned men were duly hanged six weeks after the attempted assassination.

Whether or not Neguib was guilty of any complicity in the Alexandria *attentat* was never proved, although at Hodeiby's trial it was said that he had allowed his spite against Nasser to turn him into a tool of the conspirators. But he had done enough for the RCC to be rid of him; and on November 14, following an announcement associating him with the Brotherhood's plot to overthrow the regime, he was relieved of his presidential duties and personally placed under house arrest by General Abdel Hakim Amer. The presidency was then offered to Lufti el-Said, an octogenarian scholar and former Foreign Minister, who wisely declined it on the grounds that the position carried no executive power and that, even if it did, he would not want it. Whereupon Nasser assumed the functions of President and the title was for the time being held in abeyance.

Chapter 5

The Baghdad Pact

During and after the Suez crisis in 1956 it became a commonplace for Anthony Eden and other British Ministers to accuse Nasser of nursing a vicious hatred of Britain and of seeking to evict every British economic and commercial interest from the entire Arab world. In fact, these accusations were based on a fundamental misunderstanding of the situation. Nasser greatly respected the British for their achievements in history and for their commercial and industrial skills. Although to start with he may have found it easier to get along with the relatively more informal Americans whom he knew, such as Kermit Roosevelt and Henry Byroade, Caffery's successor, he liked and trusted every ambassador whom Britain sent to Cairo and he was also on excellent terms with a number of British politicians and journalists. Far from wanting to expel British interests, he actively sought to expand Anglo–Egyptian trade and to bring British companies to invest and operate in Egypt. He wanted Britain to participate in building and financing the High Dam at Aswan and, even after Suez, he offered concessions to British and other European oil men to prospect on Egyptian soil.

Nor did Nasser reject out of hand any prospect of ultimately cooperating with Britain and her Western partners in some kind of defence arrangement for the Middle East. As he told me in our talks after we had signed the 1954 treaty, the soldier in him said that such cooperation made excellent sense; but so soon after the struggle with Neguib, he had not achieved a sufficiently strong standing with the people suddenly to reverse the policy of strict neutrality which had been initiated by the Wafd at the end of the Farouk era. He must therefore first consolidate his political position and strengthen the Egyptian army with modern weapons.

74

But here again, he looked to Britain as well as the United States, as he showed by the 'shopping list' of arms which he asked me to take home with me.

Admittedly Nasser had been bitterly anti-British in his youth and during his years as leader of the Free Officers. He had been anti-British because he could not abide the kind of domination and humiliation to which Egypt was then subjected by the British, from Lampson, who treated Farouk as a puppet, down to the ordinary private soldier who called the Egyptians 'wogs' and ridiculed the King in public with bawdy songs. And he had made it his overriding ambition to remove the British military presence which brought such disgrace upon his country. But, having now achieved this ambition, he genuinely hoped, as he himself put it, that 'another page' in Anglo-Egyptian relations would henceforth be written and that, to quote the preamble of the treaty itself, 'a new era of firm friendship and mutual understanding' would begin. Nothing emerged more clearly than his desire for this new relationship both in his talks with me and also in subsequent discussions with Stevenson and his successor as British Ambassador, Sir Humphrey Trevelyan.

But, as the appetite can grow with eating so Nasser's ambition expanded with the success he achieved in October 1954. Ever since the Palestine War he had thought not only as an Egyptian, but also as an Arab. On the second anniversary of the revolution, July 23, 1954, he had declared that 'a new era of relations with the Arabs, based on true and frank fraternity' had opened up and that the aim of revolutionary Egypt was that the Arabs should become 'one nation' capable of defending themselves and 'collaborating for the common welfare'. In the circumstances Nasser could not rest content merely to bring about the withdrawal of British forces from Egypt: the same had to apply to all Arab territory. To this end, therefore, Cairo's 'Voice of the Arabs' radio now expanded its broadcasts to four hours a day, becoming the foremost vehicle for 'anti-imperialist' propaganda in the Arab world. Likewise, political and diplomatic pressure was brought to bear upon those Arab rulers and their henchmen who, like Farouk and the former Pashas of Egypt, had welcomed the presence of British forces to preserve their own positions as much as to protect their national frontiers.

Nor was the anti-imperialist campaign solely directed at Egypt's Arab brothers. In his famous *Philosophy* Nasser had described how Egypt formed the centre of three concentric circles embracing the Arab, Islamic and African worlds. Therefore, in fulfilment of what he regarded as his duty to encourage nationalist movements throughout Africa as well as Asia, he espoused the cause of the Mau Mau rebellion in Kenya and, in July 1954, initiated a radio campaign in Swahili to arouse the African inhabitants of Britain's East African colonies.

Such actions were of course hardly likely to smooth the future course of Anglo-Egyptian relations, at least so long as Britain wished to remain an imperial power and believed that troops and bases on Arab territory were essential to the protection of her oil interests in Iraq and the Persian Gulf. Moreover, following the shock administered by the Mossadeq Government's action in kicking the Anglo-Iranian Oil Company out of Iran in 1951, the British had become more rather than less wedded to such beliefs. And accordingly, at this very juncture Whitehall veered still nearer a collision with Egypt by proposing that Iraq should renew her defence relationship with Britain within a Middle East alliance embracing Britain, Turkey and Pakistan, later to become known as the Baghdad Pact.

Iraq had been Britain's closest Arab ally since the end of World War I, when she had become a British mandate after the Turks were driven out, and the remains of the former Ottoman Empire were divided between the victors – with Syria and Lebanon going to France, Palestine and Transjordan to Britain, while Saudi Arabia alone regained her independence. From then on, the effective ruler of the country had been Nuri es-Said, a cunning, charming and ruthless patriot of the old school. Nuri had fought against the Turks with T. E. Lawrence under the banners of the Hashemite Sherif Hussein of the Hejaz, whose great-grandsons, Feisal and Hussein, were now respectively Kings of Iraq and of Jordan, as the former state of Transjordan had been renamed. Although in his earlier days a fervent champion of Arab independence, he had become increasingly conservative, as well as anti-Egyptian, with the passage of time. Having fought with Britain against the Ottoman Empire, worked with the British throughout the duration of the mandate and depended upon Britain for arms and advice ever since Iraq obtained her independence in 1930, he could not conceive of a world in which he and the British were not working hand in glove. When Anwar Sadat visited Baghdad in 1956 he told him in so many words that Iraq and the other Arab states could not survive without Britain's help. Thus, even if he had not held the Egyptians as a race in almost total contempt, he would have had no sympathy for Nasser's desire to evict the British military presence from the Arab world. And when London suggested that the arrangements should be renewed whereby Britain maintained an air force base in Iraq and that the renewal should be under the umbrella of a defence pact comprising Britain, Iraq, Turkey and Pakistan, plus if possible the United States, Nuri saw every reason to accept and no cause to refuse.

But for Nasser there was every reason to oppose this British initiative. For one thing, it was the same idea as the Middle East defence pact which Egypt had turned down in 1951. It would link Iraq with NATO and, since Iraq was a member of the Arab League, this would put the League's neutrality at risk and could involve other Arab states in NATO's disputes should Iraq herself become involved. For another, Nasser feared that, if by accepting Britain's proposals Iraq obtained large quantities of British arms, with her rich oil resources, added to her improved military strength, she would become the predominant Arab power and in consequence the centre of political gravity in the Middle East would shift from Cairo to Baghdad.

Even if other Arab states did not feel tempted to follow Iraq's example as a means of acquiring modern arms cheaply and quickly, Nuri's action seemed to strike at the very roots of Nasser's policy of Arab unity and independence. Seen from Cairo, the wily British, having been finally forced to abandon their bases in Egypt, were clearly trying to stage a re-entry on the Arab scene via Iraq. Was not the argument which ultimately persuaded the doubters in the House of Commons to accept a withdrawal from Egypt that it was in Britain's interest to 'redeploy' her forces in the Middle East? Already every Arab nationalist believed that the state of Israel had been established in order to create a beach-head for continued Western dominance over the Arab world. Britain's approaches to Iraq seemed designed to extend still further the old imperialist principle of divide and rule. And if Nasser strove by every means to thwart these dispositions, it was not, as was currently suggested by Eden and others, out of personal jealousy against Nuri, however little sympathy might exist between these two political opposites. Rather was it because he seriously believed that Nuri's policy would divide the Arab League and weaken what little cohesion it possessed, and so would enable the imperialists, just as they had planned, to pick off the Arab states one by one and impose their will upon them.

When the news of the British approach to Iraq was first mooted Nasser sent his Minister of Guidance, Salah Salem, on a tour of Arab states in the summer of 1954. At this point, far from seeking to overthrow Nuri, Nasser was looking for ways to improve relations between Iraq and Egypt which had been cool, to say the least, ever since Nuri's Fertile Crescent scheme had been ditched in the early forties in favour of an Arab League centred on Cairo. Therefore, when Salem met Nuri with King Feisal and the Crown Prince, Abdulillah, at the Iraqi mountain resort of Sarsank, he was under instructions to handle his hosts with great tact.

Nuri was in high spirits and insisted that, before they got down to serious business, he should take his guest to a Kurdish wedding ceremony. Then, when the discussions started, Salem explained, with a moderation quite out of keeping with his ebullient and emotional nature, exactly why Egypt was opposed to Iraq getting involved with NATO. His Government felt, he said, that at least until they had had time to evaluate British and other Western policies towards the Arab world, it would be advisable not to get entangled in any foreign commitments. This would give the Arab League time to close and strengthen its ranks and would prevent the West playing one Arab state off against another. And when Nuri objected that Iraq was threatened by Communism

nd needed support to counter such threats, Salem quietly replied
hat the best way to stimulate the growth of Communism in
raq would be to engage in foreign pacts which nationalist opinion
esented as subservience to imperialism.

Nuri and his royal assistants, having not yet finally decided
xactly how they would respond to the British proposals, con-
ined their replies at this stage to explanations as to how vulnerable
nd exposed Iraq was to attack and penetration from Russia. But,
vhen it came to drafting a joint statement summarising the con-
lusions of the meeting, Nuri completely outwitted Salem, who
eturned to Cairo with a statement saying that the Egyptians and
raqis would examine ways of strengthening the Arab League
ecurity pact and would hold talks with the United States and
3ritain to this end. Which ambiguity not only left Nuri a free
and to conclude an alliance with the West, but also suggested
hat Egypt might even join the alliance as well. On top of this, the
uckless Salem was quoted as saying at a press conference in reply
o a loaded question that 'if two or more Arab peoples wish to
inite in some form, Egypt does not object', which was widely
nterpreted as meaning that Egypt had finally withdrawn her
pbjections to the Fertile Crescent concept and would no longer
pbject to Syria being taken under Iraq's wing.

Infuriated by the ineptitude of his emissary, Nasser had to
alm the indignant protests which poured forth from anti-Iraqi
lements in Syria. But he was even more disturbed that Salem
hould have given his blessing to the idea that Iraq and Egypt
hould consult the West about strengthening the Arab League.
He therefore lost no time in telling Nuri's ambassador in Cairo
hat such action would be inconsistent with Egypt's policy of
ndependence. Nuri promptly hastened to Cairo where, in one
pf the very few encounters that ever took place between the
wo leaders, he told Nasser that he could not depend on the Arabs
o defend Iraq. Only Britain could help and, although he under-
tood Egypt's suspicions of the British, he had decided to go
ahead and accept their new proposals.

Nasser stated his case with equal bluntness and, while he
admitted that so far the Arab League had proved a weak reed, he

argued that this was no reason for still further weakening it b
encouraging the imperialists to prolong and strengthen their gri
on the Arabs and to play them off against each other. Then
month later, after the Anglo-Egyptian treaty had been signed, th
'Voice of the Arabs' broadcast a call to Arabs everywhere t
follow Egypt's example and throw off the yoke of foreig
occupation. 'Egypt,' it proclaimed, 'achieved this in only tw
years. Listen to her when she says there can be no alliances excep
with the Arabs – You brother with the bowed head in Iraq
brother on the outskirts of Palestine, in Jordan and in Nort
Africa, you must remember the past two years . . . you will the
raise your head in pride and dignity. Iraq . . . will be liberated b
the liberation of Egypt. The imperialists will be driven to work fo
your friendship. . . . Raise your head now, my brother, for victor
has been won for you by your Egyptian Arabs.'

The purport of those words could scarcely have been mor
ominously clear and Nuri back in Baghdad was not so foolish a
to think that he could altogether ignore so emotive an appeal t
the proud and prickly people of Iraq. Moreover, Nasser's plain
spoken arguments in Cairo had shown clearly enough that h
would fight all the way to prevent what he regarded as a
attempt by Iraq to defect from the Arab confederacy. Nuri there
fore decided to disarm his adversary by outright deception. Mus
Shabander, his Foreign Minister, was sent to a meeting of Ara
Foreign Ministers in Cairo which had been called in an attemp
to unify Arab League policy. And after the meeting had come t
a somewhat indefinite conclusion, Shabander announced at a pres
conference that Iraq would not after all join the alliance betwee
Turkey and Pakistan. Instead she would merely replace th
existing treaty with Britain by an agreement similar to tha
which Egypt had just concluded, which would include a com
mitment to reactivate the British air bases if Iran should b
attacked.

Nasser was amazed, although he found it hard to believe tha
Iraq had so swiftly abandoned her foreign alliance policy. But
few days later, on January 1, 1955, Nuri himself seemed to confirm
his Foreign Minister's pronouncement. Speaking in the Iraq

Parliament, he stated that he would enter into a bilateral agreement with Britain, which in some undefined way would also take account of the security of Turkey and Iran, but which would not involve any commitment not approved by Iraq's Arab League partners.

Even with this confirmation Nasser could scarcely credit such a volte-face. The conspirator in him told him that Nuri was engaged in some trick, seeking to buy a brief respite from the propaganda barrage of Cairo's radio broadcasts. Just how right were his suspicions was soon to be proved. Five days after Nuri's statement .Adnan Menderes, the Turkish Prime Minister, descended on Baghdad with a large delegation which included his Foreign and Communications Ministers and nine members of the Turkish National Assembly. Then, on January 12, a communiqué was issued from Baghdad which proclaimed that Iraq and Turkey had agreed to sign a mutual defence pact as soon as possible, that they hoped 'other like-minded states' in the area would join them and that they would 'make every endeavour to persuade those states to sign the treaty simultaneously with them'.

This was even worse than Nasser had feared. Not only was Iraq to form with Turkey the nucleus of a multilateral alliance with Britain, which would link her with NATO; she was also going to canvass other Arab states to join as well. Bitterly reflecting to Stevenson that Nuri had played him false at the instigation of Britain and Turkey, he reacted angrily. The 'Voice of the Arabs' returned to the attack against Iraq's threatened defection. So did the Egyptian press. But for the moment Cairo's propaganda campaign stopped short of actually inciting the Iraqi people to revolution. Before going to such lengths Nasser wanted to see if he could induce Nuri to retreat by pressure from within the Arab League.

Here he had in Saudi Arabia an influential ally and, if riches meant power, a powerful one as well. For this vast desert kingdom, owning some of the richest oil resources in the world, was currently engaged in a bitter quarrel with Britain over possession of the oasis of Buraimi on the borders of the British-protected Trucial States. Besides, ever since King Saud's father, Abdel Aziz

Ibn Saud, the founder of the kingdom, had evicted Sherif Hussein from the Hejaz in 1924 and annexed this territory to Saudi Arabia, he and his family had been dire enemies of the Hashemite dynasty. And thirty years later his successor was still carrying on the feud against the Sherif's great-grandsons, Feisal of Iraq and Hussein of Jordan, advised by a sinister Syrian diplomatist, Yusuf Yasin, who made it his business to foster the maximum enmity between his royal master and the two young Hashemite Kings.

With a natural ally of such wealth and influence as the Saudis, Nasser decided to summon a meeting in Cairo of the Prime Ministers of Iraq, Syria, Lebanon, Saudi Arabia, Jordan, Yemen and Libya, which at that time were, apart from Egypt, the only independent Arab states. Except for Nuri who pleaded a 'diplomatic illness', all those invited accepted and the first meeting was held on January 22. But right from the start, things went badly for the Egyptians. The Iraqis were not represented at all for the first five days and when they finally appeared on the scene they were led by a former Prime Minister, Fadil Jamali, who was pathologically anti-Egyptian. Moreover, at the very first meeting, it became all too clear that the Syrians, Lebanese and Jordanians were out to prevaricate and were not prepared to condemn Nuri's policy as Nasser had hoped. Fares el-Khoury of Syria, Sami es Solh of Lebanon and Tawfik Aboul Huda of Jordan all proposed a postponement until the Iraqis could attend. And after Nasser with difficulty persuaded them to start on the discussions, the Syrians opened up with a pedantic statement saying that, while they would not themselves join any foreign alliance, it would be pointless for them to oppose the Iraqis for doing so at this conference, since such a decision could not bind any future Syrian Government.

This statement reflected the current division of opinion among the Syrians who, having gained their independence from French rule with the end of World War II, had only recently emerged from a succession of army putsches involving four coups d'état and eleven changes of government in less than three years. Syria was torn mainly between those who supported the conservative

People's party in their desire for union with Iraq and the Baath
(Renaissance) party's adherents who favoured a broad Arab union
based on socialist principles. For fear of antagonising the Baathists,
Fares el-Khoury, though himself mildly pro-Iraqi, had to disclaim
any intention of joining Nuri's new alliance. At the same time,
rather than upset the People's party, he had to refuse to go along
with any condemnation of Iraq. And for all the efforts of the
'Voice of the Arabs', Nasser could not as yet impose his ideas on
Syrian opinion. For it was not only in pro-Western circles that his
regime was still regarded with reserve and even with suspicion.
The same was also true of other quarters, especially where the
influence of the Moslem Brotherhood was strong and where the
execution of the three Brotherhood leaders, following the
Alexandria incident, had outraged large numbers of people in
Damascus, as well as Baghdad and other Arab capitals.

Nor were the Syrians alone in their ambivalence. The Jordanians too said that, while they disliked foreign pacts, they were
awkwardly placed to condemn Nuri's initiative since they depended on Britain's subsidy to maintain the Arab Legion which was
commanded by a British General with British officers in all key
positions. Only a few weeks earlier Aboul Huda had held discussions in London about revising the Anglo-Jordanian treaty, in
which the British Government adamantly insisted that any
changes in the treaty could only be considered as part of a new
defence system for the Middle East. In other words, if Jordan
wanted the British subsidy to be paid in future to the Government
and not direct to General Glubb, she would have to join the Turco-
Iraqi Pact.

Lebanon too was under some pressure to follow Nuri's lead.
And her delegation to the Cairo conference made much of the
fact that the Turkish Prime Minister had, on leaving Baghdad,
called in at Beirut to dangle before them the considerable advantages which Lebanon would enjoy if she joined the Turco-Iraqi
alliance. Turkey, so Menderes had said, had an army of ten divisions with the most modern equipment and there were now
50,000 tractors working on the land, all thanks to the generosity
of the United States. He had also hinted that Turkey would

support the Arabs against Israel if they agreed to sign up with him and Nuri.

All this had clearly made a deep impression on the Lebanese Government and not least upon their pro-Western President, Camille Chamoun. Added to the fact that, as Sami es-Solh told the Cairo conference, he had been warned that the United States would not help the Arabs at all if they persisted in their opposition to foreign pacts, Menderes' pressures made him all the more reluctant to condemn Iraq. Besides, Chamoun was convinced that Nasser's hostility to the Turco-Iraqi alliance was a matter of personal jealousy caused by Nuri's frustration of his plans to dominate the Arab world. He did not wish Lebanon to compromise her neutrality by joining the Baghdad Pact on the same terms as Iraq. But he nevertheless believed that Turkey could and should be encouraged to support the Arabs in their resistance to Israel. In a letter to his Chargé d'Affaires in Cairo, Nadim Dimechkie, Chamoun suggested that Nasser be asked if this together with the large-scale arms aid which the West would feel obliged to give to any Arab allies, would not help to strengthen the Arabs as a whole. But when he suggested that Nuri be invited to hold his hand, while a conference of the Arab League, Turkey, Iran and Pakistan investigated these possibilities, Nasser pooh-poohed the idea, saying that Nuri had refused to suspend his discussions with the Turks to enable any alternative to be worked out. And in the circumstances, Sami es-Solh joined his Syrian and Jordanian colleagues in declining to censure the Iraqi initiative.

Against these prevarications Nasser argued his case with patience and persistence. Far from the Turks being allowed by their American and British NATO partners to support the Arabs against Israel, he said, it was more likely that they would be drawn into an alliance with Israel, which was after all the creature of American and British policy. The proposed Baghdad Pact was a deliberate device to disrupt the Arab world and bend it to the will of the West. Admittedly, the Arab League security pact was, as Nuri had described it, 'ink on paper' and no more. But this meant that it should be strengthened, not weakened still further. 'If we all stand together,' he argued, 'the Western powers will be compelled in the end to come to terms with us.' The West needed the Arabs as much as the Arabs needed them. 'Our strategic position, our resources and manpower are essential to them,' he went on. The Arabs were about 50 million people and the West had lost much in the way of military manpower since India and Pakistan gained their independence. This meant that in the next war forces which had previously been available from Australia to defend the Middle East would be needed to protect South East Asia against the Chinese threat. Therefore, if the Arabs could only keep their unity, the West would be compelled in their own interest to supply arms and economic aid as a deterrent to any aggressor and a means to counter internal subversion. The main threat from Russia was not open aggression but Communist infiltration. So far the Communists were not a homogeneous group in Egypt. Lacking organisation and a popular base and branded as a party which acted on orders from abroad, they were no great threat and could do little more than exacerbate already existing tensions, as they had done in the burning of Cairo in 1952. But if given a pretext such as an alliance between Egypt and her former occupiers which they could represent as a submission to imperialism, they would gain immeasurably in popular appeal.

These arguments made considerable impact on the conference as a whole. Nevertheless they failed to convert those who had already spoken against condemning Nuri who, they believed, had special problems arising from Iraq's more exposed situation and who should therefore be allowed to make whatever arrangements he thought necessary for his security. And when Fadil Jamali turned up in Cairo half-way through the conference, he was quick to seize on this permissive attitude. The Arab League could not defend Iraq, he insisted. British and American support were essential and, if such support had strings attached, Iraq had to accept the strings. Jamali also made much of Menderes' hints of Turkish aid against Israel and even claimed that, with Eisenhower in the White House, American policy was to be transformed. The President, he claimed, had personally assured him that the United States would no longer support Zionism, but would rather seek cooperation with the Arabs and would influence Turkey to do the same.

This was too much even for Jamali's most credulous listeners. Bahieddin Bashayan, Iraq's new Foreign Minister, therefore thought it wise to revert to consideration of the merits of Nuri's initiative. But, in an attempt to minimise its implications, he offered an explanation of the proposed agreement with Turkey which bore so little relation to the original announcement as to be equally incredible to the conference. Bashayan followed this up by privately suggesting to Nasser that, if Cairo Radio would stop attacking Iraqi policy, he would try to persuade Nuri to abandon his ideas of a multilateral alliance and sign instead a seven-year agreement with Britain similar to the Anglo-Egyptian treaty. Nuri, he claimed, was not all that wedded to the alliance policy which had been sprung upon him by Menderes as a fait accompli concocted between Turkey and Britain.

But Nasser was not to be bought off by such vague promises. Whoever might have first conceived the plan for the proposed pact, Nuri was now, as always, wedded to the British and he was not going to be talked into a divorce by Bashayan who, as Nasser knew, had little influence over his Prime Minister. If Nuri was to be talked into retreating, it could only be done by mobilising pressure from the Arab League. But since at this stage Nasser had no really constructive alternative policy to offer, his largely negative arguments had failed to mobilise more than the anti-Hashemite Saudis and their Yemeni neighbours on his side. In a last despairing throw he suggested that the Arab League security arrangements should be strengthened by the formation of a joint military command. Such a command would coordinate training, communications and the manufacture of weapons; it would also decide on the distribution and size of each member state's peacetime contribution and the extent of its commitment in time of war.

The Prime Ministers of Lebanon, Syria and Saudi Arabia warmly welcomed the proposal, while the Jordanian, inevitably in the light of his special ties with Britain, reserved his position. But Jamali effectively wrecked the scheme by insisting that, while raq might join in these arrangements, she must still reserve her right to enter into whatever foreign alliances she deemed necessary. Whereupon Nasser promptly withdrew his proposal, acidly remarking that, if the Iraqi reservation were accepted, the joint command would extend the Arab League's commitments further than ever and 'we could find ourselves stretched on the rack of alliances far into Asia and into the Western defence system'. Then, with a final dramatic gesture he proposed that the Arab League security pact be annulled and that the League should become an organisation for cultural cooperation.

In the ensuing consternation Nasser did not pursue this last suggestion which he had thrown out more as a *coup de theâtre* than as a serious proposition. The conference had by now clearly shown that, try as he might, he was not going to get his own way. True, he had wrung from all concerned an assertion that they would not join Iraq in her defection. But Nuri was going to proceed with his policy in open contradiction of his public promises to keep in step with the Arab League, and the Arabs were too divided and irresolute to stop him. Chamoun made a last-minute effort to persuade the Iraqis to hold their hand while discussions took place about an alternative arrangement. But Nuri adamantly refused any delay and Chamoun's mission returned to Cairo empty-handed. There being therefore no point in further prolonging the conference, Nasser forced a vote to wind it up on February 6.

All in all this first exposure of Nasser to the cross-currents of inter-Arab politics was a depressing experience which left its mark upon him. Though never exactly starry-eyed about the possibilities of Arab cooperation or about the strength and cohesion of the Arab League, he had at least expected that his fellow Prime Ministers would be prepared to use such assets and resources as they had, and in particular their nuisance value, to force the Western powers to deal with them as a united body. In his private conversations with them outside the conference chamber he had specifically not ruled out the possibility of some defence cooperation, and perhaps even an ultimate alignment, with the West. But he insisted that the Arab League should first be built up as an effective body capable of negotiating from strength, not as a mere junior partner. And he was disgusted to see that his Arab colleagues, while paying lip service to the idea of unity, would do nothing to preserve and reinforce it and would not even condemn so obvious and deliberate a defector as Nuri' Iraq.

In Nasser's eyes the weakness of the Syrian and Lebanese attitude had been greatly to blame for his failure to carry the Cairo conference with him. He accepted that the Jordanians could not in their special situation speak out against the designs of their British patrons. But he could not excuse Chamoun or Fares el-Khoury for their ambivalence. Nor did he even trust them not to go back on their assertions that they would not join the Turco-Iraqi alliance.

Nuri might be the principal villain of the piece, but Chamoun and the dithering Khoury were not much better. And since he had failed to win over the Governments of these three countries, Nasser now decided to appeal to the people to change the Governments. The 'Voice of the Arabs' henceforth let fly against Nuri, Chamoun and the Syrian regime with a violence hitherto unequalled in modern inter-Arab relationships. The people of Iraq, Syria and Lebanon were told without any mincing of words to rise and rid themselves of those leaders who would betray them to the imperialists. Nuri and his henchmen, it was said, pretended that the Arabs were in danger of attack by Russia. But, in fact, their most real danger lay in the plans of the imperialists, whose oppression the Arabs knew only too well, to return and dominate the Arab world through their beachhead in Israel and with the help of their stooges such as Nuri and Chamoun. Nor was Jordan left out of account. For although, at this point, the King and his Government were spared this kind of abuse, General Glubb was subjected to violent attacks as an agent of British imperialism, who was exploiting his position as Hussein's army commander to serve British and not Jordanian or Arab interests.

With this war of words raging against Nuri and Glubb, there could scarcely have been a more unfortunate moment for Anthony Eden to pay his first, and only, visit to Nasser's Egypt. Up to this point Eden had kept a relatively open mind about the new regime in Cairo. He had been thankful to get the issue of the Canal Zone bases settled and he had instructed me to stay in Egypt for a few days after signing the treaty, in order to sound out Nasser on the possibilities of cooperation in the future. But, despite the advice of his ambassador, he could not or would not see that, by simultaneously reinforcing Britain's military presence in Iraq with an alliance with Nuri and the Turks, he was bound to undo much, if not all, of the good which the evacuation agreement had done for Anglo-Egyptian relations.

Therefore, when Eden stopped off in Cairo in February 1955 on his way to a conference in Bangkok of the South-East Asia Treaty Organisation, he spoke bluntly to Nasser about his plans with Iraq and about the radio campaign against Nuri. But there was never any real chance of an understanding between these two men. Nasser, for his part, spoke more in sorrow than in anger. He declared his desire for good relations with the West and his delight that the evacuation agreement had at the time so greatly improved the atmosphere between Egypt and Britain. But as Eden admitted in his memoirs, he was 'not open to conviction on the Turco-Iraqi enterprise', which he thought was most ill-timed and would seriously impair effective cooperation between the West and the Arab world. As for his attacks on Nuri, Nasser rather naively asserted that they were an internal Arab affair and need therefore be no concern of the British. Eden coldly retorted that Nuri was Britain's ally and attacks on him could not be calmly ignored as a mere internecine quarrel between Arabs. And although the timing of the new pact might be unfortunate for Egypt, it was essential for Britain.

Apart from these contentious issues, Nasser found himself thoroughly ill at ease with Eden who, he said afterwards, had a supercilious air about him throughout their talks. After dinner at Stevenson's embassy, he sat back on the sofa, when Nasser was speaking, with his eyes slightly averted and a look on his face which suggested that he was saying to himself 'What can this young officer tell me about international politics?' In short, if Nasser had felt that he had made little impression on Dulles, he knew that, with Eden, he had made even less.

Four days later this fact was brought home to him when, on February 24, Iraq and Turkey signed the formal treaty which was to be known as the Baghdad Pact and which was joined by Britain in April and by Pakistan and Iran later in the year. A further last-minute attempt by Chamoun to bring about a meeting of minds between Nuri and Nasser came to nothing. For, as Nasser had guessed, Nuri was not to be deterred by any intercession. From now on, therefore, it was to be war to the knife between the two of them. But what neither Nasser nor any other Arab leader could possibly have guessed at the time was that, within another four days, Israel was to break out in a massive attack on the Egyptian army in the Gaza Strip, and in so doing to implant in his conspiratorial mind the ineradicable suspicion that the Baghdad Pact and the Gaza Raid were part of a concerted Western plot to destroy the Egyptian revolution and to reassert the domination of imperialism over the entire Arab world.

Chapter 6

The Russian Arms Deal

Coming as it did immediately after Nuri's final 'defection', the Gaza Raid marked the first crucial turning point in Nasser's attitude towards Israel and the West. Up to this point he had had some reason to hope that the West, or at least the United States, would be sufficiently gratified that a new regime had replaced the corruption of the Farouk era to be ready to support him with arms and economic aid. Ali Sabry's mission to Washington and Dulles' visit to Cairo had been most disappointing. But Eisenhower's subsequent promise to Neguib of large-scale aid, once Anglo-Egyptian differences had been got out of the way, had been followed up in November 1954 with an agreement to supply $40 million worth of economic assistance. And even though the Americans had been canvassing countries such as Lebanon to join the Western alliance, the fact that they had left the British to make the running for the Baghdad Pact suggested that Dulles, if only out of his known jealousy of Eden, might be induced to help Iraq's Egyptian rivals, despite Cairo's hostility to any foreign entanglements.

Certainly no one could deny that, in their attitude to the Arab-Israeli conflict, Eisenhower's Government were an improvement on their predecessors who had been instrumental in creating the Israeli state and had shown little but hostility to the Arabs in general and to Egypt in particular. Nasser, as usual avidly scanning the foreign press, was delighted to read in the American papers, in the spring of 1954, that Henry Byroade, the American Assistant Secretary of State, had publicly told Israel that, to live in peace with her Arab neighbours, she should 'drop the attitude of the conqueror' and had criticised her for using German reparations payments to bolster her economy 'while doing nothing towards compensation of Arab refugees'. Still happier was he to learn that Byroade had claimed that the Arabs had a right to some assurance that Israel's policy of unlimited Jewish immigration would not bring about further attempts at territorial expansion which could only be at their expense.

Such statements had inevitably raised Egyptian hopes of a real friendship with the Americans as the leading Western power. But the Gaza Raid dealt a bitter blow to any optimism in this direction. As Nasser saw it, the combination of this Israeli attack and the Baghdad Pact represented a two-pronged assault on the Egyptian revolution which the Western powers had decided was a threat to their hegemony in the Arab world. No longer did he see America's apparent hesitation to join the Baghdad Pact as possibly indicating an understanding of Egypt's attitude and a desire to help her on her own merits. Dulles, he now believed, had been holding back solely because Israel, supported by the Jewish 'lobby' in the United States, objected to anything which would reinforce Iraq, one of her sworn Arab enemies. Thus all along the line there must have been an underlying agreement between Britain and America to use Nuri and the Israelis respectively as the instruments with which the new Egypt would be isolated and brought to heel.

As later events, such as the High Dam negotiations, were to show, Nasser continued to seek American and British assistance and it was only when he had exhausted all possibilities of Western help that he felt obliged to turn to the Russians. Also he managed to maintain friendly relations with individual Britishers and Americans. But from Gaza onwards he never again felt it possible to secure with Washington or London that relationship of real trust for which he had originally hoped.

Likewise his attitude to Israel was transformed by the Gaza Raid. Until then Nasser had not been greatly preoccupied with Israel as a threat to Egypt. Short of formal recognition, he was prepared to concede Israel all the benefits of peaceful co-existence and was only too ready to agree with Washington and London to leave the Arab-Israeli issue, as he put it, 'in the freezer'. In January 1955, he wrote in the American quarterly, *Foreign Affairs*, 'War has no place in the constructive policy which we have designed to improve the lot of our people. . . . A war would cause us to lose, rather than gain, much of what we seek to achieve.' And although he maintained the claim which Egypt had asserted since 1948, under Article X of the Constantinople Convention, to deny passage through the Suez Canal to Israeli ships or cargoes while a state of war existed, he and his predecessors had in fact allowed over sixty vessels bound for Israel to transit the Canal between 1951 and 1954.

As a pan-Arabist he naturally felt the greatest sympathy for the Palestinians who had been evicted to make way for the Jewish state and he was dedicated to obtaining some form of restitution for them. But the bitterness which he had felt over the Arab armies' humiliating defeat in 1949 had been directed more at those rulers who, like Farouk, had sent their soldiers to do battle with defective arms and no coordinated planning, rather than towards the Israelis for whose courage and military skill he had, as a soldier, a very high regard. An Israeli officer, Major Yeruham Cohen, whom he met and talked to during truces in the Palestine fighting, afterwards wrote that Nasser seemed more inclined to blame the British than the Israelis and that, after their final meeting, they 'parted with the hope that the day would not be far off when we could be friends without barbed wire coming between us'.

Nasser disliked the Zionist idea of a sectarian state which made second-class citizens of all non-conformists and hence cut against the grain of Arab-Jewish relationships over more than a thousand years. But he knew that Israel was there to stay and that the international community would not allow her to be destroyed. He therefore had no time for those, like the Moslem Brotherhood, who went about demanding a holy war against the Israelis. Apart from anything else, as he succeeded in convincing the ardently pro-Zionist M.P., Richard Crossman, he was principally concerned about the need for internal reforms in Egypt. Certainly, after he got the British to remove their troops, his first objective was to set the parlous Egyptian economy to rights.

In fact, so far was Nasser from spoiling for a fight with Israel at that stage that, from the autumn of 1953 until the Gaza Raid, he maintained a secret contact with the Israeli Prime Minister, Moshe Sharett, through the press office of the Egyptian embassy in

Paris and periodically through other channels as well. Sharett had been Foreign Minister from the inception of the Jewish state until January 1954 when he succeeded Israel's first Prime Minister David Ben Gurion. He was known to have been opposed to Ben Gurion's aggressive and uncompromising attitude towards the Arabs, which had led to such actions as the Israeli attack on a Palestinian refugee camp in the Gaza Strip in August 1953, in which twenty Arabs were killed and sixty wounded including a high proportion of women and children. He was equally appalled when two months later Israeli troops destroyed the village of Qibya in Jordan, killing sixty-two of its inhabitants, again mostly non-combatants. And when Ben Gurion elected to retire for a while to his desert settlement at Sde Boker in the Negev, Sharett's accession to the premiership seemed to offer some prospect of quiet, if not of peace. Nasser's hopes in this respect had been further strengthened by the initial success of a mission led by an American, Eric Johnston, who had been commissioned by Eisenhower in 1953 to secure the agreement of Israel and her Arab neighbours to a scheme for sharing the waters of the Jordan river as a first step towards a possible peace settlement. Nasser had given Johnston all the help he could, in the belief that by thus nibbling at the edges of the problem it might ultimately be reduced to negotiable proportions.

Certainly, as he told General Burns, head of the United Nations Truce Supervisory Organisation (UNTSO), one of the most important contributions which each side could make to achieving peace was to avoid frontier clashes, which could only arouse passions and harden postures. And since Sharett became Prime Minister, there had been no major incident on the Israeli-Egyptian border. True, in July 1954, there had been a clumsy attempt by Israeli agents, acting at the instigation of Ben Gurion from his Negev retreat, to wreck the Anglo-Egyptian negotiations by exploding fire bombs in British-owned cinemas and the U.S. Information libraries in Cairo and Alexandria, in the hope that Britain and America would blame the Egyptian Government for failing to keep order if not for inciting the violence. Also, in September of the same year, a freighter flying the Israeli flag became the first such ship to request passage through the Suez Canal. This was firmly refused in accordance with Egypt's claim to belligerent rights under the Constantinople Convention; and the ship and its crew were detained for a few weeks pending an investigation of charges that they had fired on Egyptian fishing vessels in the Gulf of Suez. But if the purpose of those who instigated these provocations was to sabotage the tenuous link between Nasser and Sharett, it certainly failed after enquiries through the Paris contact were able to establish that Israel's Prime Minister was in no way responsible and had in fact roundly condemned those who were.

There was therefore every reason why Nasser should pursue his efforts to reach some understanding with Sharett. At the very least, he hoped that it would show the Israelis that the new Egypt harboured no aggressive designs on them. At best, it might have turned a fragile and uneasy armistice into a peace settlement. But time and the shadow cast by such militants as Ben Gurion and his followers were against a successful outcome. Sharett convinced Nasser that he wanted a settlement and that he understood that something had to be done for the Palestinian refugees. But he could only offer compensation for the loss of their homes; he could not concede repatriation which, he said, would lead to the Jewish population being swamped by the returning Arabs. The Arab states would therefore have to undertake the task of re-settling the Palestinians.

Nor could Sharett meet Nasser's other cardinal requirement – the cession of the southern Negev to create a contiguous border between Egypt and her sister-state, Jordan. He insisted that the Negev had been awarded to Israel under the U.N. partition plan of 1947. Nasser replied that this argument was inconsistent. Israel was now claiming all the territory which she occupied at the time of the armistices in 1949. Yet when the armistice was concluded with Egypt, Israeli forces had not yet occupied the southern Negev. Peace, he said, had to be based on give and take and Israel could not expect the Arabs to agree to her keeping the Negev because the U.N. had awarded it to her and northern Galilee because she had conquered it.

But it was no use. Sharett was simply not in a position to negotiate any territorial concessions whatsoever. Nor could he offer
enough to placate the Palestinian outcasts. Yet, if he lacked the
means, at least he appeared to will the end. And even though, in
mid-February 1955, Ben Gurion returned from his desert sojourn
to become Israel's Defence Minister, Nasser still hoped that Sharett
would be able to maintain that state of tranquillity which they
both agreed was in the interests of both their countries whether or
not they might ever reach a full settlement. Indeed, so hopeful
was he that during a routine inspection of his troops in the
Gaza Strip early in February, he personally assured them that
there was small likelihood of their being attacked.

Then, within the next few days, the blow was struck that
shattered all his hopes and set in motion a chain reaction of events
which were to change the face of the Middle East. On the night
of February 28, 1955, an Israeli force, acting on orders from the
Defence Minister, Ben Gurion, crossed the armistice lines and
destroyed the Egyptian army headquarters in the Gaza Strip,
killing thirty-eight people including a number of civilians and
wounding a similar number. General Burns was promptly called
upon to investigate on the spot and, after collecting the necessary
evidence, he reported to the U.N. Security Council that this
incident, 'the most serious clash between the two parties since the
signing of the General Armistice Agreement' in 1949, had been a
'prearranged and planned attack ordered by the Israeli authorities'.

The Israeli Government protested that the raid had been a
response to an ambush by an Egyptian force perpetrated on an
Israeli patrol inside Israeli territory. There were also mutterings
from Tel Aviv that Israel was entitled to stage reprisals for attacks
on her territory by Egyptian 'fedayeen' commandos. But none of
these excuses or explanations were borne out by the overwhelming evidence of Burns and his UNTSO investigators.

Admittedly, even in the tranquil period of Ben Gurion's brief
retirement, there had been the inevitable occasional border incident. For, in the absence of any peace settlement to confirm the
terms of armistice, Israel's frontiers were a matter of continuing

dispute. Each side was, for instance, in the habit of sending parties across the armistice lines to gather intelligence about its opponent's positions. And three days before the Gaza Raid an Israeli cyclist had been shot at inside Israeli territory by a party engaged in an espionage mission from Gaza. But the circumstances of the raid proved beyond any doubt that this highly organised operation had been planned many days before that incident. And as for Israel's talk of fedayeen activity, even Anthony Eden admitted in his memoirs that the fedayeen raids on Israel did not begin until the spring of 1955, several months later.

During the sleepless nights which followed the Gaza Raid, Nasser made a number of decisions. First and most important, he decided that, by whatever means were available, he had to buy the necessary arms to deter any further Israeli attacks. Second, having failed to thwart the Baghdad Pact, he resolved to strengthen the Arab League security arrangements with a series of defence treaties between Egypt and her closest Arab allies. Third, in order to appease the demands of Gaza's Palestinian refugees and of the militants in the Egyptian army for some measure of retaliation against Israel, he agreed that fedayeen volunteers from the Gaza Strip should be trained to conduct sabotage and hit-and-run guerrilla operations inside Israeli territory. Fourth, he ordered that the radio campaign should be intensified against Nuri and his friends who, together with the Israelis, were seemingly being used by the imperialist powers to mount a two-pronged attack on Egypt. And in addition, he decided to supplement his war of words with a campaign of intrigue in Iraq designed to foment rebellion against the Government.

In the matter of arms purchases, Nasser's first thought was to approach the American and British Governments once again, although more as a means of testing their good faith than from any serious hope that they would satisfy his needs. For, so far at least, London had not responded to the 'shopping list' which he presented after the 1954 treaty was signed and there had been no sign of the Americans delivering the large quantities of arms which Eisenhower had personally promised to Neguib once Egypt had cleared up her differences with Britain. An American military mission had recently shown up in Cairo for discussions about the supply of weapons for the Egyptian army. But after several weeks of argument, it became clear that Dulles was insisting upon Egyptian participation in a Western defence system as an absolute precondition of American arms deliveries.

Nasser naturally objected that the Western powers were trying to mobilise Egypt to fight their enemies, whereas if Egypt were to get involved in hostilities with her enemy, Israel, she would quickly be denied all aid. Besides, as he had said for the past two years, any defence cooperation with the West must be undertaken by the Arabs as a united body, not piecemeal. But once again his arguments went unheeded. The Americans took the line that Nasser's talk of uniting the Arab world was nonsense, since the West had already 'lined up' Iraq, Jordan and Lebanon, not to mention non-Arab states in the area such as Turkey, Iran and Pakistan. All that they would concede was to submit Egypt's immediate requirement of $20 million worth of arms for further discussions with Washington. Whereupon an argument developed over Egypt's need to pay for the arms in local currency, since her total hard currency reserves then amounted to no more than $20 million. And as yet another deadlock set in, Washington piled on the agony by agreeing in April to supply arms to Nuri's Iraq.

Nor did Nasser fare any better with the British. The best he could get from this quarter was a decision to suspend the export of a consignment of Centurion tanks which Israel had ordered, but which it was felt, after Gaza, should be withheld as a mark of Britain's censure. But since the French continued to supply Israel with arms far exceeding the level which it had been agreed between Paris, London and Washington should be necessary for Israel's defence needs, Britain's gesture had little real effect on the local balance of power. And, so long as British deliveries to Egypt remained a trickle, it came as small comfort to the Egyptians. For at this point they had no more than six serviceable military aircraft and enough tank ammunition for a one-hour battle. Moreover, contrary to Israel's constant complaints about being surrounded by overwhelming numbers of hostile Arabs, the total strength of all the Arab League armies was only 205,000 of which

100,000 were Egyptians, while Israel could mobilise 250,000 men in forty-eight hours.

Faced with this imbalance of strength, Nasser frequently complained to the British and American Ambassadors about what he termed the persistent 'cheating' by the French over arms supplies to Israel. But nothing had been done to stop it. On the contrary, in July 1954, France signed an agreement to supply Israel with jet fighters which far outstripped in speed and armament anything possessed by the Arab air forces. Largely out of pique against Arab nationalism, which they blamed for the loss of their hegemony in Syria and Lebanon and for the current threat to their supremacy in North Africa, the French were getting their own back by helping the Arabs' enemy. And as Israel waxed stronger than ever in consequence, so Nasser interpreted American and British reluctance either to intervene with the French, or to respond to his requests for arms, as proof that the West as a whole were in league with Israel against the Arabs, or at least against those Arabs whom he represented.

If there was one way in which the United States and Britain might have eradicated these suspicions and made good the damage done by the tragic coincidence of the Gaza Raid with the Baghdad Pact, it was by promptly responding to Egypt's desperate appeal for arms. But, as ill luck would have it, at this stage of the Cold War against Russia and international Communism, both powers were living in a world where neutralism was considered as virtually akin to hostility. They also could or would not see that, even if Nasser had not yet become the hero figure that he later represented for every Arab nationalist, Egypt was, for better or worse, the centre of the Arab world; and for Nasser to talk of uniting the Arabs was not to be laughed off as a mere illusion of grandeur.

Because they ignored these truths and therefore seemed to go on dealing with the Middle East as if the Egyptian revolution had never taken place, Britain and America failed to seize the current opportunity to dispel Nasser's suspicions with substantial deliveries of arms. Only economic aid was to be forthcoming and, although Nasser continued for another seven months to hope against hope that Eisenhower's promise would be honoured, in the meanwhile he felt it necessary to reinsure by sounding out the Communist powers as the only practical alternative suppliers of the arms that he so desperately needed.

The first opportunity for enquiring in this quarter came in April 1955 when Nasser, accompanied by Salah Salem, attended the first gathering of thirty newly independent African and Asian states at Bandung in Indonesia. The conference owed its inception largely to Pandit Nehru and Chou En-lai, respectively Prime Ministers of India and China. Having recently met Nasser on a visit to Cairo, Nehru had been anxious that he should come to this meeting which was being called to demonstrate the solidarity of the neutral, non-aligned states of Africa and Asia. India's leader had shown much sympathy with Nasser's opposition to the Baghdad Pact, partly because as a neutral he suspected all power blocs and alliances and partly because his Pakistani neighbours were to be associated with it.

Nasser never really warmed to Nehru's lofty intellectualism, which made him feel inferior and he resented being lectured on the need to democratise his regime. But politically he had much in common with India's Prime Minister and he required little persuasion to attend the Bandung gathering and to visit India on the same trip. Nor was he disappointed by his reception at the conference. The attitude of those countries whom he regarded as stooges of the West, such as Thailand and the Philippines, greatly irritated him, although they were only a small minority in an overwhelmingly neutralist gathering. Also he was nettled when Nehru tried to prevent the inclusion of the Palestine question on the agenda. But he was delighted when the conference nevertheless decided to proclaim 'its support for the rights of the Arab people of Palestine and for the implementation of the United Nations resolutions', which called for their repatriation. Nasser was also much flattered by the attentions shown to him by the leaders of Asia whom he met for the first time. Chou En-lai invited him to share his table at several of the functions laid on by Indonesia's President Sukarno, who was host to the conference; and by all save the few pro-Western representatives Nasser was hailed as a leading figure in the emerging 'third world' of Afro-Asia.

When Chou asked about the situation in the Middle East, Nasser and Salem therefore seized the opportunity to stress the real threat which Egypt now faced from Israel and her desperate need of arms which the Western powers were withholding in the hope of forcing her and the other Arab states to yield to their demands. Then he asked without further ado whether Chou could sell him any arms, to which the Chinese Prime Minister replied that he was himself too dependent on Russian supplies to have any to spare. But he suggested that Egypt should acquire arms direct from Russia and promised to take the matter up with Moscow.

A few days after the Egyptian delegation had returned home from Bandung, Salem received a call from Daniel Solod, the Russian Ambassador in Cairo, who confirmed that Peking had passed on the Egyptian request to his Government. Russia, he said, would be delighted to oblige with the supply of any quantity of arms, including modern tanks and aircraft, against deferred payment in Egyptian cotton and rice. Moreover, he added that Moscow would be prepared also to help Egypt with any industrial project such as building a new Nile dam at Aswan to increase the storage of water for irrigation and hydro-electric power.

It was a remarkable offer by any standards and it showed how far Russian policy had developed in the last few years. During the Farouk era, Moscow had persistently opposed Egypt and the Arabs on the Palestine issue and had voted with America for the U.N. partition plan and the creation of the Jewish state. She had even engaged in an undignified race with the United States for the honour of being the first to recognise an independent Israel. And during the truces in the Palestine fighting, she had allowed her Czechoslovak satellite to supply Israel with the arms she needed to win the war. However the Egyptian revolution had caused some second thoughts in the Kremlin and the temptation to seek an influence over Arab policy by switching to support for anti-Western nationalism had become irresistible. In February 1953 Russia had seized on a bomb attack on her embassy in Tel Aviv to break off diplomatic relations with Israel and in March of the following year she vetoed a resolution in the U.N. Security Council which claimed to assert Israel's right of passage through the Suez Canal. Also in 1954 Moscow weighed in on the side of Arab neutralism with warnings to the Arab states not to allow the West to inveigle them into alliances.

Realising that, in view of her geographical position, Syria, more than any other Arab state, would decide whether or not Iraq could recruit any more Arab members for the Baghdad Pact, the Russians singled out Damascus for special attention. The Syrian Communist party leader, an outstanding young product of Moscow's training schools called Khaled Bagdash, opened an intensive campaign to denigrate the West and to persuade the Syrian electorate that the Soviet Union was their best friend. Also Molotov, as Russia's Foreign Minister, told the Syrian Government that Moscow supported Syria's neutrality and would help in safeguarding her independence in whatever way they thought best.

The Anglo-Egyptian treaty of October 1954 had come as something of a set-back for Russia's new strategy. Moscow viewed with some anxiety the evidence that the element of hate in Egypt's long-standing love-hate relationship with Britain seemed no longer to be uppermost. But, given the prevailing Western mania for pacts and bases, Russia's Middle East policy could only stand to gain in the long run. For to win, all that Moscow needed to do was to support neutralism which the Arabs, with few exceptions such as Nuri, craved to the point where neutrality became synonymous with independence; whereas the West, who regarded neutralism as defection, made enemies in the Arab world whenever they denounced it. And while Britain and America persisted in their attempts to lure the Arabs into their defence alliances with promises of arms, the Russians would have been insane not to seize the opportunity to offer aid without strings and so to pose as the true friend of modern Arab nationalism.

Nevertheless, Nasser's initial response to Solod's offer was one of caution, not unmixed with suspicion. He remembered all too well how Russia had opposed the Arabs in earlier days and had helped to arm Israel during the Palestine War, knowing that an embargo had been placed by the West on arms supplies to the Arabs. He did not therefore need to be told that Moscow's sudden conversion was dictated by opportunism rather than altruism. Nor was he short of advice from his RCC colleagues to beware of mortgaging Egypt's cotton crop to the Russians who, if it suited them, could use their position as Egypt's virtually sole patrons to put pressure on her in the same way as the British had done in the past. Besides, Nasser still preferred to buy arms from Britain and America, if this could be done on acceptable terms. Despite all their differences, he was used to dealing with Westerners; he had no experience of the Russians; and the Egyptian army was accustomed to handling Western equipment.

At the same time Russia's proffered support was clearly something which could be turned to Egypt's profit. When Turkish troop concentrations were reported on Syria's borders in March 1955, Cairo Radio was quick to warn the Turks not to threaten their Arab neighbours who were opposed to the Baghdad Pact and to 'remember that Turkey too has a neighbour who is stronger than she is'. Also in the following month Egypt had found it useful to conclude a commercial agreement with Russia. Nasser's first reaction to Solod's offer was, therefore, immediately to inform the American and British Ambassadors and to warn them that, if he could not get the arms he wanted from the West, he would have to accept the Russian proposal. But this time it was the turn of London and Washington to talk of blackmail. And although Stevenson and Byroade, the new American Ambassador, advised their Governments that Nasser meant what he said, the only result of this manoeuvre was a retort from London warning Nasser that, if he took arms from Russia, he would get nothing more from Britain.

Meanwhile the Russians, rightly suspecting that Cairo was trying to play them off against the West, were pressing for serious discussion of their offer. And when, in June, the Western powers had shown no signs of succumbing to his threats, Nasser agreed with his RCC colleagues that it would be unwise to keep Solod waiting any longer. Discussions were then started with the Russian embassy and at the end of June Solod suggested to Salem that the

Egyptian Government should invite Dmitri Shepilov, then the editor of *Pravda*, to visit Cairo at the time of the third anniversary of the revolution. Shepilov, so Solod confided, played an important part in shaping Russian foreign policy and was shortly to succeed Molotov as Foreign Minister. With the RCC's agreement Salem therefore despatched the suggested invitation and in July Shepilov arrived in Cairo where in a few days he completed the draft of an agreement whereby Egypt would buy $80 million worth of Russian arms, including MIG fighters, Ilyushin bombers, Stalin tanks and other equipment, to be paid for in Egyptian cotton. The arms were to be of Russian manufacture, although the deal was officially to be handled by the Czechoslovak Government, which Nasser felt would make it sound less sinister to the outside world, since Israel had herself been armed by the Czechs during the Palestine War. And as Egyptian technicians took off for Prague to look over the assorted equipment promised by the Russians, the draft agreement was sent to Nasser for signature.

But still Nasser hesitated in the hope of some eleventh-hour change of heart on the part of the West. The previous trickle of British arms supplies had recently shown some signs of expanding with the sale to Egypt of thirty-two Centurion tanks and two destroyers. And in the hope that this example might help to break the American log-jam, he summoned his Air Attaché in Washington for urgent consultations. As the Air Attaché entered his office, Nasser pointed to a paper on his desk which, he said, was the draft of the Russian agreement. This agreement, he asserted, had not yet been signed by him and it would lie on his desk until every possibility had been exhausted of obtaining from the West the arms that he needed for Egypt's defence. Byroade was informed accordingly and the Air Attaché took off for Washington to make one final attempt to break the deadlock. But it was all in vain. As the American Admiral Radford later summed it up to a congressional committee, 'The Egyptians wanted to buy the kind of weapons we didn't want them to get.' The deadlock therefore became total and, as it turned out, the only weapon that the United States supplied to Egypt throughout he whole of Nasser's reign was a silver-engraved pistol which Dulles presented to Neguib in 1953 as a gift from Eisenhower.

So, in September, after vainly waiting for another two months for an answer from Washington, Nasser announced to the world that he had signed an agreement for the supply of arms from the Soviet bloc in exchange for Egyptian cotton. To the *New York Times* correspondent, Kennet Love, he added in a reference to the imbalance of arms created by France's supplies to Israel, 'Now we will be meeting Mystères with Migs.' Much as he regretted having to give armaments priority over social requirements, he had been left with no alternative, he said. 'I cannot defend Egypt with schools and hospitals and factories, and what will be the use of them if they are destroyed?'

In April of the preceding year when Nasser took over from Neguib as Prime Minister, he had said that it was 'useless to talk of neutralism unless you are strong enough to protect your neutrality'. This did not mean that he had any doubts about the desirability of neutrality for Egypt. It did mean that to safeguard Egyptian neutrality in the immediate future two things were essential. The British occupation of the Canal Zone had to be ended and the army had to be strong enough to protect Egypt's borders. Gaza had made rearmament more urgently necessary than ever and had added to the earlier list of requirements such weapons as bombers, which would serve as a deterrent to any further comparable Israeli aggression. And this Nasser was now about to achieve by the arms deal with Russia.

But Gaza and the Baghdad Pact taught him yet another lesson. The strength necessary for Egypt to preserve her neutrality had to be sought collectively with those other Arab states which were not under the dominance of the imperialist powers. Consequently in March 1955, after Khoury had been ousted from office in Syria, Egypt seized on the change of regime in Damascus to sign with Syria and Saudi Arabia a defence agreement, under which all three countries pledged themselves to resist Israeli aggression, to keep clear of all foreign alliances and to participate in a joint military command to coordinate training and organisation from a centralised headquarters. On top of this had come the

Bandung conference, which proved to be yet another turning point for Nasser – and not solely because it was there that the Russian arms deal was conceived. For the spirit of collective and determined neutralism which he found among most of his African and Asian colleagues at Bandung, and which was reflected during his visit to India on the way home, suggested to him that given the necessary will and organisation, it could be developed into a positive force, instead of remaining a mere negative nuisance to the existing power blocs. This was where his doctrine of 'positive neutralism' was born. And since he himself wanted to have a hand in shaping its future growth, he persuaded his Bandung colleagues to establish in Cairo the headquarters of the organisation which was to be known as the Afro-Asian People's Solidarity Movement.

Neither of these two initiatives worked out very satisfactorily. Late in 1957, a conference in Cairo of the Afro-Asian movement suggested to Nasser that this body was falling rapidly under Communist influence. And for fear that he might be drawn off his neutralist course and find himself exclusively aligned with the Soviet bloc, he was obliged to take control of the movement by placing his own nominees in leading positions in the secretariat. As for the tripartite alliance with Syria and Saudi Arabia, this initiative was to become little more than a diplomatic gesture against Nuri's Iraq. Endless discussions took place on questions such as the defence budget and the combined General Staff. Egypt demanded control, but refused to pay because she was too poor, while the Saudis said that they would pay but would not allow any other country to control their army. Nor were any of these problems resolved until, after six months of fruitless argument it was agreed to forego the over-ambitious attempt to create an integrated army command. So in October 1955, the tripartite alliance gave way to separate military alliances between Egypt, Syria and Saudi Arabia.

But of all the decisions which Nasser made in the aftermath of the Gaza Raid the most ill-fated was the launching of fedayeen attacks on Israel. Nothing could have played more completely into the hands of Israel's hard-line elements. During most of the following summer Sharett came under ever increasing pressure to hit back with savage reprisals for every fedayeen incursion or to make way for a more resolute successor. After barely surviving a series of motions of censure for his weakness, he was finally driven to resign. In November 1955 Ben Gurion took over the premiership again. Sharett reverted to his former role as Foreign Minister and seven months later he was removed altogether from office and succeeded by Mrs Golda Meir. Thus, with Ben Gurion back in full control and threatening to the *New York Times* that Israel would use force if necessary to prise open the sea-lane to Elath through the Gulf of Akaba which Egypt had closed since 1948, it was clear that the hard-liners were again directing Israeli policy. Nor was Israel content only to retaliate against fedayeen incursions. She now developed a provocation tactic of her own. Israeli tanks or armoured cars would drive head-long at an Egyptian frontier post, their crews shouting insults at the defenders. Inevitably the Egyptians would then open fire and, as the first attacking wave receded, Israeli reinforcements would pour in and wipe out the post.

Still, despite the rising temper of his army commanders, Nasser remained as loath to be drawn into a military confrontation with Israel as he had been to engage in a political showdown with the West. With an army, which was as always much more of a bureaucracy than a fighting force and which would require many months of training to be able to handle the new sophisticated weapons promised by Russia, he was not going to repeat the callous adventurism of Farouk and his Ministers in plunging into the war of 1948. Nor, having vehemently criticised Nahas' reckless collision with the British in 1951 without any planning or preparation, was he anxious to provoke a hostile reaction from the Western powers, however suspicious he might be of their inten-tions. Indeed, after the Gaza Raid, Nasser proposed to General Burns as head of UNTSO that each side should pull its forces back one kilometre from the demarcation line. And when, after months of fruitless argument in the U.N. armistice commission, the Israelis stubbornly insisted that such disengagement would involve for them an unacceptable renunciation of sovereignty, he decided unilaterally to withdraw Egyptian troops in the hope of reducing the risk of a major collision.

At the same time, Nasser had felt obliged to demonstrate to the militants in the army and among the Palestinian refugees in the Gaza Strip that he would not take Israel's attacks lying down. Hence his decision in the spring of 1955 to let the fedayeen loose upon Israel's frontiers. But with his forces getting the worst of every exchange and the Israelis inflicting casualties far exceeding anything caused by the fedayeen, these Egyptian harassments were no more than a minor irritant. Indeed, in some ways they were a positive help to Israel, for they served as a demonstration to Israel's supporters in the West, which Ben Gurion was not slow to exploit, that Israel existed in a continuing state of siege and could only survive by periodic massive reprisals against her besiegers.

Certainly there was no let-up in these Israeli retaliations. In August, while Sharett was still Premier, their forces struck again at the Gaza Strip, killing thirty-nine Egyptians and Palestinians in an attack on the village of Khan Yunis in retaliation for a fedayeen raid two days before, in which seven Israelis had been killed and a radio transmission mast damaged. In the following month, in open breach of the Israeli – Egyptian armistice terms, Israel occupied the demilitarised zone of El-Auja on the Negev border which contained a road junction of key importance to any would-be aggressor from either side. In October, her troops attacked Kuntilla seventy miles to the south. And in November, within a few hours of Ben Gurion publicly proclaiming his readiness to meet Nasser to discuss a mutual settlement, they struck hard into Sinai from their new base at El-Auja, killing another seventy Egyptians. To which Nasser's only reply was to claim that the Egyptian army had successfully driven out the invaders by a counter-attack which actually never took place.

In December, the Israelis turned their attentions on Syria and in a raid near Lake Tiberias killed fifty-six Syrians, in retaliation for the harassment of some Israeli fishing boats on the lake which had in fact caused no casualties whatever. Sharett protested vigorously to Ben Gurion about this action, although he defended it in his public statements as Foreign Minister. Nasser too issued a warning to Israel that another such attack would lead to counteraction by Egypt in defence of her Syrian ally. But Ben Gurion's immediate response was to renew Israel's threat to divert the Jordan river for the irrigation of the Negev by digging a canal in the demilitarised zone on their border with Syria. And he was only prevented from carrying out this scheme by strong pressure from the Americans, to whom he had just put a request for large-scale military aid, which included 50 jet aircraft, heavy tanks, and artillery.

Then in April of 1956 Ben Gurion's troops were on the march again with yet another strike, allegedly against fedayeen bases in the Gaza Strip, which resulted in the death of another sixty-three Egyptians and Palestinians. Dag Hammarskold, the U.N. Secretary-General, promptly hastened to Cairo and Tel Aviv to try to reduce tensions. And for a while hostilities were largely confined to angry verbal exchanges inside and outside the United Nations. But for all Hammarskold's strenuous attempts at mediation, fifteen months after Gaza, Nasser was little better placed than before and was heading for the very confrontation which he wished to avoid. By his harassment of Israel, his violent attacks on the Baghdad Pact and his arms deal with Russia, he found himself steering on a collision course not only with the belligerent Ben Gurion, but also with such Western leaders as Dulles and Eden, who regarded his neutralism as a cloak for an implacable hostility, abetted by Russia, towards every American and British interest in the Middle East.

Chapter 7

Conflict with the West

Israel and Russian arms were not the only flash-points in Nasser's relations with the Western powers at this juncture. In spite of the RCC's renunciation of Farouk's claim to the unity of the Nile Valley under the Egyptian crown, the Sudan continued to be a bone of contention between Egypt and Britain. In 1953 there had been ominous rumblings from Cairo, with Neguib alleging that the British were delaying the elections in order to handicap the pro-Egyptian NUP and working for the secession of the three southern provinces from the Sudan so as to maintain British control over these areas. These allegations had been followed by countercharges from the Umma party leaders that the Egyptians were intriguing against Sudanese independence, which were echoed in parliamentary statements by Eden and his deputy, Selwyn Lloyd. Then, early in 1954, Hussein Zulficar Sabry, Ali Sabry's elder brother and Egypt's representative on the Governor-General's supervisory commission, alleged in an obvious attack on the British that 'Sudanisation' was being deliberately held up by 'other members' of the commission. The Pakistani Chairman retorted that Sabry's claims were slanderous and once again the Umma leaders joined in the fray with accusations that it was the Egyptians who were trying to impede the Sudan's progress towards independence.

Such accusations rang all too true, for it was an established fact that Salah Salem, Egypt's Minister for Sudanese Affairs, was spending lavish sums of money in an effort to induce the people of the Sudan to opt for some link with Egypt when they came to determine their future status. It was well known too that the NUP was largely, if not entirely, financed from Cairo. Also in 1953 and 1954 the Egyptian Government had sent every one of their officials of Sudanese origin back to the Sudan on special holidays' at the time of the elections.

But, as it happened, this policy of bribery and intrigue backfired on Cairo. As the Umma party multiplied their protests against Salem's activity, supplementing them with plentiful evidence of Egyptian scheming, Sudanese opinion became increasingly apprehensive and disinclined to favour any link with Egypt beyond that which geography had unalterably prescribed. In this atmosphere the NUP leader and Prime Minister, Ismail al-Azhary, found it more and more necessary to lean towards total independence for the Sudan and away from any thoughts about a union of the Nile Valley. Besides, Azhari, who had also taken part in the Bandung conference, had been no less smitten than Nasser by the emphasis which the Third World's leaders had placed on the importance of absolute independence. And he was convinced that, if there was ever to be a true union between the Sudan and Egypt, it would have to spring from the active desire of the people and could never be imposed by bribery or force.

Thus, a little more than a year after Cairo's hopes had been raised by the NUP's victory at the polls, it was becoming clear that Azhari was only interested in Egypt's support to oust the British. For all his early protestations favouring a link with Egypt, he was in practice little less dedicated to Sudanese independence than the Umma opposition. This was a bitter pill for the RCC to have to swallow. And rather than do so, Nasser agreed to make one final effort to woo Sudanese opinion by bribery and every other available means. In September 1954 Salem, on a visit to Khartoum, devoted special attention to the Khatmiyah sect which, like the Ansar for the Umma party, was the NUP's main popular support and which, rumour had it, was sponsoring a campaign against any formal ties with Egypt. But Salem's efforts went unrewarded, although not unremarked by the Umma who made them the pretext for yet another protest about Egyptian intrigues, which once again found sympathetic echoes in Whitehall.

Eight months later Cairo tried another tack. In April 1955 talks

were held with the Sudan on the problem of revising the 192
Nile Waters agreement which the Sudanese Government ha
refused to confirm on taking office in 1953, on the grounds tha
the agreement did not take proper account of Sudanese require
ments, and that it had been imposed on the Sudan at the time b
the co-domini, Britain and Egypt. Nasser had already begun to to
with the idea of building a new dam at Aswan in order to increas
the amount of water available for irrigation of Egypt's cultiv
able acreage and to provide hydro-electric power for new indus
tries. And with the disappointment administered by Azhari'
change of front to his hopes for some form of Nile union, the age
old fear that the safety of Egypt's life-blood might be threatene
from the Sudan was beginning to haunt him. But negotiation wa
to prove at this stage no less futile than intrigue. For on the ver
next day the talks were broken off and, to add further fuel to th
flames of discord, the Sudanese delegate was arrested by an over
zealous Cairo policeman for trying to get a poem printed whicl
had been written by a Sudanese poet in praise of Neguib.

Britain, of course, had been watching these various man
œuvres with considerable suspicion, not unmixed with deligh
that the Sudanese were palpably determined to keep the Egyptian
out. In June, Eden, now Prime Minister, suggested to Nasser tha
talks be held in Cairo to settle the composition of yet anothe
commission, this time to supervise the process of self-determina
tion by the Sudanese people. Nasser agreed readily enough; bu
when, after two months of arguing, the talks had produced n
agreement, it was finally decided to let the Sudanese Parliamen
resolve the issue. Then, in this very same month, the new
reached Cairo and London that the Sudanese army garrison a
Torit in the southern Sudan had mutinied. Their action was i
part due to resentment that, under the Sudanisation processes
their British officers had been replaced by northern Sudanese whc
the troops feared would maltreat them as inferior Africans anc
non-Moslem infidels. But another major cause had been th
impact of Egyptian propaganda designed to persuade the souther
ners that they should regard Egypt as their protector agains
northern oppression. There is also some evidence to suggest tha

Salem hoped that a rebellion in the south might bring about the downfall of Azhari, of whom he had now come to despair completely as a potential ally of Egypt.

But, if such were Salem's plans, he was quickly disappointed. A state of emergency was promptly declared from Khartoum; the mutiny was speedily suppressed by northern troops; and the mutineers surrendered on the assurance of the Governor-General, Sir Knox Helm, that their fears and grievances would be looked into. Meanwhile Salem, not to be denied, had suggested, in a desperate attempt to turn the situation to Egypt's advantage, that Egyptian and British troops should be dispatched to the southern Sudan to quell the rebellion and maintain order. But this was too much for Nasser. British and Egyptian forces were scheduled to be completely withdrawn from Sudanese territory within less than three months and it would strike at the very fundamentals of his policy to invite Britain to prolong her military presence in the Sudan by so much as twenty-four hours. Thus, even if Nasser had thought that there might be some advantage in sending Egyptian troops to keep order in the southern Sudan, the fact that the British would be there as well would have caused him to reject Salem's suggestion.

Besides, Nasser had by now come to the conclusion that bribery and conspiracy in the Sudan had proved completely counter-productive and should henceforth be abandoned. In later years he was to tell Trevelyan and others, including myself, that his Sudanese experience taught him that bribery was a bad method of conducting policy because the people who took bribes were interested in the money and not in the policy. At the time, of course, Nasser kept quiet about the bribery, while admitting to Trevelyan that he had been using propaganda in the Sudan to counter Azhari's 'suppression' of the Egyptian point of view. But by way of demonstrating his change of approach, he dismissed Salem from his posts, took personal charge of Sudanese affairs and appointed Abdel Kader Hatem, another former Free Officer, as Minister of National Guidance. Salem thus became the scapegoat for the failure of a policy which Nasser had himself approved, but for which, since he had been given a virtually free hand in its execution, he had been held largely responsible by Sudanese opinion.

In the ordinary way these changes, together with the cessation of Egyptian bribery, might have brought about a greatly improved atmosphere in Anglo-Egyptian and Egyptian-Sudanese relations. In some superficial respects this appeared to be the case when, in November 1955, British and Egyptian forces were withdrawn on schedule and Khartoum proposed a resumption of the talks with Egypt about the division of the Nile waters. But this time the atmosphere was unhappily soured by a foolish piece of scheming by Whitehall behind Nasser's back.

Since the withdrawal of the Anglo-Egyptian forces would have left the Governor-General in the invidious position of having to exercise responsibility without power over a prolonged period of time, Helm suggested that the co-domini should immediately declare the Sudan independent and the Condominium at an end which would enable him to transfer his governmental functions to the Sudanese. But when Trevelyan put this idea to the Egyptians, Nasser interpreted it as requiring him to admit publicly that the Sudanese wanted total independence without any links with Egypt. No doubt they did, he said. But, for internal reasons, he could not be seen to concede it. Neguib and the old-guard politicians might be discredited, but their obsession about the unity of the Nile Valley lived on in the minds of many Egyptians. He therefore could not accept the Governor-General's proposal.

Yet heedless of Nasser's objections, Helm was authorised by Whitehall a few days later to suggest to Azhari that he should proclaim the Sudan an independent state and to tell him that, if he did so, Britain would support him. Needless to say, and as Trevelyan had warned the Foreign Office would happen, Nasser was informed of the Governor-General's approach within a matter of hours by an Egyptian agent in Azhari's office. From this he assumed, not unnaturally, that the British were trying to cheat him. For although in the past Britain had more often than not acted unilaterally in performing her functions in the Sudan, the essence of the Condominium was that the co-domini should operate by consultation and agreement; and Trevelyan's action in

onsulting him about Helm's proposal had suggested that White-
all was at long last prepared to observe these conventions.

Then, on January 1, 1956, with Helm out of the country taking
is annual home leave, Azhari elected to put the British proposal
nto effect and declared the Sudan an independent sovereign
tate. Nasser had no alternative but to accept the fait accompli and
oin with Britain in recognising Sudanese independence. But,
onvinced that the whole business had been a British intrigue
lesigned to worst the Egyptians and poison their relations with
Khartoum, he refused to discuss Sudanese matters any further
vith Trevelyan and designated Zacharia Mohieddin to act in his
olace. And the net result of this unfortunate piece of double-
lealing by Whitehall was to deepen still further Nasser's inherent
listrust of British policies and methods.

Thus the year which began with Britain and Egypt falling out
over the Baghdad Pact was to end with yet another unhappy row
about the Sudan and with London and Cairo engaged in ever-
ncreasingly hostile exchanges. But this is not to say that at no
point was there a break in the gathering storm-clouds. For one
hing, in April 1955, on the very day that Britain formally joined
he Baghdad Pact, Eden finally accepted the advice of his Cairo
embassy and assured Nasser that Britain would not attempt to
ecruit any other Arab states as members of this alliance. In
eturn Nasser toned down his attacks on the Pact. Despite press
eports that Britain and Turkey were still trying to persuade
ordan and Lebanon to join, Cairo Radio maintained silence. Nor
lid Nasser react when Eden, in reply to Tel Aviv's objections,
publicly stated that the Pact, far from being a threat to Israel, was
n fact a 'truly desirable development' for her. Then, in August,
Dulles made a further contribution to Arab–Western understanding. Following up an earlier appeal by Eden for a settlement
of the Palestine problem, he publicly expressed his sympathy for
the tragic plight of 900,000 refugees' whose grievances, he said,
were every bit as important to any ultimate settlement as the
question of frontiers.

Naturally the announcement of the Russian arms deal provoked
a shocked and hostile reaction in Washington and London, as

well as Tel Aviv, where Ben Gurion described it as being 'for on
reason only – to destroy the state and people of Israel'. Nasser ha
anticipated Western disapproval and, on the day that he finall
decided to accept the Russian offer, he told the British Ambas
sador that General Amer would not be able to take up an invita
tion by Britain's Chief of the Imperial General Staff to visit Britis]
forces in Germany and the United Kingdom. So he was no
surprised when Trevelyan told him of London's serious mis
givings that Egypt seemed about to embark on a course whicl
would involve her in an arms race with Israel, and in a dangerou
dependence on the Communist bloc, for spare parts and replace
ments, as well as for training and technical assistance. Nasse
replied, reasonably enough, that he had no intention of substitut
ing Russian for British domination but that Gaza had made i
imperative for him to buy arms wherever he could. Britain an
America only had themselves to blame for the fact that he had ha
to turn to Russia to get what he needed. He also complained witl
some acidity that the Foreign Office had leaked to the Britis]
press his prior intimation to Trevelyan that he had made a dea
with Russia, thereby putting him 'in a corner'.

The American Government took the matter every bit a
seriously. When Dulles learned from Byroade of Nasser's inten
tion to sign the Russian agreement, he sent Roosevelt to Cairo t
try to get the Egyptians to reverse their decision. But, as Roosevel
was soon to realise, Nasser was not to be talked out of the deal
All he could do was to persuade him to say, when he announce
the agreement, that the arms were solely for defence and that onc
Egypt's security had been assured he would work to reduce th
tension with Israel. But in the meanwhile Dulles had decided t
send Byroade's successor as Assistant-Secretary of State, George
Allen, to deliver a personal letter from him to Nasser. And wher
the news of this move broke, the Associated Press added the glos
that Allen was bringing an ultimatum. Once again, therefore
Nasser felt that he was being 'put in a corner'. Not only did he
strike out the passage in his speech which he had agreed witl
Roosevelt, but he also gave Allen very short shrift when he callec
to deliver Dulles' message.

The RCC were even more angered by what they considered to be the gross impertinence of a Government which had refused to supply the arms which they needed, yet reserved the right to tell them that they should not seek these supplies elsewhere. Some members argued that Egypt should break off diplomatic relations with the United States and that demonstrations should be organised against the American embassy to show Washington the strength of feeling in Cairo against Dulles' unwarranted interference. But Nasser wisely talked his colleagues out of such hot-headed action. Earlier in the year he had met President Tito of Yugoslavia with whom he had cruised up the Suez Canal on board an Egyptian naval training ship. And from this most skilful diplomatic tightrope walker, who managed not only to get substantial aid from the West but also to become the only leader of a Communist state to receive payment from Moscow in United States dollars, Nasser had learned with fascination about how to play the West and the Soviet bloc off against each other. As Tito had told him, the golden rule in this game was to maintain all possible contacts with both sides and he was not going to let the RCC push him into breaking it out of mere irritation over an impertinent intervention by Dulles. Besides, Nasser knew that, in this dispute, he held all the cards and that the only way the West could strengthen their hand would be to reverse the decision not to arm Egypt. Therefore the storm would either blow itself out or would bring him some benefit.

Events were to prove this judgement correct. The defiance of the Western 'imperialists' which Egypt had demonstrated was loudly acclaimed by nationalist opinion throughout the Arab world, especially in Syria. And Washington and London soon saw that, since they themselves had no alternative to offer, it would serve no useful purpose to go on haranguing Nasser on the dangers of doing what he had done when he could justifiably reply that the dangers of doing nothing were for him infinitely greater.

Moreover, at least on the Palestine issue, it did not seem that the Russian arms deal had adversely affected Britain's open-minded attitude. For early in November, speaking at London's Guildhall, Eden stated as his opinion that both Israel and the Arabs would have to make some compromise over the question of frontiers i order to reach a settlement and he hinted that the eventual solutio should lie somewhere between the existing borders which Israe had gained by conquest in the 1948 war and the lines agreed in th U.N. partition plan, to which the Arabs were now demandin; that Israel should withdraw. Ben Gurion immediately rejecte Eden's proposal which, he claimed, would 'truncate the territor of Israel for the benefit of her neighbours'. But Nasser welcome the Guildhall pronouncement as marking the first occasion o which a major Western leader had taken a constructive line o the Palestine conflict.

Then, as 1955 drew to its close, the West seemed to hav learned the lesson of the Russian arms deal, when America an Britain announced their decision to help with the World Bank i financing the new High Dam at Aswan, on which Nasser had se his heart. Egypt's Finance Minister, Abdel Moneim Kaissouny promptly set off for the United States accompanied by a staff o technical advisers to hold discussions with American, British an World Bank officials. Nasser felt for a fleeting moment that th West were beginning to understand that the Russians offers to help Egypt were not so much bluff and that, if the wanted to maintain their influence in the Nile Valley, they coul not afford to be less forthcoming. Admittedly, the United State and Britain were still denying him the arms that he needed. Bu Eisenhower had at least decided to reject Israel's request for fifty jet aircraft, plus tanks and other heavy equipment, to balance Russia's promised deliveries to Egypt, on the grounds that he existing weapon strength was far superior to that of her Arab neighbours. And if he could get economic aid from the West an arms from Russia, by Tito's rules he should be well served.

Also among the credit items in Egypt's relations with th West, Nasser enjoyed an excellent personal relationship with Trevelyan and, until the autumn of 1955, with Byroade also. Fo Trevelyan he had the greatest respect as a man of brilliant intellec who, unlike Nehru, never talked down to him. Despite suc upsets as had occurred over Azhari's declaration of Sudanese independence, he had implicit trust in Trevelyan's persona ntegrity. Nor did he ever waver in that trust, even in the final wful denouement of Suez, when he knew that Britain's Ambassador had been kept as much in the dark about Eden's intended ttack on Egypt as he was himself.

Nasser also had a high regard for Byroade's brilliant military ecord as a young brigadier in World War II. Sometimes he vould be taken aback by the American's breezy manner and inconventional habits. Although he liked informality, he never eally got used to being called Gamal by foreigners, however well hey knew him. Yet, for all this, he found in Byroade a warm-hearted, sympathetic friend who fully lived up to the pro-Arab promise of his earlier speeches. Nasser had been somewhat offended to learn that the absence of a number of Western Ambassadors from the reception committee at Cairo airport when he returned from Bandung had been prompted by advice from Byroade. (He was still more put out when he heard from his telephone tappers that American diplomats were jokingly referring to that conference as the 'Darktown Strutters' Ball'.) But he accepted the explanation that the absent Ambassadors had intended no offence and had merely felt that, in the circumstances of this particular event, the Prime Minister's reception at the airport should be kept as a purely Afro-Asian affair. And it was not until Byroade made the mistake of attacking Nasser to his face in front of his RCC colleagues, in the autumn of 1955, that this close personal relationship was brought to an end.

Even then he remained on the best of terms with Kermit Roosevelt and another of the CIA's Middle East representatives, Miles Copeland. He knew well enough that Roosevelt had been largely instrumental in organising the coup in Iran which led to the ousting of the anti-Western Prime Minister, Mohammed Mossadeq, and his replacement by a Government more amenable to Western oil interests. But he was so convinced of this particular American's sympathy and good faith that, when told to beware of him by his own intelligence service, he replied that Roosevelt's activities outside Egypt made no difference to his feelings of friendship for the man. Indeed he jokingly suggested that Roosevelt and Ahmed Hussein, Egypt's Ambassador in Washington at

the time, should exchange places. Roosevelt should represen
Egypt in America, while Hussein who was, he said, for eve
making excuses for Washington's attitude, should become Ameri
can Ambassador in Cairo.

But the hopes aroused by promises of Western help for th
High Dam were soon to be overtaken by further recriminations
In November, following a state visit to Amman by the Turkisl
President, King Hussein and General Glubb had indicated to
London that Jordan might consider joining the Baghdad Pact i
Britain provided her with more arms. Whitehall's response was to
send the King ten Vampire jet fighters; and on December (
General Templer, Britain's CIGS, followed up with a visit to
Amman. Templer's instructions were to promise Jordan enough
tanks and artillery to equip a new armoured and infantry division
and to offer a new agreement to replace the Anglo-Jordaniar
treaty which Aboul Huda had tried to revise a year earlier.

Trevelyan in Cairo was told to assure Nasser that Britain wa
not pressing Jordan to join the Baghdad Pact. But Templer's owr
reports of his conversations with the Jordanian King and Government showed all too clearly that such assurances were far from
the truth. For both Hussein and his Ministers had been left in nc
doubt that the British Government felt that it was high time that
they made up their minds about the Pact and that the supply of
British arms would depend on their attitude towards it. Moreover
Nasser did not even need to be informed of this by his ubiquitous
intelligence service. For, while Templer was still in Amman, four
Jordanian Ministers resigned from the Government in protest
against joining the Pact. And when, a few days later, Hazza
Majali, a known pro-Westerner, formed a new Government, all
the signs suggested that Jordan was about to succumb to British
pressures and link up with Iraq.

Once again Nasser felt that he had been deliberately deceived
and that Eden's earlier assurance that Britain would not try tc
recruit any other Arab states for the Baghdad Pact had been a
trick to get Cairo Radio to stop attacking Nuri. Promptly he gave
orders for the war of words to be resumed against Britain and
Iraq. And Egyptian intrigues against the Nuri regime were

enewed to such effect that the Egyptian Military Attaché in Baghdad was declared persona non grata and a member of his taff put on trial for plotting the assassination of leading Government officials.

Completely unmoved by Trevelyan's denials that Britain had been pulling the wool over his eyes, Nasser contended that the imperialist powers were trying to isolate Egypt by bribing and blackmailing her sister Arab states into joining the Baghdad Pact. Syria, he said, would be next on the list for this kind of treatment and, surrounded as she was by allies of the West, she would be unable to resist. How could he be accused of picking a fight with Britain when the British and their agents, such as Nuri and Glubb, were thus intriguing against Arab interests and trying to impress the Arab states one by one into serving the needs of the West in the Cold War? Had he not said, after the British finally agreed to withdraw their troops from Egypt, that the Arabs would gladly give the West facilities on a collective basis if the Russians attacked the Middle East? Yet the Western powers' only response had been to work ever harder to ensure that the Arabs should not act collectively in this or any other set of circumstances, but rather as individual satellites, obeying London's and Washington's orders.

So saying, Nasser lashed out with renewed vigour against Britain's 'stooges' in Jordan. And just as he had been able to raise enough wind to get Fares el-Khoury ousted in Syria in the previous January, so now with Hazza Majali he managed to stir up such a cauldron of popular antipathy to the Baghdad Pact that the Government were forced to resign after several days of fierce rioting in Amman and other towns in Jordan. Wherefore Hussein thought it prudent to appoint as Prime Minister the more cautious Samir Rifai, who promptly proclaimed his opposition to any new pacts and then made swiftly for Cairo to talk things over with the Egyptians.

After this victory Nasser's anger subsided sufficiently to encourage Trevelyan to revive the idea of a stand-still agreement on Baghdad Pact membership in a conversation early in January 1956. Despite the injury done by the Templer mission, Nasser did not reject the idea, although he equally did not accept it. Then, when Selwyn Lloyd visited Cairo on February 29 on his way to a meeting of the South-East Asia treaty members in Karachi the proposal received yet another airing. Lloyd expressed interest in it, but he felt that he should consult both his Cabinet colleagues and Britain's Baghdad Pact partners before giving a considered reply.

At this very moment, however, King Hussein elected to dismiss General Glubb from his post as Commander of the Arab Legion and ordered him to leave Jordan for ever within twenty-four hours. To say the least, this was churlish conduct towards a man who had given two decades of service to the Jordanian army however much the young King may have felt that he could never grow to his full stature in the shadow of this venerable British oak. But, graceless though the manner of Glubb's dismissal might be the decision was Hussein's and nobody else's; and it was taken because, in the King's own words, so long as Glubb remained in command in Jordan, so long would every Jordanian Government consult him or the British Embassy before their own sovereign when faced with some important political decision.

Admittedly Cairo Radio had attacked Glubb for 'plotting to bring Jordan into the Baghdad Pact, and had even called him a helpmate of the Israelis, for ordering that Arabs infiltrating Israel's borders be shot. No doubt, too, the Egyptian Military Attaché in Jordan had played on the jealousies and pressures against Glubb which were building up amongst the Arab officers in Hussein's army. Certainly Nasser made no secret of his pleasure and relief when he was told that this 'imperialist' influence had been removed from the Arab world. But, as such an experienced and trusted friend of the Hashemite monarchy as Sir Alexander Kirkbride was to assert, after talking to the King at the time, Eden was completely wrong in attributing the responsibility for Glubb's dismissal to Nasser rather than Hussein. Indeed, when first informed that Glubb had been relieved of his command, Nasser thought that it was the British Government who had decided to recall him and therefore congratulated Lloyd on the 'wisdom' of the decision. Yet, against all such expert testimony, Eden persisted in his belief that Glubb had been the victim solely of

Egyptian intrigues and, from these false premises, decided that Nasser was the incarnation of all the evils of Arabia who would destroy every British interest in the Middle East, unless he himself were speedily destroyed.

Nothing revealed this thinking more clearly than Downing Street's reaction to an olive branch extended by Nasser at the end of March. Having received no reply from Lloyd about a possible renewal of the stand-still agreement on the Baghdad Pact, he himself resurrected the idea in interviews with the *Sunday Times* and *Observer* newspapers. For, as he told several Arab ambassadors in Cairo, he had formed the opinion that, after the upheavals in Jordan, no other Arab state was likely to join a Western alliance. And with Iraq now completely isolated, he felt that it was time for Egypt to try to consolidate the Arab League rather than continue to flog the dead horse that the Baghdad Pact had become. But, to Nasser's surprise, his gesture only provoked still more anger in Whitehall when the *Sunday Times* and *Observer* interviews were published. Instead of welcoming the revival of what had originally been a British proposal, Eden personally ordered the Foreign Office to make a blistering attack on his new-found enemy. Nasser's actions, the statement said, did not match his professed desire to cooperate with the West. On the contrary, his real aim was to eliminate British interests from the Arab world. As for his suggesting a moratorium on Arab recruitment for the Baghdad Pact in return for a cessation of Cairo's propaganda against it, this was quite out of the question, since the terms of the Pact made it open to any state to join if it so wished!

In his masterly account of his missions to Cairo, Baghdad and Aden entitled *The Middle East in Revolution*, Trevelyan comments that Nasser took this riposte as a declaration of war. From my own vantage point as a Foreign Office Minister at the time, I can testify that this was exactly what Eden intended it to be. Nasser certainly responded in kind, and abuse of Britain and the Baghdad Pact now poured forth from Cairo's transmitters with renewed frequency and fervour. Nasser also gave the British lion's tail a further twist by proposing, in association with King Saud and Syria's President, Shukri Quwaitly, to pay Jordan the equivalent of the

British subsidy, if Eden should withdraw it in retaliation for Glubb's dismissal. Trevelyan protested that this offer was clearly intended to sabotage Britain's treaty with Jordan and denied Nasser's counter-claim that Templer had warned that the subsidy would be cut unless Jordan joined the Baghdad Pact. But after London's disingenuous disclaimers that Templer had brought no pressure on Hussein to join the Pact, Nasser refused to accept this further denial. The offer to replace the subsidy was renewed and, amid a chorus of complaints from the British press that the Egyptians were further undermining Britain's position in the Middle East, he accepted a request from Aden's Yemeni neighbours to join the military alliance between Egypt and Saudi Arabia.

By April 1956, relations between Egypt and Britain had reached a lower ebb than at any time since the revolution nearly four years earlier. But the British Prime Minister was not the only sworn enemy of Egypt among the leaders of the West. Both Dulles and the French Premier, Guy Mollet, also looked on Cairo as an essential threat to their designs which could only be removed by destroying Nasser. Mollet was convinced that Nasser was almost solely responsible for the nationalist rebellion in Algeria which had started in November 1954. Jacques Soustelle, French Governor General of Algeria throughout 1955, publicly proclaimed that Egypt was 'the head of the octopus whose tentacles have for so many months been strangling French North Africa . . .'.

In fact France had long been at odds with the new wave of Arab nationalism and in sympathy with the Zionist cause. After she had been forced to relinquish her mandates and concede independence to Syria and Lebanon at the end of World War II, she had provided facilities on French soil for secret training, as well as arms, for the Haganah, the Israeli underground army, in its struggle against the British mandatory authority in the middle forties. Successive French Governments had also refused to cooperate with Britain in preventing the departure from French ports of illegal Jewish immigrants to Palestine. More recently France had been supplying Israel with arms in complete disregard f the policy of balanced deliveries agreed with the United States and Britain. And when Eisenhower turned down Ben Gurion's request for jet aircraft and tanks to compensate for Egypt's arms deal with Russia, the French had been quick to supply what the Americans had refused. So much so that Nasser promptly concluded a second arms agreement with the Russians which provided him with more modern MIG fighters and which brought the total of arms purchases from Russia to over $300 million.

Mollet and Soustelle grossly exaggerated the contribution which Egypt was making to the Algerian rebellion. And in their obsessive belief that Nasser was another Hitler, bent on creating an empire for himself, they failed to see that the Algerian people so craved their independence that they were prepared to fight for it if necessary. France had just lost Indo-China and had been forced to concede independence to Morocco and Tunisia; and Mollet knew that his political survival depended on his avoiding the final added humiliation of letting Arab nationalism take over in Algeria. However, his accusation that Egypt was helping the rebels was not altogether unfounded. Nasser admitted to Kennet Love, without the smallest hesitation or apology, that he had sent arms to help in starting the revolution. The nationalist leader, Ahmed Ben Bella, a former sergeant in the French army who had been highly decorated for bravery in World War II, was a personal friend of his and had come to Cairo to seek his aid. Besides, however imprudent it might be, it was Nasser's policy to support nationalism in its fight against oppression whether in the Middle East, North Africa or Black Africa.

Nevertheless in March 1956, the possibility of some understanding between France and Egypt seemed to emerge momentarily following a fortuitous visit to Cairo by Mollet's Foreign Minister, Christian Pineau. Nasser had earlier sent Abdel Kader Hatem to propose to Pineau a deal whereby, if France would cease arming Israel, he would refrain from attacking French 'imperialism'. Pineau countered by saying that there could be no deal unless Egypt stopped helping the Algerian rebels, which Nasser had flatly refused to do. But when Pineau met Nasser face to face, he found him altogether different to what he had been led to expect. Far from the ranting Hitler-type demagogue of Mollet's imagination, he appeared to Pineau as a resolute but reasonable Arab nationalist whose main concern for the Algerians was that they should be allowed freely to determine their own future, and in what form, if any, they should be associated in that future with metropolitan France. He had very frankly refused to promise that Egypt would stop sending arms to the rebels, but he had given his solemn word that no Algerian nationalists were being or would be trained in Egypt.

Moreover, Nasser seemed so anxious to help in bringing about a negotiated settlement that, a month after his visit, Pineau persuaded Mollet to allow a series of secret meetings to take place between two French representatives and two leaders of the FLN, the Algerian nationalist movement, to discuss terms. But when the existence of these contacts leaked to the French press, Mollet took fright and recalled his emissaries. The fighting in Algeria immediately became more intense. And by the middle of 1956, with Cairo Radio cheering on the rebels with ever-increasing vehemence and the number of French troops engaged in suppressing them raised to 250,000, relations between France and Egypt rapidly deteriorated. Then, five months later, as the French fumed with indignation over the nationalisation of the Suez Canal Company on July 26, Mollet's Government engineered the arrest of Ben Bella and four of his associates by forcing their aircraft to land at Algiers. The French authorities had earlier granted the FLN leaders a safe-conduct to fly between Rabat and Tunis for meetings with the rulers of Morocco and Tunisia designed to explore the possibilities of a negotiated peace. And the treachery of the subsequent hijacking not only put paid to any hopes of a Franco–Egyptian understanding over Algeria, but also made Nasser more determined than ever to help the FLN to make an end to French dominion in North Africa.

Both Eden and Mollet fell out with Nasser through a miscalculation of his objectives that was at least partly deliberate. For both men needed a whipping boy to explain away the failure of their policies in the Arab world. Jordan had gone sour on Eden with the sacking of General Glubb and the Algerians were giving the lie to Mollet's claims that they really wanted to remain part of metropolitan France. And the easiest explanation of both these failures was to blame them on Egyptian intrigues. With Dulles, however, the quarrel with Nasser was much more unfortunate and unnecessary. True, the two men had been poles apart in their thinking when they met in Cairo in 1953. Dulles, with his obsession about alliances and bases, could never really understand the neutralist idea. Nor did the two Russian arms deals exactly help to endear him to Egypt. But, for all this, Dulles did realise, as he said in a broadcast following his visit to Cairo, that the Arab peoples were 'more fearful of Zionism than of Communism' and were afraid that America would 'become the backer of expansionist Zionism'. Nor did he altogether share Eden's and Mollet's view that Nasser had become no more than Russia's newest puppet. Had he done so, he would never have been as eager as he was initially to help in financing the High Dam at Aswan.

Dulles, however, hoped that Western aid for this venture would act as a sweetener for some settlement of the Arab-Israeli conflict which he felt depended primarily on Egypt taking the lead on behalf of the Arabs. Prudently enough he did not seek to attach any such condition to his terms for financing the Aswan project, for he knew all too well that to do so would have met with an immediate rebuff from Nasser on the grounds that the two issues were in no way connected and that he could not buy economic aid at the price of selling out his Palestinian brothers. Nevertheless, towards the end of 1955, in the early stages of the High Dam negotiations, Dulles despatched an emissary to the Middle East in the person of Robert Anderson, a Texas oil millionaire who later became Secretary of the Treasury in the Eisenhower Cabinet, to sound out Nasser and Ben Gurion in the greatest secrecy on the possibilities of a negotiated settlement.

There could hardly have been a more awkward moment for such a mission, coinciding as it did with the Israeli strike into Syria in December 1955 which brought Nasser to issue his public warning that further attacks would involve retaliation by Egypt as Syria's ally. However Nasser was ready enough to tell Anderson what he could and could not do in the way of negotiating with Israel. Direct discussions across the table with Ben Gurion were impossible, he said, especially after the series of massive assaults on Egyptian and other Arab territory which had followed the Gaza Raid. But he was perfectly agreeable to someone acting as go-between to explore what, if any, common ground existed between Egypt's and Israel's terms for a settlement.

Unluckily, however, due to a lack of experience of such negotiations, Anderson frequently misunderstood Nasser's meaning and, in consequence, on several occasions painted a dangerously over-optimistic picture of the Egyptian attitude when reporting home. And when, in some subsequent encounter, Anderson realised that he had misinterpreted Nasser's intentions, his attempts to correct the record were read in Washington as showing that the Egyptian leader was repeatedly going back on his word.

In the event, although the Anderson mission was in fact baulked by Ben Gurion's insistence on direct negotiations, Dulles concluded that it was Nasser who had wrecked his peace initiative. Henceforth he saw no useful purpose in helping Egypt. True, he strongly differed from Eden and Mollet in believing that economic pressure rather than armed force should be used to topple Egypt's leader from his perch. But from now on Dulles was nevertheless at one with his British and French allies in resolving that Nasser was a net liability to the West and should be eliminated at the earliest possible opportunity.

Chapter 8

Dulles' Renege on the High Dam

After the first Russian arms deal in September 1955, Nasser told the London *Times* correspondent, James Morris, 'I do not want to spend money on war. I want to build our High Dam at Aswan and our new pyramid.' Of course, he needed arms to defend his country against Ben Gurion's belligerence, else he would not be able to sleep at night. But his overriding aim was to build the High Dam.

Despite his comparison of it with the pyramids of Egypt, Nasser's ambition was no mere exercise in Pharaonic ostentation. In the first decade of this century a dam had been built at Aswan by British engineers to help in increasing the area of cultivation in Egypt. In 1912 and again in 1933 the dam was heightened and, thanks to these efforts, another million crop acres were provided for Egypt's farms. But welcome as these additions to the country's fertility might be, the population proved more fertile still. Whereas when the dam was first built there were some 12 million mouths to feed, by the 1930s there were 17 million; and by 1955 the population was 23 million and rising at a net rate of one thousand in every twenty-four hours. Yet for all the effort and ingenuity of British and Egyptian irrigation experts, the area under cultivation was less than three per cent of the entire country. Whereas at the time of Mohammed Ali a hundred years before, there was one acre of cultivated land per inhabitant, now there was only one half acre per person. If only therefore to catch up with the rise in population, it was essential to devise a system which would bring water to a million and a quarter acres of desert and convert 700,000 acres to permanent irrigation.

But the problem was not only how to increase the amount of water available for irrigation. It was also a question of conservation, of ensuring that the life-giving flood, instead of wasting itself in huge spates which frequently did more harm than good, would be saved to provide perennial irrigation, even in abnormally dry years. The first Aswan dam was not, and could not be made, big enough to satisfy this requirement. Only the High Dam of Nasser's dreams could satisfy these requirements.

As early as the autumn of 1952, only a few months after the revolution, the RCC had persuaded the West German Government to help prepare a project for the new dam, by way of counter-balancing the huge reparations, amounting to nearly £300 million, which they were paying to Israel as compensation for Hitler's atrocities against the Jews. And in November 1952, the two firms, which the Bonn Government had nominated for the task, were invited to send technical experts to Aswan to draft the designs. But Nasser knew all too well that there was nowhere near enough foreign exchange in his treasury to finance so huge an undertaking. Approaches were therefore made to the United States, Britain and the World Bank; and in 1955, after the World Bank had consulted expert opinion as to the practical feasibility of the project and pronounced it as technically sound, it was agreed in principle that the West should help to finance the High Dam's construction, with the Bank contributing one half of the necessary foreign exchange and the American and British Governments the other.

Both Dulles and Eden were then most eager that their two countries should provide the necessary financial aid. Eden wanted at all costs to 'keep the Russian bear out of the Nile Valley', as he put it to me at the time. He knew that the Soviet Ambassador in Cairo had offered Russian help over the dam when he first responded to Nasser's enquiry about arms purchases. Also, Nasser had told Trevelyan that, although the Russians came last on his list of preferred helpmates, he would accept Russian aid if he had to. Thus, the possibility that the High Dam might become a permanent monument to Russian generosity and technical achievement was assuming nightmarish proportions in Eden's mind. When news of the Russian arms deal reached London, his determination to exclude 'the bear' from the Aswan project became more intense than ever. And his anxieties grew greater still when, a month later, Ambassador Solod announced in Cairo that Moscow would supply technical assistance and equipment to any Arab state that required it and repeated Russia's offer to help in building the High Dam with equipment, technical assistance and money repayable in goods over twenty-five years.

Dulles did not altogether share Eden's fears, believing that the Russians would not be able or willing to fulfil a promise of such huge proportions. But he was anxious to strengthen America's economic influence in Egypt and to regain some of the popularity which the United States had lost by refusing to supply arms. Both he and Eisenhower had been impressed by the views expressed to them by Eugene Black, the President of the World Bank, who, on taking office, had visited Cairo and other Arab capitals and had returned firmly convinced that the United States should help the Arabs equally with the Israelis. Black was also persuaded that Egypt held the key to any Middle Eastern settlement and he strongly advised that, if the experts appointed by the Bank to investigate the Aswan project agreed that it was 'good and sound', American aid should be given along with the necessary loans from the Bank.

Accordingly, in November 1955, after the experts had so reported, Egypt's Finance Minister was invited to Washington to begin the negotiations with Black and representatives of the American and British Governments. In the following month it was announced that the Bank and the two Western powers between them would guarantee the finance required to build the High Dam. The whole project was to cost $1,000 million, of which $400 million would be in foreign exchange. The World Bank would lend $200 million of the necessary foreign currency and the United States and Britain would between them make a grant of $70 million towards the first stage of the project, with the understanding that they would in due course contribute the rest of their half share.

Inevitably there were conditions to this offer. For one thing, the World Bank's loan was to be contingent on America and Britain paying their share. For another, in aide-memoires

Western conditions

addressed to Cairo, the two Governments required that Egypt undertake to concentrate her development programme on the High Dam – one third of her internal revenue was to be diverted for ten years to this purpose – and that her resources should not be squandered on other projects. Egypt was also required to impose controls to curb the growth of inflation from the immense expenditure of public money which the dam would involve. Contracts for the construction work were to be awarded on a competitive basis, but help from the Communist-bloc countries was to be refused. And to qualify for a World Bank loan Egypt had to undertake not to accept other loans or agreements without the Bank's approval.

Not surprisingly Nasser exploded with indignation when he read the terms set out in the Western aide-memoires. Haunted, as he was, by the spectre of the Khedive Ismail struggling to free himself from the bonds of his European creditors, he declared that the Western Powers were asking for complete control of the Egyptian economy. By making their contributions on a stage by stage basis, they were asking him to walk into a trap. If he agreed, they would then be able to blackmail him into accepting new conditions at every stage. In the end he could find himself forced, as Ismail had been, to accept the imposition first of advisers and then of administrators nominated by his creditors and installed as his Ministers of Finance, Trade and so on, until ultimately he would have surrendered all of Egypt's hard-won independence.

For reasons again connected with Ismail's downfall, he suspected that the World Bank was more responsible than the two Governments for these stipulations. And it was therefore agreed in Washington that Black should hasten to Cairo to explain personally to Nasser why such requirements had been put to him. Dulles saw Black before his departure and lectured him on what he contended was his duty as an American citizen. The West, he said, had to get the credit for the High Dam. 'So go and get things straightened out with Nasser and don't act like a banker,' he said. Likewise, when Black saw Eden on his way through London, he was again told that it was of cardinal importance to forestall the Russians in their bid to secure this project. And Eden was as deaf as Dulles to Black's perfectly proper rejoinders that, as President of the World Bank, he was debarred from favouring any particular country in his dealings and that he had to act not only like the banker that he was by profession, but as the world's banker that he had now become.

On his arrival in Cairo, Black decided to see Nasser alone to explain his position. First, he repeated to him what he had said to Dulles and Eden. 'I am a Wall Street banker by profession and proud of it,' he said. 'But now my job is somewhat different as the banker for the United Nations. Although born an American citizen, I serve not one country but all the countries, including yours, who elected me to my present office. And in that capacity my job is to promote sound and practical development, not to play politics for or against any nation.' Nasser replied with his usual courtesy that he appreciated Black's explanation of his international role. Adding with a wry smile that he had checked up on Black with Nehru and Tito who had commended his sincerity and impartiality, he said he had not until then clearly understood the position of the World Bank which he thought was somehow an agent of United States policy. He then went on to explain the objects of his revolution and to stress that their fulfilment would depend in large measure on the building of the High Dam.

With such friendly, if frank, exchanges the interview got off to a reasonably good start, with Nasser showing the quiet and amiable rationality with which he conducted almost all his discussions with foreign representatives. But when Black began to argue the case for the various conditions attached by the Bank to their proffered help, all Nasser's worst fears were aroused. Angrily he refused to admit inspection of Egypt's financial administration by outsiders, and he also demanded an undertaking by all the parties concerned to see the dam through to its final construction. This reaction was probably due in part to the fact that he found himself, as always, out of his depth in discussing economic questions. But he was also convinced that Black's high-powered financial arguments were a deliberate attempt to blind him with science and so to drive him into accepting international control of Egypt's economy.

In fact, so bitter did this exchange become that Dulles, on learning of what had happened, cabled to Kermit Roosevelt, currently in Athens on CIA business, to fly immediately to Cairo to smooth things over. Roosevelt did as he was bid and, at their next encounter, Black was able to persuade Nasser that the World Bank's requirements were standard procedure and presaged no particular designs on Egypt. From then on their discussions ran more smoothly; and as Nasser's confidence in Black's patent honesty developed, he reverted to his customary rationality, frequently overruled his own advisers and finally agreed to the Bank having reasonable rights of inspection of the measures which Egypt was to take to combat inflation. Thus after two weeks of intensive negotiations, he and Black concluded an agreement for the World Bank's loan of $200 million which was publicly announced on February 8, 1956.

In a final interview before returning to his Washington headquarters, Black reminded Nasser that the World Bank's loan depended on agreement being reached with the American and British Governments on the terms of their grant. It would be unwise, he said, for Egypt to haggle about the conditions laid down in the joint aide-memoires. These conditions, like the Bank's, were in Egypt's own ultimate interest and the all-important thing was to get started on the dam. But Nasser was not so easily persuaded to abandon his stand. He might now be prepared to accept inspection of Egypt's finances, but he was not going to be kept dangling on a string until the dam had been built. Therefore, as Black left Cairo, he produced for Washington and London a list of amendments designed at least to commit the Western powers to see the project through to its completion.

What Nasser did not know at the time was that, whether or not he accepted the West's conditions, Dulles' enthusiasm for the High Dam had already begun to cool. Nor for that matter did Black, until he arrived in Rome on his journey home, where he met Byroade returning to his post from consultations in Washington. Byroade quickly told him that the State Department were going sour' on Nasser, who they alleged had wrecked the Anderson mission, and he implored Black to strain every nerve to win them back to support for the High Dam. But when Black returned to Washington, Dulles avoided him and, try as he did to rekindle enthusiasm for the Aswan project with speeches praising Nasser for what he was doing to develop his country, he made little or no headway.

The Senate's attitude to foreign aid in general had hardened considerably in recent months. And apart from the always influential Zionist lobby, there were a number of southern Senators who represented the cotton-producing states and were anything but keen to help Egypt to produce more cotton in competition with their constituents. Also there were those who disliked helping 'dictators' on principle and still more who resented Nasser's arms deals with the Soviet bloc. And when Black finally got to see Dulles, the Secretary of State said that his contacts in the Senate told him that there was not enough money available in the existing appropriations to help both Nasser and Tito. In their present mood the Senate would reject any increase in the appropriations and the Government had therefore to decide which of these two they should help. Dulles felt that it would be better to give the money to Tito, who was moving away from the Communist bloc, rather than to Nasser, who too many people thought was moving towards it. Besides, he was no longer convinced that the Egyptian economy would stand the strain of the huge expenditures required to build the High Dam, for all Nasser's undertakings to curb inflation. And when Black retorted that the Egyptian economy was no weaker than it was when Dulles was telling him to go to Cairo and forget that he was a banker, the Secretary of State peremptorily brought the discussion to an end.

Dulles of course had other reasons for no longer wanting to help Egypt, apart from those which he gave to Black. Firmly believing that Nasser had killed his peace initiative two months before, he now wanted to bring him down. He was convinced that the Russians would not bail Egypt out over the High Dam, as they had done with the arms deals, because such an immense project would involve too great a strain on their resources. He was therefore more inclined to think that, by refusing American money and so collapsing the entire arrangement with the World Bank and the British, he would leave Nasser with no hope of fulfilling his dream. The resulting general disappointment among the Egyptian people would then be enough to oust him from power.

But Dulles was not yet quite ready to take this plunge. For one thing, Eden still seemed keen to go ahead with the agreed arrangements and was willing to accept some of the Egyptian amendments to the two Governments' aide-memoires. Glubb had not at this point yet been dismissed by King Hussein and Eden was far less sanguine than the American Secretary of State about Russia's inability to help build the High Dam. Besides, Cairo was still arguing about the terms and, if the Americans held fast, maybe Nasser would get them off the hook by himself repudiating the whole deal. For these reasons, therefore, Dulles adopted the same temporising tactics as had been applied to Egypt's repeated requests for Western arms.

As a result, there was a lull in the negotiations which was to last for the next five months. During this period the last remnants of Britain's military garrisons left Egypt, amid a minimum of exultation on the part of the Egyptians; and the civilian contractors took over their allotted tasks in the Canal Zone bases in perfect harmony with the Egyptian troops who moved in after the British forces withdrew. Antony Head paid a courtesy call on Nasser; Selwyn Lloyd gave an interview to *Al-Akhbar* in which he expressed the hope that 'the present lack of confidence' between Britain and Egypt would soon be dispelled; and Nasser replied with a statement to the London *Daily Herald* saying that he agreed with Lloyd and hoped that those 'newspapers and politicians in Britain who are anything but helpful' would respond accordingly. True, Eden had in the meanwhile declared his own personal war against Nasser, following the Glubb episode in March, and British officials were therefore busily discussing with their American opposite numbers the possibilities of organising a coup in Egypt on the lines of the one which had overthrown Mossadeq in Iran. But, on the surface at least, relations between

Britain and Egypt seemed to have calmed down somewhat after the bitter exchanges earlier in the year. Trevelyan, who had not been able to see Nasser for six weeks after Glubb was sacked, now had several long talks with him about restoring mutual confidence, of which one successful result was an agreement in June finally to liquidate the Egyptian sterling balances held in London.

But if, superficially, Egypt's ties with Britain seemed slightly less embittered than before, her relations with the United States had taken a serious turn for the worse. In April, the Russian leaders, Marshal Nikolai Bulganin and Nikita Kruschev, had visited Britain for talks with Eden and his colleagues. There was some blunt speaking by Eden about Britain's determination to fight if necessary to preserve her oil stake in the Middle East which took Kruschev visibly by surprise. Possibly on that account, the Russians decided that it would be good diplomacy, in the wake of their second arms deal with Egypt, to demonstrate their peaceable intentions in the area. At a press conference on the day of his departure from London, Kruschev therefore suggested that Russia would be prepared to take part in a United Nations embargo on the delivery of arms to such trouble-spots as the Middle East.

Nasser was naturally much concerned; and his anxieties were still further sharpened by grossly exaggerated intelligence reports that the United States, Britain and France had agreed at a NATO meeting in Paris to supply Israel with sufficient arms to counterbalance those possessed by all her Arab neighbours put together. With Ben Gurion in power in Israel, he could not possibly afford to see his enemy equipped with such an arsenal, while his only supplier was offering to impose a ban on further deliveries. Even during the lull before the Gaza Raid Nasser had been under the strongest pressures from his RCC colleagues to rearm Egypt's pathetically weak forces. As he confessed to me in the autumn of 1954, he had not as yet established any great popular following: his position therefore depended almost entirely upon the army's support; and however much he might prefer to spend money on economic development, he could not afford to deny his army the weapons they needed so desperately. Gaza therefore made the

Russian arms deal inevitable and this had given Nasser a much needed breathing space as well as boosting his prestige both with the army and with the public. But now this source of supply seemed threatened, and at a time when Israel's attacks on Egypt and her other Arab neighbours were becoming ever more violent and frequent.

Desperately he cast about him for an alternative source of supplies which would not be affected by a United Nations embargo and which was capable of meeting his needs. To this problem there was only one possible answer – Communist China. Admittedly, Chou En-lai had told him at Bandung that he should seek arms from Russia since China did not have enough to spare. But, if Russia were unable to send him arms direct, China could act as the intermediary.

But there was another problem. Despite the friendly contacts which Nasser had established with Chou at Bandung, Egypt had not as yet recognised Communist China and to do so at a moment when American aid for the High Dam was still hanging in the balance would be to risk serious repercussions. True, Israel had recognised the Peking Government in 1950 without incurring any apparent wrath in Washington. But that had been in President Truman's term of office when Israel could do no wrong in American eyes. And although Eisenhower and Dulles were clearly less biassed in Israel's favour than Truman and a lot better disposed towards the Arabs, their hatred of the Peking regime nevertheless bordered on the pathological. Still, as Nasser saw it, the need to be insured against an arms embargo outweighed every other consideration, so long as Israel maintained her aggressive posture. Therefore, on May 16, 1956, he announced Egypt's decision to recognise Communist China and to exchange ambassadors with Peking.

Dulles was outraged and Ahmed Hussein, Egypt's Ambassador in Washington, hastened to Cairo to tell Nasser what he already knew, namely that his decision had done a terrible injury to the prospect of American aid at Aswan. The only possible hope of holding the Americans to their offer, Hussein said, was for Nasser to accept without further haggling the conditions laid down in he aide-memoires. But still Nasser hesitated, haunted by the ghost of Ismail, to agree to what he believed could end in abandoning Egypt's independence to the mercies of the Western powers.

In the following month Black paid another visit to Cairo on his way to Riyadh to discuss Saudi Arabia's membership of the World Bank. And when Nasser complained that he had received no response to his suggested amendments of the conditions, Black again strongly urged him not to prolong the argument any further. But Nasser once more demurred, saying in a hurt tone that he could not understand the discourteous silence with which his perfectly reasonable requests had been met in Washington. And to Ahmed Hussein's pleadings he retorted that, if the Americans were now to run out on their pledges, he could and would get the necessary foreign exchange to build the High Dam by nationalising the Suez Canal Company and bringing its fat revenues into the Egyptian treasury. Ahmed Hussein expressed shock and horror at this suggestion, but Nasser quietly told him that if he kept his nerve, everything would turn out all right.

However, after yet another month had passed with no word from Washington about the dam, Nasser came to the conclusion that Dulles and Eden were going to renege on their offer. He had for long suspected that they were holding out on him in the hope of extracting some concession towards Israel, such as reopening the Suez Canal to Israeli ships. And he had decided in his turn to gamble on the belief that, after what had happened over the arms issue, the West would be afraid to withdraw their support for fear that the Russians would again step into the breach. But in the past month his complacency had been somewhat shaken and, after further prodding from his ambassador and from Mahmoud Fawzi as Foreign Minister, he finally agreed to force the Americans into the open by withdrawing his objections to the aide-memoires and accepting the conditions as they stood.

Ahmed Hussein lost no time in returning to his post, bearing what he still hoped would be good news to the State Department, if not to Dulles personally. On his arrival on July 17, he telephoned to Black in a state of great excitement to tell him that there was no longer any Egyptian obstacle to an agreement. Then two days later he was received by Dulles to whom he related Nasser' decision to accept the Anglo-American terms. Robert Murphy in his memoirs states that the ambassador accompanied his state ment with a demand that the United States should underwrite the expenditure of hundreds of millions of dollars on the High Dam over a ten-year period and that he threatened that the Russian would do so if the Americans refused. But Murphy was no present at the meeting, which on the American side was attended by Herbert Hoover Junior, the Under-Secretary of State, and George Allen; and it is hardly likely that Ahmed Hussein, having worked so hard to persuade Nasser to drop this very demand as a written amendment to the terms, would have reintroduced it even as a verbal condition.

However, according to Allen, the ambassador did make probably on Nasser's instructions, a scarcely veiled threat that, in case Congress and other influences should force the United State to withdraw support, the Egyptians had the necessary Russian offers 'in their pocket'. But, whether or not Ahmed Hussein referred to the Russian alternative, it could have made no differ ence whatever to the outcome of the meeting. Dulles, for whom Nasser's recognition of Peking had been the last straw, had finally decided to pull out. So had Eden, as he admitted in his own memoirs. Which explains why no protest was sent to Washington when, in June, I reported to Lloyd a conversation with Cabot Lodge, the American Ambassador to the United Nations, in which Lodge warned me that Dulles would not be prepared to risk a certain rebuff from Congress by going ahead on the High Dam

Accordingly, when Ahmed Hussein had made his statement Dulles replied that the United States Government had now come to the conclusion that the Egyptian economy would no stand the strain of building the High Dam and that they were therefore withdrawing their offer of financial support. Twenty four hours later, Eden announced that Britain too was withdraw ing her contribution. And since the World Bank's $200 million loan was contingent upon the matching contributions by the two powers, this also automatically lapsed. Dulles had collapsed the house of cards. Indeed, if the mixed metaphor may be forgiven, as the consequences were to show, he had pulled down the pillars of the temple on Western influence not only in Egypt, but throughout the Arab world as well.

When the news of America's decision was flashed around the world, Nasser was returning with Nehru from Yugoslavia, where they had been staying at Tito's summer residence in Brioni, following three days of discussions among the three 'non-aligned' leaders of a wide range of topics from the war in Algeria to nuclear disarmament and relations between the Third World and the rival power blocs. Although by no means taken by surprise, his first reactions were highly confused. Dulles' explanation that the weakness of the Egyptian economy had caused America to withdraw made him suspect that the World Bank had for some reason changed its mind about Egypt's capacity to build the dam and had pressed Dulles to pull out on that account. He therefore felt that Black had been guilty of monstrous perfidy in encouraging him to accept the West's terms without further argument, when he must have known that the deal would never go through, whatever Egypt might concede. Later Nasser came to realise that these suspicions were entirely without foundation and that Black had not been consulted about the renege, although Dulles afterwards tried to persuade him to declare his agreement. And as a result, he developed a warm, personal friendship with the World Bank's President, who became an honoured guest on his annual visits to Egypt. But for the moment he angrily compared Black to de Lesseps, the builder of the Suez Canal, who ranked in modern Egyptian mythology higher than almost any individual foreigner as an alien bloodsucker who exploited the toiling masses and the penurious resources of Egypt to serve the requirements of nineteenth-century imperialism.

But angered as he was by Dulles' action and more especially by its accompanying slur on Egypt's economy, and hence on her creditworthiness, Nasser was not immediately sure of his next move. For while he hoped that the Russians would fill the gap left by the West, he had no guarantee to this effect. Still less did he know what their terms would be if they were prepared to assist him. He was due to visit Moscow in the following month which would give him an opportunity to sound out Kruschev in person. But for all Solod's talk about Russia being so anxious to help, he knew that in the spring of 1956 the Russian Ambassador had told his Indian colleague in Cairo that Moscow had not yet decided whether or not to finance the High Dam. And two days after Dulles announced his withdrawal, Shepilov, now Russia's Foreign Minister, was reported to have said that Moscow was not considering aid for the Aswan project.

At the same time the idea of raising the necessary foreign exchange by nationalising the Suez Canal Company, which had so horrified Ahmed Hussein, was not entirely new. The Company's existing concession was due to expire in 1968, only twelve years hence, and for the past two years an Egyptian Government commission had been working on the question. Also, at his first meeting with Tito in the previous September, Nasser had told the Marshal that he would have to take over the Company at some stage because Egypt, as an independent nation, could not allow foreigners indefinitely to control such an important element of her national revenue and resources. Nasser had not been satisfied with the modus vivendi agreed in 1949, whereby the Company increased their payments to Egypt to 7 per cent of the Canal's gross profits, and raised the number of Egyptian directors to five against twenty-five French and British board members. Egypt, he felt, still had too little say and too small a share of the revenue. In the previous October therefore the Egyptian Government had repudiated the arrangement. But when they tried to get better terms, the Company made it very clear that they would only concede a greater Egyptian share in the profits and management of the Canal, if Egypt would agree to extend their tenure beyond 1968. In the event, save for a few minor concessions on foreign exchange, the Egyptian negotiators were unable to secure any improvement on the 1949 agreement. In particular, they failed to persuade the Company to increase the number of Egyptian pilots, although there was a current shortage of some 20 per cent and, at the time of nationalisation, only 40 of the total strength of 205 pilots were Egyptian.

Yet, while Nasser felt that he had every possible moral justi-ication for taking over the Company, he was equally well aware hat to do so would not of itself solve the problem of building the High Dam. He would have to compensate the shareholders or forfeit what little was left of Egypt's creditworthiness after Dulles' attack upon it. Even if he could then find enough foreign exchange to start work on the dam out of the Canal's revenues, which in 1955 totalled $91 million gross and $32 million net, he would still need technical help with the actual construction. He discounted the possibility of a military reaction from the powers although he thought that Eden would not be averse to war if world opinion were not against him and if the risks to British oil supplies could be avoided. But with America and Britain now actively opposed to the very idea of the High Dam and presumably certain to raise the roof if he nationalised the Canal Company, he could hardly depend on the consortium of British, French and German firms which had offered to build the dam, even if he could raise the necessary foreign exchange. The more he pondered the quest-ion, the more he realised that, once again, he would be driven to depend on the Russians to supply both the cash and the construc-tors. Therefore, before he made any decisive move he would have to secure some reasonably firm undertakings from Moscow.

While he brooded on these problems, Nasser not surprisingly launched a bitter attack on Dulles' perfidy in a speech opening a new pipe-line from Suez to Cairo. 'When Washington . . . broad-casts the lie . . . that Egypt's economy is unsound,' he declaimed, 'then I look them in the face and say, drop dead of your fury for you will never be able to dictate to Egypt.' Then he and General Amer went to work on the Russians through the new ambassador, Yevgenyi Kiselev. And although his colleagues at the time have insisted with me that he had obtained no guarantee of Russian aid when, a few days later, he proclaimed the nationalisation of the Canal Company, there can be little doubt that, during that hectic week of consultations between Cairo and Moscow which followed Dulles' renege, Kiselev received authority at least to assure Nasser that Russia was prepared in principle to provide the neces-sary help. Nasser was a gambler, it is true, and in later years he would frequently take risks without consulting his colleagues. But at this point, although he had just been elected as President, allegedly by a 99 per cent vote of the Egyptian electorate, his position was still that of first among equals within the RCC. Thus when he submitted his decision to nationalise the Canal Company to his Cabinet colleagues, it is inconceivable that they would have approved it, as they did with complete unanimity, if they had received no such assurances from Moscow.

But while the wires between the Egyptian and Soviet capital hummed with messages about the High Dam, Nasser said not word to the Russians about his intentions vis-à-vis the Canal Company. His conspiratorial mind would not allow him to tell anyone not involved in the take-over, so as to guarantee the element of surprise which he felt necessary to ensure that the Company's offices should be acquired without bloodshed or resistance on the part of the employees. Colonel Mahmoud Yunis, who had been appointed to run the nationalised undertaking and to organise the take-over, was instructed to treat the affair as a highly secret military operation and to shoot on the spot any member of his team who violated secrecy. And to avoid any possibility of leakage through the telephoning of last-minute instructions, Nasser personally arranged that, directly he heard the name of de Lesseps mentioned in his broadcast speech, Yunis and his subordinates would move on the Company's offices in Ismailia, Suez and Port Said.

With his plans thus laid, Nasser addressed his compatriots in the main square of Alexandria. And in a speech, delivered partly in classical Arabic and partly in the vernacular which he had learned to use for his more declamatory passages, he first reminded his audience of the humiliations which had been heaped upon the Egyptian people by their oppressors before the revolution gave them back their long-lost sense of dignity. 'In the past we were kept waiting in the offices of the British High Commissioner and the British Ambassador, but now they take us into account,' he said. Then he went on to defend his decision to buy arms from Russia after the Gaza Raid had rung the alarm bells throughout Egypt. 'Whether these are Communist arms or not,' he told his hearers, 'in Egypt they are Egyptian arms.' No longer would Egypt tamely accept that for every rifle supplied to 70 million Arabs, two should be given to the one million Israelis by their imperialist backers, America, Britain and France.

Then, after a passage devoted to Palestine and Britain's promotion of Zionism as a means of combating Arab nationalism, he turned to the negotiations with the West on the High Dam. The terms laid down by Washington, London and the World Bank he described as 'imperialism without soldiers'. He had declined Russia's offers of help in the hope of getting a fair deal from the West, but the wording of the announcement of America's withdrawal showed that the West wanted to punish Egypt for her refusal to take part in their military blocs and to poison her economic relations with other states. Here he came to the passage which was his secret signal to set Yunis' take-over operation in motion. Mr Black, he said, had made him feel he was 'sitting in front of Ferdinand de Lesseps'.

Nor was this his only reference to Egypt's folk-ogre. For in leading up to his announcement of the decree by which the Canal Company was to be nationalised, he dwelt at length on the history of the Canal since its construction. Confusing its architect with the Pharaohs of old, he implied that, under de Lesseps' brutal direction, more than a hundred thousand Egyptian workers had died to build a canal which was to belong not to them or their country but to a foreign company who extracted the profit for their own enrichment and never for Egypt's benefit. 'Instead of the Canal being dug for Egypt,' Nasser declaimed, 'Egypt became the property of the Canal and the Canal Company became a state within a state.' But now, he concluded, the days of alien exploitation were over; the Canal and its revenues would belong entirely to Egypt. And so saying, he read out the terms of the nationalisation decree, ending with the triumphant cry, 'We shall build the High Dam and we shall gain our usurped rights. . . .'

This was defiance in the grand style and it won for its author an acclaim from Arab nationalists everywhere greater than any he had ever achieved before. The agreement over the withdrawal of British troops had gained Nasser considerable applause; but it had been qualified by doubts, sown by the Moslem Brotherhood in Egypt and elsewhere, about the commitment to reactivate the Canal Zone bases in the event of war, which the critics claimed constituted a virtual alliance with the former occupying power. Likewise, the Russian arms deal had been welcomed as a timely and well merited rebuff to Western attempts to impose servilities on the Arabs as the price of supplying them with the arms they needed to defend themselves against Israel. Yet, while Syria followed Egypt's suit with a similar arms deal with Russia in the spring of 1956, there were some raised eyebrows in other parts of the Arab world, notably Saudi Arabia, where the idea of any involvement with the Communist bloc was regarded with abhorrence. But about this latest act of defiance there were no such reservations. The nationalisation of the Suez Canal Company was hailed as a master-stroke for Arab independence by rulers and populace alike from Morocco to Muscat, save only for Nuri and his followers in Iraq. Nasser was now the unrivalled champion of Arab nationalism and liberation.

Chapter 9

Eden's Ultimatum

On the several reactions of the three Western powers to the nationalisation of the Suez Canal Company, Nasser's calculations were correct in the case of Britain and the United States. Rightly he estimated that, while Eden was itching to use force against him, Britain's armed strength was so spread about the world that it would take two months to mobilise and organise the necessary expedition. Rightly, too, he assumed that, in an election year, the American Government would be extremely loath to take part in any military action to restore the status quo on the Canal. He had no illusions about Dulles' feelings towards him. But he believed, correctly as it turned out, that Dulles did not share Eden's craving for armed action and preferred to use economic pressures to induce Egypt to negotiate a settlement. And he felt that, while the differences between the two Western leaders might be more in method than in aim, they were still deep enough to mean that, in the two months which Britain would require to mobilise her forces, the weight of world opinion and the influence of Washington, not to mention that of Moscow, would be able to bring about a conclusion acceptable to Egypt.

Where Nasser's calculations went wrong was in his assessment of France's reaction. For he failed completely to forsee that, coming on top of the Algerian rebellion, the nationalisation of a company in which France held the major shareholding was bound to make Mollet no less keen than Eden to seek a military show-down with Egypt. Instead Nasser dwelt on the jealousies and dissensions which divided Britain and France in the Middle East. The French, he recalled, had opposed the Baghdad Pact, partly from a long-standing resentment that Britain should still aspire to a leading role in the area after they had been shown the door in Syria and Lebanon, partly because their new-found friends in

Israel had objected to it as a dagger pointed at their throat. And while he made some allowance for French bitterness about his support of the FLN in Algeria, he wrongly assumed that their forces would be too taken up with the rebellion to be able to participate in any military action against Egypt. Consequently he estimated that, while Mollet might be as keen as Eden to destroy him, the most that either would do would be to bluster and threaten in the hope of frightening him into accepting some kind of international authority to control the Canal.

Least of all, as he later told me, did it enter Nasser's head at any stage in the Suez crisis that France and Britain would risk destroying every vestige of their influence and good name in the Arab world by using Israel as their stalking-horse for an attempt to seize the Canal by force. And when Khaled Mohieddin sent him a message in September 1956 that, according to one of his Communist friends in Paris, the French were planning to attack Egypt in league with Israel, Nasser dismissed the information as a hoax designed to lure him into making some false move against Israel. Indeed, so much did he discount the possibility of the Israelis becoming involved that, when he later decided that Britain's troop movements demanded that precautions be taken against a possible invasion from that quarter, he pulled back some 30,000 troops from the Sinai area to strengthen the defences of the Canal and the approaches to Cairo and Alexandria.

In the light of all his careful calculations Nasser was somewhat surprised to hear from his embassy in Paris that Mollet's Foreign Minister had not only protested in the sharpest possible terms against the nationalisation of the Canal Company, but had also gratuitously insulted the Egyptian Ambassador, addressing him as a judge censuring a convicted criminal. Pineau was no doubt smarting from the blows that he felt had been dealt to his earlier personal trust in Nasser. Yet, whatever the reasons, his rudeness was never forgiven by the Egyptians.

On the other hand, Nasser was not the least surprised when Britain reacted by blocking the undrawn residue of the Egyptian sterling balances amounting to some £130 million, by re-imposing the embargo on arms sales to Egypt and by taking steps to protect the funds held by the Canal Company in London from seizure by the Egyptian Government. All these measures were predictable, even though the reblocking of the sterling balances was in breach of the recent currency agreement. Equally expected were the declarations of Eden and Hugh Gaitskell, the Labour Opposition leader, bracketing Nasser with Mussolini and Hitler and accusing him of megalomaniacal ambitions. Likewise the demands from both sides of the House of Commons that the Suez Canal could not be allowed to remain under Egypt's unfettered control. Even the sneers of the London *Times* that an international waterway of such complexity and importance could not be properly run 'by a nation with low technical and managerial skills such as the Egyptians' came as no great surprise to Cairo.

After all, Britain was by far the largest user of the Canal and in those days was almost entirely dependent upon it for the passage of her oil imports. It was therefore inevitable that, in the state of shock which nationalisation had induced, British public opinion would share Eden's refusal to be side-tracked into what *The Times* called 'quibbling' about whether or not Egypt was 'legally entitled' to take over a company which was nominally an Egyptian registered enterprise, but which in practice possessed an international status of supreme importance to world commerce. Likewise, it was natural that Nasser's offer to compensate the shareholders at the value of their shares immediately prior to the issue of the nationalisation decree should be overlooked against the wider implications of this act of seizure.

Nasser had made allowance for these British reactions and for the obvious attempts by Eden to rally support for his counter-measures from the Americans and the French. He knew too that Nuri, together with the King and Crown Prince of Iraq, had been dining at Downing Street on the night that the Canal Company was taken over and he assumed, quite correctly, that Nuri had encouraged Eden to react as sharply as his strength and preparations would allow. Nor did any of this worry him unduly, as was clearly shown by the studied silence with which he reacted to the reblocking of Egypt's sterling balances. For Nasser had his plans well laid.

In the first place he had decided that, if Britain attacked Egypt, he would not call on his fellow Arabs to join the fighting which would only cause them great loss of life, and to no purpose since no Arab force could withstand an invasion by any Western power. He would therefore bow to the inevitable and rely on the force of world opinion expressed through the United Nations to bring the invaders to withdraw. If the Canal Zone alone were occupied, he would sit it out in Cairo. But, if the invaders made for the capital, he and his Government, accompanied by such army and air force units as remained intact, would withdraw up the Nile, if necessary as far as Aswan. Meanwhile, arms and ammunition were to be deposited in hiding places in houses and flats in Cairo and other cities, on which guerrilla forces would draw to conduct resistance against the occupying army. Finally, the resistance groups would have strict instructions to assassinate any President or Prime Minister appointed by the invaders within twenty-four hours of his taking office.

At the same time, Nasser was determined to refrain from any act which the British might inflate into a pretext for using military force. Although he could not resist sending back Eden's note of protest with only a slip attached saying, 'Returned to British Embassy', in every other way he leaned over backwards to avoid any provocation. He called off the fedayeen harassments of Israel and kept the Negev border quiet for the next three months. He even permitted ammunition, including bombs, to be removed from the ordnance stores in Britain's former Canal Zone base right up to a few days before the Anglo-French invasion. Although he knew perfectly well that this war material was being sent to Cyprus to be stockpiled for possible use by Britain against Egypt, the 1954 treaty allowed Britain the right to move such equipment into or out of the base and he was not going to offer Eden a casus belli by breaking this agreement. Also to avoid any suggestion that he was molesting British or French citizens Nasser decided not to enforce the clause in his nationalisation decree which forbade any Canal Company employee, including pilots, to leave their posts without permission of the nationalised authority. Ali Sabry announced shortly after nationalisation that mployees were free to leave at the customary month's notice.

As for interfering with shipping, which Eden, Mollet and other Anglo-French spokesmen had claimed would result from allowing the Canal to be 'subjected to Colonel Nasser's whim', this was the last thing Nasser wanted to do. True, during the first three months after nationalisation, Egypt only received about a third of the Canal's revenues because Britain, France and other user nations insisted upon paying their transit dues to the former Company's account in London or Paris. But even this was a lot more than the pittance which she had been getting hitherto. Besides, to interfere with ships paying dues outside Egypt would have been to break the Constantinople Convention which he had undertaken to uphold. By thus putting himself completely in the wrong, he might have offered Eden the very pretext which he was seeking for an armed assault on Egypt. Consequently, Ali Sabry was authorised, at the same time as he announced that the Company's pilots were free to leave, to repeat the pledge that the Convention would be safeguarded and freedom of navigation ensured as before.

Nor was Nasser's avoidance of provocations designed merely to keep him out of trouble. At this point, he also hoped that, when tempers had cooled in Britain and France, a negotiated settlement of some sort might be worked out and he was fully prepared to meet Eden and Mollet to this end at some neutral rendezvous such as Geneva. He had no very clear idea what form such a settlement might take and he was certainly not prepared to compromise on the essential principle that 'the Canal belonged to Egypt' and that its management and revenues should therefore no longer be the preserve and the property of a foreign-owned concern. But he was prepared to concede that, in view of the Canal's international importance, the user nations should be given some element of participation in matters affecting their interests. Accordingly he despatched the Amin brothers to London and Washington to test the ground for a settlement and to reassure leading British and American politicians that, under Egyptian management, the Canal would continue to be open to the world's shipping and would never be employed as a weapon against any user nation.

Mustapha Amin was sent to Washington where he succeeded in so mollifying official opinion as to convince Dulles that negotiations between Egypt and the user nations was a real possibility, which in turn made him all the more opposed to Eden's evident intention to force the issue to a war with Nasser. By contrast, Ali Amin's task in London was a lot more difficult than his brother's. Although he managed to smooth many ruffled feathers among the leaders of the Labour opposition and to impress some Conservative M.P.s as well, he met with total failure in his efforts to bring about a meeting between Nasser and Eden or any other British representative. Not only did Eden reject the idea out of hand, but he also embarked on a series of actions which were to make it progressively more difficult for Nasser to hold to his initial conciliatory line.

Some 25,000 reservists were recalled to Britain's armed forces; naval, military and air force units were moved from England to bases in Cyprus and Malta. And little secret was made of the fact that the purpose of these troop movements was to make ready, in the words of the military commanders' directive, for 'operations against Egypt to restore the Suez Canal to international control', which were to be undertaken jointly with French forces. 'Black' radio broadcasts emanating from Cyprus, Aden, Turkey, Iraq and France started a campaign aimed at inciting the Egyptian people to rise and overthrow Nasser. Also secret plans were concocted with Nuri to stage a pro-Iraqi coup in Syria, Egypt's closest ally.

Added to all this, Eden and Lloyd lost no opportunity publicly to denounce Nasser and to discredit his promise to compensate the Company's shareholders while at the same time building the High Dam and developing the Canal from the revenues of the nationalised enterprise. On August 8, in a television and radio broadcast which was relayed around the world, Eden stated in so many words that he would never negotiate with Egypt's President. 'Our quarrel is not with Egypt, it is with Colonel Nasser,' he said, unable as always since the Glubb episode even to accord his sworn enemy anything but his former military title. Then, forgetting that it was he who had gone back on his assurance not to canvass other Arab states to join the Baghdad Pact, Eden went on to say, 'Colonel Nasser conducted a vicious propaganda campaign against our country. He has shown that he is not a man who can be trusted to keep an agreement.' For the moment, he might be 'soft-pedalling'. But 'with dictators you always have to pay a higher price later on, for their appetite grows with feeding'. Then, ignoring alike that Nasser stood only to gain by the maximum traffic through the Canal and that, with or without the Company in charge of its management, Egypt had controlled the Canal's terminal ports at Suez and Port Said ever since the waterway opened, Eden concluded with the thoroughly disingenuous statement that, 'if Colonel Nasser's actions were to succeed, each one of us would be at the mercy of one man for the supplies on which we live . . . [and] how can we be sure that the next time he has a quarrel with any country, he will not interfere with that nation's shipping?'

Finally, following the visit of Dulles and Mollet to London in early August, the three Western Governments issued a communiqué announcing that an international conference of the twenty-four principal maritime nations was to be summoned to establish 'an international system' to ensure that the Canal would continue to be operated 'as guaranteed by the Convention'. And as if this wording did not imply plainly enough that Egypt was either unwilling or unable to manage the Canal for the benefit of the users, the three-power announcement added for good measure that nationalisation threatened 'the freedom and security of the Canal'. Egypt, it said, had the right to 'nationalise assets not impressed with an international interest', but not to undertake what amounted to 'the arbitrary and unilateral seizure by one nation of an international agency'.

Up to this point, Nasser had had every intention of sending representatives to attend whatever international meeting might be summoned to discuss future arrangements for the Canal. But Eden's violent language, added to the tripartite communiqué's public accusation that Egypt had acted illegally and its clear suggestion that the proposed conference would seek to reverse the act of nationalisation, left him with no alternative but to refuse the three powers' invitation. Even so, in a speech challenging Eden to name one international agreement which he had broken, Nasser expressed his willingness to attend a conference without prejudice, of all the forty-five nations who used the Canal, as distinct from the twenty-four whom, he felt, the three Western sponsors had carefully selected so as to give them a built-in majority for their proposals. And when the nations invited duly assembled in London on August 16 with only Egypt and, because of her current Cyprus dispute with Britain, Greece, absent from the conference table, Ali Sabry was sent to England as the President's personal representative with orders to maintain contact with any delegations who might wish to consult the Egyptian point of view.

But this gathering of Canal users, in which Britain's allies in NATO, SEATO and the Commonwealth outnumbered the rest by two to one, was hardly likely to come up with any negotiable solution. Nobody knew this better than Nasser. And it therefore came as no surprise to him when, on September 2, at the conclusion of the London conference, Robert Menzies, the Australian Prime Minister, arrived in Cairo, accompanied by representatives of the United States, Iran, Ethiopia and Sweden, to present a plan, endorsed by eighteen of the assembled nations, which required that nationalisation be revoked and the Canal's management returned to some unspecified international agency. Menzies had clearly shown his partiality on the Suez Canal issue when, in mid-August, he attacked nationalisation in a BBC broadcast as an act of lawlessness which threatened Britain's standard of living. Echoing Eden, he had then concluded, 'To leave our vital interests to the whim of one man would be suicidal. . . . We cannot accept either the legality or morality of what Nasser has done.' And he was not exaggerating when he confided to the British Lord Chancellor, Lord Kilmuir, before leaving for Cairo, that the odds were ninety-nine to one against his mission bringing about a solution. For what he was commissioned to seek was not a settlement but a surrender.

Nor did Menzies in any way try to sugar the pill which he was to ask the Egyptians to swallow. From first to last he made it clear hat his proposals were being offered on a take-it-or-leave-it basis. Also, while disclaiming any desire to utter threats, he bluntly told Nasser that current British and French troop movements were not a matter of bluff but an indication that both countries meant business which Egypt would ignore at her peril. Whereupon Nasser was only with difficulty prevented by the American representative, Loy Henderson, from terminating the meeting there and then. And although he consented to continue discussions in deference to Henderson and the other members of Menzies' delegation, he refused point-blank to accept what he called a plan for 'collective colonialism'. Moreover he did so with such an uncharacteristic lack of grace that Menzies, in reporting to Eden, remarked that, far from being charmed by Nasser, he found him gauche, awkward and irritating.

No doubt it was this sense of irritation which led Menzies, on his return to London, to give reporters at the airport the misleading statement that 'Egypt will have nothing to do with any peaceful solution of the Canal problem which does not leave Egypt as sole master of the Canal.' In fact, Nasser had only a few days earlier told Robert Anderson for President Eisenhower's information that he would agree to a new convention on freedom of navigation through the Canal and would consider giving some association of user nations the right to consultation on tolls and other management matters. Even if this had been said largely to humour the Americans, the reasons which Nasser gave Menzies for rejecting the internationalisation plan were not without validity. For as he put it, quite apart from issues of sovereignty, the plan 'would plunge the Suez Canal into the turmoil of politics instead of . . . insulating it from politics', as its sponsors claimed they wished to do. Moreover, he had not failed to reiterate his earlier proposal, which Eden and Mollet had contemptuously ignored, that a conference of all user nations should be called to consider any necessary revisions of the existing Constantinople Convention. If he was unimpressed by Menzies' contention that to internationalise the Canal would offer Egypt the status of a landlord letting his property to a number of tenants, it was because he remembered that Egypt had been in that position before, namely in all the time when she had owned the freehold of the Canal Zone, while her British 'tenants' had dug themselves into a military occupation which lasted for seventy-four years. As Nasser saw it, internationalisation could lead to even more foreign interference in the running of the Canal than the Canal Company's concession which he had just terminated.

Nor was Menzies correct in claiming, as he later did, that his efforts in Cairo had been sabotaged by Eisenhower's statement at a press conference on September 5 that 'the United States is committed to a peaceful solution' and would not give up hope of negotiating a settlement 'even if we do run into obstacles'. Contrary to his assertion that this announcement allowed Nasser to feel that 'he was through the period of danger', Menzies had in fact been rebuffed as soon as he produced his proposals and well before Eisenhower's conciliatory words were relayed to Cairo. Besides, from the moment when the idea of internationalising the Canal's management was first bruited abroad from London, Nasser had attacked it as a veiled form of imperialism. And as Eden and Mollet had intended, and Menzies had known when speaking to Kilmuir, the eighteen power plan was so structured as to oblige Nasser either to reject it or to accept a humiliating defeat.

As for Nasser feeling, after Eisenhower's statement, that 'he was through the period of danger', the truth is to the contrary. For, as Menzies' delegation departed, his belief that the British, and now the French as well, were preparing to attack Egypt was growing stronger not weaker. Although Dulles had supported the idea of internationalising the Canal to preserve the appearance of Western solidarity, he had equally advised Fawzi at all costs to keep talking with Britain and France. For, as he put it, despite American opposition, the French were determined 'to wage the Algerian war in Egypt' and had the fullest encouragement of Eden to do so. Moreover to add point to Dulles' warning, more British reinforcements had recently been sent to the eastern Mediterranean, and French forces, including paratroops, had been moved to Britain's bases in Cyprus.

Hence, in a farewell interview with Byroade on the day that

the talks with Menzies came to an end, Nasser said he felt sure that the British and French troop concentrations would remain in the area until a pretext was found for them to move in on the Canal. Likewise Anwar Sadat sounded the alarm in the official newspaper, *Al-Goumhouriya*, by saying, 'It has now become quite clear that Eden wants nothing but war. ... He has no other course open to him than either to declare war or resign.' And in mid-September Lloyd's of London seemed to endorse these apprehensions by raising war-risk insurance rates on ships trading with Egypt or transiting the Canal by as much as 250 per cent.

Of all possible pretexts for Anglo-French military action the one which gave Nasser the most anxiety was a breakdown in the functioning of the Canal. As he well knew, the Suez Canal Company, actively supported by Eden's and Mollet's Governments, were doing their utmost to precipitate this by encouraging the non-Egyptian pilots, who numbered 165 out of the total 205, to quit their jobs and return home. Mahmoud Yunis, the new manager-in-chief of the Canal, had in his possession letters showing that Jacques Georges-Picot, the Canal Company's Director-General, had written to the pilots offering up to three years' salary in advance if they would refuse to work for the nationalised authority. Also when the Egyptian Government, anticipating an early walk-out of foreign pilots, had tried to advertise for replacements in the French and British press, among others, the Company had offered the newspapers money to refuse the advertisements.

Moreover, after the Egyptians had announced at the end of August that, in the first full month of its new management, the daily average of ships transiting the Canal had risen from forty-two to forty-four the Company and the two Governments redoubled their efforts to bring the Canal to a stand-still. The pilots were now not only offered money to quit, but were also bluntly told that, if they stayed at their posts, they would forfeit their pensions. And on September 15, all of the foreign contingent, save the eleven Greeks, whose Government had refused them permission to resign, packed their bags and left for home.

For the next two weeks therefore it was touch and go whether the nationalised authority would be able to maintain the flow of traffic between Suez and Port Said. Yunis scoured the world for pilot replacements. In addition to Egyptian volunteers, he had some success in Germany and Russia, whence he managed to recruit a number of canal and river pilots. He also collected a handful of Americans and other nationalities. But until the new recruits could be initiated in the special hazards of the Suez waterway, the burden of operating the Canal fell very largely on the original forty Egyptians and their eleven Greek companions.

Nevertheless, by the almost superhuman efforts of Yunis and his small band of dedicated pilots working round the clock, which wrung praise even from Georges-Picot himself, the traffic of ships was not only maintained but increased during this critical fortnight. Indeed, Yunis' deputy was able to proclaim to the world in the first week after the foreign pilots walked out, 'Send us more ships: we can handle them. The more ships we have, the more money we can earn.' Then, as the crisis engineered by the Company subsided, Nasser told his Cabinet colleagues that the risk of war had substantially receded. Eden and Mollet had been disappointed in their hopes that the pilots' defection would cause such chaos as to give them a pretext to take over the Canal with military force. Two weeks later Lloyd's of London drew the same conclusion when they brought war-risk insurance rates on Suez shipping back to normal.

Meanwhile, as a device to maintain some degree of control over his two bellicose allies, Dulles had proposed the formation of a Suez Canal Users' Association (SCUA). Although never very precisely expressed, it seemed that his idea was to set up an organisation which would hire pilots, receive all transit dues and, in some undefined way, generally supervise the Canal's management without prejudice to Egypt's sovereignty. Mollet made no secret of his contempt for this proposal or of his suspicions of what had prompted Dulles to put it forward. But Eden was prepared to give it a trial, although his introduction of it to an emergency session of Parliament contained the ominous rider that, if Egypt would not cooperate with SCUA, Britain would be free to 'take whatever steps are open . . . to restore the situation'. Whereupon Dulles hastened to tell a Washington press conference that, whatever Eden's interpretation of his proposal might be, it was not the intention of the United States that SCUA should 'shoot its way' through the Canal. However on the next day, September 15, Nasser torpedoed the entire project when he told a graduation parade of air force cadets that SCUA would lead to 'international anarchy'. It was, he said, as silly as suggesting an association of users to run the Port of London and insisting that all ships using the port should pay their dues to the association. But then, he added, SCUA was never intended to protect the users of the Canal who were protected anyway by the nationalised authority. Rather was it designed to 'usurp' Egypt's sovereignty and rights to control the Canal which Britain had, only two years earlier, recognised in the 1954 Anglo-Egyptian treaty as forming 'an integral part of Egypt'.

With SCUA therefore a non-starter and the danger of war through a breakdown of the Canal seemingly subsided, Nasser's thoughts began to turn back to the possibility of some negotiated settlement. Apart from the fact that he had personally wanted an agreement from the outset of the crisis, provided it did not prejudice Egyptian sovereignty, there were two other important reasons for seeking a settlement. The first was financial. Britain's sterling restrictions were beginning to pinch. Also Britain and France were still prevailing on some 65 per cent of the shipping using the Canal to pay their dues to the former company and not to the Egyptian authority. And he did not see how this could be changed without taking measures against such shipping which would have played right into the hands of Eden and Mollet.

The second reason for conciliation was political. At this point pressures had begun to build up from certain Arab countries and from India, Russia and Tito's Yugoslavia in favour of an agreed settlement. At the time of nationalisation Nasser had won the widest acclamation from all his fellow Arab leaders, except of course for Nuri. Even those, such as Habib Bourguiba of Tunisia and King Idris of Libya, who had little love for Egypt's leader, had at least paid lip service to his defiance of the former imperial powers. But as the crisis wore on, with its accompanying risk of war and with no sign of Britain and France accepting nationalisation, the oil-producing Arab states, especially those without pipelines to the Mediterranean ports, began to fear for the safety of the Canal as the main outlet of their exports to the West in those days when super-tankers did not exist. Naturally enough such fears found a ready echo in Iraq and by the beginning of October the oil-rich Sheikhdoms of the Persian Gulf, not to mention Iran, were all urging Cairo to seek some compromise with the West. Added to this, King Hussein, whose country had suffered three savage Israeli raids in less than a month with the loss of over a hundred Jordanian lives, was beginning to look to Egypt's Iraqi rivals to protect Jordan's borders.

Nor were these the only Arabs whose attitude suggested some reservations in their support of Egypt. From early in the crisis the Sudanese Government had warned Nasser, through their Foreign Minister, Mohammed Mahgoub, that Egypt would most likely find herself at war with the West once the American presidential elections had taken place in November. Mahgoub had added that, in that event, she could not expect any help, except for supplies, from her Arab sister states. At the time, Nasser had discounted such risks on the grounds that, after so long a delay as November, Britain and France would not be able to mobilise enough sympathy from their friends to sustain a war against Egypt. Likewise, when Abdel Kader Hatem, his Minister of National Guidance, warned him that nationalisation would bring war with the West, he had tersely replied that it was Hatem's duty to 'strengthen the people's will to resist the imperialists' and not to moan about the dangers. But a few weeks later Ali Sabry, from his vantage point in the wings of the maritime powers' conference in London, was reporting that the British and French mood was growing uglier every day. And in September Salah Salem returned from a visit to Britain at the time of SCUA's inception in a state of great agitation and excitement saying that war was imminent and that Egypt was facing total destruction at the hands of a thoroughly enraged Eden.

Apart from these alarming counsels, the Indians were urging Nasser to recognise SCUA or some variant at least for the purpose of consultation and liaison with the nationalised authority. Tito was also advocating some gesture towards the West. As for the Russians, they were faced with the imminent threat of revolt in Hungary and with the simultaneous defiance of the Poles, who had dismissed the Russian Marshal Rokossovsky from his post as Poland's Defence Minister. Kruschev was therefore in no position to give Egypt much practical support if it came to war. Hence he too was advising Nasser to reach a speedy agreement with Britain and France.

With such powerful pressures favouring conciliation, Nasser contacted Fawzi, who was currently in New York for a somewhat belated meeting of the U.N. Security Council to discuss the crisis, and told his Foreign Minister that he would accept an international advisory group, such as the Indians were suggesting, to work in consultation with the nationalised authority. Two weeks later, on October 19, he repeated in public the offer, which Ali Amin had brought secretly to London in August, to negotiate in person a settlement with Eden and Mollet. Fawzi meanwhile informed Hammarskold of his readiness to discuss the establishment of an international board; and Hammarskold, in turn, summoned Lloyd and Pineau to meet the Egyptian Foreign Minister in a private session under his chairmanship.

Lloyd had earlier spelled out for Hammarskold the six principles which, he claimed, must govern any Suez settlement. This list consisted of free transit through the Canal without discrimination, agreement between the Egyptian authority and the users on tolls and charges, allocation of a fair proportion of dues for development, arbitration to settle disputes, insulation of the Canal from the politics of any country and respect for Egypt's sovereignty. The six principles had been incorporated in a draft resolution sponsored by Britain and France for the Security Council debate. And as soon as the talks under Hammarskold's chairmanship opened, Fawzi announced that Egypt would not only accept them, but would agree to the establishment of an international association which would represent the users and so ensure that the future management of the Canal acted in accordance with these principles.

With the help of this major Egyptian concession, an agreement of principle was speedily achieved. And the three Foreign Ministers decided to meet again at Geneva on October 29 to spell out such essential details as the composition and powers of the users' association. Yet, no sooner had these agreed decisions been taken than Lloyd and Pineau returned to the Security Council debate and insisted on pressing to a vote a rider to their draft resolution which complained that Egypt had 'not yet formulated sufficiently precise proposals to meet the requirements set out above'. What is more, they demanded that Cairo should submit promptly a plan 'not less effective' than the proposals conveyed to Nasser by Menzies and that meanwhile the Egyptians should agree to SCUA receiving the dues paid by all ships using the Canal.

Even the enigmatic and imperturbable Fawzi was astonished by this contemptuous disregard of the far-reaching concession which he had made to get an agreed settlement and which Lloyd and Pineau had welcomed at the time as a major advance. As for Nasser, back in Cairo, he was completely dumbfounded. But what neither he nor his Foreign Minister knew – although Fawzi had had an uneasy feeling that Pineau had not been dealing with him in complete good faith – was that, at the very moment when the Security Council was about to vote on the Anglo-French resolution, Mollet was bringing Eden into his plans to seize the Suez Canal and topple Nasser by force with the aid of the Israelis. The decision by Eden and Mollet to submit their dispute with Egypt to the United Nations at this late hour had never been intended as a serious move, but rather as a device to set the stage for war by inviting a Russian veto for the Anglo-French resolution and so proving to the world that redress had to be sought by other means than debate in the Security Council. Therefore, whatever concessions Fawzi might have made in private session with Lloyd and Pineau would have made no difference. For, as the Russians predictably cast their veto, Mollet, with perfect timing, approached Eden at the moment when his frustration at finding no pretext for war was at its zenith and showed him the way to settle with Nasser by military action.

The plan was first mooted to Eden by the acting French Foreign Minister, Albert Gazier, and General Maurice Challe at a highly secret meeting on October 14 at Chequers, the Prime Minister's official country residence. Its origins lay in a scheme concocted in the previous October by Ben Gurion and his Chief of Staff, General Moshe Dayan, for the seizure of Gaza, as the source of Egypt's fedayeen activities, and Sharm es-Sheikh on the Tiran Straits, whence the Egyptians maintained their blockade of the Gulf of Akaba against ships and cargoes bound for Israel's back-door port of Elath. Mollet had pledged in a number of secret encounters with Dayan and other Israelis, beginning early in September, that if this plan were to be expanded to include a thrust across the Sinai Peninsular in the direction of the Suez Canal, French forces would join in and seize the Canal, while the Israelis took whatever territory they wanted to finish off the fedayeen and to put an end to Egypt's blockade. But Ben Gurion had hesitated, partly because he did not want to get involved directly in the Canal dispute, but mainly because he feared that, while his forces were advancing into Sinai, Nasser's Ilyushin bombers might raze Tel Aviv and other Israeli cities to the ground.

If only therefore because Britain, unlike France, possessed bomber bases near enough to Egypt to be able to destroy the Ilyushins as the Israelis began their advance, Mollet suggested that he invite Eden's cooperation in the conspiracy. The Israelis agreed and, after a number of meetings on both sides of the English Channel, some between Mollet and Eden, others between Lloyd or his deputy, Pineau and Ben Gurion, the three Prime Ministers agreed upon the final arrangements. Israel was to launch her attack on October 29, paradoxically the date set for Fawzi's further encounter with the British and French Foreign Ministers at Geneva. As soon as Dayan's troops began their advance into Sinai, Britain and France were to issue an ultimatum to Israel and Egypt requiring them to cease fire, to withdraw their forces ten miles either side of the Suez Canal and to 'accept the temporary occupation by Anglo-French forces of key positions at Port Said, Ismailia and Suez'. When Israel had agreed to these terms and Egypt had rejected them, British bombers were to destroy the Egyptian air force and disrupt Egypt's communications and military capability in preparation for an Anglo-French invasion by paratroops from Cyprus and sea-borne forces from Malta. Then, when these forces had occupied the Canal from Port Said to Suez, a further attack was contemplated, aimed at the occupation of Cairo, if Nasser had not yet been overthrown by the combination of these defeats with a radio and leaflet campaign to rouse the people of Egypt against him.

Small wonder that Pineau who, unlike Lloyd at that stage, knew in New York what was being concocted between Paris and Tel Aviv, should have suggested to Fawzi's discerning eye that he was not negotiating in good faith. Which doubts caused Fawzi to ask Trevelyan on his return to Cairo whether Britain seriously intended to seek a settlement at the follow-up meeting in Geneva. And when Trevelyan, in all innocence, confirmed that this was so, he expressed his surprise that in that case Egypt should be asked virtually to spell out an entire new treaty before actual negotiations had started.

But, since Fawzi, equally with Nasser, could not imagine Britain and France being so insane as to attack Egypt in league with Israel, he and his President were both lulled into accepting that the feverish peripatetics of British and French leaders between London and Paris in the second half of October were, as the London *Times* announced, for consultations about further negotiations with Egypt. Besides, far from there seeming to be any immediate danger of Israel attacking Egypt, all recent indications suggested that Jordan was currently the most probable victim of Ben Gurion's aggressiveness. So much so that, when Hussein seemed to be turning to Nuri for support against the Israeli threat, Nasser called a meeting with King Saud and President Quwaitly of Syria and persuaded them jointly to offer Jordan financial help, together with a ticket of admission to the combined Egyptian–Syrian command.

Preferring the company of his fellow Hashemites in Iraq, Hussein rejected the offer and asked Nuri instead for a joint command arrangement for the Jordanian and Iraqi forces. But although Nuri agreed, the plan became hopelessly lost in fractious arguments over who should be the supreme commander. Then, after the third and most ferocious of the current series of Israeli raids had struck the village of Qalqilya on October 10, Hussein appealed to Nasser to help divert the threat to Jordan by sending back some of the troops whom he had withdrawn from the Negev border. Nasser refused on the grounds that the threat to the Canal and Port Said from Britain and France made it impossible to send any troops back into Sinai. But a week later, the nationalist movement in Jordan, led by the pro-Egyptian Suleiman Nabulsi and spurred by Nasser's defiance of Western threats, won a handsome victory at the polls. Whereupon Hussein, realising that his options were now exhausted, bowed to popular feeling, appointed Nabulsi as Prime Minister and, on October 24, agreed to join the Egyptian–Syrian alliance.

At this self-same moment the final arrangements were being made for the Anglo-French-Israeli invasion of Egypt. Also on that day Russian tanks rolled on their inexorable way into Budapest to crush the two-day-old revolt against Russian domination. And by the most poignant coincidence of all at this time when Britishers and Egyptians were about to kill each other, only a few hours before these awesome decisions were taken, Egyptian army buglers, with Nasser's officers standing at the salute, had sounded the Last Post at the annual Anglo-Egyptian ceremony at El-Alamein commemorating the British soldiers who died on that fateful battlefield of World War II.

Hardly had the last notes of the Egyptian bugles died away than British, French and Israeli forces began to take up their allotted positions for the combined assault on the Suez Canal. And on the afternoon of October 29, Dayan's army launched its four-pronged advance against Egypt. Two thrusts, including a paratroop drop close to the town of Suez, were aimed at the Canal, while the third and fourth prongs were respectively to seal off the Gaza Strip and to seize Sharm es-Sheikh. On the following morning Mollet and Pineau hastened to London for discussions at Downing Street, and at 4.15 p.m. the Foreign Office duly delivered the prearranged ultimatums on behalf of the two Governments to the Egyptian Ambassador and the Israeli Chargé d'Affaires. Simultaneously Eden announced to an astonished and deeply divided House of Commons the action which he had taken in association with his French ally.

In a matter of minutes the news of the Anglo-French ultimatum was hurtling round the world. Nasser immediately summoned his Cabinet. But before all his colleagues had had time to assemble, General Abdel Hakim Amer descended on him, accompanied by Salah Salem, and demanding a private audience. There could scarcely have been a greater contrast in attitudes than was evident on this occasion. Although astonished by the news, Nasser was, outwardly at least, completely calm and had already decided to reject the ultimatum out of hand. But Amer and Salem were in a state bordering on panic and both of them unhesitatingly announced that Nasser and his colleagues should go at once to the British embassy and offer immediate surrender to the demand being made upon them.

Nasser made no immediate reply to this effusion. Instead he summoned Boghdady and asked Amer and Salem to repeat in front of him what they had just said. This Amer did, adding that the army was in a hopeless condition and could not possibly resist an invasion by two imperial powers. Egypt would be completely destroyed by Anglo-French bombardments from the air and the sea. This would set her back a thousand years and his conscience would not permit him to let the Egyptian people undergo such punishment. Salem then said that he fully shared Amer's views and that the Government should surrender at once, or it would be too late to prevent the total devastation of the country.

To all this Boghdady retorted that whether or not Egypt could win the forthcoming battle was beside the point. If she did not fight now, she would never have the will to do so in the future. Her leaders, he contended with perhaps rather more courage than common sense, should go to the front and, if necessary, die there. 'Our place,' he concluded, 'is now on the Canal, not in Cairo. If we lose and we are not killed by the British, we should commit suicide rather than fall into their hands as prisoners.' Whereupon Zacharia Mohieddin was sent for and, when he had spoken in similar vein, Nasser quietly instructed him to get a lethal dose of potassium cyanide tablets for every member of the Cabinet. Then

e turned on Amer and Salem and roundly told them that he
hared Boghdady's view. There could be no discussion of the
ıltimatum which was unacceptable from start to finish. He would
ıever submit without a fight to the indignities of its terms.

Amer then withdrew his demand for an immediate surrender
ınd agreed to fight on. But Salem was not convinced by the brave
vords which he had heard and, as he left with Amer for army
ıeadquarters, he appeared to be more nervous than ever. Nasser
ıoticed this and, fearing lest Salem should further weaken Amer's
esistance, promptly instructed Boghdady to see that Salem was
ent to the Canal Zone, where he would be placed under the
urveillance of Kemal el-Din Hussein, who had been appointed as
political overseer of the area. Then, before leaving for the front
ıimself, he held a brief meeting of his full Cabinet; and without
mentioning anything that had just passed between him and his
Commander-in-Chief, he told his colleagues that he intended to
 summon Trevelyan immediately and tell him that Egypt rejected
he Anglo-French ultimatum.

This statement met with acceptance by more or less all of those
present. A few Ministers felt that there might be danger in such
putright rejection and suggested that the matter should be more
fully discussed before so crucial a decision was reached. But
Nasser, after his interview with Amer, was in no mood to allow
ıny opportunity for the spread of defeatism. Egypt, he said, was
being asked to prostrate herself before her former British occupiers, allied to her sworn enemy, Israel, and to the hated French.
About such a proposition there could be no discussion.

The few doubters were therefore silenced. And in an atmosphere
of fatalistic calm the Cabinet unanimously agreed to reject the
ultimatum. Thus the Egyptians entered the war, which Eden and
Mollet had forced upon them, unprepared in every way, save in
the grim determination which Nasser imbued in them to hold out
until the force of world opinion could be mobilised for their
rescue.

Chapter 10

War over the Canal

Even after he had received, and rejected, the Anglo-French ulti-matum, Nasser could still scarcely believe that Eden and Mollet were about to launch a war against Egypt in collusion with Israel. True, he had for long thought, as had most informed Arab opinion, that the Western powers had created Israel to serve as a beachhead to maintain their presence in the Middle East and their influence over individual Arab states. Also he had suspected that there was a definite link between the promotion of the Baghdad Pact and the subsequent sudden increase in Israeli aggressiveness towards her Arab neighbours and especially Egypt. But he still could not believe that any Western power would be so crazy as to spell out the underlying alliance between imperialism and Zionism by aiding and abetting an Israeli aggression against an Arab state.

Under the Tripartite Declaration of 1950, subscribed by the United States, Britain and France, the signatories had pledged themselves to action, within and without the United Nations, to resist any attempt by either Israel or the Arabs to change the 1949 armistice boundaries by force of arms. Egypt had admittedly never accepted that this declaration of itself entitled Western forces to enter Egyptian territory in fulfilment of their Govern-ments' pledges. Indeed, in the 1954 treaty with Britain, the Egyptians had specifically excluded an attack by Israel as consti-tuting grounds for Britain to reactivate the Suez Canal bases. Nevertheless, the three Western powers, as they had consistently reaffirmed, regarded themselves as bound to act against any aggressor. But now Britain and France were acting not against but with the aggressor and were proposing to invade not his terri-tory but that of his victim. More fantastic still, while they claimed to be 'separating the combatants', by the terms and timing of their

ltimatum to both sides, they were actually ordering the victim
o withdraw some 135 miles to the west bank of the Canal and
elling the aggressor to advance, according to the current positions
f the invading armies, between 65 and 115 miles!

The whole idea seemed so grotesque that, for the first twenty-
our hours after the delivery of the two Governments' demands,
Nasser believed that the ultimatum must be a bluff or a ruse to
elp Israel to achieve an easy victory in Sinai by drawing Egyptian
orces away from the Negev border to protect Port Said and the
Canal. Indeed, from his intelligence appreciations, so certain
vas he that this was the intention that he immediately ordered the
eturn to Sinai of many of the units of his Eastern Command
vhich he had withdrawn two months earlier when he feared a
irect Anglo-French attack on the Canal. Nor was it until
3ritish Canberra bombers began attacking Egyptian airfields on
he evening of October 31, in fulfilment of Eden's pledge to Ben
Gurion to destroy Egypt's air force, that he was forced to accept
hat the ultimatum meant what it said.

Realising now that he was about to be confronted with the
overwhelming military superiority of Britain and France, as well
s Israel, Nasser hastened to army headquarters to tell Amer to
ancel all previous orders and instruct all units in Sinai to con-
luct a fighting withdrawal back to the Canal. In addition, he
ordered that the plans for guerrilla resistance should be put into
ffect immediately. Zacharia Mohieddin was placed in overall
ommand of partisan activities, while Kemal ed-Din Hussein took
harge of the guerrillas in the Canal Zone. Caches of arms were
idden in selected houses and flats in every city and town of
Lower Egypt, together with such other accoutrements of underground warfare as radio transmitters and printing machines.
Other arms were distributed to anyone who volunteered to serve
s a guerrilla by army trucks parading the streets with loud-
peakers calling on the people to help resist the oncoming
nvaders.

It was, to say the least, a somewhat haphazard method of
organising popular resistance. But, as the British forces were later
o discover in Port Said, it was by no means ineffective. Nor were

the guerrilla bands that much more disorganised than the army. For all the Russian arms shipments, the Egyptian regular forces were quite unprepared to fight a war. Of the 200 new Russian tanks, only about fifty were as yet in service. Of the 100 MIG fighters, only some thirty were operational and of the fifty Ilyushin bombers, only twelve. Most of the pilots and tank-crews who were to man these new weapons were still learning how to handle them in training schools in Russia. The new Egyptian air force was therefore a sitting target for the British Canberras and of the thirty Ilyushins which managed to escape to Luxor in Upper Egypt, only twelve survived to fly on to safety in Saudi Arabia, the other eighteen being hunted down and destroyed by further British bombing attacks in Upper Egypt.

To add to Nasser's anxieties, just as he was contemplating the wreckage of his Russian air force, a message reached him from Kruschev via Shukri Quwaitly, who was currently visiting Moscow, which bluntly told him that Russia would not risk getting involved in a third world war for the sake of the Suez Canal. If there had to be such a war, the Russians would choose a more appropriate time and place. Meanwhile, Kruschev advised that Egypt should make her peace as soon as possible with Britain and France whose superior strength would make further resistance futile. Russia would give her all necessary moral support but could supply no further assistance at this stage.

So shaken was Nasser by Kruschev's brutal candour that he promptly put the telegram in his private safe and, for fear of lowering morale among his Ministers at this crucial moment, told not even his closest confidants of its contents. There the secret lay until 1960 when an argument developed with the Syrian members of the combined Cabinet of the United Arab Republic who were then advocating an immediate attack on Israel. Nasser warned that such action would be opposed by the West and, when the Syrians answered that Russia would then fight for the Arabs, he opened his safe and produced Kruschev's message as proof that she would not. Meanwhile, to his colleagues of the moment, he pretended that the Russian leaders were offering Egypt more aircraft plus technicians, which he dismissed as

indly but impracticable gesture, so long as the Egyptian pilots
vere still undergoing training in Russia.

Nasser did not, of course, expect the Russians to declare war
n his behalf or to send him 'volunteers' even though, as he was
oon to learn, the French were helping Israel by flying interdiction
nissions which released Israeli pilots for operational duties with
he advancing armies. For he realised only too well that the war
vhich had now broken out in the Middle East had caught the
Russians at a moment when they could think of nothing but their
wn problems in Hungary. But what astonished and dismayed
im was that Kruschev seemed to have gone out of his way to
lisown Egypt in her hour of trial.

Dejectedly he now appealed to Eisenhower for help. Also,
partly out of disillusionment with his Russian friends, partly too
o impress on Washington that he was not the Soviet puppet
vhich Eden and Mollet claimed him to be, he simultaneously
rdered the Amin brothers to reprint on their presses for circula-
ion throughout Egypt a million copies of a *Life* magazine article
evealing Russia's brutal suppression of the Hungarian revolt.
Washington's immediate reaction was suspicious. Was Nasser,
hey inquired, asking for American help so as to give himself an
xcuse for inviting the Russians in, if the United States turned him
lown? However, when Nasser blandly denied having asked for
Russian intervention, Hare was able to assure him on Eisenhower's
uthority that, while America could not be expected to go to war
with her own allies, she would nevertheless do all in her power to
top the fighting by diplomatic action within the United Nations.

In fact, the only offers of active military help which Egypt
eceived in these critical days were from Syria and Jordan, with
vhom a plan had been hastily prepared, following King Hussein's
lecision to join the Egyptian-Syrian alliance, for an advance to the
Mediterranean coast designed to cut Israel in two, should she
lecide to attack Egypt. But by this time the first reports of the
Anglo-American conspiracy with Iraq to mount a coup d'état in
Damascus had begun to filter through to the Egyptian intelligence
ervice. Nasser therefore feared that for Syria to engage the bulk of
er army in a second front against Israel might only serve the

conspirators' purpose without materially helping Egypt. Beside
there was also the risk that, if Syria and Jordan joined in the battl
France and Britain might claim this as a pretext to reoccupy thes
former mandates of theirs, in the same way as they were nov
seeking to do with Egypt.

For these reasons the Joint Command Headquarters in Cair
telegraphed on November 1 to Amman to 'halt all offensive pr
parations and postpone Operation Beisan (against Israel) unt
further orders . . .' Moreover when, in response to Arab Trad
Union demands for the sabotage of Western-owned oil pipeline
the Syrians decided to blow up the three most important pumpin
stations on the Iraq Petroleum Company's pipeline to Tripol
Nasser opposed even this limited demonstration of Arab solida
ity. The Joint Command telegraphed to Damascus saying tha
sabotage of the pipelines would be 'injurious to the interests c
other countries not implicated . . .' and should therefore be calle
off. The message arrived too late to prevent the demolition team
fulfilling their allotted task. Nevertheless, Nasser's advice mad
some impact on the excitable Syrians, sufficient at any rate to ob
viate any similar action against the American-owned Trans-Arabi
pipeline (Tapline) which escaped unscathed from the Suez War.

Having thus decided that he must face the tripartite invasion c
Egypt alone, Nasser now set about supervising the final plan c
campaign. Sinai was to be evacuated and left to the Israelis, whil
in Port Said and the other Canal townships, only token resistanc
was to be offered to the Anglo-French invaders, so as to minimis
loss of life and property by naval and air bombardment. Ther
directly the invading armies had taken up their occupation rol
guerrilla resistance would begin and would be complemented b
a major propaganda campaign in the United Nations and amon
the non-aligned countries to drum up such overwhelming con
demnation of the aggressors as would force them to withdraw
Meanwhile, Britain and France were to be denied the fruits c
their military victory in a Samson-like gesture on the part of th
Egyptians which would bring all traffic through the Suez Cana
to a halt by the sinking of blockships at both ends.

By a curious coincidence the officer designated to carry out th

iece of sabotage, Colonel Haney Amin Hilmy, was the grandson
f an Egyptian army major who had been appointed to the self-
ame task by Ahmed Arabi at the time of the 1882 revolt when it
vas learned that British forces under Sir Garnet Wolseley were on
heir way from India to crush Arabi's nationalist uprising. But,
nlike his grandfather who dallied too long and so failed to make
is move before Wolseley arrived on the scene, Hilmy succeed-
d in sinking his blockships. Indeed, as Nasser later told me with
ome amusement, far from being hindered by the invaders, he
vas actually helped by them. For on November 1, as the first
lockship, loaded with cement, was being towed into position in
he deep-water channel of Lake Timsah, half-way down the
Canal, British bombers sent her to the bottom and so obviated the
eed for Hilmy's men to do more than cut the tow-rope.

Nasser's decision to rely on world opinion to evict the aggres-
ors was very soon justified. The Arab states reacted with predict-
ble wrath. Syria and Saudi Arabia followed Egypt's lead in
reaking off relations with Britain and France. Jordan and Iraq
roke with France, though not with their British patrons; and as
he demonstrations and strikes persisted in every independent
Arab state in protest against the Anglo-French action, Britain's
Baghdad Pact partners advised her to stay away from future
neetings or risk expulsion. More important still, in the world at
arge, a chorus of denunciation of the aggressors and of sympathy
or the victim began to mount. Not only Russia and China, but
lso Britain's Commonwealth partners, such as Canada, India,
'akistan and Ceylon, joined in the general condemnation of the
ripartite assault on Egypt. The United States delegate, Henry
Cabot Lodge, presented a resolution to the U.N. Security Council
vhich called on Israel to withdraw and on all other U.N. mem-
ers to refrain from using or threatening force in the area of
onflict. This and a similar Russian resolution were promptly
ullified by British and French vetoes – the first ever cast by these
wo nations since the U.N.'s inception. Whereupon Lodge sup-
orted a Yugoslav proposal to summon a special emergency session
f the General Assembly, where the veto power did not apply, to
xpress in valid form the indignation of world opinion and to call

for an immediate cease-fire and the withdrawal of the Israel
army from Egyptian territory.

Thus, even as the Anglo–French armada was steaming toward
the beaches of Port Said from its base in Malta, Nasser could fee
reasonably confident about the ultimate outcome. Since Kruschev
message he had been in such a state of nervous tension that h
had refused to sleep alone and insisted on Boghdady sharing h
room at the RCC building on Cairo's Gezira island, which h
made his headquarters during the crisis. But as his gamble c
world opinion began to show signs of paying off, so he regaine
his calm and, in a defiant broadcast to his people reminiscent c
Winston Churchill after Dunkirk in 1940, he proclaimed that h
would never surrender, but would stay and resist the invaders unt
they were finally forced to withdraw. To give point to his word
he refused to allow his wife and children to leave Cairo, althoug
he moved them from his house in Heliopolis which was only
stone's throw from the military airfield at Almaza to the saf
residential quarter of Zamalek. And when Abdel Kader Hatem
warned him that, if the British carried out their threat to bom
Cairo Radio and the 'Voice of the Arabs' off the air, there woul
be no suitable alternative transmitters available to maintain con
tact with the people, Nasser replied that he would tour Cairo an
other cities in an open car and call on the populace to resist b
loud-speaker.

Hatem's fears were confirmed on the very next day when
further wave of British Canberras, early in the morning c
November 2, knocked out the two radio stations. And withi
minutes, a British radio transmitter in Cyprus had tuned in on th
vacant wavelength with exhortations to the Egyptian people t
rebel against Nasser who had gone 'mad and seized the Sue
Canal ... rejected a fair solution ... exposed you to Israe
attacks ... betrayed Egypt ... (and) adopted dictatorship
Therefore, the broadcast concluded, the Egyptians should accep
the proposal of the Allied states which would bring them 'peac
and prosperity ... (or) bear the consequences of Abdel Nasser
mad behaviour'.

By any standards of psychological warfare it was a pathet

ffort at subversion. And although suddenly stricken by an attack
f laryngitis, Nasser could hardly wait to expose the hollow pre-
ension that submission to a renewed occupation of Egypt by
oreign troops would bring peace and prosperity. On that same
lay, while loud-speakers relayed his voice to the people of Cairo,
.e adopted the custom of the early Caliphs of Islam and, from the
ulpit of the Al-Azhar mosque, proclaimed that the National
.iberation Army, as the guerrillas had been officially styled,
vould fight from village to village and house to house. To deafen-
ng applause he announced that £300 million worth of military
quipment left in the British ordnance depots in the Canal Zone
iad been seized and the small arms distributed to the guerrillas,
vhile the tanks and heavy equipment had been handed over to
he army. With the help of these weapons and a united will to
esist, he concluded, 'God will render us successful.' Then, to the
lelight of the Cairo populace with their penchant for spectacle and
o the anxiety of his bodyguard, and even some of his colleagues,
.e toured Cairo in an open car to show the people that, as he had
·owed, he was still amongst them and that the voice they had
.eard from the Al-Azhar mosque was live and not just a record-
ng. Likewise, for the next three days until an alternative system
·f radio transmission could be rigged up, Hatem's officials also
oured the streets of Cairo and other cities in cars with loud-
peaker equipment to bring the news to the people, while
Jamascus Radio helped out by broadcasting the Egyptian com-
nuniqués as they were relayed by telephone from the Joint
Command Headquarters in Cairo.

There can be no doubt that Nasser's leadership at this critical
uncture established him finally and completely as the 'rais', the
aptain of the Egyptian ship of state, whose word henceforth was
aw for every member of the crew. True, he was well served by
xtremely capable assistants such as Fawzi and Kaissouny among
he civilian members of his Cabinet. Among his military col-
:agues too he could count on such outstanding administrators as
Boghdady and Zacharia Mohieddin. (For although the RCC had
een formally disbanded following Nasser's elevation to the presi-
lency, a majority of its members were still very much an integral

part of the regime.) But from the moment when he received th
Anglo-French ultimatum, Nasser assumed complete charge of th
situation and, whereas formerly he had always consulted his co
leagues before taking any important decision, he now told ther
what he wanted done and brooked no argument with his judge
ment.

Had his gamble with world opinion failed and Egypt foun
herself forced to surrender her control of the Canal and accep
another foreign occupation, it would of course have been a ver
different story. It is even possible that the populace would the
have turned against him. For although, eleven years later, he wa
not allowed to 'abdicate' following Egypt's further humiliatin
defeat at the hands of Israel, this was precisely because he had bee
ever since 1956 the absolute ruler of his people and, for all h
mistakes, after fifteen years of his leadership, few could imagir
Egypt without him as President.

But as it happened, the gamble paid off. Nasser's judgemer
was vindicated. And the Anglo-French threat to impose anoth
alien occupation upon Egypt was doomed from the start, largel
because the United States insisted on upholding the will of th
United Nations General Assembly, where no less than 65 nation
including America and Russia, voted against Britain, France an
Israel who could only rally two friends – Australia and Ne
Zealand – to their support. From that moment the 'rais' could nc
lose the war even though he was sure to lose every battle. Fror
that moment, therefore, he ceased merely to be first amon
equals among the leaders of the revolution and became th
supreme and undisputed autocrat of Egypt.

Yet while Nasser might safely conclude from the U.N.'s ma:
sive condemnation of the aggression that rescue was already i
sight, he was not at all happy with the way in which his clo
friend and companion, General Amer, was conducting the can
paign. For one thing, as he remarked somewhat bitterly to Bogl
dady, he was not being kept posted on the course of the army
withdrawal from Sinai to the Canal. And when Boghdad
remonstrated with Amer over this, the General curtly retorte
that he was much too busy to communicate with anybody sav

is army commanders. For another, there was an unreality in the
rmy communiqués' claims to be holding the Israeli advance at
ll points which was horribly reminiscent of the announcements
sued by Farouk's Generals at the time of the Palestine war in
948. Indeed Amer, from the depths of despair and defeatism with
vhich he had reacted to the news of the Anglo-French ultimatum,
ad now become positively euphoric about the army's prospects
f withstanding the Israeli thrust into Sinai. When Nasser ordered
he retreat to the Canal, he had argued hotly against it, protesting
hat, although heavily outnumbered, the Egyptian army had
iflicted serious damage on the Israelis in more than one engage-
nent.

Amer was quite correct in saying that the Egyptians in Sinai
ad been by no means lacking in either courage or effective-
ess. In several places they had fought stubbornly and heroically
gainst an enemy with a numerical superiority of never less than
hree to two and with infinitely better organisation and technical
kill, who had been hardened to the inevitable bloodshed of war
y such techniques as bayoneting sacks filled with live cats during
heir training. Even the ranks of Tuscany in the shape of Israel's
military historians could not afterwards forbear to cheer such
allant actions as the stand of an Egyptian infantry company at
he Ruwafa Dam in north-east Sinai against repeated assaults by
n Israeli armoured brigade equipped with American Super-
herman tanks.

But the performance of the Egyptians in Sinai was beside the
oint. The main enemy now was not Israel but Britain and France,
vho were menacing Port Said, the Canal and Cairo. And Nasser,
uspecting that Amer's abrupt changes of mood were due to his
nown predilection for hashish, began seriously to doubt his
riend's capacity to command the army in this highly dangerous
ituation. Hence, when the withdrawal from Sinai had been
ompleted on November 3 and an effective cease-fire between
Egyptian and Israeli forces existed everywhere, except at Sharm
s-Sheikh which fell two days later, he and Boghdady decided to
o at once to the Suez Canal front to supervise the conduct of the
ext stage of the war, the descent of the Anglo-French forces upon

Port Said. Zacharia Mohieddin was put in charge of the Government in Cairo and over the protests of the commander of the
presidential bodyguard, who feared that British bombers might
attack Nasser's car, the two leaders set off for Port Said via
Ismailia.

The original Egyptian plan had been to abandon the city of
Port Said which, surrounded as it was by lakes and marshlands,
was anyhow virtually indefensible against a well-organised
assault. Then, as the Anglo-French invaders debouched onto the
narrow causeway which linked the city with the road to Ismailia
and Suez, the Egyptian army would pounce on them and seek to
delay for as long as possible their progress southwards. However,
after the uproar in the House of Commons and in the outside
world which followed the British bombing attacks on Egypt,
Nasser decided after all to make a stand in Port Said. He realised
the difficulties of defending the city. But he wanted to buy time
for sympathy and support for Egypt's plight to gain still more
ground in the United Nations. Besides, he felt that for the army
to fight alongside Port Said's civilian population would help to
raise the people's morale for the subsequent guerrilla resistance.
And since he no longer felt confident that the mercurial Amer
was able, or even willing, to carry out this change of plan, he
decided to go in person to the Canal front and ensure that his new
orders were being put into execution.

In fact Nasser never got to Port Said. On arrival at Ismailia
he was told by Kemal ed-Din Hussein that the road to the
north was unsafe. Not only was there the risk of British bombers
strafing it, but the Israelis, from their positions ten miles east of
the Canal, also had it under constant aerial observation and, in
their trigger-happy mood, they might attack anything moving
under cover of darkness. Hussein therefore advised, and Boghdady agreed, that it would be better to wait until morning to see
how the situation developed before moving any further. For
which advice Nasser was to be exceedingly grateful, since on the
very next morning British and French paratroops descended on
Port Said and would almost certainly have captured him, if he
had arrived there as intended on the previous evening.

News of the paratroop attack reached Ismailia within a matter of minutes and Nasser, realising that he would now have to leave the conduct of his forces in Port Said largely to the discretion of the local commander, returned post-haste to army headquarters. Here he found Amer in a state of almost total nervous collapse, with tears coursing down his cheeks and clearly unable to make any decisions. There was nothing for it but to order the Commander-in-Chief to return to his quarters and personally to take command of the army. But no sooner had Nasser added this burden to all his other responsibilities than he discovered to his astonishment that the orders to make a stand at Port Said had not been relayed to the local army commander, Brigadier Moguy, who decided, in the absence of contrary instructions, to ask the invaders for a truce after they had sealed off the city and cut off the fresh water supply to its inhabitants.

Moguy's purpose was partly to spare the citizens of Port Said from bombardment, partly also to gain time for his soldiers to shed their uniforms and turn themselves into partisans along with the civilian population, before a formal cease-fire required them to hand over their arms and ammunition. But this did not square with Nasser's new thinking and, although the real blame lay with Amer for not passing on the change of orders, Moguy was later to pay for his action by the loss of his army career. Meanwhile, he was curtly told that the truce was unacceptable and that honour demanded continued resistance by him and his garrison. Cairo Radio, now back on the air, hastened to deny that the city had surrendered, although not before Eden had told the House of Commons of the cease-fire to rapturous applause from the Conservative benches. And at 10.30 in the evening Moguy's troops resumed the battle with the paratroops. But Nasser could not postpone Eden's petty triumph for very long. For on the following morning, November 6, the Anglo-French sea-borne forces reached the beaches of Port Said. Moguy was taken prisoner and as his soldiers, after a brief but tough battle, shed their uniforms for the civilian attire of the partisans, organised resistance came to a stop.

Confident though he was that world opinion would ultimately

come to Egypt's rescue, the fall of Port Said and the physical reoccupation of Egyptian territory by British forces was a bad moment for Nasser. For just as the abortive negotiations with America and Britain for the financing of the High Dam had made him think of de Lesseps and the Khedive Ismail, so now this British invasion of Egypt could not fail to conjure up the ghosts of Sir Garnet Wolseley and Ahmed Arabi and the memory of those seventy-four years of British occupation which followed Arabi's defeat. Determined not to give Eden or Mollet the smallest pretext for continuing or extending their occupation of Egyptian territory, he made it known that any attacks on British or French residents would be severely punished. In fact, so much did he impress this on all concerned that, even after British bombers had smashed the Egyptian air force and attacked a number of industrial targets in Cairo and the Nile Delta, there was not a single demonstration against the British embassy, which was guarded both before and after Trevelyan's departure by its customary complement of two policemen armed only with truncheons.

But what Nasser did not know in this moment of anxious historical reflection was that Eisenhower had already forced Eden to agree to an immediate cease-fire and that Eden in his turn had persuaded Mollet to abandon the attack on Egypt. Eisenhower had made it clear that, with the Suez Canal blocked, the United States would not help to save the now tottering British pound or to finance alternative supplies of oil from dollar sources, unless the invasion of Egypt was halted and an immediate truce brought into operation on the Canal. Therefore, no sooner had Port Said fallen than, at 2 a.m. local time on November 7, the Anglo-French forces proclaimed a cease-fire and brought their advance to an abrupt and final halt, although at this point they had only progressed as far as El-Kap twenty-three miles to the south.

In the meantime the Russians, anxious to distract the world's attention from their brutal intervention in Hungary, had publicly warned Eden, Mollet and Ben Gurion not to continue their aggression and had alluded ominously to the power of the Soviet Union's rocket arsenal. Ben Gurion was also accused of 'acting as an instrument of outside imperialist forces' and was told hat the Russian Ambassador was being withdrawn from Tel Aviv. Kruschev furthermore proposed to Eisenhower that their wo countries should help to stop the war by forming a combined American–Russian naval and air force under a United Nations lirective. And a few days later, he followed this up with a warn-ng that, if the occupation of Egyptian territory were not promptly nded, Russia might send 'volunteers' to the area.

But while Nasser was not slow to use these Soviet utterances to olster public morale with the claim that Egypt was not without owerful friends and supporters in Russia as well as America, he vas under no illusion that Moscow intended to do any more than ulminate against his attackers in an attempt to regain prestige in he Arab world. He also knew, as the White House remarked, vhen describing as 'unthinkable' the idea of a joint American–Russian peace-keeping force, that the Russians were seeking not o much to help the Egyptians, as to divert towards Britain and France some of the odium which they had incurred in the United Nations and elsewhere by their barbarities in Budapest. For even as the Kremlin's threats were reverberating around the world, Kruschev was telling the Egyptian Ambassador, Moham-ned el-Kouny, that 'geographical obstacles' made it quite impos-ible for him to send any material help to Egypt.

Besides, as Kruschev had made all too clear in the message which he had sent to Nasser through Quwaitly, Russia would not isk starting a third world war for the sake of Egypt and the Suez Canal. So far everything had worked out very nicely for the Soviet leaders. Quite apart from the position of influence in the Arab world which they had acquired at the Western powers' xpense by their arms deals with Egypt and Syria, the West was leeply divided by the rift between Eden and Mollet and their American and other NATO partners. And if the Russians had in fact intervened on Egypt's behalf, their action could only have erved to heal the breach in the Western alliance and to bring the NATO powers together to resist the Russian interloper by every neans short of war.

Nearly two and a half years later, at a time when Kruschev was publicly scolding Nasser for locking up Communists in Egypt and

Syria with an excess of zeal which he said was due to 'youthfu
passion and hot-headedness', Moscow Radio accused Egypt o
ingratitude for what they claimed to have been Russia's decisiv
help in stopping the Suez aggression. Nasser then angrily re
torted that, instead of Egypt being grateful to Russia, the Russian
should acknowledge the debt they owed to the 'passion and hot
headedness' with which the Egyptians had fought single-hande
to prevent their country being turned, among other things, int
'a rocket base against the Soviet Union'. Meanwhile, acknow
ledging for his own part that if any one power had played a
decisive role in halting the Anglo-French invasion, it was th
United States, he told the American Ambassador, on the day afte
the cease-fire had been proclaimed, that he hoped for improve
relations with Washington in the difficult times that lay ahead
More in amazement than in anger he said that he could no
understand why Britain and France had embarked on such a craz
venture. But the fact remained that they had done so and, in th
doing, had forfeited their influence throughout the Arab world
This meant that, for the time being, relations between Egypt an
the West would have to be channelled exclusively through th
United States. Nasser therefore hoped that, despite their close tie
with the three aggressors, the Americans would work for a
understanding with Egypt and the rest of the Arab world. B
pursuing a policy independently of these three allies, he said, the
should have no difficulty in reaching such an understanding an
Hare should realise that any efforts made by Washington in thi
direction would be warmly reciprocated in Cairo.

From what Nasser and Fawzi told me soon after the 1956 war
there can be no doubt that this statement reflected a genuine hop
that, after the unhappy outcome of the High Dam negotiation
with Dulles, a new chapter would now be opened in American
Egyptian relations. Indeed, it is probably true to say that no
until the assassination of President Kennedy in 1963 put the avow
edly pro-Zionist Lyndon Johnson into the White House di
Nasser finally abandon hope of reaching an understanding wit
the United States. After the let-down over the High Dam he ha
been understandably encouraged by America's uncompromisin

opposition to the action of her two principal allies in the past few weeks. He was impressed that Eisenhower should have risked losing the American-Jewish vote in the presidential election, which had taken place in the middle of the fighting, by his out-right condemnation of Israel's aggression against Egypt. And he was anxious to help Washington in every possible way to hold to what appeared to be the new course of friendship with Cairo.

Partly for these reasons, Nasser went out of his way to give the lie to the accusations that he was playing Mussolini to Kruschev's Hitler which Eden had so assiduously been pouring into American ears ever since the dismissal of General Glubb nine months earlier. On November 21, he issued a statement, for distribution by every Egyptian diplomatic and press agency, in which he categorically denied that he was, or would ever become, 'the stooge or satellite or pawn or hireling of anybody'. Then he went on, 'Just as Egypt is determined to have political independence, so also Egypt is determined to have and to maintain ideological independence from all foreign ideologies such as Marxism, racism, colonialism, imperialism and atheism, all of which incidentally are European in origin.' And he concluded by saying, in reply to the charge that he was seeking to carve out an empire for himself, that 'the concept of Arab imperialism is a foreign fiction or foreign propaganda based on ignorance or worse'.

But whatever hopes may have been aroused in Cairo by America's attitude during the Suez crisis, the United States Government were all too soon to show that their policy towards Egypt differed from that of the British and French in method only. Dulles, on recovering from an operation on the cancer which was to kill him less than three years later, told Selwyn Lloyd, much to his astonishment, that, had he not been removed from the conduct of American policy by illness, Britain would not have had to endure the weight of censure which Eisenhower and his deputies, Herbert Hoover Junior and Cabot Lodge, had heaped upon her. Even so, he added, having embarked on their venture, Britain and France should have seen it through instead of stopping short of bringing about Nasser's downfall.

Dulles had, from the start of the Suez crisis, been opposed to the

idea of trying to topple Nasser by military action and had felt
that economic pressures would be more effective, as well as less
likely to outrage world opinion. But he was no less convinced
than Eden and Mollet that Nasser had to be removed by one means
or another. And it was no doubt this conviction which led him to
comment as he did to Lloyd on the failure of Britain and France
to carry out their original plans.

Therefore, when the Egyptian Government followed up
Nasser's talk with Hare with a request for emergency supplies of
food, fuel and medicines, Washington bluntly rejected this cry
for help. Cairo then asked that some of Egypt's dollar funds
amounting to $27 million, which the United States had blocked,
should be released to purchase these desperately needed supplies
wherever they could be found. But still Washington refused to
help. And after the Russians had stepped in with an airlift of drugs
and medicines and massive shipments of wheat, Nasser, more
cast down than ever by the inhumanity of the American rebuff,
bitterly accused Washington of trying to starve the Egyptian
people.

Fawzi complained privately to Cabot Lodge, whose reply was
that Egypt should have agreed to stand with the United States
against the Russian and Communist threat as Iraq, Tunisia and
Saudi Arabia had done. Why, Lodge asked, had Nasser been so
unfriendly to America in the past? But when Fawzi retorted, 'Do
you only want yes-men as friends?' he had no proper answer. And
as Nasser told me, in an interview in the early spring of 1957,
he drew from these exchanges the reluctant and inescapable
conclusion that there would be no point in even asking Washington to replace the military equipment which had been captured
by the Israelis in Sinai or destroyed by British bombing. He had
therefore gone straight to the Russians, who had of course undertaken to supply all that he required from them.

Nasser warmly acclaimed this prompt response in a public vote
of thanks to the Soviet Government. Also in a speech which he
delivered on November 9, once again from the pulpit of Al-
Azhar, he acknowledged his gratitude to his Syrian, Saudi and
Jordanian allies for their offers of help in the war just ended. Like-

wise he was loud in his praise for the solidarity shown by the Arab world as a whole, as evidenced by the strikes and demonstrations staged by the Arab Trades Union Federation from as far east as Qatar and Bahrein to Tunisia and Morocco. But because of Washington's churlish refusal to help with relief supplies after the cease-fire, he was precluded from any public expression of thanks to the country which he knew had been above all others instrumental in stopping the aggressors in their tracks and to which, as he readily admitted to me and many others in private conversation, he would have liked to be able to accord its due of tribute.

Yet, apart from his disillusionment with the United States, the situation could hardly have been more favourable for Nasser at this point. Messages of congratulation over the halting of the 'tripartite aggression', as it had come to be called, were pouring in from every Arab capital and from virtually every other country, except for a few NATO partners of Britain and France. Not only his fellow Arab rulers but, far more important in his sight, the Arab masses too hailed him as their hero and saviour, while Kruschev, Tito, Nehru, Sukarno and Chou En-lai all cabled their encomiums to Cairo. Indeed, Nasser was rapidly approaching the pinnacle of his prestige as an Arab leader and as a power to be reckoned with in the councils of the world. His enemies had been thwarted in their attempt to overthrow him and, with his control of the Suez Canal no longer challenged, he could dictate to the world about such matters as the nature and timing of the salvage operations necessary to clear the waterway of the sunken Egyptian blockships, and so reopen it for the use of the world's shipping. Nor was he slow to exploit his advantage in this respect. For in the same speech as he delivered in praise of his three Arab allies two days after the general cease-fire, he vowed that 'so long as there is ... one single foreign soldier in Egypt, we shall not begin repairing the Canal ...'

In the event, Nasser was to modify this reservation and, although the Israelis were still in Gaza and Sinai, on the departure of the last British soldier from Port Said on December 23, the United Nations salvage teams under the direction of the American

General Raymond Wheeler were allowed to begin their clearing operations in January 1957. It was after all vital to the Egyptian economy to secure the earliest possible resumption of normal traffic through the Canal; and the sooner Wheeler's men got started, the sooner the revenues would begin to flow into the Cairo treasury. But, even so, the last blockship was not removed until the first week of March when, after another two months of protracted argument by Ben Gurion, Israel too was finally induced to withdraw her forces from Sinai and the Gaza Strip under the threat of sanctions by the United Nations.

Nasser's stubbornness in this respect was not merely designed to flaunt his new-found power. On the contrary, he felt he genuinely needed to use every available lever to force the invaders to withdraw. Ben Gurion had argued with vehemence in the United Nations that Israel should be allowed to keep Gaza which, as a part of the former area of Palestine, he said had never been Egyptian territory. He also laid claim to Sharm es-Sheikh to prevent Egypt from reimposing the blockade of her back-door. Eden too had wanted to maintain what he called the 'gage', which he had gained at Port Said, in spite of the harassments which his troops were suffering every day at the hands of Kemal ed-Din Hussein's partisans of the National Liberation Army. Also, with Dulles now recovered from his operation and once again in complete control of American foreign policy, Nasser was afraid that Washington might not show the same determination to twist the aggressors' arm, as Eisenhower and Hoover had done when they were in charge of the State Department.

True, largely as a device to save British and French face, a United Nations force (UNEF), drawn from 'neutral' nations in Europe, Asia and Latin America, had been formed to replace the Anglo-French forces in Port Said and to police the cease-fire area. But this did not altogether reassure Nasser. For although Eden had accepted UNEF and the French contingent of the invasion forces had returned to the war in Algeria directly the cease-fire sounded, the British did everything in their power to delay their withdrawal, insisting for instance that every single unit of UNEF should have taken up its allotted station before British troops moved out. Also, Nasser suspected that UNEF might be used by the Western powers as an instrument to impose their ideas of internationalising the management of the Suez Canal. And he felt that the Americans might be working up to some such scheme to save at least this much from the wreckage of Eden's and Mollet's plans. After all, back in August, Dulles had spoken most emphatically to Eden of the need to make Egypt 'disgorge' what she had gained by nationalising the Canal Company, and he had been a prime sponsor of the internationalisation scheme which Menzies had brought to Cairo.

These suspicions were however laid to rest when Hammarskold arrived in Egypt, together with the advance guard of UNEF, on November 16. Hammarskold had always got on well with Nasser who regarded him as scrupulously fair in his dealings with Israel and her Arab neighbours. Moreover, since the major border clashes over the past two years had been largely of Israel's seeking and Hammarskold's severest censures had therefore been directed at Tel Aviv rather than Cairo, he had enjoyed a consistently good press in Egypt, where he was thought to be generally pro-Arab in sympathy. His handling of the Suez crisis from July onwards and his efforts prior to the invasion to bring about a settlement behind the scenes in New York had won much praise in Cairo, as had his subsequent untiring efforts to mobilise United Nations action to halt the 'tripartite aggression'.

Before leaving for Egypt, Hammarskold had told the British and French Governments that their troops would have to leave Egyptian territory before the clearing of the Canal could begin. Therefore, if there was one man who could disabuse Nasser of his suspicions about the underlying aims of UNEF, it was he. After Nasser had let off steam about the danger of major riots in Port Said if the U.N. force appeared to be conniving at any undue protraction of the British occupation, Hammarskold reassured him by proposing a formula setting out UNEF's rights and obligations. This provided that the U.N. troops should act solely as a buffer between Israel and Egypt at such potential flash-points of conflict as Gaza, the Negev border and Sharm es-Sheikh. Their presence on Egyptian territory would be entirely conditional upon

Cairo's continued acceptance and did not in any way prejudice or limit Egypt's sovereign rights. But in return, the Egyptian Government were to undertake, in exercising their sovereign rights concerning the presence and function of UNEF, to be guided in good faith by their acceptance of the U.N. resolution which established the force.

Nasser would have greatly preferred UNEF to have pulled out, once the three invading armies withdrew from Egypt. For the idea of any foreign troops remaining indefinitely on Egyptian soil was repugnant to him, even if they were drawn from such non-aligned and friendly countries as India, Indonesia and Sweden. But when Hammarskold made it clear that to insist on such conditions would only exacerbate the situation and help to prolong the stay of the British army in Port Said, he did not press the point and accepted the suggested formula without further argument. Nor did he insist that UNEF should be stationed on the Israeli as well as the Egyptian side of the border after Ben Gurion had rejected the idea out of hand as an infringement of Israel's sovereignty.

What is more, after Mrs Golda Meir had finally told the United Nations on March 1 that Israel would withdraw from Sinai and Gaza, Nasser agreed with Hammarskold that fedayeen infiltrations would in future be forbidden and that UNEF should be empowered to arrest any suspected infiltrators. Also, though the Israelis had refused to allow the border line to be clearly marked, on the grounds that the armistice which established it was 'vanished and dead', he further agreed that the Egyptian police and army would give UNEF all possible help in maintaining peace and quiet on Egypt's frontiers with Israel. As a result, once the fedayeen had been placed under restraint and the local Bedouin realised that border crossings would not be tolerated either by the U.N. force or by their own authorities, frontier incidents became almost a thing of the past between Egypt and Israel for all of the next ten years.

In fact, such was the soothing influence of Hammarskold that Nasser accepted virtually everything he proposed in respect of UNEF's functions and presence on Egyptian soil, even though Israel declined to be in any way similarly committed. Most notable of all he agreed that, when the Israelis pulled out, United Nations troops would take over at Sharm es-Sheikh instead of Egyptian forces.

Nobody knew better than Nasser that this meant the end of Egypt's blockade of Elath which a glance at the map would show was in practice a far more valuable gain for Ben Gurion than any concession regarding the use of the Suez Canal, however important that might be for Israel's prestige. And because he realised the importance of this Israeli acquisition, and remembered the Moslem Brotherhood's attacks on the 1954 treaty with Britain, he felt it necessary to protect himself against any possible criticism that he had conceded too much to secure Israel's total withdrawal. On his instructions, therefore, Fawzi told Cabot Lodge, before the final U.N. vote demanding Israel's withdrawal, that Washington should understand that Egypt was not giving up any of her rights in the Gulf of Akaba as the price of American help in getting the Israelis out of Sharm es-Sheikh. For these reasons, Cairo could give no undertaking that Israeli ships would be allowed to sail to and from Elath indefinitely as a condition of Israel's withdrawal from Sinai.

Yet for all these explicit reservations, Nasser equally knew that, to get the Israelis out, Dulles had been obliged to concede the substitution of UNEF for Egyptian forces at Sharm es-Sheikh and hence the de facto lifting of the Egyptian blockade. He therefore told his Cabinet colleagues that it would be impolitic to challenge this American decision for fear of so exasperating Dulles that he might abandon his pressure on Ben Gurion and allow Israel to keep her own troops at this strategically vital location.

Nor was Nasser being over-cautious in this assessment. For in the previous month Dulles had informed Tel Aviv in a confidential memorandum that the United States believed that no nation had the right to blockade the Gulf of Akaba and that they were 'prepared to exercise the right of free and innocent passage (through the Gulf) and to join with others to secure general recognition of this right'. To this the Israelis had replied that they would agree to evacuate Sharm es-Sheikh only if the UNEF replacements remained there until a peace treaty was signed with

Egypt, or some other permanent agreement was reached which would safeguard freedom of navigation through the Gulf of Akaba. And although Nasser was not informed of the precise terms of Tel Aviv's reply, he knew that to insist on Egypt resuming control of Sharm es-Sheikh would only prolong Israel's occupation.

Thus, just as the Negev and Gaza borders were to enjoy a period of relative peace and quiet over the next ten years, so too in the Gulf of Akaba a regular traffic in oil and other cargoes necessary for Israel's economy now began and continued to Elath until that fateful day in 1967 when Nasser, by the most costly miscalculation of his career, was led into reoccupying Sharm es-Sheikh with Egyptian forces. And with one exception, the Egyptians were steadfastly to observe all the arrangements and conditions which governed the Israelis' withdrawal.

The exception was the Gaza Strip, where the departure of the Israeli occupation forces on March 6 and the arrival of UNEF led to vehement demands by the local Palestinian population for the return of an Egyptian administration. So much so that both Cairo and UNTSO headquarters agreed that, if the popular clamour were not appeased, there would be nothing but riots in the area and UNEF's position would become intolerable, if not untenable. However, for Cairo to send even a purely civilian administration back to the Gaza Strip was not without its risks. In her speech to the United Nations on March 1, Mrs Meir had made it a condition of Israel's withdrawal that not only the military occupation but also the civil government of Gaza should in future be conducted by the United Nations. She had also given notice that, if this condition were not fulfilled, the Israelis would reserve the right to take whatever action they thought fit.

Nevertheless Nasser decided that the risk of Israeli retaliation had to be accepted. He had already given way over Sharm es-Sheikh and over much else concerning UNEF's presence and powers. He had also allowed the clearing of the Canal to begin, even though Egyptian territory was not itself cleared of foreign invaders for some two months thereafter. And he could not, on top of these concessions, ignore the daily demonstrations of the

Gaza populace in favour of a return to Egyptian rule. Five days after the Israelis departed, he therefore appointed and despatched from Cairo a civil governor for the Gaza Strip together with the necessary staff. But to lessen the chances of Israeli counteraction, no Egyptian combat forces went with the administrators and, until the eve of the 1967 war, the only military presence in the area consisted of the blue-bonneted soldiers serving under General Rikhye, the Indian commander of UNEF, plus a few hundred Egyptian troops engaged in police duties. Tel Aviv protested loudly but no more. The world had tired of the Suez crisis and Israel could drum up little support outside Britain and France. For though she claimed that Egypt's action constituted a breach of faith, in fact it was merely in defiance of a reservation made unilaterally by the Israelis and never accepted by the U.N. or anyone else as a valid condition of their surrendering or abandoning their conquests.

But if Nasser was to feel some degree of satisfaction at having successfully called the Israelis' bluff over Gaza, it was small compared with the triumph which he was able to claim when, on March 29, the Suez Canal was reopened and the first convoy of ships sailed from Suez to Port Said. Britain and France, in a desperate last-minute attempt to save face and salvage something from the ruin of Eden's and Mollet's policies, tried to persuade the United Nations to impose conditions on the future functioning of the Canal. In particular, they sought to have their original six principles spelled out in the terms of the internationalisation proposals which Menzies had vainly tried to get Nasser to accept. But with Hammarskold and an overwhelming majority of the U.N. solidly against them, the most that London and Paris could achieve was an undertaking by Egypt not to discriminate against British or French shipping. And although both Governments tried to boycott the Canal after it was reopened to traffic, they were obliged by their ship-owners to abandon this fatuous gesture in a matter of a few weeks.

For the rest, Egypt pledged in an announcement made on April 14 that the Canal would be run for the benefit of the users and in accordance with all the requirements of the Constantinople Convention. The users were assured that 25 per cent of all gross receipts would be set aside for maintenance and development and that tolls would not be increased by more than one per cent in any year. Cairo further agreed to accept the decision of the International Court of Justice in any dispute regarding the Convention and, by the same token, invited Israel to submit to the Court her case regarding the use of the Canal. Meanwhile, the ban on Israeli ships transiting the waterway was to be maintained in accordance with Egypt's rights under Article X of the Convention, although cargoes of non-strategic goods were in fact allowed to pass to and from Israel until early in 1959, when they were stopped on the grounds that Tel-Aviv was using the Canal to develop trade with Africa and Asia to the detriment of the Arab states. Egypt also undertook to begin negotiations for the compensation due to the Canal Company, which resulted in an agreement in the following year. Finally, she agreed to settle the claims of those British and French residents whose property had been sequestrated or, in the case of former Government employees such as teachers, whose pensions had been stopped when, with the Anglo-French invasions, they had become enemy aliens and had either been deported or left of their own free will.

On balance Egypt, and Nasser personally, gained substantially more than they lost by the Suez war of 1956. Egypt was confirmed in her control and management of the Suez Canal. And contrary to all the forebodings of the British and French press, traffic through the waterway was not only maintained but increased in each successive year, with no discrimination shown by the Egyptian authority towards any of the users regardless of the state of relations between their Governments and Cairo. Thanks to the moral support of the overwhelming majority of the United Nations, Nasser had thwarted all the designs of Eden and Mollet to overthrow him and make him 'disgorge' the fruits of nationalising the Canal Company. And though Israel too had gained a vital interest by ending the blockade of the Gulf of Akaba, along with her allies in aggression, she had been forced to withdraw from every inch of Egyptian territory which her armies had overrun.

Against this list of credits had to be set the loss of Egyptian life amounting to a thousand soldiers killed, not to mention the many hundreds of civilians who died in the fighting in Port Said. In addition, some six thousand Egyptians and Palestinians, most of whom had been cut off in the Gaza Strip, had been captured by the Israelis, although these were all speedily repatriated following the cease-fire. By comparison, the invading armies suffered very slightly, Israel losing 171 killed and the Anglo-French forces only 26.

Added to this debit in human tragedy, General Amer had been tried and found wanting as Egypt's Commander-in-Chief. To do him justice, he offered to resign after his collapse. But Nasser declined to part with his friend, much to Boghdady's dismay, and decided instead to make an example of Sidky Mahmoud, the Commander of the Egyptian air force, who had taken altogether inadequate precautions to protect his aircraft from being destroyed on the ground by British bombing attacks. However, when Amer pleaded for his subordinate, Nasser relented and agreed to give Sidky Mahmoud a second chance.

But most important of all the results of the war was the effect which Nasser's success in turning defeat into victory was to have on his relations and prestige in the Arab world. Admittedly, as the Suez crisis had developed, some Arab rulers had begun to have second thoughts about Nasser's precipitate action in nationalising the Canal Company without consulting his Arab League confederates. King Saud, for instance, was no longer so keen on being allied to such an impetuous associate. And from now on he began to swallow some of his traditional antipathy for the Hashemites and to reinsure with closer ties with his fellow Kings in Jordan and Iraq. Also Nuri contended – and managed to persuade a number of Western observers, including myself – that, having in the previous autumn withstood the storm of popular Iraqi agitation against him as the friend of the Suez aggressors, he had nothing to fear from Nasser's enhanced prestige.

Yet under the surface in Iraq, no less than in the clamorous demonstrations in every other independent Arab country, Nasser was now acclaimed and idolised as some latter-day Saladdin. The martyr to Western vengeance had become the hero and the architect of Western humiliation and defeat, whose very name struck a magic chord in the heart of every Arab nationalist and whose photograph was to be found in souks, cafés, taxis and shops from the Atlantic to the Indian Ocean. More than ever before, Cairo was now the centre of the Arab world, the fountain-head of the new nationalism which was sweeping through the Middle East and along the North African shore, to which the leaders of all 'progressive' thought in the Arab world would flock to imbibe of its wisdom and inspiration. As for the Egyptians themselves, all their initial reservations about this austere young Colonel had now vanished and, traditionally accustomed as they were to deify their rulers, from now on they looked upon the 'rais' no longer as the mere leader of a military junta but as a god and saviour of his people. Songs were composed to give praise to the new deity and throughout the land of the Pharaohs Nasser's subjects gave thanks to divine providence for having sent him to deliver them from the hands of their enemies.

Nor was this meteoric rise in Nasser's reputation unmerited. For whatever Egypt's failures on the field of battle, throughout the crisis, his political footwork had been virtually faultless. From the moment when he declared the nationalisation of the Canal Company, he contrived never to give the slightest pretext for armed intervention by any of the user nations. While he rejected Menzies' proposals for international control of the Canal, he was consistently prepared to try other methods of reaching an agreed settlement. Then, in October, when his fellow Arabs and other friends, such as Tito and Nehru, had advised him to make yet another effort to resolve the issue, he agreed to a basis of negotiation which even the Foreign Ministers of Britain and France were unable to reject as offering no solution. Hence, when the tripartite invasion descended upon him, he was in the strongest possible position to call on world opinion to come to his rescue. Yet even with all this in his favour, including the moral support of the world's two super-powers, America and Russia, he knew and accepted his weaknesses. Thus, when the occasion demanded, he was as ready to make concessions to Hammarskold and to the

United States as he was to exploit his strength, whenever he could be certain that his case was unanswerable. In short, Nasser's performance had been that of a veteran in the art of diplomatic dealing, a *tour de force* as adept in its execution as his handling of the later crisis of 1967 was to be maladroit.

Chapter 11

Union with Syria

It would have required a man of almost superhuman qualities not to be carried away by the idolatry with which Nasser was now hailed by the Arab masses. And for all the skill and judgement which he had shown in steering the Egyptian ship of state between the treacherous reefs and shoals of the Suez crisis, the rais was no superman. Immediately the fighting was over and his attackers had withdrawn, he went to work to exploit his new popular status in the Arab world, and especially in those countries whose foreign policies he wished to control.

First on his list was Jordan, where a nationalist majority had been in power since the previous October under the serpentine Suleiman Nabulsi, whom Nasser neither liked nor trusted, but whom he relied on, for the time being at least, to toe the Cairo line in international, and especially inter-Arab, affairs. In January 1957 Nasser's efforts in Jordan were rewarded when Nabulsi accepted the offers of aid from Egypt, Syria and Saudi Arabia in place of the annual British subsidy for the Jordanian army. Better still, in March, he declared an end to the 1948 treaty with Britain and requested the British garrisons to leave Jordanian territory within six months. To Nasser this declaration meant that Jordan, without Glubb or the British treaty to inhibit her actions, was now a completely independent state. Accordingly, as the ally of Egypt and Syria, she could be expected to play a full part in strengthening the united front of Arab nations.

But as it happened, King Hussein had very different ideas. He might have deemed it politic, following the nationalist victory in the 1956 elections, to sign up with Egypt and Syria and to renounce his treaty with Britain. Also, at the time of the Suez war, he could hardly have failed to offer his help to Egypt. But as he had told the British Ambassador after he dismissed General Glubb, ie did not want to be left a prey to the Egyptians, still less the Russians, and he therefore hoped that Jordan would be allowed to stick to her old friends'. Moreover he was still tied by blood relationship to Iraq where his cousin King Feisal sat on the throne and he had only joined the Egyptian–Syrian alliance after he had failed to reach agreement with the Iraqis on the unification of the Hashemite armies. Nor had he forgotten that Nasser had refused to send his troops back to Sinai to divert the Israeli threat to his kingdom when, in the previous September and October, Ben Gurion's forces were raiding at will along the Jordanian border. And he now feared that cooperation with Egypt, as Nasser envisaged it, would be very much a one-way traffic. Having broken his treaty ties with Britain, he had no desire to become subservient to Cairo. He also profoundly distrusted the Syrians, whose leaders he regarded as predominantly Communist in outlook, and whose continued retention of 5,000 troops in the Mafraq area of northern Jordan since the Suez crisis filled him with a disquiet which was in no way relieved by Syrian protestations that they were only there to defend their Jordanian allies.

Moreover, Hussein had recently found a new friend and patron in King Saud who had begun to share his anxieties about being allied to Nasser and who had offered to send troops to counter the Syrian threat to Jordan. Saud was still a powerful influence in Arab councils as the guardian of the holy places of Islam, as well as being one of the richest of Arab rulers. And as Hussein rightly guessed, his was the only one of the three countries offering to replace the British subsidy which was in fact able and willing to pay up. Besides, while Nasser might be worshipped by the Arab masses, apart from Syria, the rulers of virtually all the Arab states were still basically pro-West and anti-Russian in outlook and did not share Cairo's belief in 'positive neutralism', whatever their peoples might think. Not only Nuri in Iraq, but also Lebanon's President Chamoun, Libya's King Idris, Tunisia's Habib Bourguiba and the Sultan of Morocco, plus of course King Saud and the rulers of the Persian Gulf states, were all agreed with Hussein in opposing any idea of having their foreign relations arranged for them by Cairo. In varying degrees they might understand the

reasons for Egypt's current disenchantment with the West an
they certainly joined in acclaiming the defeat of the Suez aggres
sion, if only not to appear to be siding with the imperialist o
Zionist enemy. But the very power of Nasser's personal charism
with the mass of their populations made them that much mor
wary of him, and that much less inclined to let him control thei
policies.

Certain of support from his two richest and most powerfu
neighbours, Hussein therefore decided to thumb his nose at Cair
once the Middle East had reverted to its normal state of uneas
truce. In April 1957, he ordered Nabulsi to resign the premiershi
and, although he allowed him to remain for the time being a
Foreign Minister, he appointed a new Government designed t
carry out his wishes. Then, a few days later, he got rid of Genera
Ali Abu Nuwar, his pro-Egyptian Chief of Staff who had playe
a leading part in the earlier intrigues against Glubb. The officia
story was that Abu Nuwar had been caught plotting with th
Syrian intelligence service against his King. Hussein, it was said
had promptly confronted him with evidence of his treachery befor
his fellow officers at Zerqa, the Jordanian army's headquarters
Abu Nuwar had admitted his guilt and begged for forgiveness
But, although the King had pardoned him, he had immediatel
fled to Damascus.

How much of this story is true will probably never be known
There are those in Jordan who swear that Abu Nuwar wa
framed to give Hussein a pretext for breaking his alliance with
Egypt and Syria. Certainly his successor as Chief of Staff, Genera
Ali Hayari, supported this theory, when he himself resigned afte
only a week in office, because he disagreed with the King'
demands that Bedouin officers should be promoted at the expens
of their more intelligent Palestinian comrades. Speaking from
Damascus, where he too went into exile, Hayari later said that, i
there had been any plot, it was on the part of the palace which ha
wanted an excuse for its political change of course. More signifi
cantly still, after a lapse of ten years or so, Abu Nuwar was no
only allowed to return to Jordan, but was appointed Hussein'
ambassador to Paris.

Yet, as was to happen all too frequently in those Arab countries where Nasser's influence and prestige among the masses brought him into conflict with their rulers, the pro-Egyptian elements in Jordan were, to say the least, tactless and overbearing in their attitude towards Hussein. Nabulsi had, for instance, tried to rush him into establishing diplomatic relations with Russia during his premiership. He had publicly vowed that Jordan would accept Russian aid if it was offered, but would spurn American support because Washington was only trying to make trouble between Amman and Cairo in a continuing attempt to isolate Nasser in the Arab world. Then, when he and Abu Nuwar were summarily sacked, their supporters organised violent demonstrations in Amman, Jerusalem and other Jordanian towns demanding their reinstatement and accusing the King of giving way to American plots to bring about their dismissal.

Taken together with the riots which had occurred when General Templer was trying to push Jordan into joining the Baghdad Pact, there was enough smoke behind all this outcry for Hussein to believe that the fire which smouldered beneath it had been lit by Nasser, despite Cairo's repeated denials of any intention to threaten Jordan's independence. And as soon as he said so, in a speech claiming that his enemies in Egypt and Syria were seeking to overthrow the Hashemite monarchy, Cairo Radio, supported by Damascus, played up to the accusation with a stream of vituperation against 'the lackeys of imperialism' in Amman, and Hussein in particular.

More agitation followed as the Nasserists in Jordan responded to Cairo's sallies. Hussein thereupon declared martial law and, after a hurried consultation with King Saud in Riyadh, he moved swiftly to snuff out the centres of potential rebellion. Nabulsi was placed under arrest, along with several other suspects, and it was announced that Abu Nuwar and Hayari were to be tried in their absence for treason. Details of a plot said to have been concocted by Egypt, Syria and Russia to overthrow the monarchies of Jordan, Iraq and Saudi Arabia were published; and the Egyptian Military Attaché in Amman was expelled, along with the Consul-General in Jerusalem, for 'incitement to assassination'. The Egyptians indignantly denied the charges and, in turn, ordered the expulsion of the Jordanian Ambassador from Cairo and recalled their own Ambassador from Amman.

For all of the next five months this war of words went on with neither side giving an inch. Hussein even went so far as to accuse Nasser of having completely sold himself to Communism, although, as Cairo was quick to point out, the Egyptian Communist party had been declared illegal and, only a few weeks before Hussein's statement, eighteen Egyptian leftists had been sentenced to long terms of imprisonment for organising underground activities. Saudi Arabia, Hussein added, had fulfilled her promises of financial help to Jordan. But not so Nasser or the Syrians, whose pretensions to serve Arab nationalism were a mere device to divert public opinion from the worsening economic and political situation in their countries.

To all this the Egyptian press and radio gave measure for measure, accusing Hussein at times of the cardinal crime of betraying the Palestinian Arabs by secretly negotiating a separate peace with Israel. But then, in November 1957, as suddenly as it had started, the spate of abuse from Cairo came to a stop. Nasser had decided to call a halt on the strength of intelligence reports from Jordan warning that, if the campaign against Hussein were pursued much longer, it would probably get out of control. In accordance with his standing orders that incitement of opposition in Jordan was not to be pushed to the point of overthrowing the King, Nasser's propagandists were therefore ordered to desist before it might be too late to avoid enraged mobs of Palestinian refugees from the camps around Amman marching on the palace.

In fact, not for the first or last time, the Egyptian intelligence had got it wrong. For at this moment Hussein was gaining the upper hand over the nationalists in Jordan and, guarded by his Bedouin troops, was actually less threatened by revolution than he had been earlier in the year. But Nasser acted on the information given to him, realising that his radio campaign had anyhow failed in its main purpose of forcing the King to align his policy with that of Cairo. By a coincidence, King Saud and Iraq's King Feisal had only three days earlier called on Cairo and Damascus to stop attacking Hussein. But although the decision to halt the radio war was bound to suggest that Egypt had succumbed to pressures from these reactionary quarters, Nasser held to his view that a revolution in Jordan, with all its unforseeable consequences, was not in Egypt's, or in the Arab world's interest.

Besides, Cairo had other problems at this juncture, notably in Syria, which was currently undergoing a combination of external threats and internal dissension which Egypt could not afford to ignore. In the summer of 1957, yet another plot, organised by the American Central Intelligence Agency and designed to restore to power a pro-Western Government in Syria, had been uncovered when an official of the American embassy in Damascus had been caught at the border, trying to smuggle a Syrian emigré into the country from Beirut in the boot of his car. Compared with the Anglo-American conspiracy with Nuri which had come to light during the Suez crisis and which contemplated a full-scale Iraqi invasion of Syria, this latest machination of the CIA was little more dangerous than a schoolboy prank. But it showed that the West had not given up trying to impose governments subservient to their interests and requirements on the Arab world; and, as such, it was a warning which Damascus, with full support from Cairo, took seriously enough to lodge a complaint in the strongest terms in the U.N. Security Council.

Added to this, early in 1957, the President of the United States had embarked, with the approval of the Congress, on a policy for the Middle East which came to be called the Eisenhower Doctrine and which appeared to Nasser and his Syrian allies to be a clear attempt by the Americans to move into the positions of influence in the Arab world which Britain and France had forfeited at Suez. The proclaimed purpose of Eisenhower's policy was to save the Middle East from Communism; and in accordance with this aim, American aid, including arms, was to be offered to any nation which required help in defending itself against Russian pressures or Communist subversion and which was prepared to renounce all offers of assistance from the Soviet bloc.

No doubt the distinguished author of this plan, together with Congressman James Richards who was chosen to hawk it around the Arab capitals, sincerely believed that this was what the Arab world needed and wanted from the United States. But, to Nasser's conspiratorial mind, the Eisenhower Doctrine was just another gambit in the Western game of trying to draw the Arabs back into a state of dependence on the patronage of the imperialists. The efforts by Britain to recruit Arab members for the Baghdad Pact had been a classic example of this kind of policy. It had failed because its underlying purpose had been exposed by Egyptian propaganda and because Britain had become discredited in Arab eyes. So now the Americans were taking over with the same aim in mind. The only difference between the two Western initiatives, apart from authorship, lay in the fact that Washington decided to approach Nasser indirectly by asking King Saud to commend their plan to him. Which only served to irritate him the more, suggesting as it did that, instead of trying to isolate him as Britain had done, the Americans were seeking to put pressure on him to join them by marshalling his fellow Arabs behind his back.

But while this somewhat silly manoeuvre might have annoyed him, Nasser showed relatively little concern about the Eisenhower Doctrine's prospects of success. In his view, if the Arab states had not joined the Baghdad Pact when he had no effective alternative to offer them, they would be unlikely to defy him by subscribing to a similar American plan, now that his Suez triumph had placed him on so high a pedestal. Admittedly the majority of his fellow rulers were resolutely opposed to Communism. But they equally knew that the 'Voice of the Arabs' could make a lot of danger-ous trouble for them by stirring up the Arab masses at the slightest suggestion that they were selling out to the imperialist powers.

Nevertheless, in August 1957, a crisis was to arise which for a brief moment threatened to upset Nasser's calculations. Claiming that they were being menaced by a hostile Syria egged on by Russia, the Turks began massing troops on their southern borders. Simultaneously Iraq and Lebanon made similar accusations against the Damascus regime. And with the Americans declaring that the Syrians were little more than tools in the hands of the Russians, nd the Russians accusing Turkey of preparing the way for an American intervention in Syria, the situation became uglier by he minute. Washington despatched a senior Middle East expert o Ankara and Beirut for urgent consultations with Menderes nd Chamoun and also with the Kings of Iraq and Jordan. Whereupon Moscow and Damascus let fly with renewed accusa- ions that the Western powers were plotting to subvert demo- ratic government in Syria and to install a puppet regime. Eisenhower responded with a warning that he would use what- ver powers were necessary to protect pro-Western governments n the Middle East. More ominous still from Nasser's point of iew, following the consultations of Washington's emissary with Chamoun, Feisal and Hussein, the Americans announced plans for n immediate air-lift of arms to the area to support not only Turkey, but Jordan, Lebanon and Iraq as well.

For a moment it seemed that the Eisenhower Doctrine might be successfully imposed after all. But then King Saud decided that t was time for him to put himself on-side again with the apostles of the new Arab nationalism, his erstwhile Egyptian and Syrian allies. To reinsure with his fellow Kings in Jordan and Iraq was one thing, and a necessary precaution against becoming too nvolved with the political force of Nasserism which might all too easily sweep away every monarchy in the Arab world. But, unlike Hussein and Nuri who had their own quarrels with, or designs on, Syria and therefore openly supported Washington's tand, Saud had no desire, for all his attachment to American oil nterests, to be accused of encouraging the United States in what eemed to be a Western war of nerves against an Arab state. He therefore quickly assured both Cairo and Damascus that he would support Syria against any aggression. Also, after his brother, Crown Prince Feisal, had asserted in Washington that the Syrians posed no threat to any of their neighbours, he went in person to Beirut and Damascus to patch things up between Chamoun and his Syrian neighbours, and to proclaim to the Syrian people on the spot his condemnation of Turkey's threats against their country.

This gesture received a warm welcome from the anxious

Syrians who, in the previous weeks, had felt themselves hemme
in on almost every side by hostile armies waiting to pounce an
tear their country apart. But it was by no means so cordiall
acclaimed in Cairo, where it was felt, not without some justifica
tion, that Saud's purpose was not so much to support the Syrian
as to wrest the initiative in the Arab world from Egypt. Withi
less than three weeks of Saud's visit to Damascus, Egyptian troop
were therefore despatched to the Syrian port of Latakia in toke
of Egypt's determination to support her ally against the menace
of the Turks and their American backers. And when Damascu
awoke to the realisation of what Nasser had done, the memory o
Saud's mere verbal guarantees was lost amid the cheers which
greeted this signal act of friendship. Nasser's gesture had foiled th
Saudis' attempt to oust Egypt's influence in Damascus. Mor
important still, when the Turks shortly afterwards withdrev
their troop concentrations from Syria's frontier, it put paid to an
remaining hopes for the acceptability of the Eisenhower Doctrine
Token though it might be, it served well enough to show that
contrary to what Washington would have the Arabs believe
when their security was threatened, they could count on Egypt
and Russia, to support them.

Moreover, for many Syrians there was more than just a sens
of relief at the arrival of these Egyptian reinforcements which, i
any case, would have hardly been sufficient in numbers or i
fighting efficiency to withstand a Turkish invasion. For wha
mattered was what they represented, far more than what the
might or might not do in the firing line. And what they repre
sented was what an increasing number of Syrian army officers an
politicians had come to regard as their country's best, if not only
salvation – union with Nasser's Egypt.

Ever since the alliance was signed between Syria and Egypt i
1955, Syrians of this school of thought had been hoping for som
closer link with Nasser as the new champion of Arab aspiration
to unity and independence. Indeed, following the signature of th
1955 treaty, Khaled el-Azm, a prominent Syrian leftist who
had been Syria's Premier in the late forties and became Foreig
Minister after the fall of the pro-Iraqi Fares el-Khoury, went t

Cairo to urge upon Nasser the need for union between their two countries.

But the response had been very hesitant and the Egyptians had not been at all willing to commit themselves to anything more adventurous than increased economic cooperation. A descendant of the Azm dynasty which had helped the Turks to govern Syria over many long unhappy years, Khaled el-Azm was not exactly the best choice for this mission. Nasser took an immediate dislike to him, saying that he was a fake socialist who was at heart the feudal lord that his appearance, together with his prodigious wealth, suggested. Nor did Nasser's puritanical nature take very kindly to the rumours which were then current that he allowed his home to be used as a gaming-house for his rich friends. Moreover, reports from Mahmoud Riad, Egypt's extremely well-informed ambassador in Damascus, had it that Azm, along with a number of the old-guard politicians in Syria, was only proposing union with Egypt in the hope that Nasser would refuse and so enable them to blame him for whatever later went wrong in their own country. Despite the fact that he had been a leading architect of the alliance with Egypt, he was therefore the last Syrian leader with whom Nasser would have been able to deal with any feeling of confidence and trust.

Nevertheless, there were many in Syria who, unlike Azm and his associates, genuinely felt the need of Nasser's strength and vision to guide them. And by 1957 they had vastly increased not only in numbers, but also in their insistence that only complete union with Egypt could save their country from disintegrating as a political entity. Despite, or perhaps because of, their relatively sophisticated political system, originating from that mid-nineteenth century period when Syria gave birth to the first Arab reawakening, the Syrians had known little stability in the years since they obtained their independence from French rule at the end of World War II. In less than three years, between March 1949 and December 1951, the country had undergone a truly bewildering series of coups d'état with a change of Government at intervals of every two to three months.

Situated as she was at the cross-roads of northern Arabia, Syria had become a prey to the intrigues of her neighbours. Iraq wanted to annex her to form part of Nuri's Fertile Crescent scheme or, as some said, to provide a throne for the Iraqi Crown Prince Abdulillah who, as the uncle of the young King Feisal, was unlikely to become King of his own country. Jordan supported Iraq, King Hussein not having forgotten that his grandfather, King Abdullah, had once planned to seize Syria from the French and had only been prevented from making the attempt by Britain's timely offer to recognise him as Emir of Transjordan when he was actually on the march to Damascus. The Turks hovered ominously in the north; and even the peaceable Lebanese were not above picking a quarrel with or countenancing an intrigue against their Syrian neighbours, especially when they felt that they could count on American support. On the other hand, the Saudis, animated by their traditional antipathy towards the Hashemites, had strained every nerve, and not a few of their purse-strings, to prevent a union between Syria and Iraq. So too had Egypt both before and after the revolution.

Not surprisingly the Syrian party political system mirrored these inter-Arab rivalries. Ever since the formation of the Arab League at Alexandria in 1945, where Syria's delegation had insisted that the constitution should provide for closer ties between individual member states, the idea of Syria uniting with one or other of her neighbours had had its advocates among her own politicians. The People's Party, composed largely of place-seekers who cared little for national independence so long as they received the fruits of office, favoured the strongest ties with Iraq, if not formal political union. The other principal party, the National Bloc, were opposed to such links which they feared would mean domination by Nuri and hence subservience to Britain. Among Syria's neighbours they favoured Saudi Arabia with whose founder-King, Abdel Aziz Ibn Saud, and his sons, Saud and Feisal, the party's venerable leader, Shukri Quwaitly, had enjoyed close relations over many years. Quwaitly's family had originally served as the Saudi rulers' commercial agents in Damascus and after he became Syria's first President in 1945, Quwaitly had helped to strengthen the Saudi Government service by recruiting lever young Syrians, such as Yusuf Yasin, who became King Saud's adviser on foreign affairs and a bitterly anti-Iraqi influence in Riyadh.

But both these main parties consisted largely of older men with old ideas about Arab nationalism. Quwaitly, the best known amongst them, for instance, had been the leader of the independence movement against the Ottoman Empire before and during World War I and, although his terrible sufferings at the hands of successive Turkish Governors and their inquisitors had made him a national hero at the time, when Syria finally won her freedom after twenty-five years of French mandate, he and his ideas were inevitably somewhat outdated. As I found from my own talks with him shortly after the Suez war of 1956, his mind was largely directed to the past and he far preferred to tell of his dealings with T. E. Lawrence in 1918 to discussing the existing state of affairs in the country of which he was still the President.

Not unnaturally the younger Syrians of the 1940s wanted something more challenging in the way of political ideas than mere warring between factions which favoured union with Iraq or advocated total independence. They were interested in an independence which transcended the boundaries of Syria and which would embrace all of the Arab world. Several years before Egypt's Wafd Government adopted neutrality as their watchword, these young men believed that not only Syria but all the Arab states should seek unity in non-alignment, disclaiming all obligations to any outside power. Also they wanted to experiment with the new ideas, imported from Europe, of social justice and a sharing of wealth. To this end they wanted to see the Pashas and the feudal lords cut down to size, as some advanced Arab thinkers in Cairo were then advocating, much to the concern of Farouk and the landed aristocracy.

A few of these young Syrians had joined the relatively small, though vociferous, Syrian Communist party headed by a brilliant young Kurd and former law student, Khaled Bagdash, who in the early thirties had so exploited his dialectical skills, engaging manner and doctrinal rectitude as to become the local party's leader at the age of eighteen. But for the majority who thought Com-

munism too extreme, there was no political group which me
their aspirations until, after World War II, the Baath (Renaissance
party came to the fore. Founded by two Syrian teachers, Miche
Aflaq and Salah ed-Din Bitar, one a Christian and the other ;
Moslem, who had met as students in Paris in the early thirties and
had shared a youthful flirtation with Communism, the Baatl
embodied in its doctrine all the frustrated hopes and nationalis
ambitions of young Syria. As Patrick Seale succinctly put it in hi
well-informed *Struggle for Syria*, 'the Baath . . . provided the Arab
national movement with a dynamic, home-grown ideology and
with specific moral and political aspirations at a time when it wa
beguiled by other creeds'.

Most significant of all for Syria's immediate future was the
welcome which this new political venture was to receive from the
younger army officers. Unlike their elders who had been steeped
in French military traditions, these young Syrian soldiers, like
their civilian contemporaries, had been suckled on the heady wine
of nationalism, made more potent by the decline of French power
in the 1940s. Sick and tired of the old political parties, with
their incessant unconstructive bickering, and wanting no truck
with the Communists who had all too often in the past tamely
toed the line laid down by Moscow or their 'parent' body, the
French Communist party, they looked for a fresh ideology and
for an opportunity, if not to impose it on the country themselves
at least to throw the full weight of the army behind its enforce-
ment.

Meanwhile a young Syrian socialist, Akram Hourani, who wa
later to join Aflaq and Bitar, had already begun what was to prove
a most successful campaign to indoctrinate the officer corps with
ideas very much akin to those of the Baath. Although a politica
adventurer with no firm loyalties or principles save a fixed determination to be, if possible, always on the winning side, Houran
was an excellent advocate with the Syrian officer corps. He had
had close contacts with the army ever since 1941, when he
gathered a group of officers to join him in espousing the German-
backed coup of Rashid Ali against the British presence in Iraq.

But Hourani was not alone in seeing the importance of the army' support for any political change in Syria. As they were to show at the time of the revolution in Egypt, the Americans also thought that, through an enlightened and politically conscious officer corps, the Arab states might democratise themselves. Also, after the 1948 war in Palestine had ended, they entertained the even more starry-eyed hope that democratic Arab Governments would come round to the idea of making peace with Israel, which the old school of Arab rulers either would not or dared not do. And in March 1949, applying this belief to Syria, the CIA helped to promote a coup d'état against the Quwaitly regime which was supported by Hourani and led by a stocky army colonel with a florid face and boisterous manner called Husni Zaim.

The CIA could hardly have chosen a man less likely to succeed in his appointed task. For, if Quwaitly was by modern political measurements an antique, Zaim was by any standards a popinjay who, in his new-found seat of power, adorned himself with resplendent uniforms and a marshal's baton costing over a thousand pounds and indulged in such fanciful notions as being able to turn the Arabs' 1948 defeat into victory by personal negotiations with Ben Gurion. All too easily flattered into changing his mind by the attentions of his fellow-Arab rulers, he first toyed with the idea of union with Iraq, but then was so impressed by the reception he got from King Farouk that he became actively hostile to any link with Baghdad. And when the twists and turns of his political manoeuvrings had alienated all his earlier well-wishers and had become so confusing that not even the tortuous mind of Hourani could follow him, Zaim was overthrown by another coup, led by another colonel and with Hourani once again among its supporters. But Zaim's successor, urged on by the People's Party, immediately espoused the cause of union with Iraq. The Baath and their now numerous adherents in the army were therefore soon driven to oppose him. And in December 1949, yet a third colonel, Adib Shishakly, seized power with, needless to say, the enthusiastic backing of that most volatile of politicians, Akram Hourani.

Unlike Zaim, with his passion for the limelight, Shishakly, for the first two of the four years that he held sway, chose to remain

in the background and to exercise power from behind the scenes
But in due course he was drawn into the open by the persisten
opposition of the People's Party to his policy of rapprochemen
with the Saudis and with Syria's former rulers, the French. At th
end of 1951, he therefore dismissed the Cabinet and, when th
President resigned in protest, he and the army took over ful
responsibility for the government of the country. From thi
fourth coup since 1949 it was but a short step to the suppression o
all party political activity and the assumption by Shishakly of th
vacant presidency.

This move proved to be his undoing. For by now Syria hac
tired of military government and, when the votes were countec
for Shishakly's presidential candidature, it was found that onl
five per cent of the electorate had gone to the polls. Aflaq anc
Bitar, now joined by Hourani, began to organise popular resis
tance in association with the other parties, whose leaders for onc
were united in a common cause. And in February 1954, thei
efforts were rewarded with Shishakly's downfall and the restora
tion of the liberties which army rule had suppressed. Election
were held, from which the Baath emerged as the new politica
force in Syria's Parliament. The People's Party suffered the loss o
half their seats and, to complete the evidence of a strong leftwar
trend, Khaled Bagdash became the first Communist to be electec
to an Arab parliament.

Yet the new coalition which now took office brought no mor
stability than the succession of military juntas which had precedec
it. The unity of purpose which inspired the parties to overthrow
Shishakly soon gave way to the old tug-of-war between the pro
Iraqi and pro-Saudi factions, to which was now added th
Baathist element, for whom the revolution in Egypt and th
emergence of Nasser as a potential champion of Arab unity anc
independence was becoming an increasingly powerful magnet
The Gaza Raid early in 1955 and the simultaneous dispute betweer
Iraq and Egypt about the Baghdad Pact still further deepened thi
divide and with it the desire for a closer association with Egypt
Azm, as Foreign Minister, became the high priest of Syriar
neutralism and, with Hourani's support, the dominant figure ir

he Cabinet. And in 1956, as the Baathist influence grew ever more ncisive, the titular leader of the coalition, Sabri el-Assali, an opportunist politician of the centre, deemed it politic to declare hat his Government favoured some kind of federal union with Egypt.

Thus, although the aging Quwaitly had still been able to drum up enough votes from the older generation of Syrians to retain the presidency in the election of 1955, the leftward and pro-Egyptian trend in Syrian policy continued to gather momentum. After Nasser had defied the Western powers by his arms deal with Russia, the Syrians had immediately followed suit. Indeed, so determined did they seem to sever all connections with the West that in the autumn of 1956 the Americans, now thoroughly alarmed at the prospect of Syria 'going Communist', joined orces with Britain and Iraq in an attempt to overthrow the eftist leadership and restore a pro-Western Government in Damascus.

The discovery of this Western conspiracy, taken together with the shock realisation in the autumn of 1956 that Britain and France had colluded with Israel to destroy Nasser and seize the Suez Canal, served still further to strengthen and stimulate the eftist and neutralist elements in Syria. The Russians also profited greatly. Having succeeded the French as Syria's main source of arms supplies, they were not slow to exploit these Western follies for the advancement of their influence in Damascus. And if Bagdash's Communists were unable to make much further head-way with public opinion, it was largely because the Baath had managed to steal much of their thunder by forcing the coalition Cabinet to adopt socialist reforms at home and to maintain close ies with Russia abroad.

Yet the more Syria moved to the left, the more frantic became the opposition of the rightists and the pro-Iraqi factions. The People's Party had been thrown out of the Cabinet after the discovery of the 1956 conspiracy. But despite the pressures of the Baath, they were nevertheless influential enough to prevent Assali following up his declaration in favour of federal union with Egypt with any concrete measure. Indeed the mere fact that they had been included in the original coalition Cabinet proved that they still enjoyed considerable public support.

Hence, by the end of 1957, Syria was in danger of being torn apart at the seams, with the Left pulling for pan-Arabism and socialism, encouraged by Russia's material help and Egypt's political example; the Right still working for union with Iraq backed by the West and Nuri; and the Centre, supported by Saudi Arabia, seeking independence in isolation from all entanglements. Confusion reigned supreme with no political party or grouping able to command an absolute majority for its policies. Even among the Baath there was some uncertainty about the wisdom of pressing for an immediate union with Egypt. To do so, it was felt, might split the anti-imperialist camp by alienating the Saudis who feared that a merger of Syria and Egypt would cause so powerful an upsurge of Arab nationalism and socialism as to endanger their monarchy, and who were therefore working to defeat the growing leftist and Nasserist influence in Syria.

Faced with the threat of political chaos, a group of young Syrian officers decided early in 1958 to force the issue by putting to Nasser a request for an immediate union with Egypt. Twenty in number, they included the Chief of Staff, General Afif Bizri, a pronounced leftist if not Communist, and Abdel Hamid Sarraj, a sallow, taciturn young man with cold eyes and a humourless expression who, as head of intelligence and security, had gained prominence for having uncovered the Anglo-American conspiracy of 1956. Bizri's presence in such company seems somewhat mysterious in the light of his subsequent defection after the union of Egypt and Syria was formed. Those most qualified to know have told me that, like Azm and others, he only went along with the idea of proposing union in the hope, aroused by previous secret contacts with Nasser, that the answer would be another refusal. Be that as it may, there was certainly no doubt about the sincerity of the other officers, and more especially of Sarraj.

Ever since he first met Nasser in 1955, Sarraj had developed such an adoration for Egypt's rais that, whenever Nasser addressed him, he would blush to the roots of his hair. The Suez war had still further deepened this admiration and with it the conviction that Syria should merge with Egypt. But he had been greatly dismayed by the constant flow of reports from Syrian politicians who visited Cairo that their talk of union had been received with the utmost coldness. Sabri el-Assali had, for instance, been told that it would take five years to build such a structure on properly solid foundations and that it was no good trying to establish it on a basis of mere emotional attachment. Wisely, however, Sarraj had not tried to force his own views on Nasser, although he subsequently took time off to pay him at least one secret visit in the spring of 1957 on the pretext of keeping him informed about the security situation in Syria.

Nevertheless Sarraj's belief in union was well enough known in his own country to earn him the disfavour of the Right and Centre. President Quwaitly, now more than ever under the influence of the Saudis, tried to have him and his associates dismissed from the army as undesirable and unreliable elements in a situation already sufficiently charged with explosive material. His attempt was thwarted by the determined resistance of the officer corps. But towards the end of 1957, Quwaitly tried once more to neutralise the leftist elements in the army. Yusuf Yasin, King Saud's adviser, paid him a secret visit from Riyadh and together the two men concocted a proposal for a realignment of Syrian policy 'along pan-Islamic lines' which, in practical terms, meant an alliance with Saudi Arabia and no one else. Yasin told Quwaitly that, if the Syrian army would accept such an exclusive association and sever all connections with the Russians, he could guarantee that they would receive the fullest American support, including whatever arms they needed. Moreover, by way of confirming this guarantee, the American Military Attaché in Damascus simultaneously informed Sarraj that Washington had lost all faith in party political government in the Arab world. The Americans were therefore ready to back a regime of young army officers of good moral standing who, as he delicately phrased it, 'would not be prepared to go all the way with Nasser'.

At the best of times Sarraj, whose conspiratorial turn of mind yielded nothing to Nasser's, would have looked on such approaches from the Americans and Saudis with grave suspicion, the more so since Prince Feisal had only very recently visited Washington. But, coming as it did on top of the conspiracies of 1956 and 1957 which he had personally unearthed and in which the CIA had been deeply involved, Yasin's proposal to Quwaitly left Sarraj in no doubt that the Americans were making yet another effort to press Syria into their service and to force a breach in her friendship with Egypt and Russia. Moreover, if Washington had mobilised the Saudis with their seemingly unlimited resources for bribery in support of this new manoeuvre the outcome could be far more dangerous than anything which had previously been attempted.

Clearly immediate action was called for and, as Sarraj pondered how he should respond, the Baathist leader, Salah ed-Din Bitar approached him with the suggestion that he and his army associates should go at once to Cairo and ask Nasser to agree to a union of the two countries. Bitar had very recently had a most revealing conversation with the Egyptian Ambassador, Mahmoud Riad, whose contacts with the Baath were extremely close. Riad had said that Egypt thought the time was nothing like ripe for union, whereupon Bitar had asked, 'What are you afraid of?' 'The fact that Egypt and Syria do not speak the same language,' Riad replied. Bitar then asked, 'But you do agree to union in principle, do you not?' To which Riad answered that, whether or not Egypt accepted union in principle, Syria was in fact not stable enough at the moment to make it a practicable proposition. 'The army,' he said, 'are too much involved in politics, there have been too many coups already and, the situation being what it is there is a danger of yet more to come.'

Bitar's conclusion from this conversation was that only the army could persuade Nasser to agree to union. No Syrian politician, including himself, had been able to convince Egypt's President that the time was right as well as the idea. For, even though he then found the Baath closer to his thinking than any other group in Syria, Nasser had nursed a contempt and a distrust for all party politicians ever since he became disenchanted with the Wafd after the revolution. But if the Syrian army could convince

im that they wanted union and that they were not just a collec-
ion of conspirators whose hobby was staging coups d'état,
e might well be won over.

Bitar therefore told Sarraj to lose no time in going to Cairo to
ut his ideas forward. 'Nasser is uncertain about you and your
rmy friends,' he said, 'so go and arrange yourselves personally
vith him.' Sarraj promptly summoned a meeting of his asso-
iates, who agreed that a deputation should leave at once. A mani-
esto was drafted for presentation to Quwaitly and it was
lecided that, in the event of Nasser baulking, the deputation
hould refuse to return to Syria until he accepted their request,
ven if they should be jailed for their persistence.

Of Sarraj's nineteen associates only one ran out and fourteen of
he others, with Bizri at their head, flew to Cairo by military
ircraft direct from their meeting without so much as taking the
ime to pack a pair of pyjamas. Sarraj himself, by agreement with
is fellows, stayed behind, with the deputy Chief of Staff and
hree other officers, to deal with Quwaitly and to hold the fort in
Damascus. Quwaitly was told about the deputation on the follow-
ng morning and was informed that Syria's future now lay in
Nasser's hands. All he could do about it as President was to await
vents and 'catch up with them' when they occurred. Bizri and
is party meanwhile arrived in Cairo at 7 a.m., where they were
met by General Amer. They were then taken to Nasser's house
nd, after four hours of animated argument, obtained his consent
o a merger of Syria with Egypt.

Quwaitly was furious when Sarraj told him what had happened
nd showed him the officers' manifesto which, couched in the
language of an ultimatum, declared that Syria was on the verge of
disintegration, that the Government had failed to fulfil their
pledge to work for unity with Egypt and that Bizri and others
representing the army had therefore gone to Cairo to seek a solution. But, when later that same day the news came from Cairo that
Nasser had agreed to a union, he decided not to fight it any
further. Instead, after remarking to Mahmoud Riad that the army
had in fact carried out a coup against his authority, he shrugged
his shoulders and sent for his Ministers to discuss how, as the

legally constituted Government of Syria, they could best adap
themselves to this momentous turn of events.

But if Quwaitly had been taken aback by what had happened
Azm, Hourani and other Syrian politicians were still mor
concerned when they learned, on Bizri's return, that Nasser ha
insisted not only that the army should get out of politics, but als
that the political parties should agree to their own dissolutior
This was not at all what they had bargained for. True, the
had never spelled out their ideas for union to Nasser or anyon
else. But in their own minds they had always envisaged a kind o
federal system with each of the two constituent regions free t
pursue whatever form of political organisation was best suited t
it. Yet now they were being told to abandon altogether thei
party games which were for them the very breath of life.

Bitar suggested at the meeting with Quwaitly that a ministeria
delegation be sent to Cairo to argue the toss with Nasser. Azn
agreed but, not wishing for a repetition of his own unfriendl
reception in 1955, he suggested that they should send Bitar
with whose party Nasser had more sympathy than any other. But
he added, Bitar should be armed with the outline of a federa
system which he could demonstrate as being more democratic an
more practicable for Syria than the Egyptian–type autocracy o
which Nasser had apparently set his sights. This was agreed an
on January 25 Bitar set off for Cairo clutching the propose
federal constitution.

But his journey was in vain. Apart from the essential logic o
his proposals, which did not impress Nasser in the slightest degree
Bitar had nothing with which to argue his case. Egypt held all th
cards and the Syrians were the suppliants. Besides, his partner i
the Baath leadership, Michel Aflaq, had for some time favoure
a full merger with Egypt, as opposed to the federation which h
knew Azm wanted so as to be free to carry on whatever politica
intrigues might suit his book. And if dissolution of the parties ha
to be the price for a merger, Aflaq still preferred to pay it rathe
than allow the kind of machinations to continue which ha
brought Syria to the brink of disintegration. Thus, after Nasse
had said that he had only agreed to union because he was s

mpressed by the sincerity of Bizri's deputation, and so appalled
by their description of the chaos in Syria, Bitar quickly gave
way. All that he could get in the way of a concession was that
sometime in the future the Syrian parties might be allowed to join
in a single political organisation with Egypt's National Union. At
Bitar's suggestion, Nasser agreed that Quwaitly should nominate
him as sole candidate for the presidency of the union. It was also
agreed that a plebiscite should be held in both countries to
approve the merger three weeks after it had been formally proclaimed in Cairo by the two existing Presidents.

When these formalities had been completed, Bitar returned to
face his ministerial colleagues in Damascus. But, apart from Azm,
who at first refused to sign away his political freedom, the Syrian
Government and the party leaders accepted their defeat with
resignation. The important thing, they said, was the union
and if they could not make their own terms, so be it. Hourani, as
ever anxious to be on the winning side, raised no objections and
Assali went so far as to say that Syria had been saved by 'a
miracle'. As for the army, Bizri was perfectly happy, indeed even
eager, to accept Nasser's conditions. No doubt he reflected that
his Communist party friends had little to lose and much to gain
by the formal abolition of the political parties of which, with only
about 5,000 card-carrying members, they were one of the smallest
groups. Sarraj, for totally different reasons since he was anything
but a Communist, was even more delighted to know that a curb
was to be put on political intrigues, which could only help him
in the discharge of his duties as head of Syria's Deuxième Bureau.

Thus, when Azm eventually fell into line with his Cabinet
colleagues, every important element in the administration of
Syria had accepted Nasser's terms. And on February 1, 1958,
standing before a deliriously excited multitude and holding hands
on the balcony of the Abdin Palace, where in 1942 Farouk and
Lampson had acted out the drama which gave rise to Nasser's
Free Officers' movement, the two Presidents jointly proclaimed
the union of Egypt and Syria under the title of the United Arab
Republic.

Chapter 12

Crisis in Lebanon: Revolution in Iraq

Why did Nasser agree to the union with Syria, a country which he had never even seen? True, he had urged the Arab world often enough to unite and, by implication at least, to unite under Egypt's leadership. But all that he really wanted with Syria at this stage, as with every other Arab state, was to gain control of her foreign and defence policies, to prevent her joining Nuri's Iraq and to keep her from defecting into any form of foreign alliance whether with the West or with the Communist bloc. Yet instead of merely controlling her external policies, he had now accepted, even demanded, full administrative authority and had hence saddled himself with absolute responsibility for governing the ungovernable Syrians.

From the outset he knew that this venture would be fraught with every imaginable difficulty, not least that of the geographical separation of the two countries which, as he told Mahmoud Riad, meant that he could never know enough of what was going on in Syria. Quwaitly told him, when he visited Syria for the first time after they had jointly proclaimed the United Arab Republic, 'You have put yourself in a predicament in a country where everyone regards himself as God!' And as he himself confided to the American Ambassador, Raymond Hare, he felt certain that the union would prove to be 'a great headache'. What is more, all his colleagues from the former RCC were in varying degrees opposed to the merger, from Zacharia Mohieddin, who felt it would be an unnatural association built on sentiment and hampered by geography, to Salah Salem who violently disliked the whole concept. Both before and after Bizri's mission to Cairo, discussions about union occupied many hours, frequently lasting until late at night. Nasser had at first been firmly opposed to the dea which he considered to be altogether premature. But, while he gave nothing away to the constant flow of suppliants from Damascus, by the end of 1957 his opposition had begun to wilt under the mounting pressures from Syria. And before Bizri descended upon him, he had come round to the idea of a federation of the two countries. Such a system, he had felt, would meet Syria's need for protection and would vest in him all power of decision in external affairs, while at the same time allowing the Syrians the fullest autonomy in internal matters and absolving him from the responsibility of running their country for them.

On reflection, however, Nasser realised that under a federal system the politicians in the Syrian region would be left free to play their party games and to undermine the whole structure of the union whenever it suited their purpose. This, as he told Khaled Mohieddin, would give him responsibility without power; and, since he was not prepared to put himself in this invidious position, he decided to offer a full merger on condition that Syria's political parties were disbanded. The all-important thing was that union, once cemented, should be indissoluble. Better the two countries should remain separate than that the cause of ultimate Arab unity should be damaged, perhaps irretrievably, by a breach between Egypt and Syria, the two current leaders of modern and progressive pan-Arabism.

At a conference with Syria and Iraq in 1963, two years after the collapse of the UAR, Nasser was to admit that the decision to ban all political parties in Syria had been unwise. It would have been better, he said, only to have disbanded those who were opposed to union and to have merged those who favoured it in a national front. He even tried to put the blame for this mistake on Bizri and his officers, who, he claimed, had initiated the idea of disbanding the parties. He had wanted a federation, he said, with only defence, foreign and economic policy reserved to the Federal Government, and he had not insisted on a dissolution of the parties. But when the officers forced the issue, he had agreed, although he 'dreaded so to venture into the unknown'.

But whether, in these subsequent recollections of his encounter with Bizri, Nasser's memory was playing him false or whether he was merely trying to rewrite the record in his own favour, the fact remains that, when Bitar tried to argue with him for federation and the preservation of political freedom in Syria, he would have none of it and insisted that all political parties be abolished as an absolute prerequisite of union. For, at the time, he was so suspicious of Syria's politicians and so convinced that, with the exception of one group, they were only preaching union to further their own individual or party aims, that he genuinely believed they were not to be trusted to work any arrangement which allowed them to retain full freedom of action.

The one exception was the Baath who had established personal contacts with Nasser in 1955, when Bitar brought a delegation to Cairo to discuss the situation arising from Egypt's first arms deal with Russia. Bitar had been greatly encouraged by the RCC's announcement in the previous year that Egypt would work for the establishment of an Arab bloc, free from imperialist influence in order to protect and promote the interests of the world of Islam and the peoples of Asia and Africa. This was a highly significant advance on the original charter of the revolution with its concentration on Egyptian requirements and its apparent disregard of the Arab world outside. Correctly assuming that this development reflected the imposition of Nasser's views upon his more inward-looking colleagues, Bitar therefore used every opportunity not only to push the idea of union with Syria, but also to encourage Nasser's growing pan-Arab inclinations.

These efforts met with more success than Nasser allowed Bitar to realise. For while he was not prepared to admit to anyone that there was such a thing as a political party which was not either corrupted or corruptible, there is no doubt that, at this early stage before the merger was made, Nasser was impressed by the patent sincerity of the Baathist leader. He might be irritated by the way in which Bitar tended to treat him as the backward pupil in need of coaching from the Baathist professor, especially in the ways of democracy. But he conceded willingly enough that, unlike Azm, Hourani, Assali and other Syrian visitors who were clearly out for their exclusive ends, Bitar genuinely believed in a union of Egypt and Syria as the first step to a wider unity embracing the whole Arab world. Hence Riad, as Egyptian Ambassador in Damascus, was instructed to maintain specially close ties with the Baathist leaders.

Moreover, Nasser found much to agree with in the underlying concept of the Baath's philosophy. He too believed that the Arabs were, as Bitar put it, 'living through a crisis brought about by a . . . refusal to continue under a system of out-of-date ideas and traditions because they desire modernisation . . . and a refusal to cut themselves away from the past . . . because it was their pride, their honour and even their refuge during the years of misfortune'. Had not the Egyptian revolution come about, like the creation of the Baath, to find a way forward for the Arabs 'between a past from which they cannot free themselves, because it is what they cling to as their own property, and a present for which they envy others without being able to adapt themselves to it (and so) live like exiles within and without themselves, never ceasing to seek a means of escape'? The Baath's ideas about land reform were also very close to those which the revolution had put into operation in Egypt. And while their approach to economic and social policy was perhaps more abstract than practical, there was much in their general thinking that Nasser liked. Finally, they were at one and the same time both pro-Russian and anti-Communist. They believed in close relations with Moscow, but were bitterly opposed to anyone who blindly obeyed orders from that or any other alien quarter without regard for national or pan-Arab interests.

No doubt the Baath's anti-Communism was also caused by a fear lest their rivals of the Left should outbid them for the support of the socialist vote. Certainly this was a more important factor than any intrinsic differences with Marxist ideology, on which the Baath had not been too inhibited to draw for much of their basic doctrine. But whatever their reasons, they were no less anti-Communist than Nasser and, at a time when King Saud and other Arab rulers were forever moaning that Syria was going rapidly to the Communist dogs, this was another important element in their favour. Nasser might believe, as he did, that Saud's alarmism was largely a ploy to justify the abandonment of his alliance with Egypt and Syria in favour of the 'syndicate of the Kings', as the new association of Saudi Arabia, Iraq and Jordan came to be called in the Egyptian press. But the fact remained that there was enough truth in these warnings for Egypt, as Syria's ally, to be glad to find in Damascus a political force with the will and the credentials necessary to oppose the Communist threat.

Thus Nasser was drawn to the Baath by the same processes of thinking which drew the Baath to seek union with Egypt, a mutual desire to liberate and unite the Arab world around them. But there was one problem. The very pan-Arabism of the Baath's philosophy had led it to create the kind of party structure most likely to conflict with Nasser's aspirations. Protesting a belief in Arab unity to the point where they denounced the existing national divisions of the Arab states as an imperialist imposition, and proclaiming the right of self-determination of every Arab from the Persian Gulf to the Atlantic, the Baath was not merely a Syrian institution, but a party with 'formations' in other Arab countries, all of which acknowledged their subordination to a unified leadership, as 'sections of one party and not as autonomous organisations'.

The abolition of political parties in Egypt meant, of course, that there could be no question of the Baath establishing an Egyptian 'formation'. But it did not and could not preclude the maintenance of Baathist groups in other Arab states, whose foreign policies Nasser was out to influence. And while he and the Baath might for the time being see eye to eye on most issues, this happy harmony could hardly last for ever. Besides, he instinctively disliked the idea of such political competition. The very nature of his mission to unify Arab foreign policy meant that the rulers of the Arab world should look to Cairo for guidance and not to the central leadership of the Baath. On this account, therefore, when demanding the dissolution of the Syrian parties, Nasser made no exception for the Baath, even though at the time they were closer to his own thinking than any other Arab political group, including some of his own more insular colleagues.

Viewed from Cairo, this all-embracing prohibition was no more than a natural and necessary consequence of the merger. But as it turned out, it was to be the beginning of a series of grievous mistakes which, three and a half years later, brought about the secession of Syria from the United Arab Republic. The first of a long list of regulations and restrictions imposed from Egypt which made no allowance for Syrian susceptibilities, it was a classic example of Nasser's ignorance of the special characteristics of his fellow Arabs and of the consequential arrogance with which he persisted in treating the Syrians like his own Egyptian subjects. For one thing, it failed to take any account of the essential difference between the political parties in Egypt which had been, without exception, steeped in reactionary ideas and opposed to reform, let alone revolution, and those Syrian politicians who had worked for their own liberation from foreign rule and feudalism. It also totally ignored the fact that Syria's experience of military rule in recent times had been anything but happy and certainly could not be compared with that of Egypt since the revolution. For, despite their fine promises at the time of each coup d'état, every one of Syria's army regimes in the years 1949-54 had in fact governed the country with a combination of ruthlessness and incompetence and with hardly any sign of that reformist zeal which had inspired their counterparts in Egypt since 1952.

Not only was Nasser personally ignorant of the modes and customs of his fellow Arabs, but from the system which he devised for handling his relations with the Arab world it would almost seem that he had little desire to improve his knowledge. At the time of the union he had never visited Syria and, apart from Bitar, had only once met such Syrian leaders as Azm, Hourani and Assali. He would cross-examine any casual visitors returning from Damascus via Cairo and he would listen with apparent interest to their opinion of what was happening and was likely to happen in Syria. But he ignored the advice of his own ambassador, Mahmoud Riad, to hold out against union which could only bring disaster in its train. Preferring to gather his information from copious reading of Arab newspapers, and especially the Lebanese press which he regarded as the surest barometer of Arab opinion, he refused to employ advisers from outside Egypt who could have taught him something of the special problems and peculiarities of the countries whose policies he sought to control. And instead of using the expert knowledge of his Foreign Ministry's officials in dealing with the Arab states, he allotted these functions to those of his former officer colleagues who were not too preoccupied with major administrative departments. Anwar Sadat, for instance, was charged with supervising relations with Saudi Arabia and Yemen, Kemal Rifaat dealt with Lebanon and Syria and so on, while Mahmoud Fawzi and his Foreign Ministry staff devoted themselves exclusively to the United Nations and relations with the world beyond the confines of Arabia. Indeed Fawzi's deputy, Hussein Zulficar Sabry, Ali Sabry's elder brother who had been Egypt's representative in the Sudan during the run-up to independence, only visited one Arab capital, Damascus, during all the five and a half years that he spent at the Foreign Ministry and that visit was only to collect some Egyptian documents after the rupture of the union.

Had the officers to whom Nasser allocated the task of overseeing relations with the Arab world known somewhat more than he did about the people with whom they were dealing, this system might not have worked too badly. But they did not. Like their own chief, they saw no reason to treat their fellow Arabs any differently from their own people. They failed to understand or to allow for the differences between the Egyptians, by tradition a comparatively docile population of settled peasants, who had unprotestingly transferred their obedience from the Pashas of the past to their new revolutionary leaders, and on the other hand, such proud and prickly people as the Syrians, Iraqis, Yemenis and Sudanese, whose background had been that curious system of democratic feudalism practised by their Bedouin ancestors which, while confering ultimate authority upon the paramount sheikh, still required that the tribe be consulted about any decisions affecting their future.

Nor were matters in any way improved by the fact that General Amer was allowed a virtually free hand to appoint not only his own Military Attachés to Arab and other foreign capitals, but also ambassadors who, with some notable exceptions such as Riad, were more often than not his own army cronies and as unsuitable to represent Egypt abroad as they were undesirable from a moral standpoint. Amer worked hand in glove in this respect with Shams Badran, a personal friend of his who had become Minister of War. And whenever Fawzi or Zulficar Sabry objected, as they frequently did, to a list of ambassadorial nominees submitted by Badran, Amer would use his superior influence with Nasser to overrule their objections.

The net result of this system was that serious and far-reaching mistakes were made, especially in dealing with the Arab world, which could and should have been avoided, if Nasser had sought or accepted better advice. That he did not do so, both in the case of Syria and on subsequent occasions, was partly because he was understandably intoxicated by the effect of his personal triumph in the Suez crisis, partly also because his successful defiance of the imperialist West and the erstwhile occupiers of the Arab world had released forces among the Arab masses which made him their prisoner. In his famous *Philosophy* he had written that 'within the Arab circle there is a role wandering aimlessly in search of a hero'. Since then he had got rid of the British occupation, thrown out the Suez Canal Company, bought arms from Russia despite howls of protest from Washington and London, and defied all the efforts of the imperialists to destroy him. Thus, with all these achievements and victories to his credit, the role had found him and he was the Arabs' appointed hero.

How then could he reject indefinitely the pleas of the Syrians for union with Egypt? Acceptance might be fraught with every pitfall imaginable and unimaginable; yet to deny the union would be to deny himself and all he stood for and to halt, if not to reverse, the momentum towards Arab unity and independence to which he had dedicated his life and which he had already done so much to set in motion. But equally, if the very nature of his mission and of his role as the Arabs' hero meant that he must take Syria under his wing, then the union had to be on his terms. If his success had been of such an order that the Syrians acclaimed him as their own leader, then he had both the right and the power to impose his will upon them. Should the political leaders object, he had the support of the masses and this was what would count in the final reckoning.

As the events of 1957 had shown in Jordan, Nasser's calculations about the power of the Arab masses could lead him seriously astray, provoking set-backs to his prestige which only encouraged the Western powers to redouble their efforts to drive wedges between the pro-Western 'syndicate of the Kings' and the neutralist alliance of the 'progressive' republics. Yet, driven by the irresistible momentum of his achievements and drawing fresh stimulus from his position as ruler of Syria, as well as Egypt, he was soon to disregard the lessons of Jordan. And by the spring of 1958, with Sarraj and his Deuxième Bureau working all out against Chamoun and Hussein, he found himself once again deeply involved in political pressures and intrigues in Lebanon and Jordan.

Hussein's response to the merger of Egypt and Syria had been to form a Federal union with Iraq less than two weeks after the proclamation of the United Arab Republic. The King had, of course, wanted some such arrangement with his Hashemite cousin in Baghdad ever since Cairo had begun to put pressure on him to align his foreign and Arab policies with Egypt. At the same time he still wanted to be master in his own house and was not prepared to accept the role of sleeping partner which was all that Nuri envisaged for him. However, in January 1958, as the Syrian officers descended on Cairo to demand union with Egypt, King Saud informed the Jordanians that he could no longer afford to pay the £5 million subsidy which he had contracted to give Jordan after she renounced her treaty with Britain. Thus, not only was Hussein faced with the fact that his Syrian neighbours were about to be ruled by his arch-enemy, but to make matters even worse his own country was threatened with bankruptcy. In desperation therefore he flung himself on Nuri's mercies and accepted Iraq's terms for the protection and support without which Jordan would have either disintegrated or been swallowed up by her neighbours.

Inevitably the senior partner in this 'Arab Union', as it was called, was Iraq, which meant that King Feisal became Head of State, with Nuri presiding over the Federal Cabinet and directing a common policy for defence, finance and external relations. Thus to all intents and purposes Jordan had effectively joined the Baghdad Pact. True, the federal constitution laid down that neither partner would be bound by any obligations undertaken by the other before union. But it was hardly likely that Jordan, having accepted a common defence system and a common foreign policy, would in practice be able to opt out of Iraq's commitments, whether under the Baghdad Pact or any other treaty. Consequently, while formally congratulating King Feisal on the formation of the Arab Union, as required by protocol, Nasser and his Syrian partners lost little time in denouncing the new federation as a 'false' union, based on the Baghdad Pact and doomed to failure because it paid no regard to the wishes of the Iraqi and Jordanian people and to their bitter opposition to any alliance with the West.

Hussein's decision to federate with Nuri's Iraq was an obvious setback for Cairo's drive to propagate neutralism. Nevertheless Nasser was to reap one important, if indirect, benefit from it. When the Eisenhower Doctrine was first announced, King Saud had felt strongly tempted to subscribe to it in order to defend himself against what he saw as a creeping barrage of Russian and Communist influence in the Arab world. But then the Americans, in addition to backing the Turks in their war of nerves against Syria, had also decided to join the Military Committee of the Baghdad Pact, which Saud had vehemently opposed from the days of the Cairo conference early in 1955. This made it difficult enough for him to accept the Eisenhower Doctrine. But when his new-found friend and America's ally, King Hussein, established a federal union with the initiators of the Pact, it only required a little added pressure from Cairo to make him finally decide to reject the American President's proposition.

Such inhibitions were not, however, shared by Lebanon's President Chamoun, who had never been opposed to the Baghdad Pact as such or to any Arab state joining it if it felt so inclined. Chamoun deeply resented Nasser's attempts to control the foreign policies of the Arab states. He was also convinced that it was Cairo's aim to destroy the Christian ascendancy in Lebanon which he, as the Christian community's leader, was determined to preserve at all costs. Thus, while he was by no means unconcerned by the threat of international Communism in the long term, he was more immediately afraid of the pan-Arabist propaganda which was being poured forth from Egypt and Syria. And although his foreign policy wore the official trappings of neutrality, he was in his heart no less drawn to the West than Nuri or King Hussein. Moreover, his Foreign Minister, Charles Malik, of Greek Orthodox persuasion, had an almost maniacal hatred of Communism and was in favour of Lebanon joining any alliance that was directed against Russia. For Malik, therefore, the Eisenhower Doctrine was a heaven-sent opportunity to obtain unlimited American aid and he was the last person to see any objection to accepting the underlying condition that recipient countries should renounce all offers of Russian aid.

Nor was Russia Malik's only bête-noire. From the days of his youth which he spent working as a journalist in Cairo, he had been bitterly anti-Egyptian and, like many Lebanese Christians, including his President, he saw in the policy of pan-Arabism a deliberate intention to create a Moslem empire from the Indian Ocean to the Atlantic in which the Christian communities of the Arab world would get short shrift from their Islamic rulers. The talk of union with Egypt emanating from Damascus after the Suez War therefore seemed to him to suggest that the first step in the fulfilment of this design was imminent and that, having regard to Syria's proximity, it would be particularly directed against Lebanon. The Lebanese had after all been a constant target of Cairo Radio ever since 1955. Syria and Egypt had been especially bitter towards them when, alone among the Arab states, they had refused to break off diplomatic relations with either Paris or London during the Suez War, on the grounds that they still had strong links with France and that they owed their independence largely to the British. In all the circumstances, therefore, it was not surprising when, early in 1958, Chamoun became the only Arab ruler to accept American aid under the terms of the Eisenhower Doctrine in order, as he put it to me at the time, to defend Lebanon 'against international Communism and international Arabism'.

Sheltering thus under the ample umbrella of American power, Chamoun felt a lot better able to resist the pressures and propaganda of Cairo and Damascus. Certainly he looked askance at the merger of Egypt and Syria. But at least he now knew that he could count on American support if Lebanon should be attacked. Consequently he was not greatly disturbed when Quwaitly publicly invited him to join the UAR, or when Nasser was quoted in the Beirut press as saying that the Lebanese could best 'preserve their independence' by casting their lot with the new union. Such impertinent suggestions, he felt, were largely bravado and posed little threat to Lebanon, provided constant vigilance was maintained. But some three months later, Chamoun's mood was to change to one of considerable alarm when, at the end of April, Nasser took off for Moscow to pay the visit which had been scheduled for the summer of 1956 but which had been postponed by the Suez crisis.

In fact, Nasser confided to his closest associates before leaving on this journey that he had every intention of keeping his distance in dealing with the Russians whose anti-imperialism, so Tito had warned him, was probably only skin-deep. He was, of course, grateful for the promises made by the Soviet leaders, in the previous January, to lend Egypt some £50 millions at only 2½ per cent interest. This had helped in the launching of the new five-year plan for the investment of £250 millions in industrial expansion. And it was hoped that Moscow would shortly confirm Russia's readiness to help finance the High Dam. Nevertheless Nasser had every intention of making it clear to Kruschev and his associates that he would allow no interference or intrigue against his regime in either region of the UAR and that Russian arms would continue to be paid for in cotton and not in concessions to the Communists in Egypt or Syria, whose parties had been declared illegal along with any other groups which took their orders from a foreign country. Likewise he informed Raymond Hare, by way of reassuring the Americans about his Moscow visit, that he had 'not escaped from one imperialism to fall under another'. For good measure, he also ordered a suspension of Egyptian propaganda attacks on the United States. And on his return from Russia, having duly delivered his speech about interference to Kruschev, he intensified his efforts to suppress leftist activities both in Egypt and in Syria.

But all this was lost on Chamoun who, with Malik doing everything in his power to make his flesh creep, could only see the most sinister purpose behind this apparent canoodling with the Russians. Unaware of what was being said during the Moscow talks, his attentions were fastened only on the tumultuous welcome which the UAR's President had received everywhere he went in Russia from Moscow to Tashkent. All that Chamoun and his Foreign Minister could see were the words of the press release quoting Kruschev as promising Nasser 'all the aid necessary to unite the Arab people', which he found as ominous as Eden had found Shepilov's statement in Cairo in 1956 that 'the Soviet Union only wanted to see Arab unity in Asia and Africa and the abolition of all foreign bases and exploitation'. Thus when Lebanon's leaders heard that Nasser had responded to these promises with a statement endorsing Russian foreign policy, they immediately concluded that he was in league with Russia and that Lebanon was now surrounded by enemies, with the 'Syrian region' of the UAR to the north and east and Israel to the south.

From then on, Malik became convinced of two things. In the first place, only America could save Lebanon from being crushed by this unholy alliance of Russia and Nasser. Secondly, despite the fact that the Lebanese constitution precluded an incumbent President from seeking a second term of office, Chamoun, as the architect of the new close relationship with America, had somehow to be re-elected when his current term ended in a few months' time. Hastening to Washington, he plugged his twin themes with Dulles and the State Department. With his lurid description of the dangers now confronting Lebanon, which he never ceased to remind his American listeners was the only Arab country to have subscribed the Eisenhower Doctrine, he obtained much sympathy for his ideas. The American Ambassador in Beirut, Robert McClintock, and Nadim Dimechkie, now representing Lebanon in Washington, might warn the State Department not to get involved in Lebanese party politics, especially with a project that was patently unconstitutional. But Malik claimed to know better what his country needed and there were plenty of people in Washington who believed him.

Chamoun himself was not so easily convinced that his continued occupation of the presidency was so essential as to justify flouting the constitution. Quite apart from antagonising the pro-Nasser elements among the Moslem majority, he feared that such a move would split the Christian community between his own followers and those of the Maronite Patriarch Meouchi, with whom he had a long-standing feud and who, he knew, would not hesitate to oppose him openly if he were to seek re-election. Besides, there had to be others capable of commanding Washington's respect and support among the Christian community which, under the constitution, had the sole right to nominate presidential candidates. Also, while Dulles had shown some sympathy when Malik suggested a two- to five-year extension for Chamoun, he and his Western partners were disinclined to promise overt support for the idea. At the same time, it had to be admitted that the arguments for a second term were compelling as well as flattering and could not be dismissed out of hand.

Thus torn between the counsels of constitutional propriety and expediency, Chamoun hesitated to come to a firm decision. But as Malik went the rounds canvassing support for his ideas in the hope of arousing enough support to win his chief over, the rumour began to spread like wildfire that the President was going to seek re-election and that Parliament would shortly be asked to approve the necessary amendment to the constitution. Immediately the Moslem opposition throughout the country began to galvanise themselves to resist any such manoeuvre. Predictably supported by Meouchi's followers, the cry therefore went up that, when his current term expired, Chamoun should hand over the presidency to a successor to be chosen by Parliament.

Though by no means a homogeneous collection, the opposition

in the towns consisted largely of Moslems, of both the Sunni and the Shia persuasion who sank their interdenominational differences to unite against Chamoun under the banners of Saeb Salam, a former Prime Minister, and of Rashid Karami, a parliamentary deputy for Tripoli. On the other hand, in the mountainous rural areas, the resistance mainly centred around the lean austere figure of Kemal Jumblatt, the socialist leader, and his followers from the Druze sect. Salam had resigned from office after quarrelling violently with the President about whether Lebanon should break diplomatic relations with Britain and France in November 1956. According to Chamoun, he had then regretted his hasty decision and had asked King Saud and the Sudanese Prime Minister, Azhari, to help in securing his reinstatement. But no sooner had Salam been taken back than he stalked out of the Government once again, allegedly at the prompting of the Egyptian Ambassador in Beirut.

Whatever the truth of this story, the incident created an intense personal as well as political bitterness between the two men. And when Sarraj offered Syrian help in arming the Moslem opposition to resist what he regarded as the opening round in yet another American conspiracy against Syria, Salam had no hesitation in accepting the offer. Consultations followed in Damascus and Cairo and, after Sarraj had persuaded Nasser that a relatively cheap and easy victory was to be had in Lebanon by supplying money and arms to Chamoun's opponents, gun-running from Syria began to assume considerable proportions. Jumblatt's Druzes, from their mountain hide-outs, virtually controlled the frontier and so ensured the passage of Syrian arms to Salam's and Karami's followers, as well as to their own secret arsenals. By the end of May 1958, with Cairo and Damascus Radios goading the Moslem community to revolt, outbreaks of violence were occurring throughout Lebanon. And after the Arab League had failed to satisfy Beirut's appeals for protection against the UAR, Malik went to the U.N. Security Council to accuse Nasser and Sarraj of promoting rebellion against Chamoun's authority by supplying arms, training 'terrorists' and generally inciting violence against the lawful Government.

A team of United Nations observers, led by representatives of India, Norway and Ecuador, was sent to Lebanon to investigate these complaints. But since they were unable to operate at night when the main traffic in arms from Syria took place, the observers reported to Hammarskold that they had found no evidence of any large-scale gun-running. Hammarskold then paid a personal visit to Lebanon in the middle of June and returned so convinced by what his observers had told him that, when Selwyn Lloyd discussed the situation with him in New York a few days later, he insisted that Malik's accusations were wildly exaggerated.

But Malik was not defeated yet. While Chamoun announced that, if the United Nations would not support Lebanon, he might seek aid from other quarters under Article 51 of the U.N. Charter, his Foreign Minister approached the State Department with urgent demands that America should immediately send large quantities of arms, if not troops, to help the Lebanese Government in their hour of deadly peril. Washington's response was to tell Malik to calm down. As their ambassador in Beirut had not ceased to point out, the Americans were already assumed to be actively encouraging Chamoun to seek a second term. And remembering the repercussions which had followed the Anglo-French attack on Egypt in 1956, they had decided on reflection that only as a last resort should they send troops to Lebanon. Nor were they to be won over when Chamoun himself echoed Malik's demands in discussions with McClintock.

So the skirmishing continued between the established Government in Beirut, supported by a majority of the Christian community, and the Moslem and Druze rebels, aided by a small pan-Arabist minority of Christians. It was a strange kind of civil war. For one thing, the Lebanese army under their Christian commander, General Fuad Chehab, adopted for the most part a neutral stand, declining to commit themselves to either side lest their own Moslem and Christian elements should also be torn apart by interdenominational strife. Chamoun too refrained from ordering Chehab to engage the rebels for fear that he would resign rather than carry out such instructions. Moreover, apart

from a few savage engagements between the rebels and the gen-
darmerie, such as the destruction of the frontier post at Shtoura
and the killing of its entire complement of police, there was little
serious fighting. Indeed Saeb Salam seemed to wage his war with
Chamoun largely by telephone, frequently exchanging ruderies
with the President by this means. Likewise he would spend hours
talking with Sarraj in Damascus and ordering ever more supplies
of arms, knowing that the authorities who were listening in were
afraid to cut the telephone wires. For, as Salam told me at the
time, the rebels could retaliate by sabotaging the sewerage pipes
of the presidential palace which ran under his stronghold in the
Basta quarter of Beirut! To complete the prevailing atmosphere
of tragi-comedy, with a curfew in force during the hours of
darkness, there was a local joke that fewer people were being
killed every day by the fighting than were normally run down by
Beirut's notoriously dangerous taxi-drivers.

By the beginning of July this somewhat whimsical struggle had
begun visibly to wane. For one thing, with the Moslems solidly
opposed to him and the Christians split into rival factions,
Chamoun eventually decided to abandon any idea of seeking
re-election and, on June 30, made an official declaration to this
effect. Besides, Nasser was becoming disillusioned with Salam
and his henchmen and with his own agents in Lebanon. Sarraj had
assured him that with plentiful supplies of money and arms, the
Moslem and Druze opposition would be able to force the Lebanese Government to abandon their pro-American policies, if not
to join the UAR. But after nearly two months of so-called
fighting, there was little sign of any change in Lebanese foreign
policy. And if Chamoun had been brought to disclaim a second
term as President, the cost of this achievement had been grossly
out of proportion to the benefits which would accrue to the UAR.
Egypt and Syria had been implicated up to the hilt in the Moslem
rebellion and had become more than ever suspect in the eyes of
the West. Sarraj had lavished several millions of pounds from the
union's coffers to support Salam with arms, propaganda and
every other practicable weapon of subversion. On top of all this,
the Egyptian Ambassador in Beirut, Abdel Hamid Ghaleb, who

was shortly to be sent home by the Lebanese Government as persona non grata, was being deplorably ham-handed in his dealings with the rebels, allowing trucks to be loaded with rifles for Salam's and Karami's guerrillas in front of the gates of the Egyptian embassy. Not surprisingly therefore Nasser was beginning to tire of this unprofitable investment in intrigue.

But then, quite suddenly and with no warning of any kind, came the explosion which threatened to set all the smouldering embers of inter-Arab conflict aflame. At dawn on the morning of July 14, an Iraqi brigade under the command of Brigadier Abdel Karim Kassem, which was on its way through Baghdad to re-inforce the Jordanian sector of the Arab Union, turned on their rulers, killed the King, the royal family and Nuri and proclaimed a new revolutionary republic with Kassem as Prime Minister and his second-in-command, Colonel Abdel Salam Aref, as Deputy Premier. The effect on Washington and Beirut was electrifying. To Dulles and the State Department the Iraqi revolution seemed to confirm all Malik's warnings. Clearly this was part of a carefully planned conspiracy between Russia and Nasser to destroy every vestige of pro-Western influence in the Middle East and, if the United States did not act immediately, and with all the necessary force, Lebanon would be the next victim, followed by Jordan and Saudi Arabia. The Turkish Government, seeing matters in a similarly lurid light, pressed for intervention by the Baghdad Pact allies in Iraq and Lebanon. And as Salam's followers danced in the streets of Beirut with joy at the news from Baghdad, Chamoun summoned the American Ambassador with-in three hours of Kassem's coup and asked for immediate military assistance. A few hours later McClintock told him that units of the U.S. Sixth Fleet were on their way at full speed, and on the following day American warships dropped anchor off Beirut and began landing marines on the beaches.

Two days later King Hussein asked Britain to send similar troop reinforcements to Jordan. On the death of his cousin in Baghdad, Hussein had assumed the nominal functions of Head of State of the Arab Union, despite Kassem's proclamation dissolv-

ing all federal links with Jordan. Hussein had also broadcast a
immediate call to the Iraqi people to crush the revolutionarie
But with anti-Hashemite and anti-Western riots erupting all ov
the country, he now felt no less threatened than Chamoun. Henc
his urgent appeal to London, to which the Macmillan Govern
ment, in their anxiety to rehabilitate Britain's tarnished repu
tation in the Arab world, responded with such alacrity that withi
a few hours of their receiving Hussein's S.O.S., British para
troops were being flown into Amman in transport aircraft fror
Cyprus.

The impact on Nasser of these developments was no les
dramatic. Although he had been expecting, and working for,
revolution in Iraq for some considerable time, he had not bee
privy to Kassem's plans. For one thing, Kassem himself, althoug
he had long been planning his revolution, had no intention c
making his move at the time when he left his base at Baquba wit
orders to proceed to Jordan. And it was only when he discovere
that the customary precautions had not been taken and that his wa
the only military formation with arms in the vicinity of th
capital on the night of July 13/14 that he decided to put his care
fully prepared plans into effect. Besides, as Cairo was soon t
discover when relations with the new Iraqi regime began t
deteriorate, Kassem was not a man who would ever share thi
kind of secret with his co-revolutionaries in Egypt or anywher
else. Thus the first intimation which Nasser received of the cou
in Baghdad came at 4 a.m. on the morning of July 14, when h
was awakened by his radio operator, a ham enthusiast wh
seemed hardly ever to sleep and who had accidentally picked u
the Baghdad Radio announcement. Nasser was at this poin
staying with President Tito in his Adriatic retreat in Brioni wher
he had gone to discuss, among other things, the results of his Apr
visit to Moscow, accompanied by Mahmoud Fawzi, Mohamme
Hassanein Heikal, a leading Cairo newspaper editor and a clos
personal confidant, and Hassan Sabry el-Kholy, his chief persona
assistant.

Immediate instructions were sent to Cairo that Kassem'
regime should be recognised without delay and preparations wer

ut in hand for Nasser and his party to leave at once on the Egyp-
an presidential yacht for Alexandria. But then, on the following
ay as they steamed down Yugoslavia's Adriatic coast, they
eceived the news of the American landings in Lebanon, which
vas followed by reports that Hussein might ask for British troops
) be flown to Jordan. To Nasser this news could only mean one
ning. As had happened at Suez, the Western powers were
lanning to crush an Arab revolution. On the pretext of an invita-
on to send in troops from their 'vassals', Chamoun and Hussein,
merica and Britain were about to marshal an army in Lebanon
nd Jordan and, with military support from their Turkish allies,
) move on Iraq and install another puppet regime in Baghdad.

As he was to demonstrate by such later actions as his interven-
on in Yemen, Nasser firmly believed that the Arab revolution
vas one and indivisible. If it were to fail in any one country, then
 would ultimately fail everywhere else. And as he brooded on
he West's reactions to the Baghdad coup, he decided that there
vas only one way for him to prevent a failure in Iraq. That was
) hasten to Moscow with all possible speed and persuade Krus-
hev to declare that any Western attempts to crush the Iraqi
evolution would meet with Russian resistance.

Therefore, while Sarraj made plans to blow up the American-
wned Trans-Arabian oil pipeline whenever American or British
rces began to move on Iraq, Nasser ordered one of his two
scorting destroyers to take him and his party to the nearest
ugoslav port. There he disembarked and, after a brief con-
erence with Tito, sent a message to Moscow announcing his
lans. Kruschev promptly replied that a Russian aircraft was on
:s way to pick him up and, on July 17, two days after he first
eard of the American Sixth Fleet's arrival off the coast of Leba-
on, Nasser was in Moscow putting his case to the Soviet leaders.
Meanwhile, to preserve complete secrecy about his sudden
hange of itinerary, the presidential yacht, as it steamed on
)wards Alexandria, continued to relay and receive radio mes-
ages as if Nasser were still on board. Because he did not trust his
yphers, the fact that he had gone to Russia was kept from even
is closest associates in Cairo. And on July 16, when he was in fact

back in Yugoslavia and about to take off for Moscow, a statement
was issued in his name from the yacht condemning the American
landings in Lebanon and declaring that any attack on Iraq would
be considered as an attack on the UAR within the terms of the
Arab League Security Pact.

Meanwhile Nasser's fears for the Iraqi revolution had been
strengthened by Amman's call to the Iraqi people to stamp out
the revolution and by Hussein's open professions to journalists
like myself that, with the support of the British paratroops, he
intended to march on Baghdad and stage a counter-revolution.
However Nasser's pleas to the Russian leaders were by no
means as productive as he had hoped. True, Kruschev publicly
condemned the American and British intervention and the Soviet
delegate to the United Nations called on the West to withdraw
their forces from Lebanon and Jordan without delay. Also Moscow announced with a few ominous overtones that Russian forces
would shortly begin exercises on the borders of Turkey. But
Kruschev made it plain that this gesture was as far as he could go
in threatening the Western camp. And the nearest that he came
to meeting Nasser's request for an ultimatum to Washington and
London was to declare on July 18 that the Soviet Government
could 'not remain indifferent to acts of unprovoked aggression in
a region adjacent to Russia's borders'.

As they bluntly told the UAR's President, Russia's leaders were
not going to risk a confrontation with America. While they
doubted that Washington would try to stage a counter-revolution
in Iraq, they did not think it wise to make such specific threats as
would oblige them to face war with America, if their calculations
should prove wrong. On the contrary, having recognised
Kassem's Government in Iraq and having issued a warning about
regions 'adjacent to Russia's frontiers', their main concern was to
cool the situation down as quickly as possible. In fact, far from
uttering threats against the West, as soon as Nasser had left
Moscow, Kruschev proposed a 'summit' conference of the leaders
of Russia, America, Britain, France and India to discuss ways of
allaying the crisis in the Middle East.

Forced to accept this half-loaf, Nasser took off on July 18 for

Damascus where Kassem's deputy, Abdel Salam Aref, was conducting talks with Sarraj and other leading Syrians. Once again complete secrecy surrounded his journey. When the Russian aircraft which carried him and his party arrived unheralded over the Syrian capital, the airport control tower was asked for landing clearance for a group of 'Russian technicians'. And only after an awestruck airport commandant had arranged for a car to take the presidential party to Mahmoud Riad's embassy was the secret let out that Nasser had visited Moscow, instead of returning to Egypt, as the world assumed, on board his yacht.

A meeting with Aref followed at which a pact of friendship and mutual assistance was signed. And the news was announced by the two leaders to the frenzied acclamation of the Damascus populace in what was to be both the first and, for the next four and a half years, the last demonstration of unity between the revolutionary regimes of Egypt and Iraq. Then, when this ceremony was over, Nasser made plans for his return to Cairo. This time the security precautions were even tighter than before. For Nasser remembered only too well how, a few days before the Anglo-Israeli attack in October 1956, Amer had narrowly escaped death when, following a visit to Syria, an Egyptian aircraft carrying certain members of his staff had been shot down by an Israeli fighter no doubt in the mistaken belief that the Egyptian Commander-in-Chief was on board. And with American and British, as well as Israeli, warplanes in the area and his presence in Damascus now known to all the world, Nasser was not prepared to run any unnecessary risk, even though he would be continuing his journey in the same Russian aircraft that had brought him back from Moscow.

The word was therefore spread that the President intended to stay for a few days in Syria and would deliver his speech on the sixth anniversary of the Egyptian revolution in Damascus instead of Cairo. On Nasser's instructions, even Heikal was not to know of the real plans and, when he said that he had to return home immediately to write his weekly editorial, he was told to take the regular commercial flight. Then an hour or so after Heikal had taken off, Nasser flew back to Egypt with the rest of his party.

But when their Russian pilot arrived over Cairo airport, one look at the runway convinced him that it was far too short for him to land and, at Nasser's suggestion, he agreed to try the military airfield at Abu Suweir. This proved to be safe enough. However, with nobody there to meet the aircraft's arrival, the only available transport to convey the President on the long hot journey to Cairo was the station commander's battered old Austin motor-car. Thus, when Nasser finally reached the gates of his house, such was the dishevelled appearance both of the car and its dust-caked occupants, that the sentries refused to allow them to enter until the President managed to identify himself to their astonished eyes.

Meanwhile in Lebanon, Eisenhower's special representative, Robert Murphy, having arrived in Beirut in the wake of the first American landings, was busily using all his diplomatic skill and experience to defuse the crisis by making it crystal clear to the leaders, both of the Government and of the rebels, that the American marines had not come to meddle in Lebanese politics, still less to establish a beachhead for a counter-revolution in Iraq. To Chamoun he added the timely advice that, having now decided not to try for a second term, he should ask Parliament to hold the necessary ballot to elect a new President without further delay.

Malik was, of course, outraged by Murphy's attitude. Believing that, with the marines in control of the situation, Washington should have insisted on Chamoun's re-election, he felt he had been betrayed by his American friends whom he had tried so hard to persuade that, without Chamoun, Western influence in the Arab world would soon be at an end. But, Malik apart, Murphy's words were generally welcomed. Sarraj, having from the first seen the campaign against Chamoun as a direct confrontation with the American 'enemy', was of course disappointed that the Syrians were to be denied a pretext for blowing up American-owned oil pipelines. But Salam, together with Karami and Jumblatt, were relieved to hear that America's intervention was not after all designed to support Chamoun in flouting the constitution. They knew too that, since leaflets to this effect were being distributed throughout Lebanon, the effect on the will of their

ollowers to continue what now seemed to be a totally unneces-
ary civil war would be considerable. They themselves might
vant to maintain their guerrilla campaign so as to claim the credit
or driving Chamoun out of the presidency. But they knew that
nany of their supporters would in all probability run out on them
n their haste to return to the normal commercial life of the
Lebanese entrepreneur.

More important still, Nasser's own suspicions were consider-
bly relieved by the reports which reached him of Murphy's
liscussions in Beirut. He had been inclined to tell Sarraj to call a
nalt in Lebanon directly Chamoun declared that he would not
fter all seek a second term of office. Now, with the Amercians
nd the British clearly intending to advance no further and pro-
laiming repeatedly that they would withdraw from Lebanon and
ordan as soon as peace and quiet had been restored, the threat to
he Iraqi revolution seemed almost to have vanished. And ob-
iously the best and quickest way to get rid of the Western mili-
ary presence was to stop the fighting in Lebanon and dispel the
hreat of similar disturbances in Jordan.

Moreover, Washington quickly followed up Murphy's talks
vith Chamoun with a suggestion conveyed to Nasser through
Raymond Hare that the nomination of General Chehab for the
residency should be supported by all the parties involved in the
risis, since it had the support both of Chamoun, and of his rival
Meouchi. Nasser immediately saw that here was the best available
olution. He knew that, prior to the American landings, the
United States Government had had little use for Chehab, who
hey felt had failed in his duty to fight for Chamoun against those
vho were trying to depose him by force. For this very reason
Nasser favoured the General as the kind of independent candidate
vho would refuse to be influenced by those powerful Christian
lements in Lebanon, especially in the older-established business
ommunity, who he felt were all too ready to serve Western
nterests. Certainly the experience of the past two months or more
howed that Salam and his friends were unlikely to get anyone
etter than Chehab by continuing their guerrilla campaign.
Besides, Nasser's experience of dealing with the Lebanese rebels

had taught him that the only way to get results in Lebanon was to work with the leaders of the Christian community rather than with Salam's profligate and disorganised Moslem supporters.

Thus, early in August, by somewhat the same process as that by which Conservative party leaders were selected not so long ago, General Chehab 'emerged' as the candidate for the Lebanese presidency, chosen by the Americans, Nasser and Chamoun himself. As a sop to the rebels it was further indicated that Karami, the least militant of their leaders, would be generally acceptable as Prime Minister in the new regime. Sarraj was ordered to stop all further supplies to the guerrillas and Salam, now claiming that he had favoured Chehab even before Nasser and the Americans agreed on him, accepted a cease-fire. Whereupon Chehab announced as Lebanon's President-elect that his first aim was to get rid of all foreign troops and to restore national unity as soon as possible.

In Iraq, the Americans and the British recognised the new republic and, at Kassem's request, Britain withdrew the RAF squadron from the Habbaniyah air-base where it had been stationed under the Baghdad Pact arrangements. King Hussein accepted the inevitable and declared that the Arab Union had ceased to exist. Murphy paid a visit to Baghdad, where he met the new leaders of Iraq, and then rounded off his peace mission with a call on Cairo. Because Cabot Lodge chose this moment to resurrect, in a speech to the United Nations, Lebanon's former complaint about interference by the UAR, Nasser came close to refusing Murphy an audience. But after further reflection, he decided to overlook Lodge's untimely criticisms and, with Hare in attendance, Murphy spent five hours discussing every aspect of the crisis which a few weeks earlier had threatened to plunge the Arab world into war against the West.

Nasser began by harking back to Dulles' renege on the High Dam which he said had been a brutal example of how Washington played fast and loose with Egypt, encouraged by the American press which, from his own close studies, he claimed to be incurably hostile to the Egyptian point of view. He then spoke at length about the enmity which Chamoun had shown toward im and all that he stood for, carefully omitting any mention of Syria's, and more especially Sarraj's, intrigues in Lebanon. But he added that this was now a matter of history. Chehab would behave differently and Murphy could rest assured that Cairo would henceforth staunchly support Lebanese independence. In other words there would be no further pressures from Sarraj or anyone else to drive the Lebanon into joining the UAR. As for Jordan, Nasser denied having played any part in the plots which Hussein claimed had been hatched by the UAR to overthrow him, although once again he studiously refrained from admitting that he had used, and would continue to use, every available means to gain control of Jordan's foreign policy. He did, however, issue an oblique warning of what Hussein should expect from Cairo in the future, by saying that he could not see how Jordan could remain independent for very long since she simply did not possess the resources necessary to do so.

Three days after this conversation with Murphy, the quarrel between Cairo and Amman erupted afresh when Hussein publicly labelled Nasser as the main agent of Communism in the Middle East and accused Sarraj and the Moslem rebels in Lebanon of conducting terrorism in Jordan. But Jordan's veteran diplomatist, Prime Minister Samir Rifai, managed to pour oil on these troubled waters with a suggestion that he and Nasser should meet for personal negotiations. And after a further two months, with the situation in the Middle East more or less restored to normality, American and British troops were withdrawn from Lebanon and Jordan.

Nasser had achieved his immediate aims. Kassem's revolution had been saved and Iraq had joined the 'progressive' camp. The syndicate of the Kings' had been gravely weakened and, from now on, both Jordan and Lebanon were to pursue a more neutral course in their foreign relations. In short, the rais' prestige stood, if possible, higher than ever among the mass of the Arab peoples. But his success had been due more to luck than good judgement on his part. He had backed some pretty inferior horses, yet had won his bet when their superior rivals failed to complete the course. And since his judgement respecting his fellow Arabs was in no way to improve in the immediate future, the happy band of brothers in revolution, which he now led, was shortly to break asunder in an atmosphere of bitterness between Cairo and Baghdad exceeding even that which existed at the time of Nuri and the Baghdad Pact.

Chapter 13

The Breach with Syria and Iraq

t had taken Nasser only six years to reach the peak of his prestige s the prophet of the new wave of Arab nationalism. But as has happened so often in the history of political mountaineering, he was to find no long and peaceful plateau at the culmination of his climb. On the contrary, he was only permitted the briefest enjoyment of his sudden supremacy and from then on, with a few short intervals of exaltation, the road was downhill all the way to the nadir of 1967. Within eight months of signing with Aref the Damascus agreement binding Egypt and Iraq in an indissoluble alliance, Nasser was to become Public Enemy Number One in Baghdad, ranking even above Israel in column inches of hatred in the Government-controlled press. And two and a half years after that, Syria burst her bonds with Egypt and seceded in resentment and rancour from the United Arab Republic.

The first signs of a crack in the edifice of Nasser's popularity in Syria had already begun to show before the Lebanese crisis in 1958. In fact, it is no exaggeration to say that the union began to break up under pressures from without and within from the day that it came into existence. All of Syria's neighbours, not to mention the Americans, British and French, were hostile to this projection of Nasser's rule and authority in the Arab world. Nuri once again toyed with the idea of invading Syria to suppress the Nasserist ascendancy on his borders. Indeed there is evidence to suggest that the brigade with which Kassem started his revolution was intended to reinforce a strike against Damascus by Jordanian units of the Arab Union army. Then, after Iraq's revolutionary regime had fallen out with the UAR in 1959, Kassem also seriously contemplated using force to put an end to Sarraj's intrigues against his authority. Likewise Turkey, Lebanon and

Jordan intensely disliked the idea of having Nasser as a neighbour. So of course did Israel. As for King Saud, he was so nervous about the possible repercussions on his position that he overstepped even the limits of the Saudi exchequer in trying to bribe selected Syrian politicians to break up the union. And after Sarraj had accused him in March 1958 of spending some £2 millions in his efforts to destroy the UAR, he was obliged to pay for his profligacy by surrendering all his political authority to his brother, Crown Prince Feisal.

Nor were the Russians at all pleased about the union of Egypt and Syria. For, just as Dulles was moved to comment that the only redeeming feature of this otherwise thoroughly objectionable extension of Nasser's power lay in the hope that it might check the infiltration of Russian influence, so Moscow saw the UAR as possibly presaging a new chapter of closer cooperation between Cairo and Washington. Kruschev might not want to provoke a confrontation with the United States. Yet he was nevertheless working his hardest to substitute Russian for American influence in the Arab world.

But more important than all these external rumblings against the union was the resentment which Cairo's dictatorial attitude created within Syria, particularly among the politicians and the land-owners and capitalists, large and small. Nowhere was this resentment greater than among the Baath. True, Bitar had accepted without protest Nasser's demand that all political parties should be disbanded. But the Baath felt that they were different to the other Syrian parties. They were an international association, with branch formations in Iraq, Jordan and other parts of the Arab world, and to disband in Syria, at the seat of their international headquarters, would seriously curtail their activities in the neighbouring Arab states. This, they felt, could hardly be to the benefit of the 'progressive' concepts for which they and Nasser were alike campaigning. Most of all they were hurt by Cairo's apparent disregard for the part which they claimed to have played in bringing about the union, and for the passionate devotion with which they believed in it as a first step to a much wider Arab unity, based on socialism, neutralism and independence. Considering that, above all other parties in Syria, they represented the purest milk, if not the intellectual cream, of Nasser's philosophy, they could not understand why they were not invited to govern the Syrian region of the union. And they deeply resented being treated equally with the parties of the right and the Communists who, in varying degrees and for differing reasons, were opposed to Nasser's policies, and were in their hearts sworn to destroy the UAR, even though they dared not publicly admit it.

At the same time the Baath were not as clever in handling Nasser as they should have been and, from the outset, they allowed their resentments to lead them into tactical errors which rankled with their new President. A few days after the proclamation of the union, Bitar and other Syrian leaders, including Quwaitly who had retired to the role of elder statesman, came to Cairo to discuss the distribution of portfolios in the UAR Cabinet. At this meeting, which was held in Nasser's house, it very soon became clear that the Baath wanted four of the most important Ministries: foreign affairs, economy, education and local government. But if there had ever been a chance that their wishes would be gratified, Bitar, who aspired to the post of Foreign Minister of the union, speedily wrecked it. For in advancing his party's claims, he made the fatal mistake of launching into an attack on Mahmoud Fawzi, Egypt's current Foreign Minister, whom he described as a figure of the Farouk era, 'a man in a tarbush', who was not in keeping with the modern image of Arab socialism. Bitar could not have picked on a worse target. For Nasser trusted Fawzi more than any other colleague outside the ranks of the former RCC. And as the tension rose by the minute, the President angrily retorted that Fawzi was one of his truest comrades, who had helped to see him through his hour of trial in the Suez crisis and who was the last man he would dismiss to make room for the Baathists' nominee. Whereupon Quwaitly, who had never had much liking for Bitar and his leftist policies, brought the discussion to an end by saying to the Baathist leader, much to Nasser's delight, 'Ha-ha, you obviously want the Foreign Ministry for yourself.'

Nor did Bitar enhance either his own or his party's prospects by criticising Sarraj, however justifiably, as an intelligence and security officer who was totally unsuited for political office because he had no understanding of how to 'steer the masses'. As for his contention that the Baathists, rather than Sarraj and his army supporters had been instrumental in forging the union, Nasser dismissed it as yet another of the Baath's persistent claims to represent Arab unity and socialism which were in no way borne out by their performance. Thus, when the UAR Cabinet list was fully published a month later, the Baath in particular and the Syrians in general had to be content either with high-sounding offices with little power or with relatively lowly executive posts. Hourani and Sabri el-Assali were named as two of the four Vice-Presidents, Boghdady and Abdel Hakim Amer, now a Field Marshal, being the other two. Fawzi took over as the union's Foreign Minister, Bitar received the relatively humble portfolio of a Minister of State, and Aflaq, embittered by not having been consulted about the Cabinet appointments, declined all offices. Several administrative departments were double-banked with Egyptian and Syrian Ministers exercising responsibility in their respective regions. Most significant of all for the union's future, while Zacharia Mohieddin remained Minister of the Interior for the Egyptian region, his Syrian opposite number was named as none other than Colonel Sarraj.

Worse was to come. Not only were the Baathists brushed aside or fobbed off with honorific and insignificant appointments; but in no time at all the Syrians were to be subjected to the crushing weight of that deep-rooted Egyptian bureaucracy which had no counterpart in Syria, yet had been for so long an endemic feature of Egyptian life, and which the 1952 revolution had, if anything, made still more cumbrous with ever-increasing state ownership and control. Decisions which had hitherto been taken with comparative speed in Damascus now had to be referred to Cairo, which involved interminable delays as the mills of Egyptian government ponderously ground out the answers. Moreover, all too often when the answers came, they paid little or no regard to the differences in character and custom which existed between the peoples of the two regions.

The extension of land reform to Syria, which was decreed in September 1958 and put into operation by so-called experts sent from Egypt, was a case in point. For, as those of Nasser's friends who knew Syria well did not cease to tell him, any attempt to impose the type of land redistribution which Egypt had adopted would not work. True, there were in Syria, as in Egypt, some land-owners with large estates, such as the Azm family. But, unlike Egypt, where the feudal classes had been largely foreigners, Syria's land-owners were nearly all Syrians. Also, in contrast to Egypt, Syria was a nation of small capitalists, who predominated not only in the sphere of land-ownership, but also in the mercantile, and even the industrial, communities of the towns.

Yet, heedless of these facts and encouraged by Syrian socialists such as Hourani who nursed an almost pathological hatred for Syria's relatively few large land-owners, Nasser insisted that one part of the union could not be treated differently to the other. Land reform on the Egyptian model therefore went ahead and, in October, the UAR Cabinet was reorganised in a way which ended the double-banking system and gave the Syrians only a third of the total of twenty-one ministries, and an unimportant third at that. As Bitar and Aflaq now saw it, these developments provided incontestable proof that a complete take-over of Syria by Egypt had begun, which would make coexistence with Nasser impossible and would eventually force the Syrians to secede from the union.

Nevertheless, for the time being, the Baath leaders refrained from any drastic demonstration. For one thing, Kassem had already begun to quarrel violently with Nasser and they did not want to be accused of providing the Iraqis with ammunition to fire at Cairo. For another, Nasser had agreed to a suggestion from Bitar that a high-powered joint committee be established to supervise the working of the union and to recommend ways and means of creating representative institutions in place of the political parties now in dissolution. The committee was headed by Boghdady and included Zacharia Mohieddin, Kemal Rifaat and Kemal ed-Din Hussein as representatives of Egypt with Bitar and Hourani acting for Syria. Boghdady's reputation in Egypt as an extremely efficient planner and administrator preceded him to Syria, where he was soon to gain great respect and admiration. But, unfortunately, he did not carry as many guns as Sarraj when it came to influencing Nasser on policy for Syria. In the event, therefore, the recommendations of his committee were more often than not ignored by Cairo in favour of the police methods of the Deuxième Bureau. Consequently Sarraj, with his ubiquitous intelligence apparatus at his back, was able to draw even more power into his hands. And the Baath, having in their innocence dreamed that through union they would democratise Egypt, were beginning to realise that their own democracy was instead being turned into a police state, run by Sarraj at the dictates of his Egyptian master.

These fears were confirmed when, in October 1959, a little more than a year after Boghdady's committee had been set up, Nasser disbanded it and, against the advice of 'neutral' friends who warned him that the Syrian people were fed up with being ruled by the military caste, he sent Field Marshal Amer to be his viceroy in Damascus with full authority over the Syrian regional government. The Baath leaders promptly met and, at Aflaq's suggestion, it was decided that they should resign from the union Cabinet. Bitar and Hourani, who was especially bitter that he had not himself been chosen as Syria's overlord, then descended on Cairo. The purpose of their visit was to inform the President of their party's decision and to remonstrate against Amer's appointment, which they felt would exacerbate existing tensions and, Amer being the kind of man that he was, could only bring Egypt into further disrepute in Syrian eyes. But, for whatever reason, be it the power of Nasser's personality or some sudden second thoughts, neither of them made any complaints when they met him, still less any mention of their decision to resign. Thus for the next two months they soldiered on, with Bitar grumbling away to Amer that cooperation with Nasser was becoming increasingly impossible, until in December he and Hourani, together with the two other Baathist Ministers, finally resigned their posts.

Far from seeing the danger in this development, Nasser was

only incensed by what he regarded as the dishonesty of the Baathist leaders in concealing from him any inkling of their discontent, or of their intended resignations, when they visited him in Cairo. Still angrier was he to discover a while later through Sarraj's intelligence network that, before their visit, the Baath party caucus had already decided that Bitar and Hourani should resign their posts. For to him, this not only proved their total lack of frankness, but also showed that the Baath had never dissolved themselves, but were, as he put it, 'still working underground' as a political party. Putting two and two together, he saw the whole affair as a conspiracy against himself and against the union. And from now on he looked on the Baath as his confirmed enemies. What is more, he decided to dispense with the services of the politicians in the Syrian element of the UAR Cabinet, which consisted thereafter entirely of 'technicians', apart from the irrepressible Sarraj, whose advice Nasser preferred to that of any other Syrian.

Of all the twists and turns which set Syria and Egypt on the collision course that was to end in rupture in September 1961, probably the most decisive was the alienation of the Baath. However much they might have exaggerated their role in creating the union and their ability to deliver a yet broader Arab unity, their fidelity to these concepts was certainly no pretence. Even when Bitar became so embittered that he finally withdrew from the Government, he made it clear that his primary aim in making this dramatic gesture had been to draw Nasser's attention to the malady of autocracy which was threatening to kill the union and that he was not resigning out of mere spite because he had failed to get his own way.

Without doubt the union had no truer friends and allies than the Baath party as a whole. Moreover, while they might not have commanded a majority in Parliament when the UAR was formed, they certainly represented the feelings of the masses in their heroworship of Nasser. Although at the outset loud in lip-service to the cause of union, the other parties, from the extreme right to the Communists, only favoured the idea for what they might get out of it, not because they thought it right for the country. Nor was it long before some of them were actively working for secession.

Foremost among the saboteurs were the Communists, who very soon realised their error in supposing that they stood to gain some advantage from the ban on all political activity. Within less than two months of the proclamation of the union and nine days after Nasser had confirmed his appointment as commander of the Syrian armed forces, General Bizri was found to be conducting a Communist campaign designed to arouse opposition to the union within the army. He was promptly invited to resign, together with a number of his officers who shared his views. Whereupon Bagdash and the Communist press came out in open defiance of the UAR Government.

For a few months Sarraj held his fire while the Communists made the most of their brief moment of freedom and the intelligence service brought their dossiers up to date. Then, in the autumn of 1958, he struck and, as Bagdash fled to safety in Russia, every other leading Communist was rounded up and jailed, together with a number of suspected fellow-travellers. The party's only newspaper was suppressed and restrictions were placed on the Russian cultural and information centres in Syria. And to round off the year, in a speech at Port Said on December 23, Nasser delivered a blistering attack on the Syrian Communist party whom he accused of being the enemies of Arab nationalism, who served an alien cause and preached an ungodly philosophy.

This attack, which was to herald an intensive and prolonged campaign against Communism throughout the UAR, was, however, aimed at a much broader front than the supporters of Khaled Bagdash. For the Syrian Communist party numbered no more than five thousand members; and although undoubtedly better organised than the other opposition groups, they could always be contained so long as Sarraj and his Deuxième Bureau continued to exercise their unceasing vigilance. Likewise the larger, though less cohesive, Egyptian Communist party were but one of the targets of the new anti-leftist campaign. Nasser was, it is true, anxious about the influence which the Afro-Asian

Solidarity Movement had introduced into Egypt during the period of leniency towards the Left which followed the Bandung conference in 1955. For these reasons he had kept in force the anti-Communist law which Ismail Sidky had enacted in the days of the monarchy. He had also deputed Anwar Sadat to warn the Egyptian Communist leaders that, if they and their followers did not toe the line and merge with the National Union, they would end as the Moslem Brotherhood had done. Sadat had spent seven hours arguing with these men and when all his threats had failed to move them, Nasser had publicly flayed the Egyptian Communist party as the 'new enemies' of Arab nationalism who, consciously or unconsciously, served the ends of Zionism and imperialism. From then on, in Egypt as in Syria, hundreds of Communists were arrested and imprisoned, many of them without even the pretence of a trial for subversive activities.

But in doing all this, Nasser was not solely trying to preserve his authority in Egypt or even to protect the union with Syria. No less important, he was hoping to show the world, and especially the United States, that his post-Suez statement, disclaiming any ideological associations with Communism, was not mere words. By the end of 1958, hopes of improving Egypt's relations with Washington had begun to revive. Following Murphy's visit and, after the thunder of the Lebanese crisis had rolled away, the United States had, largely on the advice of Raymond Hare, resumed economic cooperation in the form of American wheat shipments under PL (Public Law) 480 which allowed Egypt to pay for these imports in local currency. On October 12, Dulles announced that deliveries to Egypt would be resumed with a first instalment of $13 million. Added to this, Hare had shown every desire to renew the close personal contacts which had existed before Washington decided, early in 1957, to withhold American aid; and Nasser had responded by granting him interviews of seldom less than two hours in length. These were frequently held in the garden of the presidential house so as to avoid eavesdropping by the ever-active tape recorders installed indoors, which Nasser laughingly claimed he did not know how to switch off.

Nasser was also hoping at this juncture for a restoration of relations with Britain. In spite of all that happened at Suez, he had sent Abdel Kader Hatem to London early in 1957. Ostensibly his emissary's visit was to attend an international parliamentary conference, but in reality he had gone to contact influential Government officials to pass the word that Cairo wanted 'the chapter of bitterness' closed as soon as possible. Negotiations followed in due course for a settlement, both of the compensation payable by Egypt to the Suez Canal Company, and of the claims and counter-claims arising between Britain and Egypt from the damage caused by the Suez War and from the measures taken against British residents and property in Egypt. Agreement was reached with the Canal Company in July 1958. Although the Anglo-Egyptian settlement was proving more complicated, negotiations were going reasonably well and, with Eugene Black about to descend on Cairo to lend his weight to achieving a solution, the prospects of at least a limited resumption of relations with Britain seemed good.

If only to maintain these hopeful developments on the Anglo-American front, therefore, Nasser wished to provide some concrete 'proof' that he was not drifting towards the Communist camp. The need for some such gesture had been greatly increased by the announcement in October that Russia was to lend Egypt 400 million roubles, or 100 million dollars, to help with the first stage of constructing the Aswan High Dam. However thankful he might be for this assistance, Nasser was determined to demonstrate, for Russian as well as American consumption, that his acceptance did not imply that he was in any way digressing from the path of strict neutrality between the two super-powers and their rival blocs, or that he would in future be any more tolerant to Communist activities in the UAR than he had been in the past.

Yet another reason for Nasser's rigorous anti-Communist drive was his growing concern about developments in Iraq since the July revolution. The first danger signal had appeared at the end of September 1958 when Kassem fell out with his pro-Egyptian Deputy Prime Minister, Abdel Salam Aref, who had gone so far as to suggest, at his meeting with Nasser in Damascus two months earlier, that the new Iraqi republic should join the UAR. Kassem had earlier told Murphy that, whereas he had initially feared an invasion by American forces from Lebanon, he was now more afraid of subversion from Damascus, whence agents were already being infiltrated into Iraq. And since he now suspected that Aref was involved and feared that his deputy might be hoping to play Nasser to his Neguib, he promptly dismissed him from the Government and sent him into exile as Iraqi Ambassador to West Germany. But in November, Baghdad Radio announced that Aref had returned to Iraq without permission and that, because of his 'repeated attempts to disturb general security', he had been arrested and was to be put on trial for 'plotting against the country's interests'. Two months later, Aref was convicted on charges of treason and found himself in the death cell of the Baghdad gaol next to such earlier 'enemies of the people', and of Nasser's Egypt, as Fadil Jamali and Nuri's Chief of Staff, General Ghazi Daghestani, whom he, as much as any of the revolutionary leaders, had helped to put in the predicament which he now shared.

Indeed from the autumn of 1958 onwards, every report reaching Cairo from Baghdad suggested that Kassem, not content with buying arms from Russia and establishing diplomatic and commercial relations with Peking as well as Moscow, was allowing the Iraqi Communists an ever-increasing amount of latitude, while going out of his way to suppress all those who advocated close ties with Egypt, let alone membership of the UAR. Restrictions were placed on members of the UAR embassy in Baghdad and the Egyptian Military Attaché was declared persona non grata and forced to leave the country. In the following January, it was reported that a Communist-oriented 'People's Militia' had been created, which would act as a supplementary police force with power to arrest and search anybody they suspected of anti-state activities. And when this was followed by reports that the regular police and the army were being infiltrated by Communists, Nasser promptly withdrew the Egyptian instructors whom he had earlier sent to train the Iraqi air force to fly the MIGs which Kassem had obtained from Russia.

But this gesture had not the slightest effect on Iraq's new leader, except to deepen still further his suspicions of Nasser and his resentment of Egypt's claim to the leadership of the new Arab nationalism. For as all who, like myself, knew him at the time will recollect, Kassem was something of a maniac, with staring eyes, an expression that was sometimes angry, sometimes frightened, scarcely ever lightened by a smile, and a medical record of schizophrenia. Although his predecessor, Nuri, was no less suspicious of Cairo, he at least flavoured his anti-Nasserism with occasional touches of humour and, in the early stages before the Baghdad Pact, he was not above visiting and talking to his rival in Cairo. But Kassem not only never met Nasser, but regarded him, almost from the outset, with such unmitigated hatred as the main threat to Iraq's new-found independence, that he was prepared to lend himself to anyone, including the Communists, who endorsed his suspicions and to strike down anyone, including his erstwhile comrade, Aref, who had a good word to say for Egypt. He even went so far as to visit General Daghestani, who was awaiting the execution from which he was later reprieved, to seek advice about attacking Syria, for which he knew that the General had drawn up plans to coincide with the intended Anglo-American conspiracy in 1956.

By February 1959, Kassem's paranoiac hostility to Nasser had reached such proportions that six members of his Cabinet of eleven, including the Foreign Minister and Siddiq Shenshal, the Minister of National Guidance and a close friend of Nasser, resigned their posts, to be followed five days later by Shenshal's successor, after what was described as 'violent friction' had arisen between him and his Prime Minister when he tried to suppress the Communist newspapers. With Aref under sentence of death, only four of the original revolutionary Government now remained of whom, apart from Kassem himself, by far the most powerful was the Minister for Economic Affairs, Ibrahim Kubbah, a well-known Marxist. And as reports continued to pour out of Baghdad, with lurid tales of murders and assaults perpetrated by the People's Militia against Iraqi moderates, including Baathists and others of similar pan-Arabist or pro-Egyptian persuasion,

Sarraj made up his mind that a Communist take-over was imminent and laid his plans accordingly to promote a coup against Kassem and his Communist allies.

Just how much consultation there was between Cairo and Damascus about these plans may never be known, although it is inconceivable that Nasser, who was in Damascus at the time, knew nothing of them and, if he did know something, unlikely that he did not insist on being kept fully informed. But, with or without his chief's complete knowledge, Sarraj now made contact with an Iraqi Colonel, Abdel Wahhab Shawaf, who was currently stationed at Mosul in northern Iraq and who was prepared to stake everything on an armed uprising against what he regarded as the criminal lunatic now engaged in selling his country out to the Communists. Syrian agents were sent across the desert via Deir es-Zor with supplies for Shawaf's projected coup, especially radio equipment which the Mosul plotters lacked more than arms. Further contacts were also made with 'nationalist' officers in Baghdad and a plan was drawn up for a simultaneous strike against the regime by Shawaf in the north taking over the Mosul district, and his associates in the capital seizing the Ministry of Defence and killing Kassem.

So certain were Sarraj and his fellow conspirators that the coup would succeed that they took few, if any, precautions to cover their tracks. The Syrian markings on the radio transmitters were not erased and at least one of Sarraj's agents was later discovered in Mosul, not even having bothered to change out of his Syrian army uniform. Rumours of discontent among the army in Mosul soon reached the ears of the diplomatic corps in Baghdad. Humphrey Trevelyan, now British Ambassador in Iraq, certainly heard that a coup was imminent; and there can be little doubt that Kassem and his security service were at least equally well informed.

Inevitably such over-confidence and carelessness were to prove fatal to the operation's chances of success. For when, early in March, Kassem sent a large group of Communists to Mosul to take part in a demonstration in favour of his regime, Shawaf decided that a counter-attack was about to be launched against him and, without any attempt to ensure that his associates in

Baghdad were ready to move, he gave his troops the order to strike.

Shawaf's moment of glory was short. The local Communist leaders were arrested and jailed and, as other army units briefly joined forces with the rebels, the Mosul radio station was seized and an announcement broadcast that the army had established a regime in opposition to Kassem's which would work for 'good relations with all states, especially the UAR'. But the expected simultaneous strike in Baghdad never materialised. Shawaf had jumped the gun. His associates in the capital were not ready and as the security service immediately clamped down on everybody suspected of nationalist leanings, those who were not whisked away to detention were frozen into immobility.

Within twenty-four hours of the first shot being fired, Kassem struck back with overwhelming force. Under orders from its commander, a well-known Communist, the Iraqi air force attacked the rebels' headquarters with rockets. Shawaf was killed, some say by one of his own men who realised that the coup had failed. Troops loyal to Kassem then entered Mosul and, as they rounded up the remaining rebel leaders, the Communists released from prison, took their revenge on the wealthier residents and the old-established families of the town. For five days, Mosul was given over to anarchy, murder, looting and burning. Lynch law prevailed, with summary executions following sentencing by political 'courts' set up to try, on charges of treason, any against whom the Communists had an old score to settle. And throughout this blood-bath, not a hand was raised in restraint by either the civil or military authorities.

Sarraj's attempted coup had aborted. Long afterwards when he and I were discussing these events, together with his role in the Lebanese crisis of 1958, he admitted with complete candour that he had helped the rebel forces in Lebanon because, he insisted, 'we were then engaged in a direct confrontation with American imperialism'. But about his part in the abortive Mosul rising against Kassem, he had nothing to say, no doubt because, unlike the Lebanon where the end-product was at least a satisfactory settlement, at Mosul he had met with an unmitigated defeat, which brought humiliation to the UAR and death in battle or by the firing squad to Shawaf and all his co-conspirators.

Revenge was swift. The Mosul mutineers were summarily convicted of treason by the People's Court presided over by Kassem's cousin, the brutal and unprincipled Colonel Medhawi, and were sentenced to be shot. The son of a butcher, Medhawi loved to boast before the unfortunate victims in the dock that 'my father butchered sheep, but I butcher traitors'. The trials over which he presided were a mockery of justice. Instead of listening to the evidence, he would make long speeches denouncing Nasser, Syria, the Americans, the British and the Israelis, usually in that order. If he heard that anyone had criticised his conduct of the court, he would at once add them to his list of diatribes, as he once did with me after I had told Kassem that Medhawi seemed to be acting more like a rabid politician than a judge. And for many months to come, death sentences and executions of nationalists became a sickeningly regular feature of Iraqi life, while Baghdad Radio and the Iraqi press, led by the Communist newspapers, kept up their attacks on the UAR, whose leaders they held entirely responsible for the Mosul rebellion.

Nasser's reaction to all this was predictable. Enraged with Sarraj for bungling the coup, he decided that, in all the circumstances, attack was the only form of defence. In Cairo, memorial services were held for the 'martyrs of Mosul' and mass demonstrations were staged to protest against the repressions of the Kassem regime. Within the same week Nasser, speaking from Damascus, launched a virulent attack on Kassem, whom he accused of trying to break up the union of Egypt and Syria, with the aid of 'Communist agents of a foreign power', and of subjecting the Iraqi people to a Communist reign of terror. There was, he said, no longer any room for conciliation with Iraq's present leadership, but the day would nevertheless dawn when the banners of Arab nationalism would fly above the city of Baghdad. What is more, despite the failure of the Mosul revolt, he gave instructions that secret contacts should be maintained with certain nationalists in the Iraqi army, who had so far escaped detection and arrest. No encouragement was to be given to them to repeat Shawaf's

attempted rebellion, at least until they had developed the necessary strength and organisation. But they were to be assured that
whenever the time might come when they could strike with rea
hope of success, the UAR would be there to give them al
possible assistance. Meanwhile, they should keep Sarraj's agent
informed about their own preparations and about the genera
situation in Iraq.

As in Nuri's day, so too with Kassem, Nasser felt obliged to
apply towards Iraq altogether more aggressive and subversive
tactics than, as a general rule, he adopted with other Arab states
where his main purpose of influencing their foreign policie
seemed to be attainable without revolution. His fear with Nur
was that, by trying to attach Iraq to the West, he would remove
her altogether from the Arab orbit and so weaken the entire Arab
structure that the West would be able to pick off the Arab state
one by one and make them into subservient satellites. Now with
Iraq under increasing Communist domination and boycotting the
Arab League at every turn, he feared that Kassem was well on the
way to committing the same cardinal sin, only with the Communist bloc in place of the West. Tito had recently paid a state
visit to Cairo and had strongly advised him to watch Russia no
less closely than the Western powers. And whatever the cost
Nasser was determined to prevent Iraq drifting into the Sovie
orbit. Hence his decision, notwithstanding the Mosul débâcle, to
maintain contact with the Iraqi army.

A conversation which Nasser had at about this time with
Kermit Roosevelt throws an interesting light on his thinking
about these problems. Talking about the question of his involvement in the internal affairs of other Arab states, he told Roosevel
that he had recently discussed with his colleagues an intelligence
appreciation on the possibilities of a well-organised coup agains
Kassem. The main question for debate was whether, and if so
how deeply, the UAR should become involved, if those who
staged the coup asked for an air-lift of troops to support them
The discussion had revealed a horrendous row of possible repercussions. Quite apart from the highly undesirable prospect o
Egyptians shedding the blood of other Arabs, there was th

possibility that the Russians might step in to preserve their Iraqi protégés. Alternatively, Israel might seize the opportunity to attack Syria or to occupy the West Bank of the Jordan, claiming the right to protect her flanks against the growing power of Nasser's Egypt. The Turks might move on northern Iraq; the British might fly in paratroops from Cyprus; or the Americans might intervene. Any one or more of these possibilities could materialise. Yet, for all this, Nasser had concluded that, whatever the repercussions, he would have to respond to the call. Kassem had become a mortal enemy of Arab unity and an agent of a foreign power, whether by accident or intent, and to ignore any opportunity to secure the true Arab revolution in Iraq would be to risk the destruction of everything that Egypt had achieved since 1952.

In the event, when Kassem was finally overthrown in 1963, it was the Iraqi Baathists rather than the UAR's agents who were principally responsible. Not surprisingly, this was not exactly to Nasser's liking. Yet he never regretted the effort or the money which he spent trying to foment resistance to what he firmly believed was a Communist conspiracy, aimed at detaching Iraq from her Arab associations as a first step to a gradual take-over of the whole Arab world. Indeed, such were the lengths to which his suspicions ran at this point that he even believed that Britain was helping the Russians in this design in order to avenge her Suez defeat. After all, she was supplying Kassem with arms, even though Iraq had left the Baghdad Pact and ordered all British forces out of the country. Moreover King Hussein was beginning to mend his fences with Kassem and to forget, if not to forgive, the murder of his cousin, Feisal, which suggested that Britain's influence was also at work in Amman. The Foreign Office had furthermore sent Trevelyan to Baghdad, who was not only one of their most brilliant ambassadors, but was also well versed in Iraqi, as well as Egyptian, affairs from the years he had spent as counsellor in the Baghdad embassy in the forties. And as Nasser believed, Trevelyan's orders were to widen the rift between Kassem and the UAR by every possible means, which was precisely the objective of the Russians and their Iraqi Communist allies.

Needless to say these deductions only served to make Nasser even more determined to quarantine the Iraqis. To this end he embarked on a policy of reconciliation with Beirut, Riyadh and Amman. In the early spring of 1959 a secret meeting took place between him and President Chehab on the Lebanese-Syrian border at which he received assurances that Lebanon would give Cairo general support. In August diplomatic relations were re-established with Jordan and, in September, Nasser and King Saud met and agreed to reconcile their differences in the interest of pan-Arabism. At the same time, in Syria security controls were tightened still further. After Bitar and his fellow Baathists had resigned from the union Cabinet, the reins of power were clutched more firmly than ever in Cairo. And with Amer and Sarraj wielding absolute power, all criticism of the UAR Government was silenced.

Meanwhile Nasser paid several visits to Damascus and other cities of the region where, in spite of the oppressions of his henchmen, his charisma with the masses ensured him a rapturous greeting from the local population who, on occasion, would lift his car onto their shoulders and carry it along the street. Amer and Sarraj of course assured him that, as these demonstrations showed, the Syrians could not be happier with their lot under the union. And Nasser rejoiced in the affection of the people and loved them for their apparent loyalty. But, in fact, these popular manifestations were misleading. For while the people undoubtedly held Nasser personally in the highest esteem, they were nothing like as happy with the union as Amer pretended.

There was, for instance, great discontent in the army because the Syrian officers who were seconded for service in Egypt invariably received postings subordinate to those of Egyptian officers sent to Syria. The Syrians frequently complained that too many Egyptian officers and government officials behaved as if they were Nasser himself. Worse still, it was generally known, and hotly resented, that Amer and his officers constantly abused their positions of authority to smuggle goods in huge quantities in military aircraft, which were either sold in Egypt at considerable profit or used to adorn their houses, wives and mistresses. A member of

Nasser's entourage one day reproached Amer for these activities, saying that he could not treat Syria as his private ranch. But to no avail. Amer simply shouted him down and told him to mind his own business.

Nor was Syrian discontent confined to the army. There was also a widespread feeling that in the economic and commercial sphere, Syria was not being fairly treated. True, her exports to Egypt had doubled since the union, but Egypt's exports to Syria had been more than quadrupled. Her former trading partners, Lebanon, Iraq and France, had been supplanted by Egyptian monopolies. In addition to Syria having to take a lot of relatively shoddy Egyptian goods in exchange for her increased exports, all her banking and credit arrangements had to be channelled through the cumbersome bureaucracy of the union. In sum, too many Syrians felt that they were getting the worst of every world. For while, as members of the union, they were subjected to the dictates and requirements of the bureaucrats in Cairo, they still had to pay customs duties on their exports to Egypt as if they were foreigners. Nor was it any comfort for them to be told that the solution of these problems lay in the creation of a unified currency. For since the Syrian pound was so much stronger than the Egyptian, such a solution could only be to Syria's detriment.

With few exceptions such as Mahmoud Riad, the Egyptians never really bothered to understand the differences between them and the Syrian people, which stemmed from centuries of tradition and which could not be bridged by the simple act of union. Riad once illustrated the problem to me by telling how a Syrian merchant was unable to make the Egyptian authorities understand that, thanks to their policies, he had made a 'loss' of 10,000 Syrian pounds in the preceding year, by which he meant that his profits had fallen from 100,000 to 90,000 pounds. To a nation of shop-keepers his protestation made perfect sense; but to an Egyptian officer or official, born and raised in a mud-hutted village among destitute fellahin, if it had any meaning at all, it was to suggest the mentality of a class which had always exploited the poor and which the revolution was dedicated to destroy. Consequently, when the Egyptians decided to apply to Syria, in addition to land reform, certain nationalisation measures which had recently been taken in Egypt, it was confidently believed in Cairo that the Syrian masses would welcome these steps towards an egalitarian society. And although Nasser was warned by several friends, who knew Syria well, that the rentier and petit bourgeois classes would stubbornly resist these measures, he insisted that all would be well because the workers and the Trades Unions of Syria would support him, as their Egyptian counterparts had always done.

In the event, Nasser was proved wrong and the rentiers and others who had invested their own savings in Syrian banks and industries, not to mention the remittances of thousands of their compatriots and relations working abroad, turned out to be not only stubbornly opposed to nationalisation, but greater in number than the trades unionists who supported it. Thus opposition from the rentiers became superimposed on that of Syria's farmers to the agrarian reforms which had been imported from Egypt. Meanwhile, discontent in the armed forces, far from diminishing, was daily gaining ground. On one occasion a riot was caused by a Syrian paratroop formation in Heliopolis in 1960. Although the incident was officially described as having been sparked by a petty quarrel between one of the paratroops and an Egyptian civilian, it was nevertheless indicative of the rising tempers of Syria's soldiers and of a growing disenchantment with their lot under the union.

To make matters worse, Sarraj fell out with Syria's military commanders when, as was inevitable, they finally came to put the army's grievances before Amer and to protest about the dictatorial powers enjoyed by a man who, for all his brilliance as head of the Deuxième Bureau, was not suited to political office, still less to the post of Chairman of the Syrian Executive Council (or regional Premier), to which Nasser had elevated him in September 1960. Sarraj sought to counter these complaints by going to Amer to warn him of the growing threat of an army revolt and to demand that the severest measures be taken against those officers who he knew were fomenting dissension. He even claimed, rightly as it turned out, that Amer's own Syrian military secretary was involved in the incipient conspiracy. But after consultation with Nasser, Amer told Sarraj that there were to be no arrests. If there were disaffected officers in the army, the answer was to win their hearts, not to imprison their bodies, he asserted. Sarraj was furious and threatened to resign. The essential thing, he insisted, was to maintain control and unless the disaffected were arrested, all control would soon be lost. But Nasser upheld his viceroy against Sarraj's protests and Amer's opinion won the day.

Amazingly enough, despite these storm signals, Nasser still thought that the union would survive all stresses and strains because he could always count on the masses to defeat any separatist movement, whether within the army or among the capitalist bourgeoisie. This was Amer's view and, since he was the man on the spot, Nasser believed that all opinions to the contrary were mere uninformed defeatism. Certain Cairo newspaper editors tried to warn him that, unless some radical changes were made in union policy, the Syrians would be bound to secede. But Nasser's only response was to invite them to accompany him to the celebrations in Damascus of the third anniversary of the union, which incidentally was to be his last ever visit to Syria. And when he was acclaimed with the usual adulation of the masses, he turned to them and said, 'You see, these people will never break with us.'

However, by the summer of 1961, even Nasser's complacency had been shaken by mounting rumours of impending rebellion in Syria. In August, therefore, he announced a restructuring of the UAR Government which gave the Syrians twelve seats in a Cabinet of thirty-one Ministers, including such important portfolios as Land Reform and Justice. Most important of all, Sarraj was removed from Damascus to Cairo, where he was made one of a list of seven Vice-Presidents and given the task of supervising internal affairs. Also, lest the Syrians should feel that, in return for their getting a larger share of portfolios, the union's administration was to become more centralised than ever, it was further announced that the Government would sit in Damascus for four months in the year.

But it was already too late to save the union and, however well intentioned, these reforms, and especially the transfer of Sarraj to

Cairo, were in fact destined only to precipitate the very breach which they were intended to avoid. For those Syrians who wanted above all things to break up the union were now convinced that Cairo was acting from weakness and fear, rather than from some last-minute desire to atone for past mistakes. The removal of Sarraj from Damascus, far from earning Nasser any credit, was seen as a panic reaction and as a golden opportunity to get a revolt under way. For, however hated he might be, Sarraj undoubtedly held the union together by the brutal efficiency of his intelligence network and by the sheer terror which his name exercised in the minds of any would-be secessionists.

Many years later, Sarraj was to tell me that, if he had been allowed a free hand at this critical hour, the handful of officers – thirty-seven in all – who led the separatist coup would never have been allowed to succeed. He was probably right. Certainly his transfer to Cairo meant that, from that distance, he could no longer maintain his former rigid control over the Syrian region. Realising this danger, he once more protested to Amer that strong measures should be taken to crush the seditious elements in the army. Then, when Amer still refused to sanction such preventive action, he decided to make one final plea to Nasser's viceroy. Resigning his vice-presidential post he hurried back to Damascus. But his dramatic gesture served only to ensure his arrest by the separatists when, on September 28, 1961, two days after he returned to Syria, army units marched on the capital and proclaimed Syria's independence.

The first inkling of the coup reached Nasser at 6 a.m. that morning when Abdel Kader Hatem, whom Amer had sent for to help him in dealing with Sarraj, telephoned to the President to say that he feared a revolt had started in Syria. On his arrival at Cairo airport, he had found that the early morning flight which carried the newspapers to Syria had returned to Cairo on being told that Damascus airport was closed. Nasser told Hatem to return immediately to the presidency, where together they heard the revolutionary communiqué broadcast over Damascus Radio at 7 a.m., which was followed by a further announcement that Amer was not to be allowed to leave Syria for the time being.

Then, as the martial music customary on such occasions blared forth from his receiver, Nasser sat for several minutes like a man in shock, too overwhelmed by the suddenness of the blow to react in any way or even to be able to feel the hurt and anger which were to follow in due course.

Later, when he had recovered sufficiently to summon his closest colleagues, he suggested that perhaps the revolt was not after all as serious as it seemed. It could, he said, be the work of a small section of the army, locally based, who had taken advantage of their proximity to Damascus to seize power and who would soon be evicted by the army as a whole and by the masses of the people, especially those in the north of Syria, who were still loyal to him and to the union. Encouraged by his colleagues' assertions that he had both the right and the duty to suppress a mutiny in what was after all part of his own army, he therefore ordered a formation of paratroops to leave immediately for Latakia to reinforce the existing Egyptian garrisons and to stimulate popular resistance to secession in northern Syria.

But the operation was bungled and, by the time the paratroops took off, it had become clear that the coup was no local affair. On the contrary, it was a highly organised revolt, spearheaded by the army and backed by considerable popular support, including the Baathists and others among the suppressed political groups. The chances of a successful counter-stroke by pro-union northerners were therefore almost nil. Consequently, when these unwelcome truths were brought home to him, Nasser quickly realised that even the most effective Egyptian reaction could at best only start a civil war in Syria from which he would lose perhaps forever the affection of the populace.

On the following day therefore, Nasser broadcast a message to the Syrian people in which, on the verge of tears, he told them that they could go their own way and that, despite the breach, their Egyptian brothers would always support them in a crisis. Hourani, embittered beyond measure because he had not been appointed as Cairo's viceroy in Damascus, now crowed with undisguised delight over the discomfiture of the man who had overlooked him and gleefully prophesied that the break-up of the

UAR would lead to Nasser's downfall in Egypt. Even Bita showed no hesitation in appending his signature to the act of secession, which he joyfully declared would release Syria from union into which she had been misled.

But if Nasser was almost in tears over the break-up of the union among the Egyptian people there was scarcely a ripple of concern and, indeed in some quarters, even a feeling of relief. The business community, which had favoured the union as a profitable enlargement of its field of investment, was naturally disappointed. So too were the army. But among the bulk of the populace who, while acclaiming Nasser as a national hero, were still untouched by his pan-Arabist message, Syria's defection was regarded as an opportunity for the Egyptian Government to spend the national revenue on national undertakings for the benefit of the Egyptians and no one else. Apart from this the general reaction was totally indifferent. For, as any foreign diplomat in Cairo could testify, the Egyptian people were so disinterested in the union that, apart from the fact that Egypt was now called the UAR, a foreigner living in Egypt at the time had no sense of awareness that any change had occurred in the country's status.

Thus the union of Egypt and Syria was destroyed and, although for sentimental reasons Nasser insisted that Egypt should continue to be known as the United Arab Republic, no amount of political contrivance on either side was to succeed in putting it together again. Inevitably, many post-mortems were held to try to pinpoint the precise reasons for the failure of this venture. Some people blamed it on the application to Syria of Egypt's nationalisation policy, although in fact by the time the union collapsed only five factories and nineteen companies had been taken over. Others contended that it was all the fault of Sarraj and his ruthless intelligence service, to which Sarraj was able to retort that, anything, security had been too lax and that, in September 1961 there were less than a hundred political offenders in Syrian prison of which 63 were Communists, 14 National party members and 9 religious fanatics of the Moslem Brotherhood.

Nasser himself told the American Ambassador that the union had been undertaken against his better judgement and that hould only have taken place after a solid foundation of common economic policies had been established between the two countries. He also admitted that Cairo had made the fatal mistake of treating the Syrians as if they were Egyptians. To other diplomats, he said that, throughout the three and a half years that it lasted, he had never felt really happy about the union, because he knew he was not fully informed about the situation in Syria and could never feel sure that the decisions he took showed a proper understanding of the Syrian people's desires. On the other hand, to his colleagues he put a large part of the blame on what he termed the feudal and capitalist elements of Syrian society who, with the help of the Saudis and the CIA, had conspired to sever the tie with Egypt in order to protect their personal fortunes. 'We committed the sin of reconciliation with reaction,' he said. He also suspected that the French had had some hand in the conspiracy in an attempt to get back at him for the failure of their Suez venture and for the help which Egypt was still giving to the FLN in Algeria.

But perhaps the truest explanation of the union's collapse lies in the fact that it was built on the shifting sands of sentiment and that those who helped to create it either had not thought it through or had naively decided, like Hourani and other Baathists, that they could use Nasser's patronage and protection for their own personal advancement. As Patrick Seale summed it up, 'Throughout the union's brief life, government in Syria bore the marks of improvisation and impermanence . . . Arabs often argue that the form union takes is of no importance. "Let there be union," they cry, "and the form will take care of itself!" But it was precisely for lack of a convincing constitutional structure, for lack of institutions in which the diverse interests and wishes of the member states might be reflected, that the union foundered.'

This was true enough. But it was also because Nasser was trapped in the role of the Arabs' champion, to which destiny and his own success had called him, that he could not deny the cry for union when it came, however unprepared he and his system of government were to answer it. And when he nevertheless responded to the Syrians' appeal, his ignorance of their ways, coupled with his distrust of all political parties and his inability to

distinguish between honest criticism and outright opposition, le
him to trust the policeman in preference to the politician as th
exponent of his will and the ruler of his subjects. Misled by th
plaudits of the populace, he therefore denied the creation of tha
'convincing constitutional structure' which could have made th
union work and therefore suffocated, and finally alienated, thos
best able and most willing to carry the message of Nasserism to a
sections of the Syrian people.

Chapter 14

Foreign Diversions and Disputes

The rupture of the UAR could hardly have come at a more awkward moment for Nasser. For, while his personal prestige with the masses, even in Syria, might have been unimpaired, he was once again involved in bitter conflict with those who controlled the destiny of the Arab states, as well as being heavily encumbered with problems and quarrels with the Soviet bloc. In 1955 he had told an Officers' Club meeting that Egypt's great strength lay in the rival interests of America and Russia in the Middle East area, and that each of the two super-powers would protect her from the other. But after six years of trying to play the super-powers off against each other, he was beginning to lose much of his earlier self-assurance and even to fear that the rivalry between America and Russia might result in more pressure than protection for his country. Certainly the problem of balancing the see-saw of relations between East and West was proving to be excessively difficult and the slightest upward move at one end seemed to plunge it to the ground at the other.

At this particular juncture it was the Western end which was uppermost. The election of John F. Kennedy as President of the United States in the previous November had filled Nasser with renewed hope of reaching a genuine understanding with Washington. Not that he had disliked Eisenhower, whether from a distance or when they met briefly at the U.N. General Assembly in 1960. On the contrary, he admired the simple honesty of this soldier-president. But he equally knew that, where America's foreign relations were concerned, it had been Dulles and not Eisenhower who made the decisions; and Dulles was, on all the available evidence, an enemy who desired his destruction and who, as he put it to me, was forever 'playing games with the reactionaries in the Arab world' in order to strike at Egypt. More than anyone,

Dulles was in Nasser's view responsible for the influence which Russia had gained in the Arab world by supplying the arms and the aid for development which Washington had refused. For Dulles had seemed incapable of understanding, as the Russians had done, that for better or worse Egypt was the political centre of the Arab world and it was therefore impossible for an outside power to have good relations with the Arabs as a whole, if its relations with Egypt were bad.

Hence, when Kennedy wrote to Nasser on his election to the American presidency to express his hope that a new understanding might be reached between their two countries, his sentiments found a resounding echo in Cairo. The new President' evident desire to understand the 'third world' offered a refreshing contrast to Dulles's rigid hostility to neutralism. Moreover Kennedy made an inspired choice in nominating the ambassador to represent him in his search for a rapprochement with Egypt John Badeau had been for ten years the Dean of the American University of Cairo and knew more about Egypt than any other living American. Yet he had no political 'record' to handicap him in his dealings with the Egyptian Government. And while Nasser was generally suspicious of Western 'Arabists', he warmly welcomed Badeau as a man whose experience would enable him to understand the aspirations of Egyptian youth who now formed more than half the total population. Thus, from the moment when he presented his credentials, Kennedy's representative was able to establish an excellent rapport with Nasser and his Ministers. At Nasser's suggestion, it was decided that the Palestine question be 'put in the ice-box', because neither America nor Egypt was likely to change her attitude about Israel, and it would be more profitable to work on other issues where a new understanding might be achieved or at least old misunderstandings could be removed.

Equally with Britain, after the diplomatic connection had been partially restored in December 1959, relations had undergone some improvement. Colin Crowe was appointed British Chargé d'Affaires until the restoration of full diplomatic relations brought Harold Beeley to Cairo as Britain's Ambassador in March 1961. Crowe had already spent several months in Egypt as head of the

British Property Commission, which was established to settle the claims and counter-claims arising out of the Suez War. In this capacity he had no diplomatic status or contacts with the Foreign Ministry and his official dealings were conducted exclusively with the Ministry of Finance. But since Nasser, even before he agreed to resume relations with Britain, wanted to be able to communicate with London on a political level, he designated his close confidant and 'mouthpiece' Mohammed Hassanein Heikal, as the political contact with Crowe, who was thereby frequently better informed of the President's thinking on current issues than many ambassadors who had full diplomatic access to the Foreign Minister and, theoretically at least, to Nasser himself.

One particular problem confronting Crowe concerned the case of a British subject of Maltese origin, James Zarb, who had been convicted of espionage during the Suez crisis, together with another Britisher, James Swinburn, and had been sentenced to ten years' imprisonment. Swinburn had been released in September 1959 after serving three years of his five-year sentence. But all Crowe's efforts through Heikal to secure a similar remission for Zarb were unavailing, until a few days before he was due to hand over to Beeley and leave Cairo. Crowe went to pay a farewell call on Heikal and, after the usual courtesies had been exchanged, Heikal said that he had a leaving present to give him from the President. He added that, for reasons of protocol which Crowe had no doubt understood, Nasser had not received him personally during his two years in Cairo. But the President had been kept fully informed of everything which had passed between them and he now wished to mark Crowe's departure with an important gift. With that Heikal handed over an envelope in which, when he opened it, Crowe discovered, much to his delight and amusement, a sheet of paper on which was written in block capitals the one word – ZARB.

Nevertheless, despite Nasser's desire to see formal diplomatic relations restored with Britain, Beeley's reception in Cairo was by no means enthusiastic. Nasser was personally friendly on the somewhat rare occasions when he and the ambassador met. His Ministers, too, were affable enough and whenever they referred to the 'tripartite aggression' they studiously refrained from any offensive or emotive remarks and spoke of it purely as a historical episode. But, try as he did, Beeley was never able in the course of the three years that this, his first, mission to Cairo lasted to get onto anything approaching the terms which his predecessors had enjoyed in the pre-Suez period.

Yet Anglo-Egyptian relations were positively warm by comparison with the treatment received by the Commission on French Interests in Egypt, the equivalent of Crowe's Property Commission. The French were allowed no such contacts as Crowe had been able to enjoy. And in November 1961, the chief of the commission, Monsieur Mattei, was arrested and charged with espionage, together with four of his French staff and six alleged collaborators. Five months later, after President de Gaulle had conceded independence to Algeria, the prosecution decided to postpone these proceedings indefinitely and the accused were all released. But, in the meanwhile, as Paris retaliated by suspending all trade and business dealings with Egypt, relations between the two countries became more embittered than at any time since 1956.

In the outside world, however, by far Cairo's most serious quarrel was with Russia, with whom relations over the past three years had degenerated at times into a personal slanging match between Nasser and Kruschev. The row began three months after the Russians announced their decision to help finance the High Dam. Late in January 1959, Kruschev elected to weigh in on behalf of the leftists whom Nasser and Sarraj were busily engaged in locking up in Egypt and Syria. In a public speech the Russian leader warned the UAR authorities not to persecute Communists who, he asserted, were among the most steadfast supporters of the Arab struggle against imperialism. At this point Nasser refrained from replying in kind, though he made it clear through private correspondence that he strongly resented this unwarrantable interference in the internal affairs of the union. This first round therefore ended with a bland statement from Cairo that the two leaders had exchanged correspondence and 'renewed their pledges of friendship and cooperation'.

But within days of the abortive Mosul rebellion in Iraq,

Kruschev returned to the charge with a speech in Moscow to a visiting Iraqi delegation in which he again warned Nasser not to pursue his anti-Communist campaign which, he claimed, was doomed to failure, as was also the attempt to force Iraq into the UAR. This time Nasser let fly and, stung by the Russian leader's obvious reference to Sarraj's role in the Mosul revolt, he retorted on the same day that Kruschev was grossly distorting the facts. Moreover, he added, the UAR did not interfere in Russia's internal affairs or support one faction against another within the Soviet Union.

Three days later, after the Syrian Communist leader, Khaled Bagdash, had joined in the fray by abusing Egypt and praising Kassem, Kruschev struck a more personal note, saying that Nasser was a hot-headed young man who took upon himself more than his stature permitted in assailing Communism in the Middle East. Whereupon, on the following day, Nasser openly denounced Moscow for 'interference in our affairs', named Kruschev as the instigator of the interference and asserted that the Communists throughout the UAR would be ruthlessly crushed as agents of a foreign power. Then, before Kruschev could recover sufficient breath to answer him, he followed up with two further speeches, disparaging the role of the Soviet Union in the Suez crisis and ridiculing Russian claims to have 'abolished tyranny', when their only elected Parliament had been dismissed by the Bolsheviks in 1917 and the Russian people had been governed ever since by a single party system in which no opposition or criticism was tolerated. Even more forthright and explicit was his statement a month later to the editor of the Indian magazine *Blitz*. 'Information,' he said, 'which we have obtained has revealed a basic Communist plan to take over Iraq and establish a Soviet state in that strategic Arab region. This would be followed by the destruction of unity between Syria and Egypt. The final Communist aim is to establish a "Red" Fertile Crescent composed of Iraq, Syria, Jordan, Lebanon and Kuwait which would enable Communist influence to penetrate to the Indian Ocean.'

As the second round in the heated debate ended on this uncompromising note, Nasser went ahead with a renewed drive against those Communists and their associates who were still at large in Syria and Egypt. Partly from a genuine fear of internal subversion, and partly in revenge for the savage reprisals against Nasserists in Iraq after the Mosul rebellion, hundreds more leftists were sentenced to prison terms of up to ten years, or detained indefinitely without trial, in conditions which in some cases amounted to serious brutality, as the prison authorities tried to break down their resistance and reduce them to total subservience. Khaled Mohieddin, who had returned from exile in 1956, managed to escape imprisonment because of his former close friendship with Nasser, although he was dismissed from his editorship of the Cairo evening newspaper, *Al-Masa*, for refusing to write that the Mosul rebels were still fighting after they had in fact been crushed. But he was almost the only exception to the rule by which the leftists of Egypt and Syria were now hunted down with a ruthlessness far exceeding that of any previous anti-Communist drive under Nasser's regime.

This uncompromising reaction to Russian pressures seemed to convince the Kremlin that public criticism of Cairo's anti-Communist policy could only be counter-productive and that Nasser was not going to accept interference from Moscow any more than he had been prepared to knuckle under to pressures from America or threats from Britian. In May 1959, therefore, after a further exchange of correspondence between the two leaders, Nasser was able to announce that he had received certain assurances from Kruschev that Russia would not interfere in Arab affairs. From then until April 1961 there was a truce in the war of words between Moscow and Cairo, with Kruschev confining his complaints to private exchanges with Mohammed el-Kouny, the UAR Ambassador to Russia, and even then only mildly murmuring that he could not understand why, if he and Nasser could deal with one another, those in Egypt who thought as he did should be persecuted for their beliefs.

Moreover, even at the height of all these polemics, Kruschev had been careful to keep matters under control. For one thing, the Russian people were kept largely in the dark about the heated exchanges which had taken place. Only a few lines of Kruschev's speeches were published in the Soviet newspapers which were themselves not allowed to attack Egypt directly, but only to quote attacks by Arab Communists such as Iraq's Colonel Medhawi. More important still, Kruschev had scrupulously refrained from making any public threats concerning Russian aid for the High Dam. The nearest he came to linking the Aswan project with Cairo's anti-Communist measures was in a long private letter in April 1959. Beginning with a sly dig at the Mosul affair by reminding Nasser of his original anxiety lest the infant Iraqi republic should become the victim of foreign aggression, Kruschev went on to contest the assertion that Russia had stood idly by when Egypt was attacked in 1956. Insisting that the fighting had been stopped by Moscow's timely reminder to the three aggressors of the power and proximity of Russia's atomic arsenal, he added that, if Nasser now found Russian aid 'a burden', he was free to refuse it. More pointedly still, he ended by quoting a Russian proverb, 'Don't spit in the well, you may need to drink its water.'

Wisely, Nasser's reply ignored this veiled reference to the High Dam. Concentrating instead on Russia's role in the Suez War, he recalled Kruschev's conversations at the time with Shukri Quwaitly and he justified his suppression of Communism by saying that local Arab Communist parties were working with Soviet support against Arab nationalism. Even if it meant incurring Russian displeasure, he concluded, he would have to continue to fight such Communists.

Kruschev did not pretend to accept this reply as satisfactory. But he made no attempt to follow up his letter with any further warnings. On the contrary, a week after Nasser, in January 1960, had set off the symbolic explosion which marked the beginning of work on the first stage of the High Dam, the Soviet Government agreed to a further loan of £80 million to finance the foreign exchange requirements of the second stage. Perhaps their decision was prompted by an announcement from Washington a few days before that the United States would support the World Bank in financing further stages of the High Dam, which Kruschev feared might help to revive American influence in Egypt. But be that as it may, Russia's leaders were clearly not going to let the fate of any number of Arab Communists threaten the superb opportunity which America and Britain had presented to them in 1956 of detaching Nasser from his Western associations, and of implanting Russian influence at the centre of gravity of the Arab world.

Thus, for the next fifteen months, relations between Cairo and Moscow continued without further incident. At Aswan there were the inevitable disputes between the Russian engineers and the local Egyptian authorities. Nasser and his advisers were frequently to regret having given the Soviet Government a virtual veto on the use of foreign contractors and equipment, which the Russians interpreted so strictly that they even refused to allow the Egyptians to employ White Russian emigrés as interpreters. The Egyptian authorities blamed Russian inefficiency whenever the work fell behind schedule. And, after frequent complaints that Soviet equipment was not up to the tasks to which it was put, Nasser decided to defy the Russian veto by ordering Swedish drills to replace the Russian types which had failed to make sufficient impression on the Aswan granite.

But, by and large, cooperation was maintained over the High Dam, despite the almost total absence of fraternisation between the work teams. Also in the sphere of general commerce, Russia's policy of low interest rates on loans, plus other inducements from technical training to barter arrangements, helped to increase the Communist bloc's exports to Egypt to three times the figure for 1952. True, the Americans and West Germans were still providing the bulk of Egypt's imports and aid at an annual average cost of £100 million. But by 1961, Soviet influence had made substantial inroads. Not only had Russia twice supplied virtually every modern weapon possessed by Egypt which, even before the Suez War, amounted to some £150 million worth of arms, including 50 Ilyushin bombers, 100 MIG fighters, 300 tanks, 500 guns and several small warships; they and their satellite partners in Eastern Europe could also claim to have collared a third of Egypt's foreign trade. And in all the circumstances it suited the Russians and Egyptians to keep their differences as far as possible away from the public gaze.

Nevertheless, the ebullience of Nikita Kruschev could not be contained indefinitely, whatever the advantages of silence might be to both sides. In April 1961, when Anwar Sadat was leading a parliamentary delegation from the UAR on a visit to Russia, he once again gave vent to his criticisms of Nasser's anti-Communist campaign. Shouting at his guests at a Kremlin reception, he said, 'If our people under a Communist system live better than yours, how can you say you are against Communism? Communism consists of ideas which you cannot shut up in prisons. You say you want socialism, but you do not understand the true socialism which leads to Communism. In the present stage of your development you are still at the letter A. In all good faith I warn you, Communism is sacred.'

Protests followed through the diplomatic channels and, when these had failed to procure any apology or retraction from Moscow, Nasser authorised Heikal to publish in *Al-Ahram* the full text of Kruschev's abusive utterance and of Sadat's more dignified reply that Egypt would find her own way to socialism and development without interference from foreign powers or ideologies. Heikal also spelled out the essential differences between Communism and Arab socialism. Communism, he wrote, imposed a dictatorship of one class; Arab socialism dissolved all class distinctions. Communism made the individual a 'working tool' of the state; Arab socialism treated the individual as the very basis of society. Communism allowed of no deviation; Arab socialism offered freedom of thought and analysis, because it was essentially humanist and flexible and, while it permitted the ownership and inheritance of private property, it ensured that such rights could not be used to exploit the people.

Such comparisons could hardly have failed to rile the Kremlin and the Soviet press was now allowed directly to attack Egypt, or at least *Al-Ahram,* for mounting an anti-Russian campaign. Then as relations between Cairo and Moscow plummeted once again, Nasser, after consulting with Tito and Nehru, weighed in with a forthright condemnation of Russia's decision to resume nuclear tests. When Syria broke with the union four weeks afterwards, Moscow recognised the separatist regime in Damascus with almost the same indecent haste as Turkey and Jordan. And two months later, when their Iraqi protégés caused a major crisis in the Arab world by laying claim to Kuwait, the Russian delegate to the U.N. Security Council vetoed Kuwait's admission to the United Nations which had been proposed by Egypt.

Nor was Russia the only 'socialist' power with which Nasser fell out over his anti-Communist policies. In September 1959, Khaled Bagdash made a speech in Peking in which he viciously attacked the UAR authorities for persecuting 'progressive' elements in Syria and Egypt. Nasser protested furiously through the Chinese Ambassador in Cairo at this 'violation of the principle of peaceful coexistence' by the Chinese authorities, in 'allowing a renegade to make a flagrant attack on the UAR which could only damage relations between the two countries'.

Even worse was the state of Cairo's relations with the rulers of the Middle East. Diplomatic ties with Iran were severed in July 1960 in protest against the Shah's decision to recognise the state of Israel. Whereupon Teheran announced that there could be no resumption of diplomatic ties with the UAR so long as Nasser remained in power. As for the Arab world, by the time Syria seceded from the union, relations with Cairo had degenerated to the lowest point since the 1952 revolution. The brittle peace which had been restored with King Hussein in August 1959 was shattered, almost exactly a year later, by a series of incidents culminating in the assassination of Jordan's Prime Minister, Hazza Majali, by two Government messengers, who escaped to Damascus after planting the fatal bomb in his desk drawer. In June 1960, two months before the murder, the radio war between Amman and Cairo had been restarted with Hussein attacking Nasser and warning him of the 'dark fate' awaiting all dictators. Shortly afterwards Amman Radio also broadcast an appeal to the people of Syria to rise and throw off the yoke of Cairo.

Nasser might have made it a rule that propaganda against Hussein should never be pushed to the point of provoking a revolution in Jordan, for fear of Israeli reactions. But at this stage he neither liked nor trusted Jordan's King and, in the radio exchanges between Cairo and Amman, there had been no shortage of personal abuse by Ahmed Said and other 'Voice of the Arabs' propagandists. Indeed, on occasion Hussein was referred to as the 'son of Zein' (Jordan's Queen Mother), which was in Arab terms equivalent to literally calling him a bastard.

Thus, when Amman Radio seemed to be actively trying to disrupt the union of Egypt and Syria by inciting Syrian separatists to rebellion, the Egyptian press and the 'Voice of the Arabs' responded with yet another stream of abuse for Hussein. As the temperature rose sharply on both sides, an ex-officer of the Jordanian army was arrested on crossing the border from Syria and charged with plotting to overthrow the Hashemite regime at the instigation of the UAR intelligence service. And when Majali was killed a few weeks later, responsibility for the crime was immediately, and inevitably, laid at the door of Sarraj's Deuxième Bureau. Cairo Radio thereupon added fuel to the fire by accusing the murdered man of being a traitor to the Arab cause for having advocated in 1955 that Jordan should join the Baghdad Pact. And as Jordanian forces concentrated menacingly on Syria's frontier, Hussein retorted by personally accusing Nasser of complicity in the murder and calling him a madman, a Red agent, a small Farouk and a blood-thirsty dictator and conspirator. Finally, in October 1960, after two months of continued invective from both sides, Hussein seemed to go out of his way to antagonise Egypt by formally recognising the Kassem regime in Iraq.

In the following March, relations between Cairo and Amman were briefly patched up 'in the wider interests of Arab unity'. The pro-Egyptian ex-Premier, Suleiman Nabulsi, was released from house arrest and, for the first time in four years, pro-Nasser demonstrations were permitted in the Jordanian capital. But the truce was short-lived. For in September, Syria seceded from the UAR and Jordan caused another breach with Cairo by conferring official recognition on the Syrian separatists within forty-eight hours of the Damascus coup taking place and before anyone could be sure that the new Government were in full control of the country.

Similarly with Saudi Arabia, relations were again soured when Prince Feisal announced from Riyadh that his Government had decided to recognise the secessionist regime in Damascus. Not that Egypt's ties with the Saudis had ever been very cordial since King Saud had remonstrated with Nasser for nationalising the Suez Canal Company without consulting his fellow Arabs. Saud had done everything in his power to wreck the UAR. He had also worked hand in glove with Hussein and had financed several 'black' radio stations to incite the Syrian and Egyptian peoples to rebel against their rulers. And even though Nasser knew that this ailing dypsomaniac was no longer in effective control of Saudi policy, he bracketed him with Hussein in a violent outburst at the end of 1961 in which he referred to both monarchs as 'agents of imperialism and reaction'.

As for Iraq, relations had gone from bad to worse since the Mosul revolt in March 1959. Although Kassem personally held aloof from the exchange of abuse between Baghdad and Cairo, other Iraqi spokesmen poured forth a continual flow of hatred on the radio and in the press against the UAR. Anyone suspected of pro-Egyptian sentiments was liable to arrest by the People's Militia and summary conviction and imprisonment at the hands of the egregious Medhawi. By way of provoking Cairo still further, in March 1960 the Iraqi Government commuted the death sentences passed on Jamali and other ex-Ministers convicted after the 1958 revolution for their anti-Nasser views, while at the same time they continued to hold Aref under sentence of death for his pro-Nasser activities.

True, even Kassem seemed now to be slightly alarmed at the speed with which the Communists were entrenching themselves in key positions in the civil service and in such important Government agencies as the Development Board. Early in 1960, his Marxist Economics Minister, Ibrahim Kubbah, had been sacked and the official Communist party was refused a licence to operate. But since the official party was a mere façade for the real Communists who were working behind the scenes in every important department of government, this was little more than an empty gesture, which did nothing to restore the equilibrium in Iraq's foreign relations, still less to mend any fences with Cairo. Indeed, Kassem's Foreign Minister went out of his way to make it clear that Iraq would not attend any meeting of the Arab League that was held in either region of the UAR.

Nevertheless, after several suggestions had been made by Riyadh, and rejected by Cairo, for mediation by the Saudis, Nasser decided to make his own bid for reconciliation with Kassem. In January 1961 Fawzi was sent to Baghdad to talk things over. But, from the very outset, it was clear that the Iraqis had no desire whatever to patch up their quarrel with the UAR. For while the Arab League's Secretary-General, Abdel Khalek Hassouna, who travelled on the same aircraft, was accorded VIP treatment on arrival at Baghdad airport, Fawzi and his party were left standing in line with the other passengers and spent over an hour having their baggage searched by the customs officials. Then to make the failure of his mission even more certain, when word got around that Egypt's Foreign Minister was in Baghdad, he was mobbed by pro-Nasser demonstrators almost everywhere he went.

Indeed, far from showing any signs of compromise or conciliation, the Iraqis were within a few months to lash out against their Kuwaiti neighbours in a venture which brought the Arab world to the brink of internecine war. Following Kuwait's achievement of independence from British tutelage in June 1961, Kassem promptly renewed the long-standing Iraqi claim that this oil-rich territory formed an integral part of Iraq, having been administered under the Ottoman Empire as part of the province of Basra. He also began to mobilise Iraqi forces with every appearance that he intended to settle the issue once and for all by the use of force. The Ruler of Kuwait promptly appealed for British help. And as Cairo, backed up by statements from Washington, Amman, Riyadh and Teheran, declared the UAR's support for Kuwait's independence, British forces hastened to the scene to confront the Iraqi troop concentrations on Kuwait's borders.

Nasser raised no objection when Beeley informed him of Britain's intervention. With no army of his own on the spot and having declared his outright opposition to Kassem's claim, he was scarcely in a position to do so. Nevertheless, he did not at all like the idea of the British interceding on Kuwait's behalf. Apart from his determination to evict Britain's military presence from all Arab territory, he feared that other Gulf states, and possibly Jordan too, would be encouraged to look to the British to protect them in the future, as they had done for so long in the past, instead of relying on their fellow Arabs for help in time of trouble. Also he had been informed by his intelligence agents in Iraq that Kassem was bluffing and that, mad though he was, he would not go so far as to try to occupy Kuwait by force, but would be content with concessions, territorial and otherwise.

For these reasons, therefore, Nasser believed that it was both safe and desirable to get the British troops out of Kuwait at the earliest possible moment and to replace them with a mixed force drawn from member states of the Arab League. Accordingly, at his instigation, the League Council met in emergency session. The Iraqi delegate promptly walked out of the meeting on being told that Kassem should withdraw his claim. And it was then agreed that the Kuwaitis should be informed that their request for membership of the Arab League could not be met, so long as British troops remained on their soil and thus denied Kuwait's claim to independent status. However, if they were prepared to accept an Arab force in place of the British, admission to the Arab League would follow immediately. Kuwait accepted these terms without hesitation and, seven days later on July 20, as the British troops began to withdraw, she became a member of the League. A mixed force, consisting of contingents from the UAR, Saudi Arabia, Jordan, Tunisia and the Sudan, moved in and Kassem withdrew his troop concentrations, though not his claim.

Nasser had gained his immediate objective and, once he was satisfied that there was no threat of an Iraqi attack on Kuwait and that the British had pulled out completely, he soon decided to withdraw his own contingent from the Arab force. For one thing, friction developed almost immediately between the Egyptian troops and the Saudi and Jordanian detachments. Besides, Egyptian agents in Iraq were reporting that the presence of UAR forces in Kuwait, coming on top of Cairo's outright rejection of the Iraqi claim, was alienating many Iraqi nationalists who were opposed to Kassem and potentially well disposed to Nasser.

Therefore, only a few weeks after the UAR detachment had arrived in Kuwait, Nasser cabled to the Ruler to say that he was withdrawing his troops because disruptive elements were trying to cause trouble between the UAR force and the Government and the people of Kuwait.

Finally, to round off Nasser's growing circle of Arab enemies, relations with Tunisia had been broken in October 1958, after President Bourguiba denounced Nasser for harbouring his arch-enemy and political rival, Salah Ibn Yusuf. Bourguiba protested that this was tantamount to interference in Tunisia's internal affairs and could not be justified by the rules governing political asylum, since Salah Ibn Yusuf had plotted to assassinate him. Cairo Radio and the Egyptian press had promptly lambasted the Tunisians as toadies of the imperialists who were 'trying to curry favour with the West'. And with Nasser persistently rejecting Bourguiba's every demand for the extradition of his enemy, the row had rumbled on until early in 1961, when it was reported that a 'discreet compromise' had been reached, whereby the Tunisian Government had agreed to resume relations without insisting on the return of Ibn Yusuf. But, due to personal dislike on the part of both leaders, the truce between Nasser and Bourguiba was a somewhat fragile affair, as later developments were to show. And when Tunisia found herself, in July 1961, engaged in a shooting war to oust French forces from their base in the Tunisian port of Bizerta, Nasser's response was confined to lending her moral support, and not much of that.

In fact, the only state with which Egypt had really close relations at the time of Syria's secession was the Sudan where, since November 1958, a military dictatorship led by General Ibrahim Abboud had been in control. Abboud's take-over was a vastly important windfall for Nasser. Having persuaded the Russians a month earlier to help finance the High Dam, he more than ever needed friends in Khartoum to settle the problems which had to be resolved before work on the dam could be started. These included the apportionment of the Nile waters between the Sudan and Egypt and the compensation due to the Sudanese for the flooding of the Wadi Halfa border area which would follow the completion of the dam. Ever since independence, successive Sudanese Governments had refused to confirm the 1929 Nile Waters agreement, which they claimed was unfair to the Sudan in that it gave Egypt twelve times more water for irrigation than the Sudanese share, and which had moreover been negotiated by their British rulers without proper consultation with the Sudanese people. These same Governments had also taken the view that the High Dam was largely a prestige project designed to satisfy Nasser's ego, and that several smaller dams would achieve better results without submerging large areas of Sudanese territory and destroying many historic monuments.

Thus the negotiations which took place periodically with the Sudan after 1956 had failed to achieve agreement on the two main issues, the sharing of the Nile waters and compensation for Wadi Halfa. Nor had the climate for these intermittent discussions been in any way improved by a bitter quarrel which broke out in February 1958 over a piece of territory on the frontier which Cairo claimed as Egyptian when, in the course of an election campaign in the Sudan, Sudanese political candidates moved in to canvass the votes of the inhabitants. An ultimatum was sent to Khartoum demanding an immediate withdrawal from the area and Mohammed Mahgoub, then the Sudan's Foreign Minister, flew to Cairo for discussions with Nasser and his advisers. After a heated exchange had failed to produce any agreement, Mahgoub telephoned to Khartoum and, in the presence of Nasser, Fawzi and Zacharia Mohieddin, said to the duty officer at his Ministry: 'Release, repeat, release.' Then, without any explanation of his instruction, he stalked out. A few hours later Khartoum 'released' the announcement that, since the talks in Cairo had brought about no solution, the Sudan was asking Hammarskold to convene a meeting of the U.N. Security Council to consider the Egyptian threat. Whereupon Nasser relented and no more was heard of Egypt's territorial claim.

In the subsequent elections the anti-Egyptian Umma party had won a handsome victory and for the next eight months no progress whatsoever was made towards a settlement of the Nile waters issue. It was therefore an immense relief to Cairo when, in

November 1958, a military coup removed the Umma-dominated Government from office and placed in power a Sudanese general who was completely under Nasser's spell. A few months later, negotiations with Khartoum were resumed and, after Nasser agreed to raise his offer of compensation for Wadi Halfa from £10 to £15 millions, Abboud readily reduced his claim from the £35 millions which previous Sudanese Governments had been demanding. The Nile waters issue was also settled. The Sudan's share of the new water supply was raised from 5 to 24 milliard cubic yards annually, while Egypt's rose from 63 to 72 milliards. And in November 1959 the agreement was finally signed which enabled work on the High Dam to begin two months later.

But, except for the Abboud regime in the Sudan, virtually every Arab ruler of importance was, for one reason or another, quarreling bitterly with Cairo at the time of the breach with Syria. Consequently Nasser was beginning to look elsewhere than the Arab world for friends and outlets for Egyptian influence. Not only did he develop an ever closer relationship with Tito; he also intensified his efforts to make and maintain contacts with the outside world. As far back as 1959 he had welcomed to Cairo such diverse personalities as General Franco's Foreign Minister, Fernando Castella, and Fidel Castro's right-hand man, Che Guevara. In the following year he himself paid another visit to India and Pakistan, as well as to Yugoslavia and Greece, and back in Cairo he received President Sukarno of Indonesia – to whom he took a violent dislike on learning that his visitor had tried to get the Egyptian Foreign Ministry to procure a lady to share his bed for the duration of his stay. More notably still, Nasser attended the 1960 session of the U.N. General Assembly. And on this his only visit to the United States, he took the opportunity to hold long discussions with Eisenhower and with such other world leaders as Kruschev, Tito, Nehru, Macmillan, Kwame Nkrumah and Castro. He also used the occasion to explain Egypt's aims and aspirations in a speech to his fellow delegates.

But it was in Africa, far more than in the rarefied atmosphere of these high-level consultations, that Nasser saw the greatest scope for Egypt to exercise her influence on world developments. I July 1960 he pledged unstinted Egyptian help in sustaining th newly independent Congolese Government of Patrice Lumumb against the attempts of the 'imperialist' powers to promote th secessionist movement of Moise Tshombe in the Katanga pro vince. In December he tried, unsuccessfully, to get Britain t agree to the establishment of Egyptian consulates in East Afric as part of the price of restoring diplomatic relations to full ambas sadorial level. Also throughout this period, Cairo Radio's Africa service, with Nasser's full knowledge and approval, poured fort a constant flow of nationalist propaganda to all of Black Afric and even to Ethiopia, whose Emperor Haile Selassie complaine bitterly that the Moslem minority in his country was being incite to revolt against their Christian rulers.

February 1961 saw Egypt sending arms to help the Congoles rebel 'Government' of Antoine Gizenga, which had been estab lished at Stanleyville on the deposition of Lumumba. Whe Lumumba was shortly afterwards murdered, Nasser accused th Belgians, as the former colonial power, of complicity in the crime And while the Cairo police turned a blind eye, a group of Egyp tian students burned the Belgian embassy to the ground. Tw months later, he was declaiming vigorously against the abortiv American invasion of Cuba at the Bay of Pigs, while in Damascu the Ministry of Education cancelled a visit by the band of th University of Michigan as a mark of its disapproval.

In the spring of the same year, Archbishop Makarios, th Cypriot leader, visited Cairo to be followed by Presidents Sekou Touré and Keita of the former French African colonies of Guine and Mali – the former somewhat startling Nasser by suggestin a form of union between Guinea and the UAR. In June, Cair took yet another step towards identifying UAR policy wit Black Africa when the Foreign Ministry announced that relation had been broken with South Africa in protest against the Pretori Government's policy of apartheid. And to round off a hecti twelve months of international activity, in September Nasse attended the Belgrade conference of the non-aligned nations along with Nehru, Haile Selassie, Makarios, Bourguiba and representatives of several other Asian and African states, both Arab and non-Arab.

Nor was all this dabbling in world affairs, and especially African issues, merely a device to add to Nasser's prestige. Of course he was happy to appear on the United Nations stage with the world's great figures, and he was naturally flattered by the attentions which they showed him, just as he had earlier been beguiled by the warmth of his reception at Bandung by Chou En-lai, Nehru and other Asian leaders. And he could not help comparing the esteem which the new leaders of Black Africa evinced for him with the bitterness of his fellow Arab rulers. Yet his desire to play a role in Africa was dictated by political more than personal considerations.

In his *Philosophy of the Revolution* Nasser had written that it was not without significance . . . that our country lies in north-east Africa, overlooking the Dark Continent, wherein rages a tumultuous struggle between white colonisers and black inhabitants for control of its unlimited resources'. Egypt's role in the world was, as he saw it, dictated by the geographical and historical fact that he occupied the cross-roads of Asia and Africa and that the centre of the three concentric circles of Arabia, Africa and Islam lay in Cairo. Africa was the continent of the future and Egypt's second line of political defence. And he felt that in its struggle against the efforts of 'the white man, representing various European nations, . . . to redivide the map . . . we shall not, in any circumstances, be able to stand idly by in the false belief that it will not affect or concern us'. 'I will continue to dream,' he concluded, 'of the day when I will find in Cairo a great African institute dedicated to unveiling to our view the dark reaches of the continent, to creating in our minds an enlightened African consciousness and to sharing with others from all over the world the work of advancing the welfare of the peoples of this continent.'

It was therefore an article of Nasser's faith to uphold nationalism and to fight imperialism in Africa, as well as in the Arab world. Even though he had little personal liking for some of the new African leaders such as Lumumba, of whose cavorting in New York's Harlem district during the 1960 U.N. Assembly's session he strongly disapproved, he could not refuse them his suppor without denying his deepest beliefs. What is more, he wa encouraged by Sekou Touré and others, and by his own Ministe for African Affairs, Mohammed Faik, to believe that the newl independent Black African states not only wanted to be unite among themselves, but were also looking to Cairo for leadership Also, as he had said in his *Philosophy*, 'the frontiers of the Sudan our beloved brother, reach into the depths of Africa'. And at thi point he was beginning to dream of a union which woul embrace Egypt, the Sudan and the Congo and so create a super state, with Cairo as its capital, stretching from the Mediterranea and the Red Sea across to the southern Atlantic.

But there were grave problems as well as opportunities i Africa. American and Israeli influences were hard at work t frustrate Nasser's dreams. In the Congo and Nigeria especially American propagandists never ceased to remind the newly inde pendent Governments of the sufferings of the African popula tion at the hands of Arab slave-traders during the eighteenth an nineteenth centuries. And the Israelis were busily engaged i offering trade, technical assistance and development aid t countries such as Kenya, Tanganyika and Ghana. Israeli agent were also stirring up trouble in the southern Sudan by helping t train the rebel Negro and Nilotic population to fight for secessio from the 'domination' of their Arab rulers in Khartoum.

As long before as April 1958, at the Accra conference o independent African states, Fawzi had asked Kwame Nkrumah Ghana's first President, why he encouraged the Israelis to pene trate the economy of his country, when Egypt and other Ara states were anxious to lend their assistance. Nkrumah had replie that, if the Arabs could match Tel Aviv's contribution in term of finance and technical expertise, he would send the Israeli packing in a matter of weeks. But neither the Arab states indivi dually nor the Arab League as a body were able to respond to th challenge with effective material help. In the event, therefore, th field remained open for Israel, America and the former colonia powers to reap a rich harvest of trade and investment throughou Black Africa.

Moreover, towards the end of 1960, Nasser's African aspirations were to suffer still further disappointment in the Congo, where Lumumba was becoming largely isolated as the pressures of Tshombe's secessionist movement in Katanga, and of the Western powers, bore down upon him. In fact, at this juncture, among the United Nations' forces which had been sent to hold the ring, Lumumba could only count on the Egyptian detachment to support him, the other elements being either neutral or actively hostile. All the major powers involved in the 'peace-keeping' operations, including the United States, were working for his downfall. Nasser was therefore obliged to undertake a painful reappraisal of his Congo policy. However much he might wish to support African nationalism, the chances of Lumumba surviving the existing pressures were now clearly very slight. Certainly they seemed on balance not good enough to warrant the UAR sacrificing the prospects of a better understanding with Washington which Kennedy's recent election seemed to hold out and which would be jeopardised by a confrontation with the Americans in Africa. And since such a confrontation appeared to be more likely if Egyptian troops remained in the Congo to fight for Lumumba's survival, Nasser, with much heart-searching, decided to withdraw his contingent.

Shortly afterwards, Lumumba fell and was succeeded by the American-backed Joseph Kasavubu. Yet although a rebel 'Government' was promptly established at Stanleyville in the interior of the Congo, Nasser nevertheless held to his decision to disengage from the Congo, rejecting alike the rebels' appeals for help and Hammarskold's efforts to dissuade him against withdrawing from the U.N. force. But then, less than a month later, Lumumba was murdered by unknown assassins believed to be acting on orders from Tshombe. Nasser was unable to hold aloof any longer. Faced by what he believed to be a major imperialist drive to retake the Congo and subject it to neo-colonial rule, he announced his decision to recognise the Stanleyville rebels as the 'legitimate national Government of the Congo'. Heedless of the danger of jeopardising his relations with the new American administration, he also sent large quantities of arms via the Sudan to help maintain the rebels' resistance against Kasavubu and his imperialist backer.

But just as he had done in many of his dealings with his fellov Arabs, so in the case of Black Africa, Nasser acted without prope knowledge of the character and susceptibilities of the people o their leaders. Of the arms which he sent to support the Stanleyvill 'Government', many were stolen en route by rebel bands in th southern Sudan; and of those which reached the Congo a larg proportion were smuggled back across the Sudanese border b Gizenga's troops and sold to the southern Sudanese rebels i exchange for beer. In the end the Khartoum authorities wer obliged to stop all further deliveries in order to prevent the south ern rebels becoming better armed than their own troops.

Besides, instead of winning the applause of such African leader as Nkrumah, Nasser's Congo venture aroused their deepest sus picions that he was setting himself up as the new Messiah of Blac Africa, if not actually seeking to carve out a new Egyptian empir with the aid of the Moslem communities in places like Nigeri Mali, Somalia and Tanganyika. Not only was Nkrumah jealou of such pretensions, regarding himself, as he did, as the 'redeeme of all Africa; he was also in no way prepared to jeopardise th substance of Israeli aid which was helping to develop his countr for the shadow of Nasser's patronage and the promises of Ara help which he felt certain would not be fulfilled.

In the event, therefore, all that the UAR's involvement in th Congo achieved was the highly dubious compliment of bein selected as the asylum for Gizenga's rebels when they were dul broken up and defeated by the central Government backed b America, Belgium and other Western countries. For when thes refugees were not wining and womanising in Cairo, much t Nasser's disgust, they spent their time inciting the Congolese an other African students, who had poured into Cairo University i the past few years, to violent demonstrations. An instance of th was the burning of the American Library in 1964, to the Egyptia Government's considerable embarrassment, as a protest again American policy in the Congo.

Admittedly Nasser was later able to make new friends in th Organisation of African Unity, especially among the forme

rench colonies through the influence which the Algerians were
ble to exercise after they had won their independence. But his
ntervention in the Congo in the early sixties brought him little,
° any, political gain and only benefited those who wished to
aint him as a megalomaniac, bent on thrusting his nose into every
vailable trouble-spot in the hope of adding to his own personal
ower and prestige. Sadder still, perhaps, it lost him much of the
onfidence and esteem of Dag Hammarskold with whom, ever
nce the Suez crisis, he had come to build a remarkably close
ersonal, as well as political, relationship and whom he looked
pon as a true friend and counsellor. For, in Hammarskold's
yes, Nasser had set out deliberately to sabotage the efforts of the
Jnited Nations to hold the ring and keep the peace in the Congo,
y first encouraging Lumumba to pursue policies which could
nly perpetuate the existing schisms in the country, and by later
ending arms and money to the Stanleyville rebels to maintain a
tate of civil war.

Yet for Nasser such risks were, at the time, a necessary element in
he struggle against imperialism in Africa. 'We are Africans,' he
ad proclaimed, 'and the people of Africa will continue to look
owards us who hold the northern gate of the continent . . . to
rovide as much help as we can in spreading enlightenment and
ivilisation to the farthest depths of the virgin forest.' And if the
orest was full of wild beasts of whose habits he had no knowledge
r experience, then the need for enlightenment and salvation from
he cunning of the white hunters was that much greater. No less
1 Africa than in the Arab world, Nasser was impelled by a sense
f destiny, the radical driven by the dynamic of his own early
uccess to transmit his revolutionary message to all who were
truggling to gain or to maintain their independence. In short,
nce again he was the prisoner of his own prestige. But, as he had
lready found to his cost, most notably in Syria and Iraq, prison,
vhether occasioned by prestige or any other factor, is not the
est place to gain experience and knowledge of the outside world.
And by 1962 Africa had begun to repeat many of the lessons
vhich the Arab nations had already so rudely taught him.

Chapter 15

The Socialist State

Apart from the quarrels which ensued with the Arab and Communist worlds, Syria's secession from the UAR had two other crucially important side-effects – on Nasser's health and on domestic policy in Egypt. Since 1956, Nasser had been suffering from diabetes. Although incurable, this complaint can be contained by treatment and, in his case, there was no cause for anxiety on the part of his doctors during the early stages. But as with other ailments, worry greatly aggravates a diabetic condition. And by the end of 1961, the stresses and tensions caused by the Syrian problem had brought about a serious deterioration in Nasser's health. On examination, his doctors decided that he was now suffering from what they called 'black diabetes', that some blocking of the arteries was taking place and that this was bound to affect his heart. But the treatment which they advised, namely that the presidential work-load should be reduced, was not one which their patient was likely to accept.

Never willing to delegate to his lieutenants, still less to assume the role of a constitutional ruler without administrative functions Nasser would only consent to spending long periods of the summer months in Alexandria, where he shut himself away from the hurly-burly of Cairo. But for the rest, he disregarded his doctors and far from reducing his work-load he now added to it by insisting, in the wake of the breach with Syria, upon a major internal reconstruction programme in Egypt. Convinced that at least part of the reason for the breach lay in a conspiracy by the feudal and capitalist classes of Syria, he was obsessed with the fear that their equivalents in Egypt would now take fresh heart and if not prevented, would use their wealth and influence to reverse everything that the revolution had achieved since 1952.

Admittedly, the political power of Egypt's feudal Pashas and

he hold of the Wafd over the fellahin had been largely broken by
and reform and by the consequential emancipation of the tenant
armer and peasant. But these measures were working very
lowly. By 1961, only a little over 10 per cent of the land had
been redistributed to some two hundred thousand families and the
ellahin were, as a whole, only marginally better off. Although
he three per cent interest rates had been halved and the time
imit for repayment raised from thirty to forty years, their
expenses, including the costs of irrigation, had more often than
not equalled the income which they could gain from working
heir tiny parcels of new land. At the same time, the old land-
owners, together with the richer peasants, still drew about 60 per
cent of the revenues of Egyptian agriculture, and could still make
an annual income of around £80 per acre from what was left to
hem after redistribution. Also the not ungenerous compensation
paid to them by the Government for the land which they lost had
been reinvested, largely in luxury building projects. These pro-
ects were attracting four times more investment capital than
manufacturing industry and were paying still further handsome
dividends to the rich.

Thus, while the feudal classes might have forfeited their former
political influence, they had lost little of their economic and
financial power. On the contrary, the feudalists of yesterday had
to a large extent become the capitalists of today. Nor had it made
much difference when, in 1961, it was decided to reduce the limit
of agricultural holdings from 200 to 100 acres after the resistance
in Syria to the UAR Government's land reforms had allegedly
caused a 'stirring' among the land-owners of Egypt. For this
further reduction of land-holdings merely added to the compensation payments to the former owners, and so helped to swell the
ranks, and the coffers, of the capitalist caste who Nasser now
suspected might be about to renew their efforts to destroy the
revolution in Egypt.

Nor were the former land-owners the only recent recruits to
the capitalist classes of Egypt. The bourgeoisie as a whole had
greatly benefited from the Egyptianisation measures which followed the revolution and which was accelerated and intensified by

the sequestrations of British and French businesses and propertie after the Suez War. Although they had been allowed no politica say under a system dominated by the military and the ever increasing bureaucracy, they had acquired considerable financia influence within the business community. Moreover this com munity still included such powerful elements as Ahmed Abboud' commercial empire, with its control of shipping lines, sugar mills textile factories and chemicals, and the Misr complex, with it labyrinthine network of associated companies and subsidiaries, al of which had survived almost untouched by the first wave o revolutionary reforms. As Nasser now recalled, the Bank Misr had, in 1958, been foremost in advocating union with Syria because its directors, supported by Dr Emary, the former Financ Minister, then head of the National Bank of Egypt, feared that with the Egyptian cotton-crop mortgaged to Russia, the nationa economy and the five-year industrialisation plan were becoming far too dependent on Soviet assistance. The Misr group's director made no secret of their hope that a union with Syria would re open the channels of trade with Western countries, such as France which were still essential for Egypt's economic needs. Also, being strongly opposed to such tentative steps as the Egyptian Govern ment had taken in the way of nationalisation since the Suez War they thought that a merger with a nation of small capitalists, such as Syria, would help to arrest any further expansion of state ownership in Egypt.

To Nasser's suspicious mind, therefore, it was only natural to suppose that, once the Misr and Abboud groups realised that the union was not going to stop further progress towards nationalisa tion, they too would be involved in the conspiracy to destroy it Having failed to achieve their ends by a merger with Syria, they were now bound to try more direct methods to thwart the progress of the revolution.

To counter any such designs Nasser decided to institute a serie of punitive sequestrations and nationalisation measures. In Octobe 1961, Zacharia Mohieddin announced the arrest of forty promi nent citizens, mostly former Wafdists, and the confiscation of th property of 167 'reactionary capitalists', including all the wealthies

amilies of Egypt. A month later 400 more persons suffered con-
iscation and some eighty banks, insurance companies and other
orporations were placed under 'emergency sequestration'. Then
n December, no less than 367 companies, including the foreign
rade enterprises of the Misr complex, were taken over and
grouped in various state agencies.

Nasser's evolution to socialism was thus an essentially pragmatic
process, based largely on reaction to the collapse of the union
with Syria, and with little, if any, ideological motivation. To be
bound by ideology was to be limited in one's sphere of manoeuvre
and this was something that he would never accept. In the early
days after the revolution, he had been not only bitterly anti-
Communist but, like several of his RCC colleagues, something
of an Islamic fundamentalist and inclined to see in the Moslem
Brotherhood the practical and patriotic alternative to the self-
seeking and unpatriotic Wafdists. Then, after he broke with the
Brotherhood in 1954, he had been encouraged by such colleagues
as Boghdady and Zacharia Mohieddin to seek an alliance with the
upper bourgeoisie, though not with the land-owners, because of
their resistance to agrarian reform.

At this point, he felt the need to create a new managerial class.
The Suez War had resulted among other things in the nationalisation of all foreign-owned commercial agencies and all commercial
insurance companies. These could not be run by the established
civil service and the bourgeoisie seemed to offer the best material
for this purpose. Unfortunately, however, in the angry aftermath
of Suez, the section of the bourgeoisie comprising the Egyptian
intelligentsia, whose education was mainly the product of British
and French schooling, had been under grave suspicion, if not open
attack, as an alien and hence undesirable influence. And having
been in consequence largely dispersed, in many cases to foreign
countries, they were not available to fulfil this need. Besides, as
time passed, Nasser began to see that a managerial class would
conflict with his desire to maintain the absolute paramountcy of
the military regime which he had established. An example of
his thinking in this regard was his decision in May 1960 to
nationalise the press. Since 1956 censorship had been lifted, but at

the same time each newspaper had had to accept a Governmen representative on its staff whose job was to ensure that editori policy toed the Government's line. But Nasser soon decide that the requirements of paramountcy demanded still tighte control. Accordingly, the ownership of such newspapers an printing houses as *Al-Ahram, Akhbar el-Yom, Rose el-Yusef* an *Dar el-Hilal* were vested in the National Union in order to preven so said the announcement, 'the domination of capitalism in th political and social media'.

Thus by 1960 Nasser had already begun to discard his ideas c entrusting the management of Egyptian life to the middle clas And when, after the breach with Syria, he began to suspect tha the bourgeoisie, and the capitalists with whom they were synony mous, were actively planning to put the revolution into revers he opted for a socialist system as the only alternative left ope to him. Or, as he put it two years later in the National Charte which formally proclaimed Egypt to be a socialist state, socia ism had revealed itself as 'a historical inevitability imposed b reality'.

In this choice he was strongly opposed by those of hi colleagues who hailed from bourgeois backgrounds. Zachari Mohieddin, Boghdady, Kemal ed-Din Hussein and Hassa Ibrahim were especially nervous that a policy of widesprea nationalisation would further damage confidence at home an abroad in Egypt's economic stability. They pointed out that, i the panic which accompanied the Suez crisis of 1956, industri investment had fallen by as much as 50 per cent and they con tended that a large-scale nationalisation programme could fatall injure the recovery which had only recently begun to take effec Besides, they argued that there was no reason to suppose tha socialism would either help the Egyptian people or be welcome by them. In their view what was wrong with Egyptian societ under the monarchy was not that there were too many capitalist but far too few. They had enthusiastically supported land reforn because it was designed to extend private ownership and give th fellahin a stake in their own country. But nationalisation was a altogether contrary approach, in that it introduced the kind o

ystem where everything belonged to everybody, yet nothing
elonged to anybody.

Nasser, however, overruled all these objections. Industrial
avestment, he said, might be recovering after Suez, but it was
eing channelled into areas of industry which brought handsome
rofits to the investors and small gain to the economy as a whole
nd to the five-year industrialisation plan in particular. Thus
vithout even consulting the majority of his Cabinet he went
head with his nationalisation policy. Yet the immediate effect of
he 1961 measures was a peculiarly Nasserist system, which bore
mall resemblance to a truly socialist society.

For one thing, there was no democratic control over the
ew state-owned industries and services or over the Economic
Agency, the Government's central planning authority, which
Hassan Ibrahim had somewhat reluctantly agreed to direct from
s inception in 1957. Instead, a new technocracy, largely staffed
y Egypt's officer corps, was superimposed on the existing
ureaucracy. In all, some 1,500 officers were appointed to senior
osts in the economic administration and what the Left chose to
all the 'popular forces' were allowed no part whatsoever in
unning or supervising the ever-growing apparatus of the state.
Nor were any of the intellectuals, on whom Heikal vented his
corn in *Al-Ahram* as cowards who before 1952 had kept aloof
rom the battle for fear of losing their jobs at the hands of the
nonarchical Establishment. All of which prompted one young
eftist editor to utter the anguished cry, 'How can there be
ocialism without socialists?'

Moreover, after the dust had settled on the 1961 nationalisation
ecrees, some two-thirds of Egypt's economy still remained in the
rivate sector. Apart from agriculture which was almost wholly
wned by land-owners and peasants, 79 per cent of the commer-
ial sphere was in private hands. So was 67 per cent of the building
ndustry, and 56 per cent of industry in general. Indeed, even after
Nasser decided two years later to apply more far-reaching
neasures – which resulted in 80 per cent of Egyptian industry
eing taken over by the state – the position of agriculture and the
uilding trade still remained unaffected. And since these two

industries employed some 57 per cent of the labour force, th
meant that more than half of Egypt's workers were still employe
by private enterprise.

More important still, these figures showed that, at the end of i
five-year course, the 1958 industrialisation plan had not mad
the expected headway. Despite all the efforts of the Governmer
to boost industrial expansion by state control and investmen
Egypt had not been transformed, as was hoped, into an industri
state. Likewise Nasser had failed in his drive to increase th
availability of employment in face of what he once describe
as 'a growth of population which could be counted in millions . .
and which had (in the past) afflicted the productive apparatus wit
a paralysis that was virtually total'. All that could be claimed fc
his peculiar brand of socialism was that the hold of the capitalis
over industry had been broken, and the strategic sectors of th
economy prised from the grasp of the bourgeoisie. But such gair
as had come from these changes were for the technocrats mor
than the people, and for bureaucracy rather than efficiency.

At the same time, it must be admitted that, in between thes
two major attacks on capitalism, Nasser did go through th
motions of creating a new representative system, known as th
Arab Socialist Union. This was to take the place of the largel
defunct National Union – the successor of the Liberation Rally
which, with only four representatives of the workers among
total of 342 deputies on the so-called Council of the Nation, ha
fallen pitifully short of the requirements of a representative Parli
ment.

In the early days Nasser used to tell foreign diplomats tha
possibly after five years of single-party government, he woul
allow a two-party system to be introduced. But, in fact, he nev
seriously intended any such thing. Apart from his deep-seate
distrust of political parties, he would never permit anyor
opposed to the regime to sit in Parliament. And he could nc
accept that representation of the people required that they l
asked to choose between one party and another. Nevertheless, h
could not altogether ignore those of his colleagues who felt th
need for some supervision of the ever-growing bureaucrat

1achine. In May 1962, therefore, he proclaimed a new National
Charter, which was designed to ensure in future that the nation's
easants and workers secured half of the seats at all levels of
gypt's political and popular organisations because, he said, 'they
re the majority of the people and the longest deprived of their
ights'. The authority of the new Arab Socialist Union was also
) be raised above that of the Executive machine and its elected
ouncils were to function at every level from the village right up
) the Parliament itself.

Among other reforms was the introduction of a new code of
ghts for women. Nasser had until recently been opposed to such
leas, believing that a woman's place was in the home and not in
1e polling-booth. But Madame Tito had talked him round by
rguing that he could not claim to have achieved a complete
:volution until he conceded equal rights for the women of
gypt. In his speech introducing the new National Charter, Nasser
1erefore declared that henceforth 'Woman must be regarded as
qual to man and she must shed the remaining shackles that
npede her freedom of movement, so that she can play a construc-
ve and vital part in shaping Egyptian society.' He also accepted
1e need for birth-control which, despite his ever-present fears of
ver-population, he had hitherto opposed on the grounds that it
1ight adversely affect the maintenance of an adequate army. And
ow for the first time the concept of family planning received the
1dorsement of the regime.

In purely abstract terms, Nasser no doubt believed all that
e said in introducing the National Charter as a means of giving
1e Egyptian people a greater say in the government of their
ountry. But then it is equally certain that he genuinely realised
1at he should delegate more of his work to Boghdady, Mohieddin
1d other colleagues. Nevertheless, just as he found it impossible
) delegate when the time came, so he was unable to fulfil the
romise which he held out that the ASU's authority would be
1perior to that of the Executive. At the lower levels, where some
,000 committees worked in the villages and townships of Egypt,
1e new system functioned reasonably well. Out of a national
1embership of four and a quarter millions, the workers and

peasants numbered more than one half. But, for all this, the ASU
was a body without a head. It might have been proclaimed as the
crucible of all the socialist forces of the country. But it soon
became, at least at the top, almost indistinguishable from its
predecessor, the National Union. Shot through with members of
the officer corps and government officials, its Executive Committee of one hundred contained only two representatives of the
non-Communist Left. True, some nine years later, Ali Sabry, who
became its chairman in 1965, was to use the ASU to conspire
against President Sadat after Nasser's death. But, so long as Nasser
lived, whenever there appeared the smallest sign that this body
was trying to exercise the powers conferred on it by the National
Charter, the Government would bear down with overwhelming
strength to reassert the paramountcy of the bureaucratic machine
and the military technicians who ran it.

In effect, therefore, socialism remained largely a slogan of the
regime, however many companies might be taken over by the
state. Akram Hourani summed up the disenchantment of the
Left by describing the National Charter with undisguised malice
as 'just words'. But, if Nasser's socialism was more of an oratorical
device than a genuine belief, it nevertheless helped to deprive him
of the services of three of his former RCC associates, including one
of the ablest members of his Cabinet, Abdel Latif Boghdady.

Neither Boghdady nor his colleagues, Hassan Ibrahim and
Kemal ed-Din Hussein, had been at all happy about the first
batch of nationalisation measures in 1961. Still more were they
disturbed when Nasser, towards the end of 1963, without even
consulting the Chairman of the National Bank, decided to plunge
ahead in his assault on the capitalist class with measures designed
to take over 80 per cent of Egyptian industry. Then, a few months
later, Boghdady was appalled to learn that Field Marshal Amer
was to be appointed to the newly created post of First Vice-
President. For he knew only too well that this step had been taken
in response to advice, following the assassination of President
Kennedy in the previous November, that Nasser should make
clear whom he wished to succeed him, should he too die pre-
maturely, so as to avoid the otherwise inevitable struggle for

ower among the five existing Vice-Presidents. Boghdady was
rongly opposed to Amer's 'promotion' not only because, as
Nasser's senior lieutenant ever since the formation of the RCC, he
felt personally slighted at being overlooked, but also because he
was certain that Amer was in no way equipped to take on the
awesome responsibilities of the presidency. Coming on top of the
renewed nationalisation drive, this was the last straw. Boghdady
and Nasser had reached the parting of the ways. Accordingly, he
resigned from the Government, along with Ibrahim and Hussein,
rather than remain associated with decisions which he deeply
believed to be as unwise as they were unjustified.

Ibrahim's and Hussein's relations with Nasser had been somewhat astringent over the past several years. Both of them were
much too conservative in outlook for their President's liking. And
though Hussein had until very recently believed that Nasser
could do no wrong, the fact that, of all the old RCC, he had been
the closest to the Moslem Brotherhood made him still more
suspect. With Boghdady however it was another story. Although
always courageously outspoken whenever he found it necessary
to criticise Government policy, he was nothing if not completely
loyal to Nasser. He had also been an outstandingly successful
Minister of Planning and Local Government. Quietly and with
great efficiency he had transformed the skylines of Cairo and
other cities, pulled down the worst of the slums, rehoused the
inhabitants in new suburban apartments and generally won the
highest praise for his achievements. Yet because of his success and
the plaudits which it had brought him, Nasser's suspicious mind
had told him that Boghdady had to be intriguing against him. As
he had several times admitted to Trevelyan and other acquain-
tances, he had been a conspirator for so long that he could not
break the habit of suspecting everybody. He therefore genuinely
believed that no-one could amass so much popular acclaim as
Boghdady had done without being tempted to use it to seek even
more power for himself. And the fact that Boghdady had begun
to fall out with him in the dark days which followed Syria's
breach with the union was for Nasser just too much of a coincidence not to suggest some devious intrigue against the regime.

Suspicion was Nasser's besetting sin and principal weakne:
For, as Zacharia Mohieddin never tired of telling him, not on
did his distrust of his colleagues cause disharmony in the Gover:
mentes, it also made him interfere continually in their work a:
so added still further to the already huge burdens which he had
bear. Moreover, the more he involved himself in the details
administration, the less time he had to argue or discuss the bro:
lines of policy with his colleagues. This inevitably meant th
the really important policy decisions were taken after consult
tion with one or two associates, and were then imposed on t
Cabinet without ever being properly thought out. But Mohie
din's remonstrances were to no avail. Nasser continued to deci
on all major issues himself and to enquire into every detail
administration. Worse still, he pried into the private lives of l
Ministers, whose telephones were tapped and any recordin
suggesting misconduct on their part kept in his personal fil
More than one Minister whom Nasser decided to dismiss f
incompetence or opposition to some policy decision was shock
to hear the record of some long-forgotten telephone conversati
with a girl-friend played back to him as proof that he was n
morally fitted to hold ministerial office.

Although himself incorruptible, Nasser did not insist on l
associates following his example. Indeed, provided always that l
knew what they were up to, and so long as they were not involv
in treachery, he was by no means averse to colleagues such
Amer, Ali Sabry and Shams Badran taking advantage of th
positions. For, in this way, he would have some evidence agai:
each of them which he could use, whenever he might decide
dispense with their services. He was also a great lover of goss
and it was because of this that Heikal, whose lively mind a:
attentive ear gleaned a great deal of chit-chat about the social a:
political goings-on in Cairo, first became one of his close ass
ciates. Heikal had first met Nasser in Neguib's house on the e
of the revolution when he was a young reporter for *Akhl
el-Yom*. At such a moment, Nasser had naturally regarded t
presence of any pressman with the gravest suspicion and h
instantly demanded that Neguib should get rid of him. But lat

through the Amin brothers, who were then Heikal's employers, he met him again and soon formed a considerable liking for Heikal's quick wit. Even before his appointment as editor of *Al-Ahram* following the nationalisation of the press, Heikal had managed to become Nasser's unofficial press adviser and, once installed at *Al-Ahram*, he was very soon to make himself the President's mouthpiece.

Nasser's liking for gossip also brought him one of his very few friendships with the opposite sex. Normally he was not at ease with women, whose conversation bored him. But one exception to this rule was Aliya es-Solh, the daughter of the late Prime Minister of Lebanon, Riad es-Solh, and a young journalist of great charm and intelligence who lived in Cairo. Although, as usual, shy at their first encounter in 1955, Nasser soon warmed to this daughter of the 'old regime'. For not only was he intrigued by her modern outlook, but he was even more beguiled by her endless fund of gossip about her native Lebanon. He did not even object to her arguing with him about politics, except in front of his wife. And he would sometimes try to flatter her by saying, for instance, that in order to please her he had mentioned her father in a recent broadcast about Lebanon, although she knew well enough that he had done so to impress his Lebanese listeners.

But, along with many other personal friendships, this one was to dissolve after the break-up of the UAR. Shutting himself away in Alexandria for long periods, especially in the summer months, Nasser grew morose and aloof towards his former associates. Prone to increasing irritability and frequently no longer even gracious with his old friends, he would sometimes say, if he thought a colleague's 'How are you?' was more than a casual greeting, 'Why do you ask? Do you hope that I am unwell?' Nor did he indulge any more in reminiscences about the revolution and those days when the Free Officers were a happy band of brothers with one simple aim in view. Even some of his sense of humour seemed to have deserted him. For, whereas in the past he had greatly enjoyed being told the jokes which were being bandied around against him, he now threatened to have any who joked about him arrested. The endless telephone conversations with the Amin brothers and other friends, which usually took place at night and frequently lasted for three and four hours at a time, were abruptly discontinued.

Nasser had never been happy to spend time giving interviews to people whom he did not know. And his own humble origins had given him a kind of inverted snobbery which made him particularly averse to mixing with what he regarded as rich people. For instance, he only once set foot inside the Gezira Sporting Club, the former social Mecca of Cairo, and because he so disliked the people he met there, he vowed that he would never go again. Nevertheless, his Chef de Cabinet, Amin Shaker, was able to persuade him in the early stages to swallow some of his prejudices and make himself available to important visitors, Egyptian and foreign, instead of remaining shut away from the outside world as he and his military colleagues had been throughout their army careers. But, in 1961, Shaker's influence was removed and an ambitious intriguer, Sami Sharaf, took over as Chef de Cabinet, bent on furthering his own career above every other interest.

A particularly disreputable character, who was more than usually addicted to loose living, Sharaf had been involved in an abortive army plot in 1954 and had distinguished himself by betraying his fellow conspirators to Zacharia Mohieddin, the Minister of the Interior, who later appointed him to a post on his staff. Sharaf became a specialist in secret police work. But there was little love lost between him and his boss and, when Nasser one day required an extra private secretary, Mohieddin was happy to pass him on to the presidency. There he went from strength to strength. His experience in snooping being regarded as a considerable asset by his new master, he set about organising a special presidential intelligence service to pry into the activities both public and private of every Minister and senior official. And when Shaker was appointed ambassador to Belgium, he was duly promoted to take his place.

Most unfortunately, Sharaf's appointment coincided with Nasser's decision to withdraw into his shell and cut himself adrift from some of his most loyal, if also most outspoken, colleagues.

Sharaf jumped at this opportunity to deploy his conspiratorial skills. Except for a few select visitors, everybody was denied access to the President. Along with every other foreign representative, save for the Yugoslav Ambassador, Harold Beeley and John Badeau saw Nasser only on rare occasions.

Thus wrapped in a protective cocoon of yes-men, Nasser became increasingly intolerant of criticism and ever more inclined to hear only what he wanted to hear and even to allow untrue and exaggerated reports of good news to be fed to the people. Saidi that he was by birth, he was now less than ever ready to listen to arguments from his Ministers and more inclined to believe that any who criticised his policies were plotting against him, especially if Sharaf's intelligence service had reported unfavourably on them. Said Marei, the Minister of Agriculture and a successful farmer in his own right, was one of the victims of this combination of intolerance and suspicion. Honest and practical man that he was, Marei told Nasser that his demand for the reclamation of more than 40,000 acres of land per year was not a practicable proposition. However, Ali Sabry insisted that, according to his so-called 'expert' contacts, as much as 200,000 acres could be reclaimed annually. And after the President had been reminded that Marei had served as a Member of Parliament in the Farouk era, he was duly dismissed from office. Likewise Sarwat Okasha, the Minister of Information and Culture, was forced to resign after he and Nasser had quarrelled about cultural policy. Okasha had insisted that quality rather than quantity should be the guideline in the dissemination of culture and he had hotly disputed Nasser's view that it should be fed to the people in the same way as information was pumped out by the press and radio. But to no avail. Hatem was appointed in his place and Okasha was obliged to accept a transfer to the chairmanship of the National Bank of Egypt.

One of the few among Nasser's close colleagues to benefit from the advent of Sharaf to the presidential entourage was Ali Sabry, who lost no time in ingratiating himself with the new presidential assistant. Sabry, then Minister of State for Presidential Affairs, was an extremely ambitious young man, a consummate intriguer and a skilled veteran of the intelligence service, in which he had spent most of his air force career. An unattractive and unscrupulous personality who hardly ever had a kind word to say about anybody, he was most unpopular with all of the old RCC especially Boghdady and Zacharia Mohieddin. But he had commended himself to Nasser as a highly efficient assistant during the years which he had spent in the presidency. And it was often enough for Sabry to speak against someone for Nasser to dismiss that person immediately. Also Sabry had few, if any, fixed principles and could be relied upon to bend whichever way the prevailing wind might blow. In July 1961, seeing that his master was moving rapidly towards his own special brand of socialism, he gave a press conference at which he extolled the benefits which nationalisation would bring in mobilising and developing the economic resources of the UAR. Athough generally regarded as anti-American and pro-Russian, he was in fact no less willing than Nasser to accept whatever aid America might offer; and he was careful not to allow the personal bitterness engendered by his abortive quest for American arms in 1953 to affect his political judgement. In short, he was everything that Nasser, especially at this moment, wanted in the way of ministerial material – an efficient secretary who would follow where his President led without argument or criticism.

True, when Nasser decided three years later to appoint Zacharia Mohieddin as Prime Minister, he told a former colleague that Sabry had been unfit for the job as he was too indecisive and could not control the Cabinet. But, in 1962, he thought very differently of him. Sickened partly by his diabetic condition partly by the hostility of his fellow Arabs, he felt himself hemmed in by adverse circumstances and, egged on by Sharaf, he longed to rid himself of those in his Cabinet who now seemed to be for ever criticising his policies. His closest colleagues seemed to be turning against him in opposition to the nationalisation programme. Worse still, he was beginning to feel completely cut off from the army over which Amer had been allowed to exercise absolute authority as Commander-in-Chief. Yet, since he never liked new faces, any more than he now liked many of the old

nes, the problem of changing his Cabinet seemed insoluble until,
n September 1962, he conceived the idea of appointing Ali Sabry
s Prime Minister.

Not surprisingly, his intention was hotly opposed by his
ormer RCC colleagues. But all that Nasser would concede to
heir objections was to entitle Sabry President of the Executive
Council, instead of Prime Minister, for which small mercy his
critics were obliged to be silent, if not thankful. However, when
it came to restoring his authority with the army, Nasser found
Amer an altogether stronger opponent. Amer had used the years
since Suez to build around himself an almost impregnable fortress
of personal popularity with the officer corps, to whom, especially
in cases of hardship, he had never refused a helping hand which
frequently contained a generous offering of cash. And for these
reasons, Nasser had preferred to try to limit Amer's interventions
in politics rather than to assert his own authority in military
affairs and so perhaps provoke a clash with the army. However,
not only had Amer used his paramountcy to protect incompetent
commanders such as Sidky Mahmoud, as well as to delve into the
diplomatic sphere: more recently he had also begun to interfere in
politics and administration. In addition to appointing his cronies
to most of the available ambassadorial posts, several provincial
governors and even one or two Ministers were his nominees.
Nasser therefore now decided that, whatever the repercussions in
the officer corps, it was high time that the Commander-in-Chief
was cut down to size; and the only way to do this was to attack
the root of his authority – his paramount supremacy over the
army.

Nasser accordingly sent for his old friend and told him that he
wanted Mahmoud replaced as chief of the air force, together with
the commanders of the navy and the artillery. As President he was
responsible for every branch of government and he was no longer
prepared to accept presidential responsibility for the armed forces
without having the power to exercise it. Amer objected strongly
to these demands and, as had happened a year before when an
abortive attempt had been made to clip his wings, he threatened
to resign from all his offices, including his vice-presidency. But

this time Nasser would not give way and Amer was obliged to agree to the changes demanded by his President. However, before the necessary orders could be drawn up for his signature, he disappeared to Mersa Matruh where he remained incommunicado for the next several days.

Nasser promptly summoned the other Vice-Presidents and declaring that Amer must be planning a coup, insisted that he be immediately dismissed. But when it was pointed out that, whatever the evidence for this supposition might be, Amer could not be condemned in his absence, he withdrew his demand. And after a long wrangle, it was finally agreed that Nasser should assume the post of Commander-in-Chief and that Amer should be demoted to Deputy Commander. Defence policy would be entrusted to a Defence Council, presided over by the President and the armed forces placed under the supervision of a National Defence Committee, consisting of Boghdady, Amer, Zacharia Mohieddin and Kemal ed-Din Hussein.

It was a brave attempt to restrict Amer's influence. But, in the event, it was no more successful than the futile effort of the previous year. Amer managed to resist almost every attempt of the new Defence Council to control and direct his actions, even to securing the annulment of the order dismissing Sidky Mahmoud from his air force command. Then, after Boghdady left the Government a little over a year later, the new 'supervisory' machinery also ground to a halt. And in fact all that this clash of wills achieved was to cast a permanent cloud over the close friendship which had existed for so long between Amer and his President.

When Boghdady and his two colleagues resigned early in 1964, more than half of the old RCC were no longer in office. Thus, eleven years after the revolution, Nasser was rapidly losing his truest friends at home, as well as quarrelling with his most important allies abroad. In due course, he was to emerge from his self-imposed isolation and to seek to renew some of his old associations. In 1965 he appointed Zacharia Mohieddin as his Prime Minister. In the aftermath of the 1967 war with Israel, he was also to ask Boghdady and Kemal ed-Din Hussein to come back and elp him through the last and darkest hours of his life. But for he moment, far from making any attempt to regain the esteem of his critics, he seemed to go out of his way to alienate them by uch actions as the nomination of Amer as First Vice-President nd hence as his chosen successor. Boghdady and Hussein, already leeply hurt by Nasser's suspicions of their loyalty, were even nore dismayed to find that their leader, while so intolerant and listrustful of their well-intentioned criticisms, could yet be so ndulgent towards Amer's continuous insubordination and inter-erence. And from this moment, both for them and for those other ld comrades of the RCC who elected to soldier on under Nasser's leadership, nothing could ever be quite the same again.

Chapter 16

Abortive Reunion with Syria

For the Egyptians one of the few redeeming features of the early sixties was the decision of President de Gaulle finally to cut France's losses in Algeria and to offer the independence for which the FLN had been fighting since 1954. For the most part Nasser's interest in the North African states was little more than marginal. His periodical rows with Tunisia were usually provoked by Bourguiba whose vanity was constantly affronted by the fact that such an untutored 'upstart' should aspire to control the policies of so intellectual and experienced an Arab leader as himself. Libya had gained her independence before the Egyptian revolution; Tunisia and Morocco had done so shortly afterwards. And, although none of these regimes were what Nasser would have called progressive and all of them had close ties with the Western powers, he never felt the concern for their political associations that he did in the case of such countries as Syria or Iraq. Libya and Morocco might have British and American bases and the French might still be clinging onto Bizerta. But, placed as they were on the western fringe of the Arab world, the North African states did not impinge on the central direction of Arab policy as, for instance, did Iraq under both Nuri and Kassem. And apart from an occasional episode involving an Egyptian Military Attaché in some piece of skull-duggery, there was relatively little interference from Cairo in any of these three North African states.

Algeria, however, had been the exception to this rule. Ever since the FLN fired the first shot in the war of liberation from French rule, Nasser had been determined, as part of his policy of ridding the Arab world of 'imperialist' domination, to see the French evicted from Algeria. To this end he had spent considerable sums of money to help the FLN with arms and propaganda. Also, in the course of his contacts with the Algerian nationalists he had formed a strong personal liking for their leader, Ahmed Ben Bella, who had been treacherously captured by the French in 1956, and had been languishing ever since in a French gaol. Consequently, when de Gaulle announced in March 1962 that a peace settlement had been agreed which would give Algeria independence after nearly seven and a half years of bloody war, Nasser immediately hailed the news as a great victory. Paying tribute to de Gaulle's statesmanship, he added that this most welcome development should open the way for a renewal of friendly relations between France and Egypt.

Two weeks later the trial of the four French officials in Cairo was abruptly stopped and all the accused released, after the prosecution had requested an indefinite postponement. In July, Algeria's independence was formally proclaimed following elections for a national Parliament; Ben Bella, released from prison after the March agreement, was named as Prime Minister by the new Algerian National Assembly; and full diplomatic relations between Egypt and France were restored.

But this single Algerian swallow was not enough to make anything like a summer for Nasser's relations with the Arab world as a whole. Syria was, not surprisingly, proving the most intractable of his problems in this sphere. Six months after secession, utter confusion reigned throughout the country. The Government remained firmly separatist in outlook. Yet Nasserism was still strongly entrenched among the masses and in certain sections of the armed forces. After the humiliation of the recent breach, therefore, the temptation to engage in intrigue against the separatist regime in Damascus was more than Cairo could resist. And in March 1962, on the prompting of Egyptian agents, a group of Nasserist officers of the Syrian army attempted a coup d'état. The President was deposed and, as unionist demonstrations took place in Aleppo, Homs and other towns, a deputation was sent to Cairo to discuss a resumption of the merger with Egypt.

But the coup proved abortive. The Nasserists were not strong enough to hold down their separatist opponents. Within a week, they were being rounded up by elements of the army and police loyal to the Government. As the deposed President returned to office, Hourani seized the opportunity to denounce Egyptian intrigues in Syria and to warn Cairo that, if these activities did not cease, he would disclose certain 'secrets and facts' about Nasser which he had learned as a member of the union Government. Thus, when the dust of the coup and counter-coup eventually settled, all that the Nasserists were to secure was the appointment of a new Prime Minister who, two months later, proposed a partial restoration of the union. But since he equally insisted that, in any new arrangement, Syria should retain her full sovereignty, it was clear that the proposal was intended more to give the Syrian Government an alibi than to heal the breach with Egypt. Not surprisingly therefore nothing more was heard of the matter after Cairo had replied somewhat acidly, through an inspired comment in *Al-Ahram*, that Egypt would be ready to negotiate reunion with any Syrian Government which represented the people and which did not merely play with the concept of unity in order to serve individual or party interests.

However the matter was not allowed to rest there. For within the next few days, an explosion took place which was to shake the very foundations of the Arab League, let alone of the Egyptian-Syrian relationship. In the spring of 1962, the Egyptian Military Attaché in Lebanon, Colonel Zaghloul Abdel Rahman, who in the absence of any Egyptian embassy in Damascus was the focal point of Cairo's under-cover operations against the Syrian regime, got himself seriously into debt by gambling in the casinos of Beirut. In a desperate attempt to recoup his losses he helped himself to his official funds. But his luck was out and, after he had gambled away half a million Lebanese pounds (over £60,000), he decided to throw himself on the mercy of his boss, Abdel Hakim Amer. Typically, the Field Marshal made good the deficiencies in Abdel Rahman's coffers without a word to anyone and allowed him to continue in his post.

Amer's benevolence was, however, poorly rewarded. Abdel Rahman went straight back to the casino and within a few days had lost another half million. This time he knew that he was finished and that not even Amer could save him. And when he was approached by an agent of the Saudi Arabian embassy, who had come to hear of his prodigious losses, he agreed to hand over his secret files on a promise of two million Lebanese pounds, to be paid into a bank in Switzerland where he would be able to escape retribution for his embezzlement. The files, which included lists of Egyptian agents operating in Syria with details of their activities, were duly passed to the Saudis who, anxious as ever to blacken Nasser's name in Damascus, lost no time in forwarding copies to the Syrian authorities. In return, Abdel Rahman received an advance of 10 per cent of the total bribe which, compulsive gambler that he was, he promptly frittered away at the gaming tables. And when it became clear that, with the Syrians raising a public outcry against Cairo, his Saudi paymasters were reneging on the rest of the deal, he tamely surrendered to Egyptian justice and was sentenced to life imprisonment for his treachery.

To Nasser's enemies in Syria this episode was a heaven-sent opportunity to depict Nasser as a blackguard and his supporters in Syria as agents of a foreign conspiracy. The fact that Sarraj had escaped from detention and fled to Cairo a couple of months before was seized upon as added proof that Egypt's President and his henchmen were plotting to destroy Syria's independence. Hourani went even further, accusing Nasser of being a tool of imperialism. As evidence for his charges, he published the minutes of a meeting of the UAR Cabinet in 1960 – no doubt the 'secrets and facts' of which he had spoken after the March coup – which showed that Nasser had argued hotly that military action against Israel would be suicidal and, to prove his point, had produced Kruschev's warning during the Suez fighting that Russia could do nothing to help Egypt.

Hourani also claimed to have inside knowledge of reports from the United States' Ambassador in Cairo, showing that the Americans were well satisfied with Nasser's policies, which had greatly helped to further their plans in the Middle East, and more particularly in Syria. This information, he added, had come to the ears of the Russians and it was because of such evidence of Nasser's 'duplicity' that relations between Cairo and Moscow had deteriorated so far. Nor were the Syrian Government exactly slow in exploiting the opportunity to denounce Cairo. These dastardly

Egyptian intrigues, they insisted, should be exposed at an immediate meeting of all the Arab states. And on July 28, armed with the documentary proof of Abdel Rahman's secret files, Damascus officially called for an urgent session of the Arab League to consider Syria's complaints of Nasser's 'flagrant interference' in her domestic affairs.

The ensuing meeting of the Arab League Council at Shtoura on the Syrian-Lebanese border was the most turbulent ever to take place since the League's inception. Immediately the Egyptian delegation found themselves opposed by an alliance of Syria, Saudi Arabia and Jordan, whose representatives launched into a chorus of denunciation, while the Yemenis and Tunisians looked on in evident satisfaction at seeing their big brother thus chastised. Indeed, apart from the fact that the Iraqis stayed away from the meeting as a mark of their continuing protest against Kuwait's admission to the League, the only crumb of comfort which fell to Nasser from this bitter encounter was the sympathy of the newly elected Algerians. Not content with having caught the Egyptians red-handed, the Syrians rose to the heights of hyperbole by repeating Hourani's allegations and charging Nasser with having worked secretly with Washington to 'liquidate' the Arab-Israeli dispute and sell out the Palestinians. Egypt was also accused of putting pressure on Hassouna, as an Egyptian citizen, to abuse his position as Secretary-General of the Arab League by favouring his own country whenever he could get away with it. Hassouna of course protested indignantly that there was not a single grain of truth in this charge. If anything, he said, Nasser had deliberately avoided seeing him for fear of giving any wrong impressions. But the Syrians would have none of his denials and stubbornly refused to withdraw their accusations.

After six days of this kind of execration, Nasser could stand it no longer and, on August 28, the Egyptian delegation stalked out of the Shtoura conference, muttering threats of Egypt's complete withdrawal from the Arab League. Hassouna was sent bundling after them to Beirut in an attempt to bring them back. But to no avail. Nasser had had enough. He was fully aware that, as a result of Abdel Rahman's treachery, the Syrians had a cast-iron case

gainst him. Even if he had been unaware of the activities of
Egyptian agents in Syria, he could hardly have said so with any
hope of anyone believing him.

But the fury of his opponents had, to Nasser's mind, revealed
something far more significant and sinister than a desire simply to
castigate him for intriguing against the ruling regime in Damascus. From all that had happened at Shtoura he was convinced that
the Syrian separatists were being incited by the Saudis and Jordanians who were merely using the Abdel Rahman affair to pin a
lot of scurrilous charges on him in an attempt to destroy his
prestige and weaken his leadership in the Arab world. The 'syndicate of the Kings' might have lost one of their number when
Feisal of Iraq was killed in the 1958 revolution. But Shtoura had
proved that they were, if anything, more active than ever in their
opposition to Cairo. Indeed not only had they recruited a new
ally in Syria, but they were even reported to be angling for the
support of Kassem's Iraq as well. The Egyptian delegation was
therefore ordered to return to Cairo immediately and three days
later the Shtoura conference broke up in disarray.

But, if Nasser hoped that his threats to pull out of the Arab
League altogether would give his Syrian opponents pause, he was
soon to be disappointed. A few weeks after Shtoura, Khaled el-
Azm formed a new Government and, for the next five months,
the witch-hunt against the unionists in Syria was prosecuted with
an ever-increasing vigour. Azm personally accused Nasser of
'wrecking Arab unity and playing off Syrians against each other'.
Nasserists were blamed for any and every disturbance and hardly
a week passed without a spate of arrests, with accompanying
revelations of plots hatched by the Egyptian embassy in Lebanon.

Nor were Cairo's other antagonists inactive in the wake of the
Shtoura imbroglio. Such hopes as Nasser still nursed that Prince
Feisal would take a more accommodating line towards Egypt
than his brother Saud were now finally shattered. Three months
before, the Saudis had gratuitously insulted Cairo by refusing the
traditional annual offering from Egypt of the holy carpet which
covered Mecca's Kaaba, the focal point of the Moslem pil-
grimage; and Egyptian pilgrims, outraged by this affront, had

immediately cancelled their hajj and returned home. Riyadh had then followed up with a series of attacks on Nasser, echoing Hourani's slanders and charging him with participating in Zionist plots and causing dissension among the Arabs. Indeed, even while the Shtoura meeting was taking place, Feisal had been playing host to King Hussein at Taif, where the two monarchs agreed to establish a joint military command and a coordinated foreign policy.

Admittedly Nasser had helped to aggravate Riyadh by twice publicly receiving a Saudi prince, Talal ibn Abdel Aziz, who had fallen out with his family when he called for democratic rule in Saudi Arabia. But such was the hostility with which the Saudis now laid into Cairo that by the early autumn it seemed that Feisal was moving rapidly, and deliberately, towards a total breach with Egypt. Whether or not this breach could have been avoided no-one will ever know. For within a month of the Shtoura confrontation, a struggle began in southern Arabia which was to end any hope of reconciliation and to involve the Egyptians and Saudis in bitter conflict for almost all of the next eight years.

On September 27, 1962, a group of Yemeni army officers, led by General Abdullah Sallal, staged a coup d'état and deposed the reigning Imam al-Badr who had succeeded to the throne on the death of his father eight days earlier. Forty-eight hours later, Cairo recognised the Sallal regime, although it had little control over the country outside the capital itself and was so insecure that in a matter of a few days it was appealing for the support of Egyptian troops. And within less than a month after the coup, as Saudi Arabia declared for the deposed Imam, Egyptian forces were disembarking in Yemen to help in maintaining the infant republic against the counter-attacks of the Imam's royalist supporters. In November relations between Cairo and Riyadh were formally broken off and, by the end of the year, Egypt and Saudi Arabia were to all intents and purposes at war with each other on behalf of their respective Yemeni clients.

Nasser's interest in Yemen prior to Sallal's coup had never been very intense. Although he had conceded the Yemeni's request for an alliance with Egypt in the middle fifties, he knew nothing of their country and had studiously avoided paying it a visit. He looked upon the Yemen as a potentially useful base for twisting Britain's tail in Aden and the Aden Protectorate, and he certainly did nothing to discourage the periodical border scuffles in which the Imam's tribesmen were prone to engage with their British neighbours. Also, even in the days when relations between Riyadh and Cairo had been most cordial, and he and Saud were at one in opposing the Baghdad Pact, Nasser disliked the idea of Riyadh exercising a monopoly of influence in the Arabian peninsula, and he regarded Yemen as a possible future challenge to Saudi paramountcy in the area.

On the other hand, to be allied to the archaic autocracy of Imam Ahmed, who consulted a fortune-teller before taking any important decision, was something of an embarrassment to him as the leader of the progressive school of Arab states. And in 1956, after the Imam, on his fortune-teller's advice, had declined an invitation to Cairo, Anwar Sadat was sent to Sanaa, the Yemeni capital, to try to persuade the aging ruler to introduce some reforms. Sadat's brief was to suggest that, if the Imam could not democratise his system of government, he should at least delegate some of his absolute powers to his son and heir who, on a recent visit to Cairo, had seemed anxious to seek Egypt's aid and friendship and who seemed to hold considerably more liberal views than his father. But as the Americans had found with Farouk in the late forties, the Imam was in no way prepared to respond to Sadat's proposals and Nasser was obliged to turn to other methods to achieve his aims.

Nor were such means in any way lacking. For in 1955, following the signature of Egypt's defence agreement with the Imam, a sizeable number of Yemeni officers had been sent to Egyptian military academies for training. Also an Egyptian military mission had been established in Sanaa. And when the mission reported through Sadat that the Yemeni army would be a fertile field for Nasserist propaganda, orders were promptly issued to start the necessary processes of indoctrination. The Yemeni officers in Egypt were the first and obvious target, though a number of contacts were also made surreptitiously with their comrades at home by the Egyptians in Sanaa. And for the next five years Cairo's propagandists worked quietly but effectively to inculcate republican ideas into the Yemeni army, while Sadat, who was in charge of the exercise, kept in contact with potential revolutionaries among the senior officers.

In 1961, after the Yemenis had taken the side of Iraq in the Kuwait crisis, relations between Cairo and Sanaa deteriorated sharply. Nasser abrogated the military alliance and began to bracket the Imam's name with King Saud and King Hussein as enemies of Arab unity. At the end of the year, Yemen and Egypt broke off all relations, the Egyptian military mission was sent packing and the Yemeni officers in Egypt were recalled. But in the meanwhile enough had been done to create a strong core of republicanism in the Imam's army and it was therefore merely a matter of time before the rebels would show their hand.

Nine months later, on September 19, the Imam Ahmed died and his son, Saif al-Badr, was proclaimed as his successor. In an attempt to impose his relatively liberal views, Badr promptly proclaimed an amnesty for all political prisoners, as well as a number of much needed social and financial reforms. But, with the autocratic Ahmed out of the way, the republican dog had seen the rabbit and was not to be baulked of its prey. Refusing to take the new Imam on trial, the rebel officers struck eight days after his accession. Seizing and destroying the royal palace, they announced that Badr had been killed and that a republic had been established with General Sallal as leader of the new regime. A number of leading royalists were quickly executed and for the first twenty-four hours it seemed that the coup had succeeded in crushing all opposition. But, directly it was announced that the new Imam had escaped to Saudi Arabia and was organising a counter-revolution, a dramatic change took place. Tribesmen loyal to the monarchy immediately took up arms against the republican regime and, as Sallal realised that he would have to fight a civil war, he unhesitatingly appealed to Nasser for support.

Sadat, who had been the first in Cairo to hear the news of the Yemeni coup, received the call for help from Sallal's Deputy-Premier, Abdel Rahman Baydani, who at this point asked only or one Egyptian fighter to fly over Sanaa as a token of Nasser's backing for the revolution. But a few days later, after Sallal's threats of dire punishment for anyone helping the royalists had failed to stop the tribesmen flocking to the Imam's standard, the republicans began to step up their demands on Egypt. Sadat was now told that troops, tanks and air support were also needed.

Nasser took three days to decide on his answer. But from the first there was never any real doubt as to what his decision would be. True, he had so little information about Yemen that he was reduced to asking Badeau, the American Ambassador, if he had any reports in his files which might give some idea of what sort of country it was. And though the only information which Badeau could find was a copy of a long out-of-date economic report from the United States embassy in Sanaa, Nasser read it with consuming interest and much gratitude.

But, aside from lack of knowledge about Yemen, the only argument against responding to Sallal's plea was that it would bring him into still deeper conflict with the Saudis and the British, since neither Riyadh nor Aden would relish having an Egyptian army on their borders. However Cairo's relations with Riyadh were already so poor that any further deterioration would have been hardly noticeable. Also Nasser had always wanted to counter Saudi influence in the Arabian peninsula. Likewise he had long since declared his intention to drive Britain's military presence from all Arab territory. And Sallal's S.O.S. offered him a chance which might not be repeated to bring pressure to bear on the British in Aden by establishing close ties with the Adeni nationalists from Egyptian bases across the Yemeni border. Besides, it was of no small strategic value for Egypt to establish herself at both ends of the Red Sea.

Apart from these considerations, there was also the standard argument that the Arab revolution was indivisible and that, if it failed anywhere, it might fail everywhere. However little he might know of Yemen or Sallal, Nasser therefore had to support the rebels against the counter-revolution of the royalists. His military advisers were firmly of the opinion that, provided Egyptian help were sent promptly enough, the Imam's supporters would be crushed well before the Saudis could galvanise themselves to join in the fighting. Thus, whether or not he later decided to keep a military presence in Yemen to twist the tails of Britain and the Saudis, his troops should not be involved in any long drawn-out campaign.

But perhaps the reason which, more than any other, decided Nasser to respond to Sallal's call was more emotional than strategic or political. For, as he confided to his closest associates, after the rebuffs and humiliations which he had suffered so recently at the hands of the Syrians, not to speak of Kassem and others, the fact that a fellow Arab state had shown to him, and the world, that his support was needed was a vindication so welcome that, whatever the cost, he could never have turned it down. Nor was this a mere matter of personal prestige. For, as Nasser saw it, if Egypt failed to regain the initiative which she had lost after the breach with Syria, the dynamic of the Arab revolution would be irretrievably lost.

Three days after receiving Sallal's cry for help, Nasser therefore agreed to send Egyptian troops, the first of which embarked on their journey on October 5. And as soon as it became known to the Saudi intelligence service that they were on their way, Riyadh began to pour in men, money and arms to help the deposed Imam. Sallal sent his own troops to the frontier where serious fighting promptly broke out with Saudi as well as royalist forces. A few days later, on December 21, King Hussein joined in the fray with a telegram to the Imam pledging every effort on the part of Jordan to help him regain his throne. And as Sallal's deputy, Baydani, proclaimed to the world that the revolutionary Government's forces were standing by to invade Saudi Arabia by land, sea and air, Nasser found himself compelled by the rush of events to sign a full-scale defence agreement with the Sanaa regime. The original Yemeni demand for one MIG fighter had already become many thousands of men. By the following year Egypt was to have 20,000 troops stationed in Yemen; by 1964 the figure had risen to some 40,000; and before the fighting was finally finished six years after that, it had grown to over 70,000, or nearly half the Egyptian army.

In the end Yemen became what Nasser called 'my Vietnam', when talking to some of his closer friends from the West, a venture more futile and protracted than any other undertaken during his reign and an endless drain on Egyptian resources of men and money to win a war which could never be won. Nevertheless, the decision to intervene was immediately followed by at least a partial revival of Egypt's lost prestige. For within five months of the arrival of the first Egyptian contingent in Yemen, the bitter hostility of Iraq and Syria had been silenced by coups which destroyed the Kassem and Azm regimes. Governments were established in both countries whose first thought was to seek union with Egypt. And for a brief moment, the progressive Arab nations appeared to be on the verge of achieving some element of solidarity.

The coup in Iraq came on February 8, 1963, when, as suddenly and unexpectedly as they had struck against Nuri, the army founded on Kassem and killed him, together with Medhawi and his other principal henchmen. Nasser was of course delighted to see the end of the Kassem regime and he was still more pleased to receive the news that Abdel Salam Aref, who had been sentenced to death for pro-Egyptian activities four years before, had been proclaimed as President of the republic. But his joy over these events was somewhat tempered by the knowledge that it was the Iraqi Baathists who were principally responsible for prompting the army to revolt and not the Nasserist elements with whom the Egyptian intelligence had been in touch ever since the Mosul rebellion. For, if the instigators of Kassem's downfall had been the Baathist International, it was likely that, notwithstanding the appointment of Aref as President, the new regime in Iraq would look more to Syria than to Egypt for guidance.

Still, anything was better than Kassem, and Nasser was not slow to congratulate Aref and the Iraqi people on being once again 'masters of their own destiny'. Two weeks later, after Iraq had resumed her seat in the Arab League Council, a goodwill mission arrived in Cairo from Baghdad and were received with appropriate expressions of the unity of purpose which now existed between the Egyptian and Iraqi elements of the Arab nation. And at the end of the visit the Iraqis announced, with more ambition than accuracy, that they had agreed with Nasser on what would be the basis for uniting the entire Arab world.

Two weeks after this, it was Syria's turn to round on those who proclaimed hatred for Nasser and all his works. On March 8, in the wake of yet another purge of unionists allegedly involved in an Egyptian plot to assassinate Syria's leaders, Azm's Government was overthrown by dissident army units led by Colonel Luway Atassi. Azm took refuge in the Turkish embassy and Damascus Radio announced that the era of bitter separatism was over and a new chapter designed to support Arab unity had begun. But once again, Nasser's joy at seeing his enemies deposed was qualified by the realisation that, as in Iraq, the decisive factor in effecting the change of regime had been the Baath. For the man who emerged from this latest coup as Syria's Prime Minister was none other than Salah Bitar, the Baathist leader, whom Nasser remembered much more vividly for subscribing the act of secession in 1961 than for his claim to have been Syria's principal pro-Egyptian advocate in earlier days.

For all the sudden semblance of harmony between the progressive Arab states, Nasser was therefore none too happy about these developments. It was galling enough to know that all the efforts of the Egyptian intelligence service had been so comparatively ineffective and that, only after Abdel Rahman had 'compromised' every Egyptian agent in Syria and so brought all their activities to a standstill, had a coup been staged which succeeded in getting rid of the Government. Several years later Nasser could jokingly tell his Western friends that the only successful coups in the Arab world were those which his intelligence service had no hand in organising. But at the time he saw little to laugh at in this inference. Besides, he now found himself confronted in Syria, and to a lesser extent in Iraq as well, with new Governments created and dominated by the Baath whom he distrusted almost as deeply as those they had overthrown.

True, in the previous year, Bitar had come to repent his support for secession. After a traumatic public self-criticism, he had broken with the leftist 'Young Turks' and other Baathist factions who fired with revolutionary romanticism, had chosen the road of total independence and derided him for protesting anew that 'Nothing Arab can be done without Egypt and Egypt is Nasser'. True too, Nasser, who had never disliked and distrusted Bitar as he did Hourani and even Aflaq, believed his repentance to be genuine enough. But he nevertheless felt that he was a highly confused personality and he feared that, if Bitar's fellow Baathists had prevailed on him in the past to deny his belief in union, they could do so again.

Moreover, Bitar had not been in office more than twenty-four hours when the new Iraqi Vice-Premier, a leading Baathist in Aref's Government, descended on Damascus to discuss joint military arrangements, which Cairo not surprisingly interpreted as a first step towards the creation of a Baathist union between the two countries. And as Nasser saw it, while the latest coups in Baghdad and Damascus might have ended the hostility towards Egypt, they had thrown up something which could be even more difficult for Cairo to handle. For one thing, it seemed that an underlying alliance might develop between Syria and Iraq which it had been Cairo's purpose to prevent since long before the revolution. For another, this alliance would, by definition, be dedicated to a proposition for Arab unity which could all too easily shift the centre of Arabism away from Cairo and so threaten Egypt's paramountcy in the same way as Nuri had tried to do with his concept of a 'Fertile Crescent' with its capital in Baghdad.

In fact, such worries were somewhat exaggerated. Even though the Baath had been able to function underground in Syria and Iraq, the measures taken to suppress the party in these countries had deprived the national formations of their former close liaison with their international 'high command'. As a result, they had become virtually autonomous underground bodies with little or no central coordination. The idea of an Iraqi-Syrian union under the supranational control of the Baath was therefore scarcely a practical possibility. Nevertheless, Nasser was nagged by the fear of a Baathist Fertile Crescent and it was in this anxious frame of mind that he received, a few days after the Bitar Government took office in Damascus, a proposal for a conference in Cairo to discuss the possibilities, not only of recreating the union of Egypt and Syria, but of extending it to include Iraq as well.

As with Sallal's appeal for support in Yemen, there could be no other answer but yes to this proposal. To have refused would have been to deny Egypt's unifying role in the Arab world. Yet Nasser was consumed with doubts as to whether this was another trick to ensnare him in some undertaking in which Egypt would bear the responsibilities and her partners would gain all the advantages. Dearly as he might want to savour again the adoration of the Syrian populace, which he had found so unforgettably warmer than anything his Egyptian subjects had shown him, he scented great dangers in reviving the union with the Syrian Baath. However much romantic satisfaction he had felt after 1958 over what he regarded as a marriage between the rich Egyptian and the relatively poor Syrian girl, he simply could not face the humiliation of a second divorce.

Still less did Nasser want to take on Iraq as a second bride, whose fractious Kurdish cousins would involve him in continual family quarrels of the kind which had kept them for so long in constant ferment against whoever ruled in Baghdad. Much as he liked Aref, with whom he felt that he could work in harmony, he suspected that the Iraqi leader's principal purpose in seeking union with Egypt was to strengthen his personal position. Aref had been nominated as President by the Baathists who overthrew Kassem solely because, long before 1958 and even before Kassem became imbued with revolutionary ideas, he had been the lynch-pin of the nationalist movement in the Iraqi army, whose support was essential to any Government. But his Cabinet was packed with Baathists who made no secret of their intention to run the country in their own way. And Nasser had no desire to become involved in internal political squabbles in Iraq by allowing Aref to use him as a weapon to resist Baathist domination. If his Syrian experiences had taught him anything, they had certainly taught him to beware of that kind of entanglement.

For all these reasons, when the tripartite unity talks opened in Cairo on March 14, 1963, Nasser approached the subject with the greatest caution. From the very first session he maintained as a constant refrain that he could never again trust the Baath after the treachery with which they had destroyed the UAR. 'If it is the Baath party which now rules Syria,' he said and kept on saying, 'then I am absolutely not prepared to hold any discussion. Unity with all of Syria, that I am prepared for. Unity with the Baath party, I say to you: "Sorry, once stung, twice wise".' While he admitted that 'mistakes were committed during the previous union', he insisted that most of them had been committed by the Baath who had 'worked to destroy the UAR from envy and jealousy'. The resignation of Bitar and Hourani had been a 'crime', as was the subsequent secession which had been planned by the Baath and their supporters in the army. 'I personally did not rule Syria,' he insisted, 'it was ruled by Syrians.' There had been a regional Executive Council of which the chairman was always a Syrian and it was not true to say that Egypt had dominated Syria. But what, he asked, was the situation now? Had there been a revolution or a coup d'état? 'Does the army or the Cabinet rule Syria? Is the regime Baathist or Arab nationalist?' Such questions, he concluded, had to be clarified before any progress could be made in discussing another union.

From start to finish Nasser's performance at the tripartite conference was a tour de force; and if he turned some of the facts about the previous union inside out, he succeeded in putting the Syrians on the defensive for all of the twenty-four days of talks. Indeed the verbatim record of these discussions is probably the most remarkable of all available revelations of Nasser's dealings with his fellow Arabs. At every session he completely dominated the proceedings, in which he alone was reverently addressed by his official style of 'Mr President' or 'Your Excellency', while other delegates were referred to as 'Brother Salah' or 'Brother Talib'. On frequent occasions he had the Syrians and Iraqis contradicting each other and quarrelling among themselves and throughout he displayed an extraordinary knowledge, not only of the utterances and intrigues of his Arab adversaries, but also of the constitutional history of America, Russia and other powers, on which he drew when discussing the form which the prospective union should take. Reluctant from the start to agree to the re-creation of the old union, still less to its extension to include Iraq, he never ceased to stress his hatred and suspicion of the Baath, who he claimed had never been truly representative of Syrian opinion; and he dwelt constantly on his fear that a tripartite union would place him 'between the hammer and the anvil' of the Baathist Governments in Damascus and Baghdad. Finally, he insisted that if any union were to be acceptable to Cairo, the existing political parties had to give way to 'popular organisations' such as the Arab Socialist Union of Egypt.

Nor did the Syrian delegates really seek to defend themselves against these attacks on what Nasser called their record of perfidy towards the union. On the contrary, they seemed to roll with every punch. While they put most of the blame for the secession on Hourani who, they said, was so embittered by his lack of authority that he had pushed Bitar into resigning, they did not dispute Nasser's indictment of the 'mistakes' made by Syria after 1958. As to the present day, they protested vigorously that Hourani, together with the reactionaries who had brought about the rupture, had now been 'isolated' and that the Baath, purged of such elements, were 'working for unity as an article of faith'. The present Syrian Government, they insisted, were a national front, not a purely Baathist regime. They even seemed ready to agree to the substitution of 'popular organisations' for political parties.

But Nasser was not prepared to let it go at this. He had plunged in the dagger of his pent-up bitterness and he was determined to give it a sharp twist. Why, he asked, had all the grievances about Egyptian rule appeared after the rupture? Bitar and Hourani had never complained to him during the union. Nor had they given him the slightest inkling that they were about to resign when they came to see him in the autumn of 1959, although their party caucus had, so he subsequently discovered, already ordered them to leave the union Government. As for the complaint, which had again been voiced after the rupture, that Egyptians had engaged in cut-throat commercial competition in Syria, nothing could be more ridiculous, coming from a people who for years past had had literally thousands of mercantile businesses, great and small, throughout Egypt, especially in Alexandria.

Nasser's pet hate was Hourani and repeatedly he came back to his accusations. How could Hourani contend that Cairo forced its rule on Syria when no law was ever promulgated by the union Cabinet before being discussed by the Syrian Executive Council? He had personally done his best to associate Hourani with his plans and had taken him on his visit to Russia in April 1958. But he had been rewarded for his efforts by a stream of bitter falsehoods. He had been accused, for instance, of insisting on the abolition of the political parties when, in fact, it was the Syrian army deputation who had pressed this demand, when they forced the union on him in February 1958. Still worse, he had been charged with paying huge sums of money to buy agents in Syria. But where and who were these agents? His supporters in Syria were entirely voluntary, he blandly asserted, and not the 'doormen of the Deuxième Bureau', as had been suggested by Hourani and his clique. As for the money paid by Cairo, this had been given to help in easing the lot of pro-Egyptian Syrians who were suffering in prison for their sympathies, not to organise espionage or subversion.

Nevertheless and in spite of all these calumnies, Nasser said that he would not oppose a new effort to strengthen Arab unity. But he was none too keen on the idea of a tripartite union in which Egypt would be caught between 'the hammer and the anvil' of her two Baathist partners. The Syrian Baath appeared to be advocating Iraqi participation as a means of deliberately weighting the scales against Egypt. After all, the Iraqi delegation had themselves admitted to the conference that their Revolutionary Command Council, who were the effective rulers of Iraq, were entirely Baathist. Seen from Cairo's angle, therefore, a tripartite union looked like a 'manoeuvre to secure two votes for the Baath against one for Egypt'. For these reasons, Nasser proposed that the union of Egypt and Syria be re-created forthwith and a study be made of the possibilities of Iraq acceding to it at some later date. This, he suggested, would give time for Iraq to 'complete her revolution', by which he meant, of course, time to rid herself of Baathist influence.

Not surprisingly, this idea commended itself neither to the

Syrians nor to the Iraqis. Nasser therefore proposed as an alternative that a tripartite union be declared in principle immediately
but that its actual formation be staggered, with Egypt and Syria
joining at once and Iraq coming in after a lapse of three to four
months. Surprisingly enough, he even suggested that, as a last
resort, Syria and Iraq might initiate a union which Egypt would
join at a later stage. But he stressed that, whichever method they
chose, they should proceed step by step. If union were to fail a
second time, it would be an even greater disaster than that of
1961. Yet, if it had to fail, it were better to do so when only two
of the three nations were involved.

However, both the Syrian and Iraqi delegations would have
none of these variations of their original proposal. Nothing
short of an immediate tripartite union would satisfy them. The
Iraqis would not hear of a union with Syria alone, protesting
their vehement dislike of any arrangement which would appear
to isolate Egypt and so play the game of the imperialist powers.
The interests of the whole Arab nation, they said, required them
to go hand in hand with their brothers in Egypt and Syria. Of
course, they had their problems arising from the overthrow of
Kassem, but why, they asked, should they have to wait in the
wings, if they considered themselves ready to play their part on
the stage? Likewise, the Syrians said that they had 'always considered Egypt as the headquarters of Arab nationalism, due to her
geographical, social and cultural situation'. Union with Iraq
alone might have certain 'party advantages', but they insisted that
'the road to Arab unity must first pass through Cairo'. Egypt's
leaders might well be suspicious of the Baath, but they should not
imagine that the Baathists were the only people who mattered in
Syria.

However Nasser was still not satisfied, the more so since he had
just discovered from a private talk with the Syrian delegation that
their Revolutionary Command Council were to consist of seven
Baathists and three non-Baathists. Up to this point, the Syrians
had stubbornly insisted in the plenary sessions of the conference
that the Council's composition had not yet been decided, but that
the new regime was more nationalist than Baathist. Nasser there-

ore protested angrily that once again the Syrians had shown that they could not be trusted. And he warned his fellow delegates that, if the Baath ruled in Syria, as now seemed inevitable, 'they will not agree with us and Egypt will withdraw from such a unity before four months have passed'. Broadly hinting that the Baath would then take over completely in Baghdad, he said that Iraq would suffer far more than Egypt from such a breach since she was nothing like as stable as Egypt had been when the rupture came in 1961.

On this note, the Iraqi delegation suggested that the conference should adjourn for a brief interval to give time for the Egyptians and Syrians to settle their differences without the embarrassment of a third party being present. This was duly agreed; and when the two delegations met a couple of days later, with Salah Bitar and Michel Aflaq now leading the Syrian contingent, the discussions seemed initially to run a lot more smoothly. Nasser, in a more mellow mood, admitted by implication that he had perhaps been a little hard on the Baath in 1958 and that he had acted too hastily in disbanding all the political parties under the previous union. 'We should,' he said, 'have dissolved the parties with which we had no common aim and united the nationalist parties.' But he added, 'At that time I did not know Syria very well. All I knew were five or six persons. And those who came to make unity were divided and estranged blocs . . . I kept telling them that the thing needed five years, because we were not acquainted with all the details of the situation in Syria.' But having nevertheless taken the step, 'the destruction of the unity began from the first days. The Government was a collection of contradictions. . . . Unity of purpose did not at all exist among those in the Government.' If a new union was to last, he went on, there had to be unity of leadership between the two countries. But this did not appear to exist. Syria was riddled with regionalism, with towns such as Damascus, Aleppo, Homs and Hama all determined to preserve their independence of any central authority. Moreover the Syrian Baathists could never see eye to eye with the Arab Socialist Union of Egypt. They could not agree on a socialist policy and, if they were each to operate in their respective regions,

they would attack each other and so destroy all hope of lastin
unity.

To all this Bitar and his colleagues protested that they were no
united in their desire for union and in regretting their past mi
takes. They admitted that, before the overthrow of Kassem i
Iraq stimulated the unionist forces to get rid of Azm's regim
Syria was fast becoming an 'anti-nationalist base'. But the rece
coup had changed all this. Hourani was isolated and would l
destroyed as a political force. The unionists in the Baath were no
the dominant element in the party and the Government, an
their first thought after March 8 had been a tripartite union wit
Egypt and Iraq. Thus it was not true to say that there was n
unity between the leaderships of their two countries. On th
contrary, the two regimes shared the common aim of 'Ara
union, freedom and socialism'.

Nasser, however, argued that mere repetition of slogans did n
resolve the essential problems. What did 'union, freedom an
socialism' really mean, he asked? He had read all the Baath's boo
and pamphlets, but had nowhere discovered any practical expre
sion of the party's policy. He had found a number of declaratio
plagiarising the works of Lenin but nothing in the way of origin
thinking.

These barbed shafts were to strike the Syrians on their sore
spot, the absence of any concrete policy in Baathist thinkin
Wilting under Nasser's well-informed cross-examination, Afl
and Bitar were obliged to admit that there were basic differenc
of policy and personality between Egypt and Syria. They co
ceded, for instance, that unlike Egypt, 'we have no need (
Syria) to nationalise companies, only perhaps the banks', to whi
Nasser readily agreed. But when they also tried to show th
Syria was more truly a supporter of Arab nationalism and th
Egypt's conversion to pan-Arabism was not as thorough as Cai
liked to pretend, they ran into a veritable storm of prote
Touched on his own sore spot, Nasser angrily retorted that 'eve
village' in Egypt had sent its sons to fight for the Yemeni revol
tion. And while he admitted that, after 1961, some peop
wanted to see Egypt revert to her old style and to scrap that of t

United Arabic Republic, he repudiated any suggestion that pan-Arabism in Egypt was only skin-deep.

With this angry exchange the atmosphere of the discussions became once again embittered. Nasser reverted to his 'hammer and anvil' hypothesis and to his belief that the Baathist leopard had not really changed its spots. Even since March 8, he asserted, the party's newspaper and official guidance still harped on the old secessionist dogmas, insisting that Egypt wanted the Syrians to be her agents rather than her partners and abusing the Cairo Government as a deviationist regime. Bitar retorted that Heikal was conducting a no less bitter campaign against the Baath in a series of articles in *Al-Ahram* entitled 'I Accuse', in which the party and he personally were being attacked for trying to discredit Nasser and blame Egypt for the rupture of 1961. Moreover, Cairo Radio was broadcasting Heikal's accusations and so stirring up trouble between Nasserists and Baathists in Syria. Yet what mattered, he said, was that on both sides there was a need and a desire for union. Speaking for his own side, Bitar made it clear that, like the Syrian officers who insisted on the merger in 1958, he could not go back to Damascus without an agreement on some form of unity. And when after some ten sessions devoted to disputing the past, the two parties finally got around to discussing the future, he proposed that, to avoid the pit-falls which had been suggested, a loose federation should be formed with a maximum of regional autonomy and a minimum of central control.

But Nasser was no more able now than at the outset of this long and inconclusive debate to see any real prospect of achieving a meeting of minds with the Syrian Baath. Wearily he replied to Bitar that his suggested union would be 'a ragged state . . . without authority' and even less effective than the Arab League. Besides, he said, whatever form the union might take, there could never be agreement unless there was a common ideological aim among the partners. If, as their discussions had shown, this common aim was lacking, it would be better to settle now for a simple alliance, and then try to develop it into a union in three or four years' time.

Yet still the Syrians refused to take no for an answer. And as the talks continued, it became ever more evident that Nasser, for all his domination of the proceedings, was once again being penned in the prison of his own prestige. Try as he might, he was not going to be able to resist the determination of Bitar and his associates to shelter under his umbrella. Sooner or later he knew that he would have to come to some agreement with them, even if he felt that it would never withstand the tests of time. However much he might dislike the idea, Egypt's leadership of the Arab world demanded that something more than a mere military or political alliance should emerge from these discussions. Bitar had made this very clear. Yet at the same time, he knew that for Egypt to unite with a Baathist Syria could only end in another disaster.

As Nasser pondered this dilemma, it occurred to him that perhaps he had been wrong to reject a tripartite union and that, instead of Syria using the Iraqis to weight the scales against Egypt, he might be able to play Iraq, or at least Aref, off against the Syrians. There would be obvious dangers and drawbacks in a tripartite system. But, if there had to be a union of some kind, it might well turn out to be better for Egypt than a merger with Syria alone, so long as the Baath ruled in Damascus. With this thought in mind, therefore, Nasser suggested that the discussions be resumed on a tripartite basis. The Syrians agreed and, exactly as he had hoped, the Iraqi delegation, on returning to the conference, adopted the role of peace-makers bent on reconciling the divergent attitudes of their Egyptian and Syrian brothers.

Moreover, the Iraqis had noticeably changed their tune about the urgency of union. In the previous few days they had received news from Baghdad which showed that the situation at home was highly unstable. The Kurds in the north were threatening yet another open revolt and there were rumblings of trouble between the army and the Baath. Consequently, when the Syrians now suggested that, to help in resolving national differences, an interval of up to three years should elapse before any new union would enter into full effect, the Iraqis jumped at the idea. 'Time,' they said, 'will be a uniting factor.' And although Nasser questioned whether such a long interval might not in fact give the saboteurs of unity an opportunity to get to work, he fell into line after the Iraqi delegates had convinced him in a private meeting that they genuinely needed at least a year and a half to sort out their internal problems.

After further discussions, the transition period was set at twenty months, subject to a referendum in all three countries which was to be held in three months' time. The union was to take the form of a federation, similar in many respects to that of the United States, which would be responsible for foreign policy, defence, finance, information and education, justice and federal communications. All other matters would be dealt with by the three regional Governments. The Federal authority would be responsible to the union's Assembly which would elect the President for a four-year term and which would consist of a Federal Council, with equal representation from each of the three states, and an elected Chamber of Deputies of which 50 per cent had to be workers and peasants. In other words, Nasser won the day with his demand that political parties should give way to 'popular organisations' such as the ASU. But, like the Federation itself, the dissolution of the parties did not have to take effect for the next twenty months.

These decisions, which were announced to the world on April 17, would have resulted in a much more practicable union than the one which emerged from Nasser's all too brief discussions with the Syrian officers in February 1958. For, unlike that arrangement, the new Federation was the product of many days of discussion and examination of constitutional structures, past and present, in such countries as America, Russia, Britain, China, and even Fascist Italy, to whose concept of workers' participation in industrial management and profit-sharing Nasser was particularly attracted.

Nevertheless the new union never got off the ground. For although the Cairo decisions were promptly ratified by all three Governments, a simultaneous Syrian announcement that Azm and other separatist leaders would be put on trial as 'enemies of the people' caused an outbreak of violent riots and demonstrations in Damascus and other cities. Nasserists then joined in the fray and

335

many were arrested and imprisoned for their pains. And as a Cabinet crisis came near to unseating Bitar from the premiership, the Baath press once again lashed out against Egypt. Heikal in particular was accused of deliberately provoking Syria by his continued charges of Baathist 'perfidy'.

In Iraq too, there were explosions, although not directed against Egypt. At the end of April, the Kurds stepped up their demands for representation in the new Government and, when these were duly refused, fighting broke out once again on a major scale between Kurdish rebels and Government forces. The rebellion was eventually suppressed, but not before the Iraqi Baathists found themselves driven to use even more brutal measures than anything imposed by Nuri or Kassem upon earlier Kurdish insurrections.

But the main cause of the new Federation's still-birth was the further worsening of relations between Cairo and Damascus. In June, following the Baath press attacks on Heikal, *Al-Ahram* published a verbatim record of the tripartite talks. Whereupon the Syrian Government exploded with indignation, protesting that the account was distorted, especially those passages relating to Syria's secession from the union in 1961. *Al-Ahram* then added fuel to the fire by commenting that the conference minutes showed clearly that Nasser had distinguished between the Syrian Baath whom he could not trust and their Iraqi fellows with whom he had no quarrel. And as tempers raged in Damascus, the Government arraigned a number of Nasserist officers for plotting against the state at the instigation of Nasser's old henchman, Abdel Hamid Sarraj. A state of emergency was declared and, after summary trials had found most of the accused guilty as charged, nineteen officers and civilians were executed by firing squads.

Syrian-Egyptian relations were back to Shtoura. A week later, on July 27, the relentlessly anti-Nasserist General Amin el-Hafiz who, as Minister of the Interior, had been largely responsible for these bloody reprisals, took over as President of Syria in place of the more moderate General Luay al-Atassi who, it was announced, had resigned for 'health reasons'. And although Bitar remained Prime Minister for the next four months, there was now no way for him to save the tripartite union. The referendum which was to have taken place at this very moment was indefinitely postponed; the Charter of the new Federation remained a dead-letter; and Nasser, more embittered than ever by this latest evidence of the savage hatred of the Baath's Young Turks, turned towards Aref and his friends in Iraq for understanding and support.

In August Aref visited Cairo and, after five days of talks, the two leaders issued a communiqué which spoke of their identity of views on the need to 'liquidate differences'. As a further token of their good intentions, the Iraqi Government announced in October that they had finally decided to recognise the independence of Kuwait, for which gesture they received a £30 million loan from the Kuwaitis. Then, after further consultations between Cairo and Baghdad, to Nasser's infinite relief, Aref and his army supporters rounded on the Iraqi Baath following an attempt to oust him from the presidency. In November the leading Baathists were deported and the party declared illegal. A Government was established which consisted entirely of nationalist and non-party members. And the Iraqis, taking their cue from Egypt, though with a ruthlessness all their own, set about arresting and executing Communists and Baathists wherever they might be found.

Syrian-Egyptian relations might be 'back to Shtoura', but thanks to Aref's coup de main, Egypt could now count on Iraq's support. By the end of 1963 therefore, with Syria isolated and, for the time being at least, the Iraqi Baath eliminated, the way seemed clear for Nasser to stage a come-back as the guide and guardian of modern Arab nationalism.

Chapter 17

Nasser's Vietnam

Had Nasser been able to gain the quick and decisive victory in Yemen that his advisers had led him to expect, he might well have been able to recover the leadership of the Arab world for more than just a fleeting moment. With no credible rival among his fellow rulers and with a friend instead of an enemy in control of Iraq, his position was now potentially no less strong than it had been before the recent series of reverses had struck him.

But the Yemeni venture did not work out as Nasser had hoped. Despite repeated claims by Sallal to have crushed the royalist resistance and defeated the Saudi and Jordanian intervention, fierce fighting continued between the republican army, with their Egyptian allies, and the Imam's tribesmen, supported by men and arms, including aircraft, supplied by Riyadh and Amman. The republican side suffered far heavier losses than their royalist opponents who from the outset of the fighting seemed to have retained the initiative. Indeed, in the first six months, almost the only joy which came the way of the republicans was when a formation of Jordanian fighter aircraft, intended as reinforcements for the Imam, took off from Amman and flew to Cairo where the pilots promptly defected to the Egyptians.

Within three months of the Yemeni revolution, therefore, Nasser had come to realise that his commitment to Sallal was going to involve him in a much longer campaign than he had bargained for. As he now saw the situation, if only because of the factor of proximity, the support that the Saudis were giving to the royalists was a lot more effective than any help the Egyptian army could bring to Sallal. Provided therefore that Saudi Arabia and Jordan agreed to a matching withdrawal, he was beginning to think that for Egypt to take the initiative in pulling out of

Yemen could do no harm and might, on balance, even help more than it would hinder the revolution. Certainly this was the view of almost every one of his Government colleagues.

Besides, Sallal was already demonstrating serious shortcomings as a nationalist leader. A complete simpleton, he had no political knowledge or touch and, far from showing any signs of being able to establish himself as an independent ruler, he was inclined to lean altogether too heavily on Egypt's support. Indeed he seemed not only content but even anxious for the Egyptians to direct the affairs of Yemen, while he acted as Nasser's viceroy; and when the Charter of the abortive tripartite union was signed seven months after the Yemeni revolution, he jumped at the opportunity further to off-load his responsibilities by immediately applying to join the new Federation. Lacking any tribal background, Sallal had virtually no knowledge of the population outside the towns and, even if they had not pledged themselves to support the Imam, the tribesmen of Yemen would never have accepted him as their ruler. Nor did he seem able to work with his own revolutionary colleagues. For within a few months of his seizing power, he had fallen out with his deputy, Abdel Rahman Baydani, who escaped to Aden pursued by accusations of treason.

Faced with the uninviting prospect of a lengthy campaign in support of so burdensome an ally, Nasser therefore proposed in December 1962 to withdraw Egyptian forces from Yemen, provided that Saudi and Jordanian help to the royalists also ceased. But Prince Feisal, for all the hopes which Nasser had earlier reposed in him, was currently little less averse than his brother Saud to the idea of obliging the Egyptians. He had after all been in charge of the Saudi Government when they refused the Egyptian carpet for the Kaaba in Mecca. He had helped to make Egyptian workers so unwelcome that most of them had left the country. He had even made difficulties for Egyptian pilgrims to Mecca by insisting that they should pay their fees in hard currencies. And in league with Hussein in Jordan, he had tried to secure the removal of the Arab League's headquarters from Cairo so as to eradicate what he regarded as undue Egyptian influence.

It was hardly likely, therefore, that he would now be prepared to let Nasser off the hook on which his intervention in Yemen had impaled him.

Apart from this, both Feisal and Hussein had been shocked by the Americans recognising Sallal's regime, subject only to his reaffirming the Yemen's treaty obligations. They felt that Washington should have withheld recognition as the British had done, albeit from a reluctance to encourage the spread of the revolutionary idea into the neighbouring territories of Aden and its hinterland Protectorate. Both Kings were therefore determined to show the Americans how foolishly premature they had been in writing off the monarchy in Yemen. Yet the harder they tried to crush the Yemeni republicans, the more Washington strove to secure a peaceful settlement. For not only was President Kennedy anxious to remove any likely causes of friction between America and Egypt, but the American embassy in Riyadh also feared that a protracted Saudi involvement in Yemen would create internal troubles which might endanger the monarchy and so threaten American oil interests.

Consequently, two months after Sallal's coup d'état, Kennedy offered American mediation to stop the Yemeni conflict. A special representative was sent from Washington to work on Feisal to accept the offer. But neither Feisal nor the Imam were interested and of the parties involved, only Sallal and Nasser showed any enthusiasm for the idea. Thus rebuffed, Kennedy handed over the peace-making role to the United Nations. But although the Saudis had meanwhile declared a general mobilisation of their forces, it was not until March 1963, four months after the American peace initiative had failed, that Dr Ralph Bunche, the U.N. Assistant Secretary-General, went to Yemen on a fact-finding mission; and not until yet another four months had passed did the first U.N. observer teams arrive on the scene. In the interval, as fierce fighting persisted with the Egyptian air force bombing areas of Saudi territory allegedly harbouring the Imam's troops, the Saudis continued to build up supplies and support for the Yemeni royalists. And by the time the observers reached the zone of operations, Feisal and the Imam were far too committed to each other and to their mutual struggle against republicanism to have any time for the U.N. mission. ₆₃

By the following September, U Thant, the U.N. Secretary-General, conceded that his peace-making efforts had failed. Whereupon the Arab League took over the task, sending a team of mediators early in October to confer with Sanaa. But their endeavours fared no better than those of the United Nations. Unable to meet with the royalists, who were considered to be rebels with no official status, or with the Saudis, who declined to parley with them, they could only talk to one side in the dispute and such proposals for a settlement as they were able to sell to the republicans were contemptuously ignored by the Imam.

Meanwhile Nasser had already begun to withdraw a portion of his troops from Yemen, supported by Amer's 'expert' opinion that the Egyptian army's task had been fulfilled and that the republicans could now be left to fend for themselves with no more than advice, training and arms supplies from Egypt. In September 1963 some 3,000 Egyptian troops were brought home and in the following month a further 9,000 were withdrawn. True, some of these were replaced by fresh contingents, at the urgent request of Sallal who, of course, did not at all share Amer's sanguine opinions. But towards the end of 1963 the trend was clearly and definitely towards reducing the Egyptian commitment.

Nobody could see this better than Sallal who, as the year drew to a close, traipsed to and fro between Sanaa and Cairo in a determined effort to keep Nasser in the fight. But, in fact, his journeyings were a lot less necessary than they seemed at the time. For even if his own constant invocations to Cairo created more annoyance than sympathy, the Saudis could be relied on to prevent Nasser disengaging from the Yemeni conflict, at least until they had filled his cup of mortification to the brim. And though in December, at the instigation of the Americans, U Thant sent another high-powered negotiator to Riyadh, Sanaa and Cairo, Feisal continued to reject this and every other attempt at mediation.

Indeed from the Saudi point of view things could have hardly been going better. For all Sallal's threats of vengeance against the royalists, the republican forces were finding it increasingly difficult to make any impression on the Imam's tribesmen, whose superior knowledge of the mountainous Yemeni terrain gave them an enormous advantage. Still less able were the Egyptians, who had been trained for conventional war, to deal with an enemy holed up in caves and mountain hide-outs which were impervious to aerial bombardment, even if they could be located. Already there were signs of failing morale on the republican side. Stories were rife of Government forces breaking out under cover of darkness to sell arms to royalist sympathisers in the rural areas in return for food to supplement their meagre rations, which prompted the current aphorism that Sallal's supporters were 'republicans by day and royalists by night'.

Moreover, Western opinion was overwhelmingly on the side of the royalists and their Saudi supporters. The American and British press were almost unanimous in backing Feisal and the Imam and condemning Nasser for once again meddling in other people's affairs in order to extend his sphere of influence. The British Government were stubbornly refusing to recognise Sallal and, after all its peace initiatives had failed, Washington was also coming round to backing Riyadh. Despite his efforts to disengage, Nasser could do no right and the wildest claims on the Imam's behalf were taken at face value. The royalists' charges that Egyptian forces in Yemen were using poison gas against their villages was, for instance, readily accepted by the Western press, although the U.N. observers on the spot could find no evidence to this effect. Cairo might protest that, while Egypt possessed, like many other countries, small quantities of poison gas for experimental purposes, she had neither the capacity nor the intention to use it in combat. But, in the current climate of world opinion, such denials carried less conviction than the lurid complaints of Egypt's enemies.

With the dice thus loaded against him, Nasser did not know which way to turn in Yemen. Amer's claim that Sallal could fend for himself proved all too soon to be starry-eyed optimism and the republicans seemed to be daily losing more ground, even though some two divisions of Egyptian troops still remained in Yemen. At the same time, every peace effort had been stultified by Riyadh and whether or not Egyptian forces were withdrawn appeared to have no effect on the obstinate determination of the Saudis to restore the Imam to his throne.

Nor was Yemen by any means the only problem with which Nasser was faced at this point. In October 1963, he received an urgent appeal for military help from his friend Ben Bella, who had become involved in a serious clash with Morocco about an area of the Sahara frontier awarded to Algeria by the French, to which the Moroccans had long laid claim. With virtually no armoured formations in an army that was still largely equipped as the guerrilla force which had fought the French occupation, the Algerians had been unable to resist the better armed Moroccan forces when they moved in to seize the disputed territory. Consequently Ben Bella appealed to Cairo for support. Despite his fears of becoming embroiled in further prolonged hostilities, Nasser responded immediately. Although unable to spare any troops, he arranged for several shipments of tanks which were despatched to Algeria with a speed and efficiency altogether remarkable for the Egyptian army. And happily for the Algerians these supplies arrived in time to enable them to hold the position until negotiations could be set on foot. Whereupon the two sides speedily agreed upon a compromise settlement.

By comparison with the conflict in Yemen and the quarrel between Egypt and Syria, this clash on the outer fringes of the Arab world had been of small intrinsic importance. Nevertheless, it was to have significant repercussions on inter-Arab relationships. Among other things it led to the recall of the Moroccan Ambassador in Cairo and to bitter complaints by King Hassan's Government of Egyptian 'hostility' during the dispute. To this extent it served still further to polarise relations between the kingdoms and the republics in the Arab world and therefore to suggest, at least to Nasser, the need for some new initiative to close the Arabs' ranks. For it was no exaggeration to say that never had the Arab world been more divided and less prepared to resist the menacing developments now confronting it in the outside world.

Foremost among these developments was the assassination of

President Kennedy in the month of November. This, in itself, was enough of a set-back for the Arab world, and especially for Nasser, who had come to regard Kennedy as the only Western leader whom he could trust. But to make things even worse, his successor was a man whose pro-Israeli sympathies had led him to oppose the application of any pressures on Israel to withdraw from Sinai after the Suez War. Nasser doubted Lyndon Johnson's capacity for handling complex international issues. Regarding the new President as no more than a shrewd political 'fixer' from his years as a United States Senator, he had no faith either in his integrity or in his judgement. Least of all did he expect that Johnson would maintain his predecessor's relatively fair-minded approach to the Arab-Israeli issue, or treat him with the frankness and understanding that Kennedy had shown in their exchanges over the past three years. No longer would Washington take the trouble to explain to Cairo policy decisions such as the 'quarantining' of Cuba during the missiles crisis in 1962. Nor would there be the same forewarning of American arms sales to Israel that Kennedy had given in a private letter to Nasser when he agreed to Ben Gurion purchasing Hawk missiles from the United States. Johnson, so Nasser calculated, would openly favour Israel and, although on his accession to the presidency he might have written to the Arab heads of state in the same vein as Kennedy had done after his election in 1960, his inherent prejudices, coupled with his lack of international experience and vision, suggested that Egypt and the rest of the Arab world would get short shrift from the White House in the years that lay ahead.

In addition to these ominous developments across the Atlantic, the Arab world was also facing a menacing resurgence of Israeli belligerence after a lull of six years, unbroken save for two border affrays with Syria in 1960 and 1962. Paradoxically this reversion followed the final retirement of Ben Gurion, who in June 1963 had been succeeded by the relatively mild Levi Eshkol. Eshkol had begun his reign with a statement that he would watch for any opening which might lead to a settlement with the Arabs and that he was willing to meet Nasser or any other Arab leader at any time to discuss peace. But, as had happened in 1955, after Ben

Gurion made similar assertions, no sooner had Eshkol spoken than a clash occurred with one of his Arab neighbours. In August, the Israeli authorities embarked on operations to divert some 75 per cent of the Jordan river for irrigation and industrial development in Israel. Syrian troops tried forcibly to prevent these depredations; and as fierce fighting erupted across the border, Israel threatened massive retaliation against Damascus.

Cairo thereupon announced that Egypt's armed forces had been placed on an emergency alert and the Iraqis offered Syria military support. At the same time Nasser privately urged the Syrians to exercise all possible restraint. With the Yemeni conflict still raging, he wanted less than ever to be faced with another round of fighting against Israel. It had after all been his policy, ever since the Suez War in 1956, to maintain peace and quiet on the Egyptian-Israeli border. Robert Murphy had remarked on the fact that when he visited Cairo in 1958, the President had studiously 'refrained from aggressive statements about his Jewish neighbours'. And Nasser himself had only recently said, in an interview with the London *Sunday Times*, that his policy was to build up the Arab world's economic strength and to raise its living standards 'until such a time as we shall have reached a stage of evolution which will permit us to exert enough pressure on the Israelis to make them understand the complete justice of our position'.

Admittedly he had periodically reaffirmed, since the lull in the hostilities with Israel began in 1957, that he would never rest until the rights of the exiled Palestine population had been restored. And whenever some important statesman, such as Chou En-lai, came to visit him in Cairo, he sought, and usually obtained, his endorsement of the rights of the Palestinians in the ensuing communiqué. Also from time to time, he had indulged in a little sabre-rattling. In July 1962, for instance, when the Egyptian army paraded its new rockets, he had declaimed to the world that Egypt had gained vastly in economic and military strength over the previous ten years. Yet realism, combined with the experience of 1956, told him that the usurped rights of the Palestinians were not to be restored by force, at least so long as the Arabs remained as uncoordinated and disunited as they had been ever since the war of 1948. And there is no doubt that what he said to the *Sunday Times* precisely reflected his thinking at the time on the Arab-Israel issue.

But, while Nasser spared no effort to warn the Syrians against precipitate action, he knew only too well that Damascus did not believe in his long-term approach. In 1960, he had had difficulty in restraining Hourani and other Syrian members of the UAR Cabinet who wanted to go to war with Israel over a border incident, and he was not at all surprised that the current Baathist regime had allowed themselves to be provoked by the Israelis. Amin el-Hafiz, who had recently taken over the presidency of Syria, was not only hot-headed, but also a bitter opponent of Egypt. Having climbed to power by rallying the anti-Nasser groups at the time of the disturbances in the previous July, and having directed the savage retribution which followed and finally nullified the tripartite union, he was in Nasser's estimation the kind of man who would stop at nothing to humiliate the Egyptians, even if it meant getting into a fight with Israel in which they declined to take part. And though this latest crisis was soon settled by the U.N.'s prompt action in bringing about a cease-fire, nobody could tell when the Syrians would once again become involved in combat with Israel over the Jordan waters or some other issue.

This danger, added to the adverse portents from America and to the intransigence of Saudi Arabia over Yemen, served finally to convince Nasser of the need for the leaders of the Arab world to meet at the earliest possible moment and to form a united front in face of whatever the future held for them. If Cairo's efforts to induce Feisal to talk about peace in Yemen had so far been in vain, perhaps he could be won over at a general conference, where the pressures favouring a settlement would be less easy to resist. Likewise the Syrians, who treated Nasser's advice with so much scorn and abuse, might be persuaded to act with rather more caution towards Israel by a gathering of their fellow Arabs.

With these objects in mind, Nasser therefore called what was to be the first of a series of Arab summit conferences. And on

January 13, 1964, the heads of state of thirteen Arab nations assembled in Cairo. Prior to the opening session Nasser took the precaution of seeing King Hussein in private to discuss the resumption of diplomatic relations which had been severed since Jordan's precipitate recognition of the Syrian separatists in October 1961. This proved to be a highly profitable move. For, by so doing, he contrived to split the 'syndicate of the Kings' and, with Aref on his side and Feisal and Hafiz unable to form a common bond on any issue, he was able to isolate both the Syrians and the Saudis.

Having thus eliminated any organised opposition, he went on to propose that a careful study be made of plans to counter Israel's diversion of the Jordan and that a unified Arab command be established under the Egyptian General Ali Ali Amer, to which all Arab League members would contribute and which was to be responsible for defending Arab frontiers against Israeli attack. In the event, this new military structure was to become little more than a paper plan, for all its imposing title. And when the Israelis began to step up their attacks on Syria and Jordan in 1966 in preparation for the Six Days War, the unified Arab command proved to be totally ineffective as a defence system. But, at the time of the Cairo summit conference, it served well enough to steal the Syrians' thunder and to silence the protests of Hafiz that the Egyptians were too cowardly to back his stand against Israeli aggression.

Nor were these the only cards with which Nasser was able to outbid Hafiz on the Israeli issue. In the previous year the representative of the Palestinians on the Arab League Council, Ahmed Hilmi, had died and, on the nomination of Nasser and Ben Bella, his place was taken by Ahmed Shukhairy, another Palestinian who had been an ambassador to the United Nations, first for Syria in the fifties, and then for Saudi Arabia. Shukhairy had just been sacked by Feisal for refusing to submit to the U.N. Saudi complaints of aggression by Egyptian forces in Yemen. His appointment as Palestine's representative to the Arab League was therefore made over the objections of Feisal and King Hussein, as well as the former Grand Mufti of Jerusalem, Haj Amin el-Husseini, who, ever since the Arab revolt against Jewish settlement and British rule in 1936, had regarded himself as the only true guardian of Palestinian interests.

However, unlike the elderly and self-effacing Hilmi, Shukhairy was an extremely ambitious man. Ignoring all his opponents, he immediately set about making himself a factor to be reckoned with in the councils of the Arab world. Among other things, he was determined to establish a Palestinian national 'entity'. This idea had first been mooted some four years earlier but had found little favour at the time. This was largely because of objections from King Hussein, whose country contained as many Palestinian refugees as all of Israel's other Arab neighbours put together and who was strongly opposed to any suggestion that the Palestinians might owe an allegiance other than to the country which sheltered them. But when Shukhairy revived the idea at the Cairo summit conference, Nasser jumped at what he saw as an opportunity to gratify Palestinian national aspirations, without provoking Israel. And after due debate the conference agreed to Shukhairy's proposal. Neither Hussein nor the Saudis were very happy about this decision. But, with a relatively small Palestinian population in Saudi Arabia, Feisal had no strong objections. And Hussein, having come to the conclusion that the Palestinian majority in his kingdom was always easier to handle whenever he and Nasser were in agreement, decided not to press his dissent at this stage, in the hope that the idea would eventually die a painless death under subsequent detailed examination.

But if Nasser was able by these devices to regain the initiative and to silence his Syrian critics on the Palestine issue, he was a lot less successful in bringing the Saudis to heel over Yemen. Discussions took place both in plenary session and behind the scenes. But, apart from persuading Feisal that relations should be restored between Cairo and Riyadh, his efforts brought little result. And although it was decided to hold further talks later in the year, Feisal made it crystal clear in an interview with the London *Observer*, three weeks after the summit meeting ended, that his Government would never accept any regime in Yemen that was 'controlled by a foreign state'. In other words, Sallal would have to go before the Saudis would agree to any settlement.

Nevertheless, by any assessment of the results of the Cairo conference Nasser gained more than he lost from this first experiment in Arab 'summitry'. And even if his euphoric comment to Hassouna that the Arab League had now become more of a federation than a mere alliance was grossly exaggerated, his delight at the outcome was in many ways well justified. In addition to Saudi Arabia and Jordan, relations were restored with Tunisia. Thus, while in no way sacrificing his paramountcy within the progressive bloc of Iraq, Algeria and the Sudan, he had also been able to resume a dialogue with the conservative leaders, or at least with Hussein who, two months later, paid a visit to Cairo and had several long talks at the presidency.

As to the Israeli issue, Nasser had managed to prick the bubble of Syrian bombast without committing himself to any action that might lead to war. In addition, he had got the conference to accept a truce in the internecine radio war and he had given a lead in this direction by halting Egyptian propaganda attacks on Saudi Arabia, Jordan and Syria. Four months later, in May 1964, he and Aref concluded an agreement for the unification of the Egyptian and Iraqi armies which, it was claimed, was a first step towards a constitutional union. Better still, in the same month, it seemed for a brief while as if Hafiz and his followers were being forced to take a back seat in Syria, when Salah Bitar returned once more as Prime Minister and called a halt to the virulent anti-Nasser outpourings of Damascus Radio.

In sum, therefore, by the spring of 1964, Nasser had re-established much of his lost leadership. But for all his skilful political manoeuvring at the summit meeting, he had not settled his Yemeni account; and because of this, his resurgence was to be as brief as the reconciliation of the Arabs which accompanied it. For of all the reverses that he was to suffer during the eighteen years that he presided over Egypt's destinies, by far the most humiliating was the disaster which overtook his intervention in Yemen, with all the shaming evidence that it revealed of the ineptitude and ineffectiveness of tens of thousands of Egyptian troops against a relatively small number of guerrilla tribesmen. Well might he call his Yemeni venture 'my Vietnam'. For with

his failure to persuade the Saudis to pull out and agree to a negotiated settlement, he now had no alternative but to pile in yet more
troops to prop up the gimcrack structure of Sallal's republican
regime.

Three months after the summit conference ended, Nasser paid
his first visit to Yemen, from which he returned after five days in
Sanaa profoundly depressed and shocked by what he saw. To
John Badeau he confided his feelings saying, 'You would not
believe what goes on in Sanaa. Half of the Ministers never go to
their offices and the other half don't know what to do when they
get there.' All his worst suspicions of incompetence and corruption at every level were now confirmed and he was obliged to
insist on a drastic reshuffle of the republican Cabinet, together
with changes in the administration, designed to delegate a number
of Sallal's powers and functions to some of his less incompetent
subordinates. For the sake of appearances, he had to sign a
communiqué on his departure which proclaimed that the union
between Egypt and Yemen was 'stronger than any form of constitutional union'. But, in conversation with old friends such as
Khaled Mohieddin, on his return he made no secret of his bitter
regret that he had allowed himself to become trapped in so humiliating a situation. Lamenting that he had been misled at the outset
into believing that a token Egyptian force would finish the civil
war in a few weeks at the most, he said that the Yemeni venture
had shown the folly of trying to impose Egyptian influence by
military action. As he had long ago told his Guidance Minister,
Hatem, Egypt could achieve far more with propaganda than with
tanks. The success of his campaign against the Baghdad Pact
proved how right he was then and how wrong he had been to
attempt a military solution in Yemen.

Yet, much as he might now bemoan this error of judgement,
Nasser could not escape from his commitment to the Yemeni
revolution. Unlike Sallal's Russian and Chinese allies who had
pledged only economic and technical assistance, Egypt was bound
to fight for the republicans by the terms of the latest treaty. And
she was therefore obliged, at whatever cost, to keep on sending
more troops to Yemen in the desperate hope that perhaps sheer

weight of numbers might eventually turn the scales. Nevertheless Nasser never ceased to hope that the Saudis would agree to a settlement. For not only was the Yemeni venture degrading Egypt's image in the eyes of the Arab world, but it was also poisoning her relations with the West. It was bad enough anyhow to have to deal with a pro-Zionist President in Washington, without giving arguments to those of Johnson's advisers to whom Badeau's desire to maintain good relations with Cairo was so much woolly thinking and whose ideas of an Arab policy involved little more than propping up Jordan as a Western outpost and appeasing Saudi Arabia to preserve America's oil interests. As Nasser knew only too well, the Yemeni republicans had few friends in the new American administration. Apart from Washington's obvious partiality for the Saudis, Sallal's peregrinations to Moscow and Peking and his apparently growing association with the Communist world was doing him no good in the United States. And as a result Badeau's influence in Washington was rapidly waning in favour of the anti-Nasser lobby.

Even worse was the state of relations between Egypt and Britain which, with Aden next door to the scene of the fighting, were once again becoming deeply embittered. Inevitably the British were blaming Nasser for the current increase in nationalist agitation in Aden, while he in his turn blamed the British for permitting gun-running from the Aden Protectorate to the Yemeni royalists. Nor were either of these charges without foundation. Nasser, it is true, was being careful at this stage not to get too deeply involved with the Adeni nationalists. But he nevertheless felt obliged to help finance one of their groups, the Federation for the Liberation of South Yemen (FLOSY), which had its headquarters in Cairo. Conversely, although the Aden authorities affected an officially neutral posture with regard to the war in Yemen, there was no disguising the fact that they, along with the Protectorate sheikhs, privately hoped that the royalists would win, if only to stop the spread of republicanism in southern Arabia. Nor could it be denied that the sheikhs were smuggling arms to the royalists supplied by various British soldiers of fortune.

Not surprisingly, these activities caused Nasser to suspect that Britain was involved in yet another conspiracy to subvert the Arab revolution. In December 1962, in a speech marking the sixth anniversary of the Anglo-French withdrawal from Port Said, he had furiously attacked the British Government for meddling in the internal affairs of Yemen. By way of showing that this was by no means an isolated case of interference, he revealed that, in the previous year, Beeley had tried to intervene on behalf of the French officials who had been charged with spying. Beeley of course protested that it was the Egyptians who were interfering in Britain's affairs by their support of FLOSY and that this attack on the British presence in Aden was wholly unjustified. But Nasser retorted that he had a right and a duty to support Arab nationalism everywhere. As to the justification for his speech, he added that Duncan Sandys, Britain's Colonial Secretary, had only recently made a vicious attack on Egypt. Nor, of course, was this the end of the matter. For as the fighting in Yemen intensified, tempers on both sides of the border grew shorter. And eighteen months later, following an exchange of aerial bombardments of Yemeni and Adeni territory, Nasser loosed off another series of denunciations of British imperialism in Aden, urging upon his hearers the need to rid southern Arabia of all traces of colonial rule.

Then, quite suddenly in July 1964, the British Government declared that Aden and the other territories comprising the South Arabian Federation would be given their independence not later than 1968. Nasser was naturally delighted by the news. For, although the announcement added that Britain intended to retain a military base in Aden, under a defence agreement to be negotiated with the Federation Government, he could at least claim that the British were now on their way out of southern Arabia. Within a few days, still more good news reached Cairo when King Hussein, following talks with Field Marshal Amer in Amman, decided to withdraw his support for the Imam and to recognise the Sallal regime.

Sallal was of course still leaning as heavily as ever on Egypt. Following London's announcement about Aden's forthcoming independence, he descended on Cairo yet again, this time with a plea to be taken into the federal union, envisaged under the recent agreement to unite the armies of Egypt and Iraq. And only with difficulty had he been fobbed off with an undertaking to coordinate policies between Cairo and Sanaa. But within less than two months all such worries paled into insignificance when, early in September 1964, Nasser received the long-awaited message from Feisal agreeing to a meeting to discuss a cease-fire in Yemen.

Understandably enough Nasser now felt that, perhaps after all, his artful manoeuvrings at the Cairo summit conference had worked the oracle and that, with Hussein finally breaking ranks and recognising the Sallal regime, Feisal had decided to go it alone no longer. But, even if the Saudis were only seeking a breathing space, Nasser was determined to grasp what seemed to be a golden opportunity to escape from his Yemeni dilemma without further loss of prestige. When he and Feisal met on September 9, he was therefore at pains to point out that he harboured no aggressive intentions towards Saudi Arabia. Tongue well in cheek, he asserted that, in sending troops to Yemen, he had merely been answering a call for help from the established Government of the country and, if attacks across the Saudi border had occurred, they were due to an excess of zeal by troops exercising the right of hot pursuit and were not part of any plan to wage war on Saudi territory.

Feisal, of course, knew that this was only part of the truth. He realised well enough that Nasser's aim in Yemen, originally at least, was to establish a republican presence under Egyptian influence in order to challenge Saudi paramountcy in the Arabian peninsula and also to stimulate nationalist resistance in Aden. And it was because he himself feared that a victory for the republicans in Yemen would have repercussions in Saudi Arabia that he had supported the Imam in the first place. But now, after two years of fighting, the Imam was still holding out. Although supported by 40,000 Egyptian troops, Sallal had made no headway against the royalists. Egyptian casualties alone were estimated at some 10,000 killed, wounded and captured. And with such blows to Egypt's pride, the Nasserist threat to southern Arabia seemed to have been effectively checked.

Feisal had therefore made his point and he was now prepared to accept a cease-fire and to seek the Imam's compliance. What is more, he gave a broad hint that King Saud, who was trying to make trouble for him by opposing any settlement in Yemen, would shortly be dethroned and sent out of the country where his intransigence could do no harm. Nasser was naturally much relieved to hear all this and, on the strength of Feisal's assurances, he agreed that, at the end of October, republicans and royalists should meet on 'neutral' ground at Erkwit in the Sudan to discuss ways and means of ending the war. Moreover, four days after the Erkwit discussions began, Riyadh announced that Saud had been deposed in favour of his brother and that Feisal had assumed the title as well as the powers of Saudi Arabia's King. And two days after that, on November 5, news came from the Sudan that a cease-fire had been agreed and that a 'national reconciliation conference' would follow in a few weeks' time.

However, as it turned out, the high hopes raised by the Erkwit agreement were not to be fulfilled. For one thing, the republicans refused to sit with representatives of the Imam's family, who they alleged had committed crimes against the Yemeni people. For another, the Imam had been most unwilling to accept a cease-fire, except as a means of lulling the republicans into a sense of false security. Feeling that he had nothing to gain from a negotiated settlement which would oblige him to participate in the government of his country with his sworn enemies, he was determined to settle the issue one way or the other by force. Early in December, therefore, after the truce had lasted barely a month, the royalists once again poured forth from their mountain hide-outs and resumed operations against the republican and Egyptian armies.

The year 1964, which had begun with such bright prospects for the recovery of Nasser's lost prestige through the skilful manipulation of the Cairo conference, thus ended in bitter disappointment and failure. 'My Vietnam' was not finished after all and the humiliation of Egyptian arms in Yemen was to continue with no hope of respite until the next truce was negotiated, whenever that might be. Inevitably too, Sallal now called for more help, not only to resist the renewed royalist onslaught, but also to surmount a revolt in his own Cabinet from which three of his leading Ministers had resigned in protest against 'corruption and incompetence' in the presidency, while the rest were threatening to do likewise if Sallal was not dismissed. Thus, as the year ended, Nasser found himself obliged to send yet more troops to Yemen and at the same time, to summon Sallal to Cairo for further lectures on how to run his Government.

There was, however, one event in this otherwise disappointing year from which Nasser had been able to draw an unqualified sense of achievement. In May 1964, the first stage of the Aswan High Dam was completed with the construction of the great wall that was to contain a perennial supply of water for the irrigation of Egypt. In token of Russia's indispensable contribution to this achievement, Kruschev had been invited to perform the opening ceremony. President Aref of Iraq was also to attend, as were Sallal, Ben Bella and other leading figures of the 'progressive' Arab states. Throughout all Egypt a mood of rejoicing prevailed in expectation of the bounteous gifts which this historic development was about to confer on the long-suffering fellahin.

Even this happy occasion was almost marred when the Egyptian press, in exulting over the building of the High Dam, claimed a major share of the credit for Egypt and played down the Russian contribution to a point where the Soviet embassy in Cairo feared an angry explosion from the impetuous Kruschev. Nor had the Government helped matters by attempting, just as the first stage was nearing completion, to persuade the Russians to turn their loan into an outright grant, which request had been summarily rejected. For his part, too, Kruschev was to make little secret of his displeasure at the attendance of Aref who was still busily hunting down Communists in Iraq. He also could not resist a slight dig at Arab nationalism by proclaiming at Aswan that the 'unity of the workers of all nations' was a more important goal than any regional unity, including that of the Arab world.

Nevertheless, Nasser was determined not to allow anything to spoil this opportunity to restore the relationship which had existed between Russia and Egypt before the Suez War. A month before Kruschev's visit, as a special gesture towards the man with whom he had quarrelled so bitterly about the suppression of Egyptian Communism, he had ordered that all those who had been imprisoned for Communist activities should be paroled. Consequently the Aswan ceremony, and the rest of Kruschev's visit to Egypt, took place in a spirit of mutual amity and good humour which had been totally missing in Russian-Egyptian relations for most of the previous eight years. Addressing the Arab Socialist Union in the National Assembly, the Russian leader delighted his hearers with a forthright call for the abolition of all foreign bases, specifically mentioning Britain's bases in Aden, Cyprus and Libya. He also conferred on Nasser the twin distinctions of the Order of Lenin and Hero of the Soviet Union. Best of all, at a farewell dinner in Cairo, it was announced that the Russian Government would lend Egypt some £100 millions to help in financing the second five-year industrialisation plan.

But greater than any honours or favours which Kruschev might bestow on him was the fact that Nasser had achieved his greatest single ambition for Egypt – the building of the Aswan High Dam. Although not as large as others of its kind, such as the Kariba project on the Zambezi, this achievement symbolised for the Egyptian people something infinitely greater and more significant than the promise of a perpetual irrigation system for the Nile Valley, important as that might be. As Nasser put it in his speech at the opening ceremony, 'There is no spot which represents the great battle of contemporary Arab man better than this site on which we stand. Here the political, social, national and military struggles of the Egyptian people intermingle and combine like the huge blocks of stone which dam up the old course of the Nile and store its waters in the biggest lake made by man to become a permanent source of prosperity.' For all the reverses which she had suffered in recent years, the High Dam stood as unassailable testimony that Egypt was no longer a backward nation of poverty-stricken peasants, but was beginning to take her place in the modern technological age.

Added to this prodigious achievement, Nasser could also claim that the long and bitter chapter of dispute between Cairo and Moscow had been brought to a close. On top of the £500 millions worth of Russian military and economic aid already supplied, he had been able to guarantee the necessary injection of foreign currency to renew the drive to industrialise Egypt. Thus, whatever might be the state of his relations with his fellow Arabs and however many humiliations he might have suffered and would continue to suffer in Yemen, at least among his own people, Nasser was more firmly entrenched than ever as the founding-father of the new Egypt.

Chapter 18

Final Breach with the West

The completion of the first stage of the High Dam and the simultaneous Russian undertaking to help in furthering the industrialisation of Egypt could scarcely have been more timely. For five months later, Kruschev was ousted from power by a 'palace revolution' within the Soviet Praesidium. And a few weeks after this earth-shaking development, on November 15, the anti-Egyptian Umma party overthrew the Sudan's President Abboud, whose cooperation on the Nile waters' issue had been no less essential to the Aswan project than the money and skills furnished by the Russians.

Nasser was seriously put out by the fall of Kruschev. Within the space of twelve months the leaders of the two super-powers, with whom he had become accustomed to working, or quarrelling, had been replaced by men whom he either distrusted or did not know at all. Violent and uncouth as he often had been in his dealings with Cairo, Kruschev had been steadfast in helping Egypt with money, technical assistance and military equipment ever since the first Soviet arms deal in 1955. And with little or no knowledge of the men who had taken over in Moscow, Nasser was afraid that, once the existing aid agreements had been fulfilled, the Soviet Government might not be so helpful in the future or might try to attach unacceptable strings to any further assistance. Indeed he could not even be certain that the existing agreements would be honoured. For it was being strongly rumoured at the time that Kruschev's recent promise of more economic aid for Egypt had helped to bring about his downfall.

Even under Kruschev the Russians had refrained from helping Egypt to achieve anything like the commercial independence for which Nasser had hoped. In return for buying her cotton crop at above world prices, Russia had been careful to ensure that Egypt received only finished goods, and not raw materials; and such finished goods as she bought from Egypt were paid for in Egyptian rather than foreign currency. In short, Kruschev's policy had been to help Russia by helping Egypt to become independent of the West at the price of becoming correspondingly dependent on the Soviet bloc. Likewise, by offering similar inducements to countries such as Syria and Iraq, he hoped to substitute Russian for Western influence wherever possible in the Arab world.

Chou En-lai had bluntly asserted, when he visited Cairo in December 1963, that Russia's intentions towards Egypt were far from altruistic. And when the Chinese leader paid a further call eight months after Kruschev had been deposed, he seemed to go out of his way to make Nasser's flesh creep with lurid warnings that the Russians would betray him as they had already betrayed the Communist revolution. Broad hints were dropped that the new Soviet leaders were contemplating a deal with Washington, which would divide the world into Russian and American spheres of influence at the expense of all lesser states. Nasser was reminded that the Russians were, after all, Europeans whose Asian territories had all been stolen from China. As Europeans they looked on the countries of Asia and Africa as their inferiors and they were only helping Egypt in order to use her as a pawn in their own game of power politics.

Chou went on to say that the same motive underlay Russia's help for North Vietnam in the current struggle against American imperialism. Indeed, when Nasser, prompted by a recent suggestion to his ambassador in Brussels from Belgium's Foreign Minister, Paul Henri Spaak, proposed that he might usefully mediate between Peking and Washington over Vietnam, Chou rejected the idea out of hand as being precisely what the Kremlin, and the Americans, wanted. For, as he put it, if the Vietnam war were brought to an end, the Russians would immediately be free to make a global deal with the Americans. Then, having ensured complete security for their western borders, they would turn on China. Besides, he added, nothing suited Peking better than for the Americans to continue indefinitely to waste their blood and treasure in a war in Vietnam which they could never win, even if their superior fire-power meant that they equally could not lose it. Wherefore, Chou suggested, Egypt's President would be more usefully employed in resolving his own internal problems than in offering his good offices where they were not wanted.

In their previous encounters Nasser had felt much sympathy for Chou En-lai's passionate determination to make China equal and ultimately superior, to the West. And even though he did not like to hear it, he knew only too well that Russia was serving her own interests in helping countries like Egypt. But he was more than a little irritated by Chou's rebuff, behind which he clearly saw a deliberate Chinese plan to harass and weaken Russia by keeping her at loggerheads with America and forcing her to maintain the utmost vigilance on both her western and her eastern fronts. This might suit Peking's policies, but it was of no benefit to Egypt. Nasser was also greatly annoyed by the Chinese Premier's evident attempt to involve him in the growing antagonism between Peking and Moscow and to persuade him to abandon his Russian ties in favour of China. Still more angry was he when the Chinese wrecked a highly important conference of the Afro-Asian nations, scheduled to be held at Algiers in November 1965, by threatening to boycott it, together with their South East Asian satellites, if the Russians accepted their invitation to participate. For in so doing, they not only forced the cancellation of the conference, but also destroyed much of what had been done to bring some cohesion to the Afro-Asian movement.

Nevertheless, convinced though he was that the Chinese were trying to make trouble between Cairo and Moscow, Nasser was sufficiently disturbed by Chou's assertions to decide on an early visit to Russia to size up the situation for himself. And although he was able to satisfy himself that there would be no diminution in Soviet aid to Egypt, he confided to his friends on his return that he had found Brezhnev and Kosygin comparatively aloof and stiff. Certainly there would be no question of establishing with them the personal relationship which he and Kruschev had from time to time enjoyed.

By contrast to the suddenness of Kruschev's fall in Russia, the changes which occurred in the Sudan were a lot less unexpected. Abboud had been conspicuously absent from the Aswan ceremony in May 1964. Deeply offended that Nasser had not asked him to play a pre-eminent part at the opening of the High Dam and had only sent him a belated invitation to be present, he had arranged to visit Peking at the time. And when the Egyptians refused to accept the Sudanese Minister of Irrigation as his appointed deputy, relations between Cairo and Khartoum plummeted to their lowest point in five years. With no further moral support from Cairo and bitterly disenchanted with the man whom he had idolised for so long, Abboud rapidly lost ground. As his enemies in the Umma party closed in upon him, he became ever more isolated. Anti-Government riots broke out in October and, although Abboud tried desperately to save his regime by agreeing to appoint a transitional Government while a new constitution was drafted, he succeeded in delaying his downfall by no more than a few weeks.

But although this meant that he no longer had friends in Khartoum on whom he could rely to align Sudanese policy with Egyptian requirements, Nasser wasted little time bemoaning Abboud's departure. The Nile Waters agreement had long since been secured and he had other more compelling problems to attend to. One of these was the Palestinian question which directly impinged on his efforts to keep Syria isolated.

Despite his success in persuading the Arab heads of state to adopt the concept of a Palestinian entity and to form a unified Arab command, Nasser could not afford to rest on his laurels. For, no matter how sincerely he might protest his determination to restore the rights of the Palestinian people which Israel had usurped, his performance so far had proved a grave disappointment to the more militant Palestinians such as Yasser Arafat and his Fatah resistance group. His photograph might be found in the tents of every Palestinian refugee camp and his name might be chanted in demonstrations against Hussein in Jerusalem and other towns of Jordan's West Bank. But his steadfast refusal to try further conclusions with Israel over the past eight years had not gone unnoticed by these dispossessed masses, who believed that only by fighting could their lost lands and homes ever be restored to them.

The Palestinians remembered all too vividly the days before 1952 when the Egyptians knew little and cared less for what the Israeli usurpers had done and were doing in Palestine. They could not forget the slanderous stories which had gone the rounds of the cafés of Cairo, Alexandria and Port Said about how Palestinians had kidnapped Egyptian officers and sold them to the Israelis in the war of 1948. And they recalled the high hopes which Nasser had aroused in every Palestinian breast when he declared that Egypt was now an Arab state, pledged to uphold Arab interests wherever they were threatened. The first Egyptian leader ever to talk in such absolute terms, he had moreover seemed ready to match his words with deeds in the early stages of his reign. For although the fedayeen raids of 1955 had been a lot less effective than was hoped, they had at least suggested that a new militancy had seized hold of Egypt's leadership. Thus, when in 1955 Nasser asked a young Palestinian student why he supported him, the answer came back without hesitation, 'Because we Palestinians see in you the expression of our own aspirations; so please do not fail us.'

Yet, however Nasser may have spoken and acted at the beginning of his reign, neither then nor at any subsequent stage had he known how to tackle the problem of restoring the lost lands of the Palestinians. If he saw himself cast in any historical mould it was as a modern Mohammed Ali, not as a resurrected Saladin. And just as he rejected the counsels of those who suggested that if he was to lead the Arab world effectively, he should appoint Arabs from other states to advise him about their countries, so he had refused to associate any Palestinians with his thinking on their problems until he and Shukhairy together brought the Palestinian 'entity' to life at the Cairo summit conference. Even then he saw as few Palestinians as possible, knowing as he did that his ideas for action on their behalf were largely limited to political posturing and that he could not satisfy their desire to fight for their rights. Yasser Arafat, for instance, never met him until three years later when, in the aftermath of the 1967 war, Heikal introduced him as the new leader of the Palestinian Resistance.

This was not to say that Nasser was lacking in sympathy for the people of Palestine. On the contrary, in the Gaza Strip which housed all of Egypt's 300,000 Palestinian refugees, he spent large sums to develop the area and to alleviate the lot of the hitherto impoverished inhabitants. Gaza was made a duty-free zone and as such became a relatively thriving tourist attraction for large numbers of Egyptians and other visitors. Paved roads, a hospital and modern sewerage were provided where none had existed before; and even when Egypt's entire output of cement was requisitioned for the High Dam, Nasser insisted that Gaza's needs should not suffer. Also the Egyptian Government underwrote jobs for those Palestinians who passed out of the U.N.'s vocational training school, some of whom were employed as teachers in village schools where Egyptian teachers did not want to go, while others according to their skills found outlets in industry or agriculture.

But, for the more militant Palestinians, this therapeutic approach was far from being enough. They wanted action not alms. They were deeply disappointed that, after all the tough talk and promising efforts of the mid-fifties, Nasser had held his fire ever since the Sinai campaign in 1956, which period of inaction, they claimed, had allowed the usurper to strengthen still further his hold on the fair land of Palestine. As his erstwhile student admirer and his fellows were now ruefully to declare, Nasser had failed' them after all.

Still greater was the dismay of Arafat and his disciples on hearing that, at the Cairo summit conference, Nasser had contended that the liberation of Palestine was not an immediate issue and that action would have to await the solution of a number of other more pressing Arab problems. The Syrians of course lost no time in telling Arafat that, when their President asserted that the Arabs collectively could defeat Israel in a comparatively short time, Nasser had retorted that Hafiz must be out of his mind. Nor did they omit to add that the most vocal supporter of Nasser's defeatist' attitude had been President Bourguiba who, claiming to be what he called 'a professor of resistance', from his own battles against the French colonial power, had declared that it was impossible to fight Israel and that the Arabs should accept the inevitable and make the best of it.

Nasser had of course been able to manipulate the Cairo conference and to show up Hafiz for the conceited ass that he was. But he equally knew that he would in future have to devote a lot more time and ingenuity to the Palestine problem if the holding operations which he had initiated were not to come unstuck. Not only was there the danger of the more militant Palestinians making common cause with Syria's Young Turks; but Shukhairy himself, as the newly elected spokesman for Palestine, was hardly the kind of man who would rest content indefinitely to play the role of political coordinator of a shadow Government waiting on the U.N. or the great powers to settle the issue. As Shukhairy never tired of telling everybody on every available occasion, with Israel continuing to ignore every Security Council resolution on Palestine, the Palestinians would have to wait for ever if they left it to the United Nations to secure the restitution of their rights.

Indeed, Shukhairy lost no time in following up the Cairo decisions by calling a Palestine Congress which met in Jerusalem in May 1964 with all the Arab Foreign Ministers in attendance and which, on his prompting, gave its blessing to the formation of the Palestine Liberation Organisation. Designed to embrace all the disparate groups of Palestine expatriates, together with those still living on their native soil in the West Bank area of Jordan, the PLO was to take the form of a Government in exile, with headquarters in Gaza, and an army which was to be recruited from the Palestinian refugees.

It did not require much military expertise to see that such an army could do little, if anything, to liberate Palestine from Israeli occupation. Yet if only to keep control of this new initiative in Egyptian hands, Nasser welcomed it with open arms. He gave orders that the PLO were to be helped in every possible way. The army would be trained by Egyptian instructors and provided with Egyptian equipment and the Gaza authorities were to give their full cooperation to Shukhairy. On the diplomatic plane, he also sent Mahmoud Riad, who had succeeded Fawzi as Egypt's Foreign Minister, on a tour of East Africa to explain the Palestinian case, in preparation for a conference of the Organisation of African Unity which he had invited to hold its next meeting in Cairo in two months' time. When the African heads of state assembled for the conference, he made an eloquent, though largely vain, appeal for their understanding and sympathy for the plight of the Palestinians. And by way of showing that, feeble as his bite might be, his bark was as abrasive as ever, at a graduation parade of Egyptian air force cadets, he denounced a recent wave of incidents on Jordan's border as Israeli aggression and declared that war was ultimately inevitable unless Israel forswore her belligerent ways.

Then, in September 1964, eight months after the first Arab summit conference, Nasser again called his fellow Arab rulers together at Alexandria, and secured their endorsement of the decision to establish the PLO as what he termed the first step towards the liberation of Arab Palestine. King Hussein, fearing that this might lead to the Palestinians in Jordan becoming a state within a state, was none too happy with the idea and joined with Feisal in objecting that Shukhairy had exceeded his functions in railroading the Palestine Congress into accepting his proposals. But, as at the previous Cairo meeting, he eventually decided to go along with the majority decision, in the interests of preserving peace with his West Bank subjects. Only Hafiz objected that Shukhairy's plans did not go far enough and, with the Syrians left blathering about the need to strike at Israel without further delay, the second summit conference agreed to follow Egypt's lead and to sanction the establishment of the PLO.

Six months later, Nasser's efforts to put himself on-side with Palestinian opinion were still further helped by a highly injudicious speech from Tunisia's President Bourguiba. In the course of a visit to Jordan in March 1965, Bourguiba announced to a Jerusalem audience that Arab policy towards Israel was too much rooted in sentiment and emotion. The Palestine problem could only be solved by moderation and reason, he said. The

Palestinians should follow the example of their Tunisian brothers and live at peace with the Jews inhabiting their land.

Bourguiba was immediately and violently attacked in almost every Arab newspaper. The Egyptian press was not slow to point out the essential difference between the small Jewish minority in Tunisia, who had done their Arab compatriots no harm, and the two million Israelis who were living in lands which they had largely seized by conquest from the Palestinian people. Shukhairy demanded that Tunisia be expelled from the Arab League. Nasser withdrew his ambassador from Tunis as a mark of protest. The Tunisian embassy in Cairo was ransacked and burned by a group of angry students and, as tempers rose on both sides, the Egyptian embassy in Tunis suffered similar treatment. The Egyptian Government promptly issued a communiqué disclaiming responsibility for the Cairo incident and, with tongue in cheek, stated that the heroic efforts of the police had failed to curb the outraged feelings of the perpetrators. Whereupon Bourguiba immediately issued a statement in identical terms about the burning of Egypt's embassy in Tunis. But, if Nasser was more irritated than amused by this piece of tit-for-tat, the whole affair had been a most welcome windfall for him. For it helped him to show the Arab militants that, although the Tunisians had supported some of his arguments at the first summit conference, in fact he and Bourguiba were miles apart on the subject of Palestine.

Nor did Nasser have to rely exclusively on Bourguiba to show he was no renegade where Israel was concerned. Within a few weeks of his breach with Tunisia, he broke off diplomatic relations with West Germany in retaliation for Bonn's decision to recognise the state of Israel. This dispute had been brewing ever since it was discovered in 1960 that the West Germans were supplying large quantities of American arms to Israel. In February 1965, Nasser decided to twist Bonn's tail by inviting the East German President, Walter Ulbricht, to Cairo. Then, having signed an agreement for scientific and technical cooperation with East Germany, he let it be known that Egypt was contemplating the establishment of a Consulate-General in East Berlin and that he himself might return Ulbricht's visit in the near future.

Indignant protests followed from the West Germans, to whom Ulbricht's Russian satellite regime was as much anathema as Israel was to the Arabs. And after the Israelis had publicly appealed to Bonn to stop German free-lance scientists helping to expand Nasser's rocket arsenal, the West German Government instructed all German technicians in Egypt to quit their jobs. The Egyptians retaliated by arresting four Germans on charges of spying for the Israelis, whereupon West Germany announced that she would establish diplomatic relations with Tel Aviv. The Egyptian embassy in Bonn was promptly withdrawn and German properties throughout the Arab world, including the embassies in Baghdad and Sanaa, were attacked by mobs of enraged students. And as Nasser called on the Arab states to sever relations with West Germany, all except the Tunisians, Libyans and Moroccans agreed to follow his lead.

But if at this point Nasser found it necessary to play to the militant gallery with belligerent words, he certainly had no intention of being drawn into any provocative action against Israel. On the contrary, his plan was to use such popularity and prestige as his political posturing might win for him to inject a further dose of realism into Arab thinking. And when, in September 1965, a third summit conference was held at Casablanca, he once again told his fellow rulers that the Arabs were in no condition to make war against Israel. Not even all the Arab states combined, let alone any single one of them, were equal to the Israelis, he said. For while they might have weapons as good as anything possessed by the enemy, they did not have the training and technical knowledge to make effective use of them. It would take at least three years for their armies to acquire such skills and, instead of uttering wild threats which deceived nobody, the Arab states should devote their energies to the training and coordination necessary to catch up with Israel.

From Nasser's point of view this was the easiest and most successful of all the first three summit meetings. For one thing, he was spared the embarrassment of Bourguiba's applause because the Tunisians stayed at home and sulked in their tents. For another, his ice-cold douche of common sense managed to make the egregious Hafiz so much the odd man out that he was constrained to suggest that diplomatic relations, non-existent since the collapse of the union, should now be restored between Cairo and Damascus. In fact, although Nasser agreed readily enough to the proposal, nothing came of this peace move. In the previous autumn Bitar had once more resigned the premiership of Syria after objecting violently to his President's hostility towards Egypt. Thus the Baathist Young Turks were yet again in the ascendant; and when Hafiz returned home, he found himself too engulfed in the prevailing tide of anti-Nasserism to follow up his suggestion for an exchange of ambassadors with Cairo.

Meanwhile Nasser had been working away at the Yemen problem. And on August 24, three weeks before the Casablanca summit meeting, he and Feisal met in Jedda where they agreed to make another attempt to impose a cease-fire on their respective clients. Much of the credit for this further hopeful development was due to the efforts of Ahmed Mohammed Numan who had become Sallal's Prime Minister in the previous April, after several months of continuous feuding within the Cabinet had brought the republican ranks to a state of chaos. Numan had lost no time in letting the Saudis know that he wanted nothing but friendship with them. He also said the same to the British in Aden. For good measure he added that he had no desire to see Yemen permanently reliant on Egypt and that he wished to elicit the support of other Arab countries in the struggle to make his country economically viable as well as politically independent. Needless to say, however such sentiments had little appeal for the more headstrong republicans. Numan was therefore soon ousted from the premiership.

But while Numan's enemies could dismiss him from office they could not so easily suppress his ideas, especially when they happened to coincide with Nasser's. Besides, by this time offers of mediation were pouring in from all sides. Hussein had submitted proposals for a compromise settlement to Cairo, Riyadh and Sanaa. The Algerians were volunteering as mediators; so were the Kuwaitis. Indeed by the summer of 1965 an atmosphere of frenzied activity had developed with Anwar Sadat flying to consult Sallal in Sanaa and Sallal visiting Nasser in Alexandria, while Feisal received royalist representatives in Riyadh and, most remarkable of all, a group of anti-Sallal republicans met delegates of the Imam at a conference in Saudi Arabia. And although Numan's successor, Hassan al-Amri, went out of his way to unsay the things which Numan had said about friendship with Britain and Saudi Arabia, this spate of consultations brought about its duly intended result when Nasser and Feisal met and signed their new agreement to bring the now three-year-old war in Yemen to an end. Saudi Arabia agreed immediately to stop all military assistance to the royalists and Egypt undertook to withdraw her forces within a year. A cease-fire would take effect forthwith and a transitional Government was to be formed by agreement between the parties and their Saudi and Egyptian patrons, after which the Yemeni people would decide who should rule their country in a referendum to be held not later than November 1966.

The Syrian Government and press promptly set up a howl of protest that Nasser had betrayed the Yemeni revolution. But aside from this partisan chorus, the Jedda decisions were greeted with immense relief in the Arab world and especially among Nasser's supporters. Unlike the previous armistice, which had been left to the Yemenis to settle among themselves, this new arrangement formed part of a written compact between the principal backers of the warring parties and it was therefore thought to have an altogether better chance of holding fast. Certainly Nasser believed this, for within four days of putting his signature to the document, substantial numbers of Egyptian troops began to embark for home. Sallal was of course greatly perturbed to see them go, fearing as always to be left to fend for himself. But publicly at least, he too was obliged to join in the general Arab welcome for the prospect of peace in Yemen.

Apart from its local impact, the Jedda agreement was for the briefest of moments to open up a new vista of understanding between Britain and Egypt. After the royalists had broken the truce agreed at Erkwit, the Egyptian press had resumed its usual periodical slanging of British imperialism in Aden. *Al-Ahram* had recently published a bitter attack on the Aden authorities who, it alleged, were acting as agents of the former Baghdad

Pact powers in a conspiracy to disrupt the Yemeni revolution. London had expressed no little indignation at these allegations, which Harold Wilson's new Labour Government considered a poor reward for the conciliatory messages that they had sent to Cairo on their election to office in the previous autumn. But, with the renewed cease-fire in Yemen, London now saw a real hope for a cessation, or at least a reduction, of nationalist agitation in Aden and hence of improved relations with Egypt. It was therefore decided to send George Thomson, the Minister of State at the Foreign Office, to Cairo for talks with the Egyptian Government about a number of issues, of which the most important were the future of Aden and the situation in Rhodesia, where the white minority, led by Ian Smith, were about to declare their independence of British control. The idea was for Thomson to explain to Nasser what Britain's intentions were towards Aden after independence and also to try to persuade him not to follow the Black African states in a mass breach of diplomatic relations with Britain, if her efforts to crush the Smith regime in Rhodesia should prove unavailing.

Nasser agreed to receive Thomson on his return from Casablanca. Nevertheless, he was personally none too happy about the proposed discussions. Earlier in the year he had received some highly disturbing information about British plans for military action in the Middle East, which his Military Attaché in London had obtained from a War Office employee. True, these plans, which envisaged joint action with the American Air Force and Sixth Fleet, were based on certain contingencies such as the outbreak or threat of a general war in the area. But remembering the specious reasons which Eden had given for Britain's actions in 1956, Nasser's suspicions had been immediately aroused; and the British Government's vehement protests in Cairo, following the discovery and arrest of the informant, only served to intensify his fears that they were engaged in some devious design.

Nor was the fact that Britain now had a so-called Socialist Government of much comfort to him. He knew little about Wilson's Cabinet beyond the fact that it contained a fair sprinkling of supporters of Israel, such as Richard Crossman. Although there were also in it a few men whom he knew and liked, such as George Brown and Christopher Mayhew, he also knew only too well that the British Labour movement had a long and strong tradition of sympathy for Zionism. Besides, he was none too keen on being drawn into a discussion on Aden which might have the effect of tying his hands. With Britain in the throes of abandoning her base in Libya, Aden and the Persian Gulf were the last toeholds of her dominion in the Arab world. Thomson's visit might therefore be intended to talk him into endorsing the plans for Aden's future independence, including the perpetuation of the British base.

At the same time, Nasser knew that he could hardly reject this British olive-branch. However deeply he might suspect its underlying motives, to do so would be to cause gratuitous offence which could be of no benefit to Egypt. In late September, therefore, as soon as the Casablanca conference adjourned, Thomson arrived in Cairo to begin his round of consultations with the Egyptians.

It was an ill-starred visit. For hardly had he landed than the news broke that the British High Commissioner in Aden had suspended the constitution, dismissed the Council of Ministers and assumed full governmental powers under a dawn to dusk curfew. These severe measures were in response to a recent outbreak of nationalist agitation, following the failure of a constitutional conference in London to reconcile the differences between the British Government and the Adeni nationalists represented by FLOSY and its rival group the National Liberation Front. But whether or not the High Commissioner's action was justified in the prevailing circumstances, it could not have been worse timed from Thomson's point of view. Only an hour or so before the news was flashed to Cairo, a member of Nasser's staff had telephoned to George Middleton, Beeley's successor as British Ambassador, to arrange for Thomson to see the President later that same morning. But as soon as he heard what had happened in Aden, Nasser immediately cancelled the appointment.

Unable to believe that such extraordinary timing could be

accidental, he was now convinced that Thomson's visit was no more than a perfidious cover-plan and that, as at the time of the Suez crisis, Britain's real intentions were to provoke a show-down with him as the principal Arab adversary of British imperialism. The suspicions aroused when he first learned of Britain's contingency planning in the Middle East now seemed to be fully borne out. The pledge of independence for Aden by 1968 was a mere blind to divert attention from the small print. Far from being about to bow their way out of the Arabian peninsula, the British were actively planning military operations against Egypt in concert with their American allies. And for these purposes they intended to stay in Aden indefinitely with a military base maintained by agreement with some puppet Government, selected by a British High Commissioner exercising the same arbitrary powers as had just been used to suspend the constitution.

The more Nasser pondered on these unhappy developments the more determined he became to leave the British Government in no doubt that he had seen through their sinister schemes. Apart from a meeting with Mahmoud Fawzi before the news from Aden reached Cairo, Thomson's attempts to confer with Egyptian Ministers met with a complete official boycott. Of the two hundred Egyptians invited to the embassy reception in his honour only thirty turned up, of whom none save Heikal were of any significance.

After Thomson had departed empty-handed, Nasser refused to have any further personal dealings with Britain's Ambassador. Two months later the Egyptian Government unhesitatingly supported the decision of the independent African states to break with Britain, if the Smith regime in Rhodesia had not been crushed by December 15. And when the appointed day arrived with Smith still firmly entrenched in office, Cairo duly severed diplomatic relations with London. As a personal favour, Middleton was allowed to stay in his embassy for a few weeks as a private citizen, after he had complained with mock bitterness to Fawzi that, if he were sent home before Christmas, he would be expected to send presents to every distant relative! Also, unlike in 1956, consular and commercial relations between the two countries remained unaffected. But, these considerations apart, the breach with Britain was once again complete.

Rhodesia had provided the pretext, but the real cause of this demonstration was Nasser's now absolute conviction that the British were engaged in yet another conspiracy, this time with the Americans, to destroy the Arab nationalist revolution. Their secret plans and their performance in Aden were alone enough to show their treacherous intentions. But this was not all. For it also seemed that they were once again trying to gang up the 'conservative' Arab states against Egypt. On leaving Cairo, Thomson had visited Saudi Arabia for talks with Feisal. Then three months later and less than a week after the breach between Cairo and London, Riyadh announced that Britain had agreed to supply the Saudis with an air defence system costing some £150 millions. And on top of all this, in the very same month Feisal paid a visit to Teheran, where he and the Shah jointly proclaimed their intention to summon an Islamic summit conference.

Nasser inevitably interpreted the Teheran decision as a deliberate attempt to submerge him and his 'progressive' allies in a gathering of Moslem states in which such sworn adversaries of Egypt as Turkey and Iran would predominate. This was threatening enough in itself. But set alongside Britain's agreement to supply Saudi Arabia with so much valuable and sophisticated military equipment, it seemed all too obvious that the imperialist powers had selected the Saudis to lead their counter-offensive against the Arab revolution. There could only be one answer to such machinations – to drive the British out of Aden, their last remaining military base in the area, with the utmost possible speed.

Support for the Adeni nationalists, including arms and explosives, was therefore immediately stepped up. Cairo Radio poured forth an ever-increasing stream of invective against British imperialism. More far-reaching still, a drastic reappraisal was made of Egypt's strategy in Yemen, from which it was decided that, whether or not the current cease-fire continued in effect, an Egyptian military presence should remain in Yemen to reinforce the efforts of FLOSY and the other nationalist groups in Aden.

Egyptian troop withdrawals were therefore promptly suspended and, in January 1966, amid loud protests from the Saudis and the Imam that Egypt had broken the Jedda agreement by failing to withdraw her forces, fighting broke out yet again in Yemen.

Among the imperialist powers Nasser's darkest suspicions were at this point clearly directed towards Britain. But his feelings towards the Americans were scarcely less apprehensive. In the past two years, Lyndon Johnson had done nothing to exorcise his pro-Israeli and anti-Arab reputation. Relations between Washington and Cairo had become decidedly sour and Nasser suspected that the new American administration were playing politics with their economic aid to Egypt. In November 1964, the new American Ambassador, Lucius Battle, had had a most ill-fated conversation about American wheat shipments with Kemal Stino, the Egyptian Trade and Supply Minister. Battle had complained of the apparent ingratitude of the Egyptians for all the millions of dollars' worth of American help which, he said, showed a grievous lack of good manners on their part. When the record of Stino's interview reached his office, Nasser, who was not in the best of moods after an argument with Amer about Yemen, exploded with rage and indignation. Seizing the first opportunity to hit back, he declaimed in a speech at Port Said that the Americans could 'go and drink the Mediterranean', for all he cared. President Johnson, he said, must realise that 'I am not prepared to sell Egyptian independence for thirty, forty or fifty million pounds.'

No less unhappily, a couple of days later, a demonstration by Cairo's African students against American policy in the Congo resulted in the burning of the United States Information Service's Library. And some three weeks after that, an aeroplane belonging to an American oil company was shot down near Alexandria by an Egyptian fighter after a misunderstanding had arisen about its clearance to overfly Egypt. Consequently, when the wheat shipment agreement negotiated by the Kennedy Government lapsed at the end of its three-year term in July 1965, there was no great enthusiasm in Washington to renew it.

Nasser was able to obtain some compensating supplies of grain from Russia and China. But, since at this point Egypt depended on America for 50 per cent of her wheat imports, by the end of the summer the shortage had become critical. Nevertheless, when Zacharia Mohieddin, whom Washington regarded as being pro-American, took over the premiership from Ali Sabry in October 1965, the American attitude towards Egypt visibly mellowed; and on November 30, the United States Government agreed to supply another £20 million worth of wheat, making a total of some £285 million of food supplied against Egyptian currency since 1962.

But the new agreement was limited to the next six months and, when the time came to renew it, a serious grain shortage had struck America and other producers. Such surpluses as existed were therefore sent to India whose need was held to be greater than Egypt's. To make up for this, Washington intended, when the situation reverted to normal, to offer the Egyptians a two-year wheat agreement. But Nasser had no knowledge of this and, before the Americans could come up with any concrete offer, he angrily accused them of playing cat-and-mouse with Egypt and of trying to starve her into submission. Rather than wait for Washington to oblige with further shipments, he took his custom elsewhere. And once he had made sure of a guaranteed supply of grain from other sources, he formally withdrew all requests for further American aid.

The President's advisers might protest that by so doing he was serving Moscow's interests more than Egypt's. They might warn him that the Russians were using him to shut American influence out of the Arab world, while they kept the door open for their own negotiations with Washington on such issues as nuclear weapon testing, where Russia's interests required agreement with the United States. But Washington's hesitation in 1965 to renew the supply of grain to Egypt was to implant in Nasser's mind an ineradicable conviction that the Americans, no less than the scheming British, were his implacable enemies. Even if he had not felt that his position as the leader of the Arab revolution required him to brand the United States as an imperialist power, nobody could now persuade him that any amount of sweet words

further
6 mos
supplies

from Cairo would ever change Johnson into a friend. Admittedly he had been only too thankful when Mohieddin's occupancy of the premiership helped to get a further six months' supply of American grain to feed his hungry subjects. But very soon after that Nasser abandoned all hope of achieving an understanding with the United States, at least so long as Johnson occupied the White House. For, coming on top of the evidence that Britain was ganging up on him with a pro-Zionist American President and a reactionary Saudi monarch, Washington's apparent attempts to put pressure on Egypt by withholding wheat shipments clearly suggested that a coordinated Anglo-American conspiracy, on the same lines as that hatched by Eden and Mollet in 1956, was now under way.

Thus, 1965 became a turning point in Egypt's relations with the West no less significant than that which ten years before had led to the first Russian arms deal. And although Nasser did not actually break off relations with America as he had done with Britain, he decided to discontinue all but the most formal diplomatic contacts with Washington. Indeed so incensed had he become with the Americans over the wheat problem, and so suspicious of their intentions, that he even turned on the man whom he had long ago appointed as his private contact with the CIA, as if to erase every vestige of such American associations.

Despite the ever-growing ascendancy of Heikal as his principal confidant, Nasser had over the years maintained close personal relations with the Amin brothers. He also kept up the habit, which began in the Suez crisis, of using them for the kind of unofficial diplomacy to which he had been addicted since those early days under Neguib when, although the power behind the throne, he himself had no official standing with the representatives of foreign powers. Ali Amin had been a kind of roving ambassador to Britain, while his brother Mustapha had been Nasser's private contact with Washington, and more recently, with the CIA representative in Cairo by the name of Bruce O'Dell.

Among other things, Mustapha Amin was detailed to keep O'Dell posted of those items of interest which Nasser, for one reason or another, did not want to be passed officially to the

American Ambassador. Not surprisingly therefore, in the spring of 1965, he told his contact that Egypt was facing a grave food shortage as a result of the cessation of American wheat shipments. Such information could hardly have been regarded as secret and no doubt Amin thought it useful to rub into the Americans the seriousness of Egypt's current plight. Yet, when it was decided to mark the discontinuance of such informal contacts with the CIA by expelling O'Dell and arresting Amin for espionage, the fact that he had said this was among the charges included in the indictment. Admittedly the tapes of Amin's conversations, on which the prosecution based its case, also revealed that Amin had been somewhat indiscreet in telling O'Dell of a visit by Egyptian physicists to China to seek help in atomic research which Russia had refused to provide. Also he was unwise enough to discuss certain financial transactions in such a way as to suggest that he was smuggling money out of Egypt preparatory to fleeing the country. But the fact that, while awaiting trial, he was assured by the Chief of Intelligence, Salah Nasr, that, provided he did not mention that he had been acting on the President's instructions, the trial would be mere 'theatricals' and he would be swiftly released, suggests that the motive for these proceedings was not exactly judicial. Moreover, when he refused to accept this 'advice', and wrote to the Minister of Justice protesting that his actions had Nasser's full approval, Sami Sharaf, speaking on the President's behalf, categorically denied this assertion.

It is just possible that Nasser was persuaded by his intelligence service that his old friend had abused his position to pass information to the Americans which he had no authority to divulge, and for large sums of money with which he was intending to abscond from Egypt. Certainly Amin's every attempt to make contact with the President before and after his trial was not only thwarted by the prison authorities, but usually followed by a denial of such privileges as special food or drugs which he needed as a diabetic. Yet it is difficult to believe that Nasser, with his consuming interest in the minutiae of government, was unaware of this travesty of justice, even if it was originally conceived by others who held a grudge against its victim.

However ill-advised Amin may have been in some of the things he discussed with O'Dell, Nasser should have known that he was no traitor and that, at any moment before or after his trial, a word from the presidency could have spared him further mental and physical suffering. But Nasser had now decided to drop the Americans altogether. And since, according to the tapes of his conversations, Amin had never failed to remind O'Dell of the close relationship which he enjoyed with his President, he presumably deemed it doubly necessary to deny his former friend and so to serve notice on the United States that he had severed all his old associations. Consequently this cruel farce was played out to the end which for Mustapha Amin meant life imprisonment and for Nasser the start of a sorry progression of errors and miscalculations which was to leave him to face disaster in the course of the next two years with hardly a single friend among the leaders of the Western world.

But if, in this particular instance, Nasser seemed to have acted with an uncharacteristic inhumanity towards an old friend, in general his attitude towards his associates had come to show an ever-increasing arrogance and disregard, especially of those who deeply, and often rightly, believed that what he was doing was wrong and foolish. Nothing could have illustrated this growing tendency more graphically than the manner in which he made his sweeping changes of policy in 1965. For, even as he embarked on the radical reappraisal of his relations with the West and of his strategy in Yemen, he decided to appoint as Prime Minister the man who, above all his other colleagues, had consistently urged that Egypt should keep a balance in her relations with America and Russia and should withdraw from Yemen whatever the cost in prestige. Yet, far from taking Zacharia Mohieddin's advice, Nasser consulted only Amer before deciding to keep his troops in southern Arabia and to abandon all hope of an understanding with the West. Used to treating Ali Sabry over the past two years as an executive secretary, he saw the function of his Prime Minister as being exclusively confined to the home front. Mohieddin might try to argue, as he did throughout the eleven months that he held the premiership, that Egypt's involvement in Yemen, having already cost the country around £500 millions, was draining the economy dry. But his President literally refused to listen and, at each attempt, he cut him short, as he did with any others of his associates who ventured to question the wisdom of the Yemeni commitment.

Besides, Nasser contended that Mohieddin had been appointed specifically to deal with a number of problems on the home front which had recently begun to cause grave concern. Among other things the government machine had, under Ali Sabry's misdirection, become so seriously disorganised and contaminated with corruption that, at the end of 1964, it had been necessary to set up a committee under Mohieddin's chairmanship to reorganise it from top to bottom. Added to this, the loss of Boghdady was making itself felt in the Cabinet and in the country at large. Public opinion had been disturbed by his resignation; and the split in the Government over nationalisation, which had helped to precipitate it, was being reflected among the people. A considerable rightist reaction was developing within the dispossessed bourgeoisie and, when the old Wafdist leader, Mustapha Nahas, died in September 1965, the enormous crowds which followed his funeral cortege served notice on the regime that, however docile they might be, the Egyptian populace with their peasant traditions had remained predominantly conservative in outlook, despite every effort to change them. Then, when the residue of the old reactionary Moslem Brotherhood chose this moment to erupt in a violent demonstration against the police in one of Cairo's suburbs, the authorities promptly proclaimed martial law. The ring-leaders were rounded up and it was announced that a major conspiracy to overthrow the Government had been unearthed.

In fact the Moslem Brotherhood was at this late stage hardly in a position to topple the regime. But, however exaggerated the case against them might have been, these events made plain that an important section of the Egyptian public still distrusted socialism and regarded the ownership of property as their inalienable right. Therefore, if Nasser for his part still insisted that without 'economic democracy' all the political gains of the revolution would be endangered, a major effort was required to sell socialism to the people.

To this end, the President had already appointed Khaled Mohieddin as editor of *Akhbar el-Yom*, Cairo's most important weekly publication, with the specific task of educating public opinion in his special brand of economic democracy. But this was clearly not enough and it was therefore decided that the Arab Socialist Union should be built up as a proselytising force for socialism. Ali Sabry was then promptly switched from the premiership, in which he had been so totally miscast, to the chairmanship of the ASU; and Zacharia Mohieddin, who after Boghdady left the Government, had been Nasser's most efficient administrator, was appointed as Prime Minister to reorganise the Government apparatus and deal firmly with the challenge from the Moslem Brotherhood and the disaffected bourgeoisie.

Nasser knew well enough that Western opinion would misinterpret the change in the premiership as a swing back to the Right. For, however misguidedly, in Washington and other Western capitals it was firmly believed that, while Ali Sabry was pro-Russian, Mohieddin was pro-American, whereas in fact the former was pro-Sabry and the latter pro-Egypt. But apart from finding some amusement in the thought that the Americans would hail what was intended as a move to propagate socialism in Egypt as a gesture of friendship towards the citadel of capitalism, Nasser was at that moment in dire need of help which only the Americans could provide at such short notice. Therefore, if Mohieddin, with his good name in Washington, could help to plug the gap in Egypt's grain supplies, nobody need point out that his political sympathies were not as the Americans believed.

In the event, Mohieddin's eleven months' tenure of office was a mixture of failure and success. The revolt of the Moslem Brotherhood and the rightist bourgeoisie was vigorously suppressed, three of the former being sent to the gallows for plotting to assassinate members of the Government. By way of preserving a balance, a number of Communists were also imprisoned, whom the Government took care to accuse of working to the orders of Peking rather than Moscow. On the other hand, the ASU's indoctrination campaign achieved only limited success in its efforts to popularise socialism. But so well did Ali Sabry succeed in popularising the ASU that Nasser began to fear lest it become a serious challenge to the supremacy of the Executive. And when Amer and the army began to envisage a similar threat to their own autonomy, he quickly forgot all the fine phrases with which he had introduced the ASU as the new instrument by which the people would control their rulers. Ali Sabry was swiftly put in his place and all ideas of parliamentary government were laid to rest.

But by far the most intractable of the problems with which Mohieddin had to cope was the economic situation. In vain did he appeal to Nasser to pull out all but a token force from Yemen, which he insisted was the only way to set the economy to rights. Although he introduced a number of austere measures to reduce demand, expand exports and curb inflation, when these measures began to bite and so to cause popular criticism, the President more often than not insisted that they be discontinued. In fact, by April 1966, Mohieddin was so discouraged that he submitted his resignation. But this was refused and he therefore soldiered on until the following September, when Nasser decided in effect to become his own Prime Minister and appointed as Mohieddin's successor Sidky Suleiman, a former army engineer with little experience of government beyond having supervised the final stages in the construction of the High Dam. Mohieddin thereafter remained one of the Vice-Presidents of the republic. But, as Boghdady had found when he was deprived of administrative office after his stand against nationalisation, the Vice-Presidents were, save for Amer, seldom consulted about policy. Thus, after more than ten years at the centre of government, Mohieddin found himself fobbed off with a grandiose sinecure with less power than ever to influence events and only prevented from resigning altogether by his absolute loyalty to the leader whom he had served and loved for so long.

The pretext for Mohieddin's dismissal was his agreement with the International Monetary Fund to a form of devaluation, which Nasser regarded as an intolerable interference in Egypt's economic affairs. But in fact the two men had anyhow reached a parting of the ways. Nasser had come to regard Mohieddin as both defeatist and obstructive. With his incurable suspicion of other people, he was also afraid that, if Mohieddin remained in office, the Americans would be tempted to try to do some private deal with him. Besides, he had decided that the West were ineluctably his enemies and in making the dispositions which flowed from this decision, he wanted nobody around him who would question his basic premise.

Chapter 19

The Fatal Commitment

By the beginning of 1966 Nasser had, politically speaking, declared war on the United States and Britain in much the same way as Anthony Eden had done against him after the Glubb episode in 1956. And, as had happened with Eden, so Nasser was now to be driven inexorably towards disaster by a chain reaction of sickness and suspicion, over-reaction and misjudgement. Desperately striving to retain the initiative in the Middle East, he committed Egypt to a series of adventures and undertakings far beyond what her capacities could sustain; so that, instead of moulding events to his design, he found himself reacting ever more impetuously to the actions of others who, whether by their own or his choosing, had become his enemies.

In his absolute determination to evict the British from Aden and thwart the sinister plans which he believed them to be concocting with their American allies, Nasser reinforced his troops in Yemen until nearly half his army was engaged in this remote corner of Arabia. Heedless of the fact that his efforts to promote the activities of FLOSY were currently doing more to create jealousy among rival nationalist groups than to make trouble for the British colonial authority, his agents continued to smuggle arms into Aden. For good measure, he even took up an offer by ex-King Saud to go to Yemen and work against his brother Feisal by bribing the tribes to defect from the Imam, which paradoxical enterprise was to be as unfruitful as it was treacherous. He also proclaimed that the Egyptian presence in southern Arabia would remain for twenty years if necessary, which Heikal afterwards spelled out in *Al-Ahram* as meaning that Egyptian troops would stay in Yemen until they had forced the British out of the area. Cairo Radio continued to lambast Western imperialism and the CIA were accused of helping the royalists on behalf of their British and Saudi allies.

In February 1966 the British Government indicated that on reconsideration they would not after all require a military base in Aden after independence. But Nasser suspected that this was just another blind. And although proposals for mediation in Yemen continued to come from various Arab quarters – including one from the Ruler of Kuwait suggesting that he and Nasser should together visit Feisal for discussions about restoring the cease-fire – they were now one and all summarily rejected in Cairo. Nasser was not going to accept any arrangement which required the withdrawal of his troops until the last British soldier had left Aden.

For a nation as lacking in resources as Egypt this decision was in itself asking too much. Yet such were the constraints under which he was now working that, notwithstanding these extensive commitments, Nasser was about to take upon himself the further and, as it was shortly to prove, fatal obligation to defend Syria against attack from any quarter.

The series of events which led to this additional undertaking had begun in June of the previous year when Ben Bella was over-thrown in Algeria in a 'palace revolution' staged by the Defence Minister, Colonel Houari Boumedienne. Nasser was deeply disturbed by this event. For one thing, it threatened the life of a man for whom he had considerable personal affection. For another, he suspected that it had been engineered by the imperialist powers, to whose interests Algeria's uncompromising nationalism had been a constant threat.

Two years earlier, in May 1963, he had paid a state visit to Algeria which, apart from the opportunity to renew contacts with Ben Bella, had turned out to be anything but happy. Not only had he arrived green in the face from sea-sickness after a particularly rough voyage in the presidential yacht, but among the functions which he had to attend was the state funeral of the Foreign Minister who had been assassinated two days before. On top of this Algeria was currently stricken by violent storms and floods. And what with the vagaries of the weather and the violence of the Algerian character, as evidenced by the Foreign Minister's bullet-riddled corpse, Nasser found little to like about the country or its people.

When Boumedienne seized power in June 1965, Nasser was therefore gravely concerned. He feared for Ben Bella's life and also for the effect which the change might have upon the balance of power in the Arab world. An emissary was sent immediately to Algiers to seek assurances on both counts. But although in the end Ben Bella's life was spared, at the time Boumedienne refused to give any guarantee of clemency. Also, far from promising any continuity in Algeria's inter-Arab relations, he quickly aligned himself with his Moroccan and Tunisian neighbours, both of whom were among Egypt's staunchest opponents. More ominous still, he began to show signs of wooing the Hafiz regime in Syria with suggestions of support on the Palestine question.

Eight months later, however, in February 1966, the Secretary-General of the Syrian Baath party, General Salah Jadid, staged yet another coup in Damascus. To Nasser's infinite relief, Hafiz was arrested and deposed and his former Deputy Prime Minister, Nur ed-Din el-Atassi, was proclaimed President of Syria. This change of leadership, which was largely the result of a power struggle within the Baath hierarchy, produced little significant modification of foreign policy beyond a slight leftward trend, to which Russia was quick to respond with offers of help and an agreement to assist in the construction of a much-needed dam on the Euphrates river. But Nasser's quarrel with Syria had recently become so personalised by his hatred for Hafiz that, with his pet aversion now finally out of the way, he had no hesitation in making immediate approaches to his successor.

Even so, he could not resist a dig at the capriciousness of the Baath by remarking on his first encounter with President Atassi, 'I am told that Jadid is the real ruler of Syria. Why don't you send him to meet me?' Also, on a later occasion, when the two Presidents met in Tripoli to celebrate the withdrawal of the American air base from Libya, he told Atassi that he had never trusted the Baath in the past and would never be able to do so in the foreseeable future. Yet, at this moment, with Boumedienne offering his hand to Syria, Cairo had no option but to try to get on terms with the new Damascus regime, if only to preserve the balance of power. Besides, the very fact that Hafiz had sent messages warning the Egyptians against having any dealings with his successor would have sufficed to tempt Nasser to sound Atassi out.

At this self-same juncture, Cairo also heard that Nkrumah had been deposed as Ghana's leader. To Nasser's way of thinking, this development only served to reconfirm his suspicions that the imperialist powers were engaged in a major counter-offensive in the Third World and that the 'progressive' countries should therefore close their ranks and sink their differences. No less worrying was the news which came two weeks later that his best, if not only, friend in Iraq, Abdel Salam Aref, had been killed in a helicopter crash near Basra. Aref was promptly succeeded as President by his brother, Abdel Rahman, who marked his appointment by pledging that there would be no change in Iraq's policies. But the new President was relatively unknown to Nasser; and to make things worse, his succession had been strenuously opposed by the Baathists who, for all the recent attempts to suppress them, still remained a force to be reckoned with. Added to all this, the stability of Iraq had been still further threatened by a fresh outbreak of heavy fighting with the fractious Kurds only a few days before Aref's untimely death.

When therefore Russia's Premier Kosygin visited Cairo in May 1966 and urged Nasser to make his peace with the Syrians, he was pushing at an open door. For the Egyptians were already striving their hardest to develop the closest attainable relationship with Syria's new leaders. Contacts with Damascus were vigorously pursued by Mahmoud Riad, with his unrivalled knowledge of Syria and more especially of the Baath. And in June, after Atassi had responded to Cairo's solicitations with warm praise for Egypt and Algeria as 'progressive forces', the first delegation of Syrian Ministers to visit Egypt for more than three years arrived in Cairo for what were officially termed 'political discussions'.

Satisfied that a new relationship with Syria was in the making, Nasser then launched into a series of violent denunciations of the pro-Western Arab rulers with whom, he claimed, cooperation against Israel had become futile and impossible. Contending that he had been deceived at the summit conferences in 1964 and 1965 by their protestations of solidarity, he declared that, in the months that followed, these 'reactionaries' had proved quite useless in the conflict with the Israeli invader and had shown that 'they hate us more than they hate Israel'. He even indulged in the fanciful threat to wage a preventive war or develop atomic weapons should Israel acquire such arms from her Western backers.

Among the targets of Nasser's renewed assault on the 'reactionaries' was King Hussein, with whom the fragile peace that emerged from the Cairo summit meeting two years before had yet again been shattered. For one thing, Hussein had in the interval become increasingly a protégé of the Americans. Moreover, he was currently engaged in a bitter dispute with Shukhairy. He might have agreed to the concept of a Palestinian entity as a means of pacifying his West Bank subjects. For the same reason he had also accepted the creation of the PLO. But Hussein had little love for the Palestinians in his kingdom, having inherited much of the traditional jealousy of the East Bank Jordanians for their West Bank cousins from the days when his grandfather, King Abdullah, had been obliged to draw on the superior talents of the Palestinians to rule his relatively backward realm. Thus, when Shukhairy tried to recruit and establish units of the PLO's army on Jordanian soil, the King stubbornly refused to countenance any such plan.

As Hussein saw it, the Egyptians had nothing to lose by letting Shukhairy operate in the Gaza Strip, which was far enough removed from the main centres of Egypt not to interfere with the daily life and administration of the country and was protected by the U.N. troops from any Israeli reprisals. But for the PLO to set up training camps on the West Bank would be at one and the same time to invite Israeli counter-action and to threaten Jordanian authority in the very heart of the country. In the interests of preserving peace and security in this sensitive border area, it had long been a rule that, apart from members of the Jordanian army and police, no West Bank inhabitant should carry or possess firearms. Therefore, if Shukhairy were to get his way, this rule would be broken and a rival army would also spring into existence, owing allegiance to an outside authority over which Amman had no control, threatening disturbances in Jordanian territory and, more menacing still, provoking the Israelis across the border.

However, Nasser did not choose to see the problem in this light. And when Shukhairy bitterly attacked Hussein for refusing to allow the PLO to recruit the Palestinians living in Jordan, he supported Shukhairy. The utmost that he would concede to Hussein was to call a conference in Cairo of Arab representatives at which the Jordanian case could be put and debated. But the conference soon turned into a one-sided contest between Hussein's representative and Shukhairy, supported by Egypt, Syria, and Algeria, from which the Jordanians only extricated themselves by announcing that they would ask the next Arab summit conference, scheduled for Algiers in a month's time, to draw up a clear-cut plan for the future of the PLO. Whereupon Nasser promptly wrecked the Algiers meeting by declaring that he refused to sit at the same table with the supporters of reaction and the friends of the dastardly Americans, who were currently trying to starve Egypt into submission by withholding wheat shipments.

Nasser knew well enough that Shukhairy's ambition could all too easily run away with him and that his fiery utterances against Israel and Hussein could cause incalculable trouble. Although Egypt's frontiers were relatively secure, thanks to the protection provided by the Blue Berets of UNEF, those of Israel's other Arab neighbours were not. On the contrary they were as vulnerable as ever to the kind of 'reprisal' raids which Ben Gurion had instigated in the days before the Suez War. Nasser was also well aware that, while the PLO were prevented from engaging the Israelis from Egyptian territory by the presence of UNEF, and from Jordan and Lebanon by order of Amman and Beirut, the Syrians were allowing Shukhairy's guerrillas, as well as Arafat's Fatah commandos, to train and operate from Syrian territory.

All these considerations made it essential for Cairo to gain some degree of control over the actions and policies of the men in Damascus. For, as the events of the past year had made all too clear, it was no longer possible to quarantine the impetuous

Syrians. Following on the loss of his friend Ben Bella in Algeria, Nasser had become dangerously isolated. No longer, therefore, could he manipulate his fellow rulers as he had previously been able to do at every summit meeting from Cairo to Casablanca.

True, the alienation of the conservative Arab states was largely the product of Nasser's own determination to expose their association with the new conspiracies which he believed the Western powers were hatching against him. But, whether or not his attacks on the 'reactionaries' were justified, the fact remained that, whatever line he took vis-à-vis Israel, he was now liable to attack from his fellow Arabs. He had therefore come to the conclusion that there was only one way to keep the initiative in Egypt's hands. That was to join in a defence agreement with the regime in Damascus and, without openly appearing to dampen their ardour, to impose a restraining influence on the Syrian army and hence on the Palestinian guerrillas operating from Syrian territory.

Much as he still distrusted Syria's Baathists, Nasser could see no other course open to him. The fact that the tone of his public utterances about Israel had recently become more abrasive did not mean that he had in any way changed his mind about the futility of the Arabs trying to restore the Palestinians to their lost lands by force of arms. On the contrary, such playing to the militant gallery was purely a matter of political necessity. No longer able to beat the Syrians and keep them isolated, he felt he had no alternative but to join them if he was to avoid the Arab world being dragged into a third round with Israel. If, as he believed, the Western powers were gunning for him again, nothing could better help their plans than for Egypt to become embroiled in a war with Israel in which the weight of world opinion would be against the Arabs because Syria had started it. Quite apart, therefore, from any questions of leadership in the Arab world, Egypt's security required that she should secure control of Syrian military planning at the earliest opportunity.

If there was ever any doubt in Nasser's mind about the logic of these conclusions, the Israelis themselves were soon to dispel it. For, early in September, the Syrians suffered a punishing attack on their territory in retaliation, so Tel Aviv claimed, for shelling by Syrian artillery and for infiltrations by Palestinian guerrillas operating against Israel with the connivance of the Syrian authorities. In fairness to the Syrians, the bombardments of which Tel Aviv complained were against fortifications which the Israelis had erected in the area of Lake Huleh, which under the terms of the 1949 armistice agreement had been made a demilitarised zone. Although successive Governments in Damascus had tried to have the issue adjudicated by the Mixed Armistice Commission ever since the fortifications were first built in 1951, the Israelis had stubbornly contended that such matters were not negotiable. And when Damascus had recently tried to raise the matter again, the only response from Tel Aviv was to issue an unequivocal warning that Syria would be held responsible for all future attacks by Palestinians or others in the area.

Shortly after this renewed outbreak on the Israeli-Syrian border, Nasser received another highly disturbing piece of intelligence about American strategy in relation to the Middle East. Amin Shaker reported from his embassy in Brussels that, according to Belgium's Foreign Minister Spaak, the Americans had recently told a secret meeting of NATO representatives that they were convinced that peaceful co-existence with Egypt was no longer possible. Nasser, they said, had poisoned all hope of the United States working with Arab nationalism by his repeated attacks on American policy and by his ever-growing cooperation with Russia. And for these reasons Washington was now working on a new policy for the defence of American interests in the Middle East which would be based on the twin bastions of Turkey and Israel.

Coming on top of existing suggestions that America and Britain were ganging up on Egypt again, together with the announcement a few months earlier that a large consignment of American military aircraft was on its way to Israel, Shaker's report could not have seemed more ominous. Nasser, more than ever convinced that the clock was being put back ten years, now decided that the recent attacks on Syria were, like the Gaza raid in 1955, the prelude to some concerted move by the West and

Israel to stamp out Arab nationalism. As he saw it, even if the Western powers, remembering the shameful débâcle of Suez, refrained from actually fighting in support of another Israeli aggression, they would certainly be deeply involved in the political and strategic planning. They would offer Israel all the necessary arms and advice for whatever military operations were intended, together with a guarantee of political support in the United Nations and of the Sixth Fleet's presence if things went wrong. Then, when the Israelis had triumphed in the field, they would move in to install whatever puppet Governments they wanted in the conquered territories.

Meanwhile, in Damascus, Atassi had for his part also begun to favour Nasser's idea of a military alliance. In the summer of 1966, Chou En-lai had paid a visit to Syria where, in language similar to that which he had used on Nasser in the previous year, he had tried to poison the Syrians against Russia and Egypt. The Egyptians, he hinted, were completely under the dominance of their Russian paymasters who were only interested in helping the Arab world for what they could gain in the way of political influence. However, if Atassi were to break with Moscow, China would be more than happy to step in and supply all Syria's needs without any strings or ulterior motives.

Atassi was not a little shaken by the vehemence of Chou's denunciation of his Russian and Egyptian friends. But he nevertheless declined the offer of Chinese help and promptly reported his exchanges to Moscow. Whereupon the Soviet Government unhesitatingly urged Damascus to seek some kind of mutual defence arrangement with Egypt. Atassi lost no time in doing so. And Nasser, delighted that the initiative had come from the Syrian side, readily agreed to begin staff talks. In October 1966, ambassadors were exchanged between Cairo and Damascus and, on November 4, a defence agreement was signed by the two Governments, which provided that aggression against either state would be regarded as an attack on the other.

No provision was made for Egyptian forces to be stationed in Syria, and Nasser, remembering Syrian complaints of the behaviour of his troops under the union, did not press for such facilities.

Nevertheless, he felt that he had secured a measure of control over Syria's military dispositions sufficient to ensure that Egypt would not be dragged unwittingly into war with Israel. Moreover, by way of underlining that Cairo intended to be the judge of when and in what circumstances the new alliance would be activated, Heikal promptly warned the Syrians through the columns of *Al-Ahram* not to assume that Egyptian forces would automatically intervene against any Israeli attack on their territory. But, no matter what caveats Cairo might issue regarding these arrangements, the fact was that Nasser had sprung upon himself the first of a series of traps which were to present him as a sitting target to his Israeli enemies in exactly seven months' time.

Within nine days of the agreement's signature, a chain of events was set in motion which was to upset all his calculations. On November 13, following the explosion of a mine which killed three Israeli soldiers on the Jordanian frontier near Hebron, an Israeli armoured force, backed by air and artillery support, struck at the Jordanian village of Samu, destroying 125 houses and killing eighteen soldiers of a Jordan army unit which had gone to the defence of the villagers. Violent demonstrations followed in Jerusalem and other West Bank towns, where the King was bitterly attacked for having abandoned the Palestinian population to the fury of the enemy by refusing to allow the PLO to defend what remained of their homeland. And as Jordanian troops moved in to quell the riots, Hussein's Prime Minister, Wasfi al-Tall, bitterly reproached the unified Arab command and the Egyptian air force for having lifted not a finger to help Jordan to beat off this savage Israeli assault.

Hussein had found the answer to the vilifications of Shukhairy and his Egyptian patrons. From now on the Jordanian press and radio maintained the derisive refrain that Nasser was hiding behind UNEF's skirts and avoiding combat with the enemy, while at the same time posturing as Israel's most redoubtable opponent and Syria's staunchest ally. Israel, it was said, was receiving military supplies via the Gulf of Akaba which Nasser had allowed to pass unhindered, knowing that they were to be used to kill Arabs whom he was sworn to defend. The unified command had been invented as an alibi for Egypt's total inactivity whenever her brothers in Jordan or elsewhere were attacked. Most heinous of all, with the encouragement and connivance of the Russians, Cairo was preparing to sell out the West Bank to Israel in return for a separate peace settlement.

To all these allegations the Egyptians could only retort, somewhat lamely, that UNEF would be ordered to withdraw at the right opportunity and that they were not going to have the timing decided for them by Hussein who, like his grandfather before him, was a creature of Western imperialism. Atassi then joined in the fray, calling on the Jordanian people to overthrow the Amman regime which he said had become 'a stumbling block in the way of the liberation of Palestine'. Shukhairy and the Fatah leadership also fulminated against Hussein for actively preventing the Palestinians from mobilising to fight for their lost heritage. But the King was not to be moved. Accusing the PLO of seeking to destroy Jordan and of 'sending saboteurs instead of soldiers to fight on our side', he demanded an Arab summit meeting to expose what he termed the machinations of his twin enemies, Israel and Arab Socialism allied to Russian and Chinese Communism. Then, when this was refused, in February 1967, he withdrew his ambassador from Cairo in protest against the attacks made upon him by the Egyptian press and by the 'Voice of the Arabs'. For good measure he also withdrew his recognition of the Sallal regime in Yemen.

By contrast with the disarray which now prevailed in the Arab camp, the Israelis presented the very embodiment of military preparedness. Unlike their fragmented neighbours, they had used the years since the Suez War not to squabble among themselves, but to work out and perfect plans to recover all and more than they had been obliged to abandon after their victory in 1956. As the Israeli air force commander was to say after the Six Days War, more than ten years of planning had preceded the assault which Israel launched against Egypt and her allies in 1967.

For all these ten years it had been an axiom of Israeli thinking that Nasser should be destroyed, or at least humiliated beyond hope of recovering his prestige as an Arab leader. After the war of 1956, Ben Gurion had told his people that, while Egypt's defeat in Sinai had 'diminished the stature of the Egyptian dictator', he had always feared that a personality might come forward such as arose among the Arabs in the seventh century and 'raised their spirits, changed their character and turned them into a fighting nation'. There was, he said, 'still a danger that Nasser is this man'. True, Ben Gurion had since handed over the premiership to Eshkol. But his words had lost none of their meaning for the Israeli army and the more belligerent politicians. What is more, in 1965, Ben Gurion had broken with Eshkol and his old Mapai party associates, whom he considered too passive towards the Arabs. Together with Moshe Dayan, the hero of the 1956 campaign, he had formed the Rafi splinter party, from which independent political base he had spent the past two years sniping at what he termed the Government's inertia.

Eshkol's policy was certainly not cast in the Ben Gurion mould of activism. For, at least to begin with, he believed in persuasion rather than coercion as a means of gaining the cooperation of the Arabs. He had permitted Israel's small Arab minority to join Israeli Trades Unions and had shown signs of wanting to release them from the system of segregation and pass laws which had restricted their freedom of movement over the previous eighteen years. He had also removed Dayan from the Ministry of Defence, together with Ben Gurion's other favourite 'hawk', Shimon Peres, who had been one of the principal architects of the 1956 war.

Initially Eshkol's relatively conciliatory approach was by no means unpopular with the majority of the Israeli people, as was shown by the failure of Ben Gurion's Rafi party to gain more than 10 seats out of a total of 120 in the 1965 elections for the Knesset. But, by the following year, Israel was beset by serious economic problems. Immigration fell to the lowest figure since 1948, unemployment rose to 10 per cent of the labour force and, most ominous of all, considerable numbers of the upper echelons of Israel's population, the intellectual and scientific cream of society, were returning to America and Western Europe to seek more scope for their talents. When the inevitable discontent began to manifest itself against the Government, the 'hawks' stepped up their campaign for a return to a more activist attitude towards Israel's Arab neighbours, partly as a diversion for Israeli opinion, partly also to rally support for the concept of a beleaguered Israel. Shukhairy, with his fiery speeches, and the Palestinians and Syrians, with their operations against the Huleh demilitarised zone, played into the hands of Ben Gurion and his supporters, who lost no opportunity to accuse the Government of irresponsibly compromising the nation's security. And as the army, led by its hawkish Chief of Staff, General Itzhak Rabin, demanded a free hand to engage in reprisals, Eshkol was obliged to abandon his passive ways. Hence the lunge at Syria in September 1966 and the destruction of Samu in Jordan two months later.

Nor was Eshkol an altogether unwilling convert to the activist idea. True, after the Samu operation, he proclaimed his hope that it would be the last of its kind and asserted that reprisals were not an integral part of his policy. But he also knew that Israel's best hope of getting the Western help that she needed to cure her economic ills was to be able to show that this 'bastion of Western democracy' was once again under siege. And if, as was almost certain, the Arabs could be relied upon to react with the required hostile threats, it could only benefit Israel to raise the temperature on her borders with at least an occasional punitive raid.

But the army and their militant supporters were still not satisfied. For although Syria and Jordan had been punished, Nasser had not; and so long as he was protected by UNEF, he could not be brought to battle. With Ben Gurion's warning constantly in mind, they were therefore determined to draw Nasser out from behind his protective screen and destroy his image as the Arabs' leader once and for all. Egypt's new commitment to defend Syria as her own territory seemed to provide the key to this problem. Hence, after the raid on Samu, the Israeli army claimed that their intention had not been to punish Jordan, but to destroy a village which had become a base for Syrian saboteurs operating behind their lines.

But Nasser was not to be lured into snatching at this obviously baited hook. And when a further series of minor raids across the Syrian and Jordanian borders, early in 1967, had failed to provoke more than furious protests from Cairo and a few feeble sallies from the Syrians, Eshkol was obliged by the pressures of his own militants to authorise another major strike against Syria. In the middle of April, with an ominous reminder to the Arabs that Israel could always count on the support of the Americans whose Sixth Fleet was never very far from the Syrian and Egyptian coasts, the Israeli air force was sent into action in retaliation for an act of sabotage committed by a group of Fatah guerrillas. And when the dust of this reprisal raid had settled, Israeli jet fighters had shot down no less than six Syrian MIGs after a chase which led them as far as Damascus itself.

Nasser was now thoroughly alarmed; and when, on April 21, a few days after this latest onslaught against his Syrian ally, an army coup in Greece installed a right-wing dictatorship, he immediately assumed that this represented yet another development of the 'imperialist' offensive in the Middle East. The new American strategy, of which Spaak had spoken, was being unfolded with awesome clarity. Greece was evidently to join Turkey as the rear base, while Israel acted as the vanguard in an operation designed to achieve Washington's long-sought aim of making Syria, like Jordan, an American satellite and thus isolating Egypt and forcing the submission of her leaders as well. Moreover, to confirm Nasser's worst suspicions, an Associated Press report three weeks later quoted a high-ranking Israeli officer as having threatened the military occupation of Damascus to put an end to Syrian and Palestinian sabotage inside Israel. Then, as these foreboding words echoed around the Middle East, General Rabin weighed in with a personal declaration that not until the Syrian Government had been overthrown could security be guaranteed for Israel or any other state in the area.

The concentration of all these threats on Syria only a few months after Egypt had underwritten her security could hardly have been more significant. Equally suggestive was the fact that, whereas Israel's attack on the Jordanians at Samu had called forth the strongest denunciation by the Western powers in the U.N. Security Council, the attacks on Syrian territory had occasioned only comparatively mild reproofs, accompanied by pious hopes that the Mixed Armistice Commission would be able to prevent a repetition of such incidents. For to Nasser these contrasting Western reactions implied that the Americans, aping Eden's tactics in 1956, were trying to keep Jordan out of the fight and to divert Israel's onslaught against their own chosen target.

The Syrians certainly believed beyond any doubt that they were about to be invaded. After Israel's air assault in April and several days before Rabin uttered his threat about overthrowing the Damascus regime, Atassi pleaded with Cairo for some practical gesture of military support. And although Nasser then temporised with a request for more information, once Rabin's statement was issued, he knew that, with no troops of his own to hold the ring in Syria, he would sooner or later have to make a diversionary move on his Sinai frontier, if only to stop the Syrians from taking some reckless action of their own. As Amman and now Damascus ceaselessly pointed out, the unified Arab command had failed to do anything to protect their territory. And whether or not Israel was about to launch a full-scale invasion of Syria, Egypt's prestige could not allow her indefinitely to be made the laughing-stock of the Arab world for sheltering behind UNEF while her allies were being slaughtered. Ever since the Samu incident five months before, there had been no let-up in Hussein's efforts to ridicule Egyptian inertia; and only a few weeks previously the Jordanian press had bitterly lambasted Nasser for fighting his fellow Arabs in Yemen, while lifting not a finger to defend Arab lives against Israeli attacks.

In fact, it is probable that at the time the Israelis were planning something more on the lines of the Gaza raid of 1955 than a full-scale invasion of Syria. For them the all-important thing was to bring Nasser to battle, and the depth and duration of their strike into Syrian territory would depend on how long it took to produce the required Egyptian reaction. To this end, they appear to have deliberately set out to persuade the Russians, and hence the Egyptians, that a major assault on Syria was imminent. By a clever combination of calculated leakage, for the benefit of the Soviet embassy in Tel Aviv, and fictitious radio messages which they rightly assumed would be picked up and relayed to Cairo by

Russian ships patrolling in the Eastern Mediterranean, they made sure that Nasser would be immediately informed that his Syrian ally was about to be invaded. Also, while being careful not to overplay their hand by massing troops on Syria's borders, and later even inviting the Russian embassy to inspect the frontier, they managed to suggest that their armoured formations were being readied for action by conspicuously excluding them from the Independence Day parade in Jerusalem on May 15.

The Israeli plan could hardly have succeeded better. The Russians, fearing for the safety of their Syrian protégés, duly passed on to Cairo the 'information' which their embassy and naval patrols had picked up. Whereupon Nasser hesitated no longer. On May 15, a state of alert was declared in Egypt; troops were despatched into Sinai; and on the following day the Chief of Staff of the Egyptian armed forces sent a written request to the UNEF commander, General Rikhye, for a limited withdrawal of his forces to enable the Egyptian army to occupy certain positions on the Sinai border with Israel and to avoid UNEF troops being caught in any cross-fire when Israeli and Egyptian units came face to face.

The second trap had been sprung and the Egyptians had come out from behind their protective screen, exactly as Israel's 'hawks' had planned. Yet even at this critical moment, Nasser was not unduly concerned about the likely effects of his gesture. As emerged all too clearly from a long discussion which I had with him a few hours before the Six Days War began, he was still living in the atmosphere of 1956. Because of this, he was convinced that the Israelis would not be prepared alone to fight a war on two fronts, if only for fear of the striking power of Egypt's Russian-equipped air force. Therefore, he believed that, unless they could count on the West joining in the fighting, at least to the extent of providing air cover, as Britain had done in the Suez War, he would be able to thwart their plans by showing that Egypt would fight if they went for Syria. If, on the other hand, the West should decide to play an active military role alongside their Israeli clients, then he reckoned that Russia could not fail to respond. In that event there would be an explosion involving the whole of the Middle East and possibly the world; and whether or not Egypt was currently threatening Israel's border would not matter one way or the other.

Such were the basic errors of judgement which led Nasser to make his move into Sinai in May 1967. Alas for him they were all too soon to be compounded by yet another fatal miscalculation. Having decided to advance to Israel's frontier, he mistakenly believed that the matter would end there. And to ensure that no further threat or provocation was offered to the Israelis, he had taken care to see that General Fawzi's letter to General Rikhye requested that UNEF be withdrawn from the border observation posts and not from such highly sensitive areas as the Gaza Strip or Sharm es-Sheikh. For Nasser knew only too well that any move by Egypt to evict U.N. forces from Sharm es-Sheikh and re-impose the blockade of the Gulf of Akaba would substantially increase the risk of retaliation by Israel.

But here again his calculations were to be falsified. Rikhye quite properly told the bearer of Fawzi's letter that he could not withdraw any part of the U.N. force without instructions from the Secretary-General, to whom he would immediately cable the Egyptian request. Two and a half hours later, on the evening of May 16, U Thant sent for Egypt's Ambassador to the U.N., Mohammed el-Kouny, and told him without equivocation that a partial withdrawal of UNEF was quite impracticable. Even if this were not so, he said that it would be contrary to the terms of the General Assembly resolution, which established the force in 1956, for UNEF to be made the instrument of any one nation's policy. Therefore General Fawzi's letter 'would be considered as tantamount to a request for the complete withdrawal of the U.N. Emergency Force from Gaza and Sinai . . .'.

True, the Secretary-General also asked Kouny if he could throw any more light on Fawzi's sudden demand and, when the ambassador confessed that he had received no instructions, asked him to seek clarification from his Government. But while Nasser might have been prepared to tell U Thant to his face what his motives were – as he certainly would have done to Hammarskold – he was not prepared to cable them half-way across the world. Knowing how weak were his cyphers, he was not going to risk some hostile intelligence service decoding his reply and revealing it to those who would use it to jeer and sneer that his Sinai move was an empty gesture. Besides, U Thant's reply to Kouny had been an adamant refusal to consider a partial withdrawal and there was no reason to believe that any amount of 'clarification' from Cairo would make him change his mind. The choice therefore lay between an ignominious retreat and the risk of asking for a complete withdrawal of UNEF which would include Sharm es-Sheikh and Gaza. And as Nasser well knew, if he chose the latter course, he would have to fill the vacuum in these highly sensitive areas with Egyptian troops; more dangerous still, he would then be faced with overwhelming pressures from Israel's other Arab neighbours to reimpose the blockade of the Gulf of Akaba which had been open for Israel's use for the past ten years.

Of the two alternatives, retreat was clearly out of the question, not only because of the blow which it would deal to Egypt's prestige throughout the Arab world, but also because it would remove any hope of deterring the Israelis or restraining the Syrians. And after pondering the problem with Amer for almost two whole days and nights, Nasser decided that he would have to risk the consequences of a complete withdrawal. Therefore, on the afternoon of May 18, Riad cabled to New York Egypt's formal request that all United Nations forces should be removed from Gaza and the Sinai peninsula.

Yet even now, Nasser hesitated to take the final step of barring Israeli shipping from the Tiran Straits at the entrance to the Gulf of Akaba. While in no doubt that he had the legal right to close this channel which was entirely within Egypt's territorial waters, he also knew how much Israel had come to depend in the past ten years upon the supply of Iranian oil through the port of Elath. And though advance units of Egypt's 4th Armoured Division swiftly moved into the positions vacated by UNEF on the Sinai border, for the time being no troops were sent to reoccupy Sharm es-Sheikh.

But the Jordanians were not going to let the Egyptians dodge the consequences of their actions. Nor were many of Nasser's own officers who, after ten years of inactivity against Israel, were itching to use their sophisticated Russian equipment to wipe out the stain of Egypt's defeat in 1956. And although Amer warned the army not to expect any dramatic moves when Sharm es-Sheikh was eventually reoccupied, they refused to be denied. Thus, as Amman Radio poured scorn on Cairo's evident hesitation to face the logical next step, Nasser, after four agonising days of deliberation, found himself obliged to take the final fatal plunge. On May 21, Egyptian troops took over once again at Sharm es-Sheikh and on the following day Cairo announced that henceforth the Gulf of Akaba would be closed to Israeli ships and other vessels carrying strategic cargoes to Elath.

Overnight Nasser became once more the hero of the Arab world. Even the ranks of Tuscany in Jordan could not forbear to cheer this singular act of defiance. The taunts and jeers of yesterday were forgotten, drowned in the euphoric chorus of jubilation. And as Arab nationalists from Muscat to Morocco again acclaimed the name of Nasser, no-one save the ever-watchful Israelis seemed to realise that the third and final trap had been sprung.

Chapter 20

The Six Days War

In the course of the inquest which followed the Six Days War of 1967, U Thant was to claim that, before he gave General Rikhye the order to withdraw the U.N. forces on the evening of May 18, Egypt had already presented him with a fait accompli by 'ousting UNEF from its posts on the (border) line and at the entrance to the Gulf of Akaba'. In fact, this was not true. As is shown by the United Nations' official chronology of these events, the only action taken by Egyptian troops prior to the issue of U Thant's order was the occupation of El Sabha, a U.N. post about a third of the way along the Sinai border and some 220 miles from the entrance to the Gulf of Akaba. And even this post was evacuated an hour and a half later, after Rikhye had objected that he had not yet received instructions from New York and could not therefore allow any U.N. posts to be taken over. Nor in fact did the Egyptians ask for the U.N. forces to leave Sharm es-Sheikh or Gaza until two days after U Thant had told Kouny in New York that there could be no partial withdrawal. Far from presenting the Secretary-General with a fait accompli in the Gulf of Akaba, in fact the Egyptians did not physically reoccupy Sharm es-Sheikh until three days after U Thant had ordered Rikhye to pull out.

Of course the primary blame for the disaster which followed this tragic chain of events must rest largely with Nasser for having taken the first step. But at the same time, it seems somewhat strange that, with so much at stake, U Thant should not have suggested that he meet Nasser in Cairo until after he had received Riad's formal request for the total withdrawal of UNEF. Even odder is the fact that, although the President warmly welcomed the idea of a visit, the Secretary-General did not set forth for yet another four days, by which time Nasser had finally decided to close the Gulf of Akaba to Israeli shipping. U Thant later complained that the announcement of this decision was made while he was on his way to Cairo. But even if he did not fully understand the purpose of Egypt's request for a partial withdrawal of the U.N. force, he could hardly have failed to realise that, once UNEF was out of Sharm es-Sheikh, Nasser would be under irresistible pressures to reimpose the blockade and that, once he succumbed to these pressures, war with Israel was probable, if not certain.

In fairness to U Thant it must be admitted that the U.N. force was at this point on the verge of breaking up of its own accord. The Yugoslavs and Indians, whose contingents comprised more than half its strength, were anxious to pull out and, when the Secretary-General consulted the contributing nations, the majority agreed that Egypt was acting within her rights and that it was not for them to oppose her request for UNEF's withdrawal. Also the reactions of the United States and Britain did not exactly help to create a favourable climate for negotiation with Cairo, both countries protesting about Egypt's action as if UNEF was some kind of occupation army placed in the Middle East to do their bidding. Likewise, Canada's Foreign Minister, Paul Martin, still further soured the atmosphere with an indignant speech demanding that, if not the whole U.N. force, at least the Canadian contingent should be flown home in twenty-four hours' time. And when U Thant finally took off for Cairo on May 22, his mission was not exactly helped by the Americans peremptorily telling Nasser that he should comply with whatever the Secretary-General suggested.

U Thant moreover did make certain proposals which were designed to lower the temperature, but which were one and all promptly and resolutely rejected by the Israelis. On May 18, he suggested, in reply to protests from Tel Aviv that Egypt was threatening Israel, that the simple answer would be for UNEF to cross over onto the Israeli side of the border, where they would be no less able to prevent an attack than from their previous positions. But Tel Aviv refused to countenance the idea, contending that any such move would be prejudicial to Israel's sovereignty. Later, when he was in Cairo, U Thant suggested that a special U.N representative be sent to Israel, Egypt and Jordan to arrange a settlement. And after this had been accepted by Nasser but rejected by the Israelis, he proposed a plan of his own for creating a breathing space in which negotiations could be set in motion. Israel would be asked for the time being not to test the blockade by sending ships to the Gulf of Akaba. Other nations would be similarly requested not to send any strategic materials. And on this understanding Egypt would refrain from exercising her right to arrest any ships bound for Elath which passed through the Tiran Strait at the entrance to the Gulf. But, although Nasser accepted this proposal as well, once again the Israelis rejected it out of hand.

U Thant had acted too late. And while the Egyptians were only too ready to cooperate with him or any other mediator in finding a way out of the current impasse, the Israelis were not. Nasser had sprung the final trap upon himself and they were not going to let him escape. His closure of the Gulf of Akaba had put world, or at least Western, opinion overwhelmingly on their side and whatever military action they might now take would be supported in the West as legitimate self-defence. From now on therefore Israel's 'hawks', claiming that Nasser would never have dared so much if Ben Gurion and Dayan had been in power, asserted an ever-increasing control over Government policy. Eshkol might argue that diplomacy be given every chance to induce Egypt to back down. But henceforth it was merely a question of how soon the army would put into operation the plans to smash Nasser on which they had been working for the past decade.

However, because it suited the military to conceal their ultimate intentions at this juncture, Abba Eban, Israel's Foreign Minister, was allowed to set off on a rapid round of visits to Western capitals. In Paris, London and Washington, Eban insisted that his people were about to be slaughtered by millions of Arabs, whose frenzied cheering when Egypt closed the Gulf of Akaba showed that they were out for Israel's blood. De Gaulle responded by proposing a four-power conference and Wilson for Britain said that he would be prepared to join in any measures by the United States or the U.N. to prevent Egypt from blocking an international waterway.

Lyndon Johnson, more assertively still, promised that action would be taken to reopen the Gulf, with or without British naval support from Aden, although in the meanwhile urging upon Eban the need for the utmost restraint on the part of Israel.

Exactly how Johnson planned to prise open the Gulf of Akaba was not explained. Certainly he met with a speedy rebuff when he tried to do so by diplomatic approaches in Cairo, although he took care to sweeten his démarche with assurances that the United States were disinclined to take any military action. And while Nasser did not reject a subsequent proposal that Vice-President Hubert Humphrey should fly to Egypt to discuss the crisis, he equally did not respond to it until a week later when he suggested that his Vice-President, Zacharia Mohieddin, should instead visit Washington and New York for conversations with the American Government and the United Nations. Consequently, when Eban returned to Tel Aviv on May 27, he found his colleagues united only in their scepticism as to the value of Johnson's assurances. Those who still wanted a peaceful settlement were afraid that Washington would not act firmly enough to force Nasser's hand, while the militants were delighted by the thought that the Western powers would in the event leave it to Israel to settle the issue in her own way.

Eshkol made a last desperate bid to forestall the 'hawks' and to give Washington a chance to make good Johnson's assurances. But the majority of his Cabinet colleagues were against him. Any chance that he might have had of winning them over was destroyed by Arab reactions to the closure of the Gulf which, by this time, had reached a veritable crescendo of ferocity. Shukhairy, now joined by the Syrian, Iraqi and Jordanian radio networks, was letting fly with renewed vehemence, declaiming that war was now both inevitable and imminent and that the day of liberation of Palestine had finally dawned. Atassi declared that Palestinian operations from Syria would be continued until the Palestinian homeland was recovered. Aref sent Iraqi troops to Jordan with a farewell message announcing that they would shortly 'avenge the martyred brethren who fell in 1948' and that 'God willing, we shall meet again in Jaffa and Haifa'. And although both the

American and Russian Ambassadors repeatedly urged the Israeli Government to exercise restraint, the 'hawks' could wait no longer. Eshkol was faced with a virtual ultimatum, either to give the army a free hand and forget about diplomacy, or risk a military coup d'état or, at least, a mass resignation of the General Staff.

By now even Eshkol was coming to the conclusion that for Israel to win a diplomatic settlement without making impossible concessions, she had to negotiate from strength and that for this purpose she had first to demonstrate beyond all doubt her military superiority over Egypt. He therefore conceded the army's terms, and agreed to reinstate Dayan as a Minister without Portfolio, while he himself continued in charge of the Defence Ministry. But the militants, including General Rabin, were still not satisfied. Nor was Dayan. And on May 31, the Mapai party's Executive Committee voted, over the opposition of Eshkol and Mrs Golda Meir, to give Dayan the only post that he wanted – the Ministry of Defence. Their decision was duly ratified by the Cabinet on the following day and, as the hero of the Suez War took over Eshkol's defence responsibilities, a Government of National Unity came into being which included such extremists as Mehachim Begin, the former Stern Gang leader and architect of the Deir Yassin massacre in 1948.

Meanwhile in Washington and other Western capitals, Tel Aviv's representatives had abruptly changed their tune on instructions from home. For fear that the Americans might in the last resort take matters out of Israel's hands by, for instance, sending tankers through the Gulf of Akaba under naval escort, the Israelis now no longer lamented that their people were about to be slaughtered to a man. Instead they contended that they could take care of themselves and force Nasser to reopen the Gulf without any help from the West. A high-ranking Israeli intelligence officer told the Pentagon that Israel had no intention of taking the blockade of Elath lying down or of letting the Egyptians off the hook on which they had impaled themselves.

But if those in Israel who wanted a show-down with Nasser feared that America might send warships to the Gulf of Akaba, the Russians were even more alive to these possibilities and to the incalculable consequences which might ensue. Although they did not activate the 'hot line' system of emergency communication with Washington until the war actually started, they warned the Americans in the most vigorous terms not to attempt any forceful intervention. Nasser had not consulted Moscow before announcing that the Gulf would be closed to Israeli shipping. And the last thing the Russians wanted was for him to be drawn into a collision with American forces, which could hardly fail to involve them as well. Realising that, rightly or wrongly, they had helped to trigger the current crisis by sounding the alarm over Syria, they were now desperately anxious to calm the situation. Among other things, after consultations with Britain's Foreign Secretary, George Brown, in Moscow, they proposed a bilateral conference with the United States, to agree on joint action by the two powers to enforce a settlement. At the same time, they urged on Cairo as well as Tel Aviv the need for the utmost caution. And when Nasser sent his War Minister, Shams Badran, to Moscow for urgent discussions on May 25, they redoubled their efforts to persuade Cairo to desist from further provocative action.

As it happened, Badran completely misinformed Cairo when reporting on his conversations with Russia's leaders who, he asserted, had promised him that they would give Egypt their fullest support. Scarcely a word of their repeated pleas for restraint was mentioned. Even when they remarked that, if the Americans became involved so would Russia, Badran chose to interpret their words as a pledge to back Egypt regardless of the risk of starting a third world war. Badran was, of course, one of the Egyptian army's leading militants and a close confidant of the Commander-in-Chief. Before leaving for Moscow, he had converted Amer to the idea of gaining the initiative by striking the first blow rather than waiting for Israel to do so. And he was not going to report anything which might create despondency in Cairo, especially at the very moment when, as he well knew, Egypt's advance formations were about to move up to the Sinai border. Besides, both the forces in Sinai and their comrades in Yemen were urging that Egypt should strike at Israel without further delay and, if only to maintain their morale and his own prestige as their spokesman in the Cabinet, Badran felt it necessary to cast no gloom upon the scene.

In fact, apart from creating some confusion at a time when the Russian Ambassador in Cairo was calling for restraint, Badran's misleading reports could at this late stage have had little effect on Egyptian policy. Living as he then was in the atmosphere of 1956, Nasser refused to believe that he was seriously threatened by an Israeli attack. In my own talks with him during those last critical days he seemed convinced that he could ride out the storm, provided he offered Israel no further provocation. He had after all moved troops into the area seven years before when Israel seemed to be on the point of invading Syria and there had been no crisis then, let alone a war. U Thant had unfortunately not understood, as Hammarskold would have done, why he now wanted UNEF to withdraw only from the Sinai border. He had therefore had to take over all the U.N. posts, including Sharm es-Sheikh, if only to forestall the Israelis. But, while he had no doubt that some Israelis were itching to fight Egypt over the Gulf, he firmly believed that discretion would prevail in Tel Aviv. Without the active cooperation of either American or British bomber squadrons, he was convinced that Israel could not destroy Egypt's air force and that her armies would therefore be exposed to merciless attack from the air as they crossed the Sinai desert. And even if all these calculations were wrong and the Israelis were able to advance into Sinai, he believed that the United Nations would soon intervene to stop the fighting and make them withdraw as had happened at the time of the Suez War. Meanwhile, he laughingly told me, Israel having had the Gulf open for the past eleven years, it was Egypt's turn to close it for the next eleven years, after which the two parties could discuss what should be done.

Nasser's complacency was to some extent encouraged by repeated assurances from Washington that Israel would not fire the first shot. For not only were the Americans straining every nerve to cool tempers in Cairo, but they were also inclined to regard Israel's latest line of belligerent talk as largely a matter of bluff. Needless to say, they were afterwards accused among other things of deliberately misleading the Egyptians with these soothing words. But there is little doubt that Washington's intentions were genuine enough. Nor were these assurances by any means the only reason for the current lack of apprehension in Cairo. For instance, when I pointed out to Nasser 36 hours before the war started that, according to information I had received in London, Israel was fully capable of doing for herself what the British Canberras had had to do for her in 1956, he refused to believe me. And he flatly contradicted my statement that over the past few weeks Israeli transport aircraft had been taking off hourly from the Dassault factory's airstrip in France loaded with the latest Mirage fighter-bombers for assembly in Israel. His intelligence service, he said, had assured him that his Russian MIGs and Sokhols were more than a match for anything possessed by Israel. (He later told me that, as a result of our conversation, he had gone immediately to Amer's headquarters and told his army commanders to expect an Israeli attack within a matter of hours. But by that time it was too late to escape the consequences of his miscalculations.)

Likewise, when Boghdady and Hassan Ibrahim wrote to Nasser warning him that his action over the Gulf would lead to war, he summoned them to his office and told them that there was no cause for alarm. According to the most reliable and recent information in his possession, Israel was not planning to attack Egypt and would not be able to do so for at least another eight months. Boghdady then tried another tack, saying that whatever happened the Egyptian army should not get involved with the Israelis. The air force might be able to take care of itself, but the army was hopelessly inferior. But still Nasser would not listen. Seemingly forgetting all that he had said at the Cairo and Casablanca summit meetings about Israel's military superiority over the Arabs, he told his old comrades that this was no occasion for such defeatist talk. Then, when Boghdady and Ibrahim, recalling Kruschev's attitude during the Suez War, asked what was Russia's position, he blandly quoted Badran's report, saying that the Soviet Union would support Egypt to the end, even if this involved another world war.

Boghdady had made no more impression upon Nasser than

those few Cabinet colleagues who had tried to warn him of the risks which he was running. Not that they or their less outspoken fellows in the Council of Ministers had been in any way consulted about the recent decisions. Indeed the Cabinet had only discussed the issue on one occasion in the middle of May, after the Prime Minister, Sidky Suleiman, had returned from a visit to the Golan Heights on the Syrian-Israeli border. A former close friend of the President, now a Minister in one of the home departments, had then caused a considerable stir by asking whether his colleagues realised that, if Egypt attacked Israel on Syria's account, the Americans would fight to defend the Israelis. Nasser, who on principle never liked his Ministers to intervene in discussions not strictly related to their own departments, had shot him an angry look, but had otherwise made no comment. Nor was he to be drawn into any discussion when, in reply to further probing from the same Minister, Sidky Suleiman admitted that, during his recent tour of the Golan Heights, neither he nor any of the Syrian staff officers who accompanied him had been able to detect any sign that Israel was concentrating troops on Syria's borders. And when Nasser later met his importunate colleague in private, he refused all entreaties to back down, replying, as he had done with Ahmed Hussein in 1956, that if he kept his nerve everything would turn out all right.

At the same time the Egyptian forces in Sinai were given the strictest instructions not to offer any further provocation to Israel. Amer's and Badran's pleas for a pre-emptive strike were resolutely denied. The army was ordered to take up defensive positions only until and unless the Israelis invaded Syria. Indeed even Egypt's adversary General Rabin was later to concede, in a statement published by the Paris *Le Monde* in February 1968, that he did 'not think Nasser wanted war. The two divisions he sent to Sinai on May 14 would not have been sufficient to launch an offensive against Israel. He knew it and we knew it.' Admittedly, a further five divisions were later sent to Sinai to lend credibility to Nasser's bluff. But since, for the most part, they were held in reserve up to a hundred miles from the frontier, the Israelis still had no serious cause for alarm. Moreover, Nasser went out of his way to reassure the Americans that Egypt would not fire the first shot. And on May 26, after his troops had occupied the Sinai border and the Egyptian Ambassador had been summoned to the White House in the middle of the night for a further lecture on the need for restraint, he readily repeated the assurance. Likewise with the Russians whose Cairo envoy called on him uninvited at 3 a.m. the next morning to urge against any aggressive action. And in public statements over the next few days, as in two television interviews with Christopher Mayhew and myself on June 3, he reiterated again and again that he would not be the one to start the shooting.

Besides ordering Amer to adopt a strictly defensive posture in Sinai, Nasser also took care to place the PLO forces in the Gaza Strip under his control as soon as Egyptian combat troops reoccupied the area. It is also probable that he would have been content to apply the blockade only against ships carrying arms to Israel, although the question was never put to the test, since not surprisingly no single ship presented itself for passage to Elath during the crisis. The general threat of war, together with statements by the Egyptian press that the Tiran Straits had been mined (which turned out to be untrue) were enough to discourage any of the mercantile nations from hazarding their vessels in the area.

Certainly Nasser could not have made it clearer to all concerned that he wanted a settlement and that he preferred not to enforce the right of blockade before there had been a chance to talk things out. To this end he told Washington and other Western capitals that he was perfectly prepared to submit the issue to the International Hague Court to decide whether or not Egypt was within her rights in closing the Tiran Strait to enemy shipping. Hints were also dropped that even the ban on Israeli ships passing through the Suez Canal would be negotiable, provided that any negotiations equally took account of the earlier U.N. resolutions which required Israel to take back the Palestinian refugees and to confine herself to the borders laid down by the 1947 partition plan. Then, when Washington proposed that oil be exempted from Egypt's blockade restrictions, he indicated his readiness to consider the question and suggested that Zacharia Mohieddin should visit Washington and New York to discuss this and all other relevant matters with the American Government and the United Nations. True, he also told a press conference on May 28 for the Arab record that he could not see how the Arabs could co-exist peacefully with Israel, whose very creation had constituted an aggression against the Palestinians. But at the same time, he equally declared his readiness to reactivate the Egyptian–Israeli Armistice Commission which had been defunct since the 1956 war.

Maxime Rodinson in his book *Israel and the Arabs* has suggested that, at this point, Nasser's object was not simply to win recognition of Egypt's rights in the Gulf of Akaba, but rather to force Israel to negotiate on all the problems arising out of the 1948 war and to make far-reaching concessions to the Arabs over the refugees and territorial adjustments. But from my contacts with him at the time, I am inclined to doubt that he had thought things through anything like as far as this. Always more inclined to reaction than to action, he had, as he saw it, merely taken the steps which U Thant and the Israeli threat to Syria between them had forced upon him. Having made his gesture and recovered his lost leadership, he would have been quite content to reach a compromise settlement on the problem of the Gulf alone. Certainly his instructions to Zacharia Mohieddin did not envisage any widening of the existing issue. Nor, when a senior State Department official, Charles Yost, was sent to Cairo for discussions to prepare the way for Mohieddin's mission, did the Egyptians make any attempt to engage him on topics outside the scope of the immediate crisis.

Since Cairo had already rejected Lyndon Johnson's suggestion that the Egyptians should simply cancel the blockade and allow UNEF to return to all their former positions, Yost promptly set about examining with Mahmoud Riad how the operation of the blockade might be modified to enable both sides to live with it. Riad suggested that the criterion be the same as the American Battle Act which forbade the export of a long list of strategic materials to the countries of the Communist bloc. This he seemed to think would offer Israel substantial concessions. But when Yost replied that the Battle Act's prohibitions included petroleum which had been Israel's principal import through the Gulf of Akaba, Riad said that the matter clearly required more detailed study, which could be undertaken when Mohieddin reached Washington. At the same time he gave his American visitor a broad hint that Egypt might be prepared to allow the flow of oil to continue, provided there was no appreciable increase in the tanker traffic to Elath.

On June 3, after two days of discussions, Yost left Cairo with at least the basis of a negotiation between America and Egypt well and truly laid. Mohieddin was to visit Washington on June 7 and, as far as the State Department could judge, there was now a reasonable chance that a settlement would be reached. Nasser had repeatedly assured them that he did not want war. And despite the Israelis' recent tough talk, Washington still hoped that they would allow diplomacy a chance to settle the dispute. But, in fact, the Israelis had no intention of letting any diplomatic settlement rob them of the opportunity of sweeping Nasser from his pedestal. And there can be little doubt that, directly they were told by the Americans on June 2 of Mohieddin's intended visit, they decided that the time had come to strike.

Dean Rusk afterwards lamented that he had probably helped inadvertently to press the trigger by passing this information to the Israeli Government. It is certainly no secret that the news caused the gravest anxiety in Tel Aviv where it was feared that an emissary so well-liked in Washington as Mohieddin would be able to extricate Nasser from his trap by charming and wheedling the Americans into agreeing a compromise. It could hardly have been through an oversight that, having helped to create an atmosphere of frenzied agitation in Israel over the recent Arab threats of vengeance, the Government did nothing to ensure that the sense of detente, now prevalent in Washington and Cairo, was communicated to their distracted people.

But Mohieddin's projected visit to America was not the only reason which decided the Israelis to strike at this juncture. On May 30, Hussein had joined in a military alliance with Nasser binding

Jordan to fight alongside Egypt in the event of war. Nothing could have suited Israel's military planners better. From that moment, they could claim before all the world that Israel was again surrounded by a ring of steel. And if Hussein could be relied on to reject a last-minute offer to leave him alone if he reneged on his alliance with Egypt, they would have a perfect pretext to seize the West Bank, which they had coveted for so long as the last remaining portion of Palestine in Arab hands. The Jordanian army presented few problems, the air force none at all, equipped as it was with a few obsolete British Hunters. But, remembering how quickly and easily Hussein had fallen out with Nasser in earlier times, it was imperative to strike before he should do so yet again.

This eleventh hour rapprochement of Jordan and Egypt was something of a shot-gun wedding. Only a couple of months before, at a meeting of the Arab League's Defence Council in Cairo, the Jordanians and Egyptians had been engaged in bitter quarrelling. Hussein's representative had poured scorn on Shukhairy's complaints that Jordan would not allow the PLO to operate from her territory. It was ridiculous, he said, to talk of liberating Palestine so long as UNEF acted as a buffer between Egypt and Israel. Nasser's support of Shukhairy was no more than a cover for his own reluctance to get involved in fighting the Israelis. If he really believed in recovering the lost lands of the Palestinians by force, he should bring his troops back from Yemen, get rid of UNEF and join with his Arab neighbours in a concerted plan of action.

With such arguments Hussein had been able to checkmate Shukhairy. Likewise, when the Syrians overplayed their hand with a campaign of sabotage in northern Jordan and radio appeals to the Jordanians to revolt against the monarchy, he could count on the unity and loyalty of his army, Palestinian and East Bank elements alike. When he decided to break diplomatic relations with Syria, scarcely a word of protest was heard in Amman. But as soon as Nasser reimposed the blockade of the Gulf of Akaba, Hussein's army echoed the widespread acclamation of the Arab world. With Egypt now in the firing line beside her Arab comrades, the King could no longer rely on his officers, and especially the Palestinians among them, to back him in opposing Nasser and Shukhairy. The situation was not the same as in 1956, when Egypt had told the Jordanians to stand aside. Then the Israelis had taken the Arab world by surprise and had reached the Suez Canal before any of Egypt's allies could have galvanised themselves for a counter-attack. But if war were to break out now, Hussein knew that, win or lose, his throne would be gravely endangered if he held aloof from the conflict. Besides, in the prevailing atmosphere of euphoria, the Jordanians no less than their Egyptian and Syrian cousins believed that, if Israel should attack, victory for the Arab armies would this time be a certainty.

After a few days of reflection therefore, during which pressures from the Jordanian army mounted steadily, the King took the plunge and flew to Cairo to offer Nasser his support. Shukhairy attended the meeting and, typically of this highly emotional yet basically good-natured man, he took all the blame on himself for the recent rows about the PLO, rejecting any suggestion from Hussein that Jordan too bore a share of responsibility. Consequently, when the defence agreement had been signed, at Nasser's suggestion and to the amazement of every onlooker, Shukhairy and the King left Cairo airport hand in hand and returned to Amman to work out plans for defending Jordan against an Israeli invasion.

But this sudden reconciliation with the PLO did not survive very long. Hussein might have pledged himself to fight with Nasser if Israel attacked Egypt. But he had no intention of allowing thousands of armed Palestinians into his country who, he felt, would be no help to the Jordanian army in a war and would be a menace to security if, after all, peace should be preserved. Although Shukhairy begged that the 5,000-strong Palestine Liberation Army, stationed across the Syrian border at Deraa, should be allowed to play a part in defending the West Bank, the King adamantly refused him. His own forces had the situation well in hand, he said, and such an influx of Palestinians would only cause trouble with the army even if, as Shukhairy was ready to concede, they were placed under Jordanian command. All that he would allow was that the PLO office in Jerusalem, closed since the row with Shukhairy began, should be reopened. Hussein had contracted his shot-gun wedding with Nasser and it was no part of the contract that Shukhairy and his Palestinians should join in the honeymoon.

But if either Amman or Cairo hoped that their defence agreement would close Arab ranks, they were in for a speedy disappointment. The Algerians and Syrians promptly denounced it as an alliance with reaction unworthy of the leader of Arab socialist unity. At the same time the Saudis, having only recently been branded by Nasser as reactionary tools of imperialism, not only protested vehemently that Hussein had joined hands with their enemy, but also suspended further military aid to Jordan. Only Iraq, who promptly adhered to the alliance and despatched troops to Jordan, demonstrated any positive support, while Hussein predictably rejected Tel Aviv's last-minute 'peace offer' and stuck firmly to his contract with Nasser.

The moment could, therefore, have hardly been more propitious for an Israeli assault. If they had planned every Arab movement and reaction themselves, they could not have organised things better. The Arabs were effectively in complete disarray. Such political unity as had been achieved between individual states had not been, and could not be, translated into a coordinated military strategy. As for the unified Arab command, for all its grandiose title, it was a head without a body, a General Staff with no army to support it. Besides, as Rabin was later to admit, the Israelis knew that Nasser was not going to strike the first blow. Nor did it need much ingenuity on the part of the Israeli intelligence service to discover that neither were the Egyptians expecting Israel to do so. As anyone could see who flew into Cairo's civil airport at that time, Nasser's much vaunted MIGs and Sokhols on the adjacent military airfield were in no way hidden or protected from aerial attack, but were drawn up in neat rows, wing-tip to wing-tip, as so many sitting targets for enemy attack.

For all these reasons, added to the copious supplies of arms and equipment with which they had been provided by America and France, the Israelis were confident that they could now take on Egypt and her allies without having to call on the West for air cover or any other form of military support. Western opinion was overwhelmingly on their side as the aggrieved party in the dispute over the Gulf. Those elements in Britain and France that were still smarting from the humiliations of 1956 were only too anxious for the Israelis to finish the job which they had then been unable to complete themselves. As for the American Government they were clearly in a very different mood to that which Eisenhower had adopted during the Suez War.

With these assurances in mind Dayan and Rabin set about completing the final details of the long-prepared plans. And early in the morning of June 5, two days before Mohieddin was due to fly to Washington, Israel struck at Egypt, Syria and Jordan in a *1967* lightning assault on the air forces of all three countries. All but a dozen of her 400 war planes, including the latest Mirage fighter-bombers, were thrown into the attack. Egypt, with the largest and most formidable air force of the three, suffered the first and heaviest onslaught as wave after wave of enemy Mystères and Mirages hurled their bombs, specially designed for low-level attack, upon the country's ten principal air bases at intervals of no more than ten minutes. The assault began at 7.45 a.m., the time when, as the Israelis rightly guessed, the Egyptians would be least prepared for an attack, with their dawn patrols returning to refuel and therefore unable to engage the enemy. By 10.35 a.m. the last of the seventeen waves had passed, leaving behind it a scene of utter devastation. Nasser's air force had been smashed, mostly on the ground, and out of a total of some 340 operational aircraft, 300 had been destroyed, not to speak of the damage to runways which prevented the few still serviceable planes from taking off.

Later that same morning, after a squadron of Syrian MIGs had tried to raid Haifa, the Israelis quickly destroyed the relatively small Syrian air force. After this it was Jordan's turn; and on the following morning the Iraqis, having tried their hand with a raid on Natanya, suffered an identical fate. Within twenty-four hours the Israelis had smashed four Arab air forces and destroyed over 400 aircraft, of which all but 24 were on the ground.

In the circumstances, the advance of the Israeli army into Gaza and Sinai, which began half an hour after the first air attack on

Egypt, was almost a formality. Operating on much the same lines as in 1956, but with new techniques as well as new weapons to avoid the hold-ups which had then occurred, they smashed their way through Sinai's desert wastes and mountain defiles. And with undisputed control of the air above them, they were able to announce on June 8 that they had gained complete control from Gaza to the Suez Canal and down to Sharm es-Sheikh. Likewise by June 7 Jordan had been forced to cede the Arab part of Jerusalem, together with Nablus, Jericho and the rest of the West Bank. On June 9, Syria joined with her allies in accepting the U.N. Security Council's demands for a cease-fire. But, in their determination to get control of the strategic Golan Heights, the Israelis pressed their attacks on Syrian territory for another two days until they achieved their objective.

Thus in six days of fighting Israel defeated three Arab armies and more than decimated the ranks of her adversaries at a cost of less than 700 of her own soldiers killed. Egypt alone suffered a death toll of some 20,000, many of whom died of exposure and thirst when their captors, having removed their boots, set them 'free' to find their way home barefooted and without food or water across the pitiless Sinai desert. And when the cease-fire finally sounded, the Suez Canal was blocked and the Israelis were masters of all Sinai, together with the Gaza Strip, Jordan's West Bank and Syria's Golan Heights.

Indeed, in the case of Egypt and Jordan the issue was decided in three rather than six days. And although Kouny, speaking for the Egyptian Government on June 7, rejected the U.N.'s first call for a cease-fire, it transpired that his instructions to do so had been based on false information from Amer, who at that moment was claiming that his forces in Sinai, far from being defeated, were regrouping for a counter-attack. But by the next day, even Amer was forced to admit that the army was broken and, having abandoned all its arms and equipment, was retreating in a state of panic and disorder across Sinai. Consequently Riad telephoned to Kouny to tell him to accept the cease-fire. Kouny's Arab colleagues in New York immediately protested that such instructions must be a trick. But a subsequent telephone call to Cairo was to bring swift confirmation from Sami Sharaf that the President had indeed been forced to sue for peace.

Nasser's agony in these hours of desolation was revealed to Boghdady who, shortly before the cease-fire was accepted, called to offer such comfort as he could. When Boghdady asked what attitude the Russians had taken after Israel attacked, Nasser replied that they had been frozen into immobility by their fear of a confrontation with America. And when reminded of Badran's euphoric report from Moscow of only ten days earlier, he had no answer. Boghdady then asked why the Russians had not at least flown in enough replacement aircraft to give the Egyptian army in Sinai some element of air cover. But Nasser could only reply that they had been too scared of getting involved with the American Sixth Fleet. At one point, he said, they had agreed, in response to his desperate appeals, to send some replacements via Yugoslavia, provided Tito concurred. But after he had obtained Tito's agreement, they had taken fright and said that they could not deliver any aircraft for several weeks and then only via Algeria which would have involved still further delays.

Boghdady also asked why Russia had sent no guns to help the retreating Egyptian forces, to which Nasser replied that they had sent a ship before the war started with several thousand guns on board. However the captain had turned back within sight of Alexandria for fear of Israeli bombing. With a final despairing gesture, Nasser said that everything had been lost, including the army and all its equipment. Amer had deceived him into thinking that the army could at least defend Egypt, even if its offensive capabilities were somewhat more questionable. He had also withheld news from the battle-front and had issued completely false communiqués claiming advances when in fact only the Israelis were advancing. To get at the truth, Nasser said, he had had to cross-examine Amer's junior staff officers.

In fact, Amer was more to blame for the past than for the immediate situation. Admittedly he had not opposed the series of military movements which led to this humiliating defeat. Indeed, towards the end he had even argued that Egypt should strike first. But his real crime was his utter failure to reform or retrain the army in the eleven years since 1956. As for the Russians, they had not after all been consulted about the closure of the Gulf of Akaba, even though they had been partly responsible for precipitating the initial Egyptian move into Sinai. And while there were ugly rumblings of public resentment against them for betraying Egypt, with armed gangs threatening the Russian embassy in Cairo for several days after the war ended, there was in fact very little that Moscow could have done in the time available to stave off defeat for Egypt. Kosygin did try to save his Syrian protégés and, when the Israelis, heedless of the fact that Damascus had accepted the cease-fire on June 9, continued to advance into Syrian territory, he used the 'hot line' to warn Johnson that a grave catastrophe might occur, involving military action by Russia, if the fighting were not immediately stopped. But his ominous words only caused the Americans to move their Sixth Fleet closer to Syria's coast, while the Israelis helped themselves to the Golan Heights. Hence the fact that Damascus escaped capture was because the Israelis did not want it, and not because Kosygin had scared the Americans into calling a halt.

Amer and the Russians were of course by no means the only objects of Nasser's resentment in the aftermath of the Six Days War. He was also very bitter about the Syrians whose harassment of the Israelis had set in motion the whole disastrous sequence of events, yet whose losses in human life and territory had been minute compared with what Egypt or Jordan had suffered. Likewise, he also blamed the Algerians for egging the Syrians on. Most of all, as he had publicly declared on the first day of the war, he believed that America and Britain had provided Israel with military help. Unable or unwilling to believe that, even with the newest Mirages, the Israelis could alone have destroyed Egypt's air force in less than three hours, the Egyptian High Command had accused the Americans and British of flying sorties from their aircraft carriers to supplement the attacks of Israel's air force.

As 'proof' of these allegations they pointed to the fact that all the attacking aircraft had come from the north instead of the east. For it never occurred to them that the Israelis had deliberately chosen the longer route so as to circumvent the Egyptian radar defences on the Suez Canal and so increase the element of surprise. With rather more justification, they also accused the American intelligence service of colluding with Israel, following the mysterious incident of the U.S.S. *Liberty*, a radio ship of the American Sixth Fleet, which had been accidently attacked by Israeli aircraft and torpedo boats while cruising a few miles off the Egyptian coast. Not unreasonably the Egyptian authorities concluded that the *Liberty* had been engaged in monitoring Egyptian operational messages and relaying them to the Israelis. Certainly, in the heat of the moment, such actions seemed too much in keeping with the persistent hostility of the Johnson administration for anyone in Cairo to believe otherwise. Consequently, as the Israelis advanced relentlessly across Sinai, Nasser had announced that diplomatic relations with the United States were at an end.

Paradoxically one of the few countries for which Nasser had any feelings of sympathy at this point was Jordan. When the cease-fire sounded, he told Hussein that he would never forget the sacrifices he had made and the loyalty he had shown in the crisis. He even said that, if the King had contacted him before finally committing his troops to action, he would have suggested that he await developments, in spite of their mutual defence agreement. He also had qualms of conscience that Hussein should have been told by Egyptian staff officers on June 5 that three-quarters of the Israeli air force had been destroyed over Cairo. And he knew that the Jordanians had therefore been led to believe that the Israeli planes, which they spotted returning from Egypt on their radar screens, were Egyptian planes engaged in raiding Israel. Still more did Nasser admire the King for not exploding with indignation when he later discovered that, even as he was being duped into believing that Israel was on the way to defeat, the Algerians and Syrians were being told by Cairo the full and grisly truth and Boumedienne was being entreated to send fifty MIGs to plug the gaping holes in Egypt's defences. He was also deeply grateful for the Jordanian army's attempts, albeit unsuccessful, to relieve the pressure on the Egyptians in Sinai by counter-attacking in the Hebron area, even though this meant abandoning all plans to save the West Bank by an offensive through Jenin designed to cut Israel in two. And as he later showed by his handling of Hussein at the summit meeting in September 1970 when the Jordanian army turned on the Palestinian Resistance, Nasser was to remember to his dying day the solidarity which Jordan had shown at this black moment of Egypt's and the Arabs' history.

No less remarkable than the reconciliation of these two formerly bitter enemies was the relationship which now developed between Egypt and France. Nasser had been much attracted and impressed by de Gaulle's defiance of the Americans which, he felt, made France a potential ally of the Third World. De Gaulle moreover had fully reciprocated Cairo's desire to reach a mutual understanding ever since he conceded independence to Algeria. Amer had paid a state visit to France in 1965; Herve Alphand, the Secretary-General of the French Foreign Ministry, had visited Egypt only three weeks before the Six Days War; and throughout the crisis, de Gaulle had kept in close touch with the Egyptian Ambassador in Paris. But what finally clinched the new relationship was the fact that, although the French had provided every aircraft with which Israel struck on June 5, de Gaulle, alone among Western leaders and with a cynicism extraordinary even in French diplomatic dealings, promptly and forthrightly denounced the Israelis as aggressors.

Nasser of course was fully aware that Israel's air force had been largely equipped by the French since before the Suez War, even if his intelligence service did not know how modern the equipment was. Indeed the French Government's announcement that, because of Israel's aggression, they were suspending all further shipments of aircraft and spare parts amounted to a public admission of the fact. And even though he initially believed that American and British planes had participated in the Israeli air assault, he must have realised that the French were at least as much to blame as their Western partners for the destruction of his air force and the consequential rout of the Egyptian army. Yet, when Paris elected to censure Israel as an aggressor, all this was forgotten and the French were acclaimed in Cairo as Egypt's only true friend in the Western camp.

The Arabs are of course renowned for their addiction to sympathy and flattery. All too often they are wooed by words, even when the wooer's deeds in no way match his protestations. Nor are the Egyptians any exception to this rule. But in this case, it was not so much that Nasser personally was gulled by de Gaulle's denunciation of Israel, although the popularity of the gesture with the Egyptian public undoubtedly helped to facilitate a rapprochement with France. Rather was it a matter of keeping a door, or at least a window, open to the West. Suspicion of Britain and America over the past two years had been largely responsible for setting Egypt on the road to catastrophe. And with his ties now broken with Washington as well as London and his relations with Russia severely strained, Nasser had no choice but to try to mend whatever fences he could with the Western world. After the Suez War when the breach had been with Britain and France, he had clung to the Americans: now in the infinitely more menacing aftermath of the Six Days War, with the Americans and British against him, he looked to the French to preserve his sole remaining link with the West. In a conversation with Heikal a few days after the cease-fire, I put this proposition to him, and reminded him of my earlier warning to Nasser that the French were arming the Israeli air force to the teeth. For once caught off guard, Heikal smiled and said, 'Shall we talk about something else?'

To say that Nasser's policy was now in ruins is if anything an understatement. In fact it had disintegrated into dust and ashes. After some thirteen years of trying to preserve a balance in Egypt's relations with the West and the Soviet bloc, he had in 1965 finally turned his back on the West as incurably hostile. From this dire decision he had slithered irresistibly from reaction to reaction and from blunder to blunder until, at the end of the road, he found himself snared in the very trap that he had tried to avoid and abandoned to the bitter humiliation of total defeat by Israel amid the taunts and jeers of his many enemies. Thus, when the cease-fire finally sounded, the man who had been deified by his own countrymen, worshipped by the Arab masses and, though often hated, at least respected in the world at large, was thrown upon the mercies of a disdainful Russia, with no army or air force to defend his country and cleaving desperately to the two nations, France and Jordan, for which until very recently he had felt little save hostility, distrust and even contempt.

Chapter 21

The Frustrations of Defeat

On the evening of June 9, the day after Egypt had accepted the cease-fire, Nasser appeared on television and, to the consternation of millions of his own subjects, announced that he had resigned the presidency in favour of Zacharia Mohieddin. For a brief moment his listeners were too stunned to react. But then, as the effect of his words sank in, a spontaneous outburst of public feeling followed which was to astonish even the most cynical of foreign observers. Men and women, who only a while before had been bitterly criticising the rais for having led their country to the most humiliating defeat in living memory, now suddenly realised that, in the prevailing storm, Nasser was the only rock to which they could cling. They had made him their political god; it was unthinkable that he should step down in favour of another at this moment of national peril and disaster. Within a matter of minutes, therefore, thousands of Cairo's citizens poured forth from their houses, apartments and cafés, commandeered buses, taxis, private cars and anything on wheels and, frantically calling their leader's name, headed for Nasser's house near Heliopolis to call on him to stay and lead them.

Of this whole extraordinary episode perhaps the most astonishing feature is that Nasser had not informed his chosen successor of his intended resignation, still less asked him if he was prepared to take over. Like every other listener to the broadcast the first that Mohieddin heard of the plan was when he switched on his own television set. Whereupon, having no desire to become President, least of all at such a critical moment, he drove with the utmost speed to Nasser's house to refuse the succession for himself and to tell the President that he could not abandon his post while the army was trapped in Sinai, however much he might blame himself for the disaster. Nasser at first insisted that his mind was made up. With Amer disgraced by the Sinai débâcle, Mohieddin was the logical successor and he had to take over. 'You are now responsible,' he said, 'you cannot refuse.' But Mohieddin was no less adamant. Besides his own reluctance to assume the leadership, he said that Nasser had no right to choose him as his successor. The fact that he was a Vice-President was neither here nor there. Only the National Assembly could decide who should be President.

So the argument continued, while in the street outside the Cairo populace kept up a constant cry for their leader to stay and guide them. Meanwhile in an adjoining room, other Cabinet Ministers had gathered for the meeting which Nasser had called to ratify the hand-over, among them Mohammed Faik, the Minister of National Guidance, who had been severely manhandled by the crowd at the gates as a result of being mistaken for Mohieddin. Eventually, after two hours of wrangling, Nasser gave way and agreed that Mohieddin should decline the presidency in a statement which would be broadcast immediately by Cairo Radio. A tape recording was duly made and sent by car to the radio station. But at the last minute, and again without telling anyone, Nasser ordered the radio station not to broadcast the Vice-President's statement. Mohieddin only discovered this later that night, after the Cabinet had adjourned. But vehemently as he protested, it was to no avail. Nasser, he was told, had decided that no further announcements should be made until the Parliament had met on the following morning.

The National Assembly's decision was a foregone conclusion. Nasser was invited by a unanimous vote to remain as President until all the traces of Israel's aggression had been removed and all Egyptian territory liberated from enemy occupation. And on his acceptance he was given full powers to organise the 'political and military reconstruction of the country'. But for Mohieddin the whole affair had been a sad disillusionment. Convinced that he had been made a cat's-paw in a scheme designed to shock public opinion into rallying to the President's support, he was bitterly hurt that he had even been denied the opportunity openly to renounce the succession. For when the National Assembly duly recorded its vote on the following day, the public were left with the wholly false impression that he had claimed the presidency and been rejected.

Coming on top of the long series of differences between him and his leader, from the start of the Yemeni war onwards, this was the final straw. And although Mohieddin stayed at his post until the immediate crisis had passed and Egypt's armed forces had been re-equipped by the Russians, in the spring of 1968 he resigned as Vice-President and never saw Nasser again except at the wedding of Boghdady's daughter. Indeed so complete was the breach between the two men that when certain Lebanese newspapers later suggested that Mohieddin was about to return to office, Nasser immediately suspected that he was intriguing against the regime. And when a book was published in 1969 by the CIA's erstwhile Cairo representative, Miles Copeland, purporting to reveal details of secret contacts between the Free Officers and the CIA prior to the revolution, Mohieddin's secretary was detained for eighty days of rigorous interrogation because Nasser believed that Mohieddin was the source of what he called Copeland's 'fairy tales'.

Whether or not Nasser's resignation statement was a piece of deliberate stage-management we may never know. Certainly the reaction of the Cairo populace, as testified by the foreign press corps at the time, was nothing if not spontaneous. Also there is no doubt that Nasser was deeply conscious of his personal responsibility for Egypt's bitter agony and defeat. And it is not impossible that his failure to consult his appointed successor was just another example of his arbitrary and impulsive methods. But if his announcement was no more than a device to restore his popular position, it was only partially successful. It might have produced the desired answer from a dazed populace and Parliament; but it failed to rally those of his subjects, especially among the already resentful middle classes, who now saw all too clearly that the leader they had once deified was not after all infallible.

Most Egyptians might have overlooked the catalogue of Nasser's errors since 1959, but they could hardly disregard this latest and most grievous of his miscalculations. They had cared little about Saudi or Iraqi rebuffs or about Syria's secession from the union and, save for those with relatives involved in the fighting, even the war in Yemen had not greatly concerned them. But they cared deeply about the occupation of Egyptian territory by the Israeli enemy and about the degrading defeat inflicted on their army, even if many of them might seem to a casual observer to be carrying on their normal easy-going way of life as though nothing had really happened. True, there was at no time any question of Nasser's leadership being threatened by revolt, if only because the masses could not conceive of anyone else taking over. But from now on, at least among the more thoughtful sections of the bourgeoisie and the student movement, there was never the same confidence in his judgement. Consequently, although he was to try once again, early in 1968, to make the ASU more responsive to popular feeling and even promised elections for a parliamentary democracy once Israel had withdrawn from Sinai, it was no longer possible to narrow the gulf between Government and people.

On the personal plane an even sadder outcome of the Six Days War was the ending of Nasser's relationship with Amer. Although this friendship had cooled somewhat after the Syrian secession in 1961 and still more following the row about the powers of the Commander-in-Chief two years later, Nasser was still deeply devoted to Amer with whom he had been associated for longer than any of his other colleagues, past or present. He had treated him as his closest lieutenant before and since the revolution, had used him to conduct every important negotiation with Russia, whether about arms or aid for the High Dam and other projects. Yet now he knew that, even if he personally had not blamed Amer for the recent defeat, his duty to the state demanded that he dismiss the Commander-in-Chief. On top of the appalling loss of life in Sinai, the army was now suffering the added humiliation of being the butt of every satirist in Egypt and outside. Nasser therefore had to make an example of the responsible commanders, if only to exonerate the rank and file and restore some element of public respect for the armed forces.

Amer was thus removed from all his offices and Sidky Mahmoud, the air force commander, together with nine other senior Generals, was sacked. Mahmoud and the others were also put on trial for gross dereliction of duty. But in deference to his long friendship with Amer, Nasser sent him word through Anwar Sadat that, if he were to leave the country immediately, he would not be arrested. He even offered to send him whatever money he might need to live on in exile. But Amer contemptuously rejected the offer. Peppering his reply with personal insults to Sadat, he said that he would stay in Egypt and vindicate himself against the attempts of the Government and the press to put all the blame on him.

Amer's defiance was to have a tragic sequel. For three months later, he was arrested, together with Shams Badran and some fifty other officers, on charges of conspiring to overthrow the President. Salah Nasr, the Chief of General Intelligence, was later to be included in the indictment and, along with Badran, was in due course sentenced to life imprisonment. Nasser's cup of bitterness had overflowed. Amer had rejected his offer of clemency and, for one in his position, there was no way of escaping the supreme penalty if he was convicted, which on the available evidence was inevitable. Nasser knew this as well as anyone and, by that curious quirk of his nature which made him often as lenient to those who betrayed him as he could be harsh to his truest supporters, he decided that, rather than be forced to sign the death-warrant of his oldest friend, Amer should be allowed to commit suicide before he could be brought to trial.

In fact, however sinister the motives of the other conspirators might have been, it is almost certain that Amer's personal intention was less to overthrow his President than to reinstate himself as Commander-in-Chief. Believing that his popularity with the army would serve him now as in the past, he allowed himself to be drawn into a scheme which the prosecution at Badran's subsequent trial had little difficulty in showing as a treasonable conspiracy against the regime. Simpleton that he was, he failed to see that it made no difference whether he intended to overthrow Nasser or was merely trying to get back his old job. For if at that stage he had succeeded in returning as Commander-in-Chief, he would have destroyed Nasser's authority as effectively as if he had seized the presidency for himself. More remarkable still, he totally ignored the fact that the army which had hitherto so revered him had been so shattered and degraded that it had lost all faith in him and every other leader.

Following Amer's suicide the post of first Vice-President was abolished and, when Mohieddin later resigned, no Vice-Presidents were appointed until, in December 1969, Anwar Sadat re-emerged from the relative obscurity of presiding over the National Assembly to become the sole deputy right up to Nasser's death nine months later. Indeed, when Mohieddin left the Government, only two out of Nasser's eleven former colleagues of the RCC remained—Sadat whom Nasser had persistently underrated as a yes-man and the even more self-effacing Hussein Shafei, both of whom had survived because not even in his most suspicious moments could the rais have regarded them as rivals to himself.

As he had shown so often before, when he met with a serious reverse, Nasser tended to withdraw into his shell and, dispensing with all but the most uncritical of his associates, to take ever more responsibility upon himself. In the aftermath of the Six Days War, he therefore became his own Prime Minister in name as well as fact. He replaced Amer with General Fawzi and appointed the highly professional Abdel Moneim Riad as Chief of Staff, who was later to be killed by Israeli shelling on the Suez Canal in March 1969. But lest Fawzi should attempt to become another Amer, he took personal control of the armed forces, naming himself as their Supreme Commander. He also intervened in judicial matters and, when the steel workers at Helwan and students of Cairo and Alexandria universities erupted in protest that Sidky Mahmoud and his fellow generals had been let off too lightly, he personally ordered a retrial which increased Mahmoud's sentence from fifteen years to life imprisonment.

Nasser afterwards confessed to me that the weeks which followed the 1967 war were one continuous nightmare. Such had been the losses in equipment as well as manpower in the recent fighting that those troops who were not either bogged down in Yemen or lying dead in Sinai had virtually no arms with which to defend Egypt. The air force had been destroyed; Cairo lay open to attack; and if the Israelis had decided to advance westwards from the Canal, there was nothing the army could have done to stop them. In a desperate attempt to muster some form of resistance, he had summoned Kemal ed-Din Hussein and asked him to form a People's Militia on the same lines as that with which he had harried the British occupiers of Port Said in 1956. But Hussein agreed to do so only if the Government were prepared to release a number of his former Moslem Brotherhood associates. To which Nasser, enraged by such conditions, retorted, 'Do you think I'm so weak that you can dictate terms?'

But if Nasser refused to submit to Hussein's demands, nobody knew better than he did how desperately weak and vulnerable was Egypt's position at this moment. With the Suez Canal blocked and the enemy encamped on its eastern bank, the revenue stood to lose some £100 millions a year. There was therefore no money to buy the arms which were so desperately needed to hold the Canal front and protect Cairo and the Delta from further invasion. And when Russia's President Podgorny visited Cairo two weeks after the cease-fire, Nasser was obliged to swallow his pride and literally to beg for Soviet help. Not only did he ask for arms as a free gift, but he also pressed for Russian military advisers and instructors. Realising that Israel's victory was due as much to technological superiority as to military prowess, he knew that the mere possession of modern equipment would not help his forces to match the enemy in the future any more than it had helped them in the recent débâcle. With Podgorny in Cairo, therefore, Nasser insisted that Soviet advisers and technicians should be attached to every brigade and, if possible, every battalion of the Egyptian army.

At first the Russians resisted these appeals. They were only too glad to help with medical and relief supplies for the wounded and the refugees from the cities in the Canal Zone, who had fled from Israeli bombardment. They were also prepared to make good Egypt's losses in aircraft, guns and other military equipment. But Kosygin had recently visited the United States for talks with Lyndon Johnson, where he had been considerably shaken by the depth of pro-Israeli sentiment in America and especially in the

Johnson administration. He was therefore afraid that, if Russia were to undertake the active role suggested by the Egyptians, she would precipitate a confrontation with the Americans. However, in the end, he and his Kremlin associates were won over; and comforting themselves with the thought that, by complying with Nasser's requests, they would be able to keep Egypt's armed forces under their control, they agreed to provide not only the arms, but also the advisers and technicians for which they had been asked. Indeed, once the decision was made, so speedily did the Soviet Government act that, within five months, Egypt's defences had been completely restored with modern weapons and with Russian instructors in every military formation above battalion level.

Nevertheless, the war, and even more the aftermath of sleepless nights and constant dread, had taken a heavy toll of Nasser's health. Not only did he lose more than thirty pounds in weight; worse still, the black diabetes was causing increasing complications, including diabetic neuritis and heart trouble. His limbs were affected and he began to drag a leg as he walked. Yet he was so afraid of reports of his illness being bandied about the world that he refused to see any foreign doctors until early in 1968 when, on the insistence of his family, a British consultant who had treated his son-in-law in England was called in. And although he continued to ignore his own doctors' pleas to seek treatment abroad or to take more rest, by the following July, his condition had become so bad that he was forced to relent and to spend three weeks in a Russian sanatorium. Three months later when I saw him in Cairo, he had regained most of his lost weight and seemed to have recovered much of his former physical robustness. But his doctors still feared for his heart and it was noticeable thereafter that, whenever he undertook a journey or engagement involving any physical or mental strain, a mobile oxygen unit would follow him at a discreet distance.

Weighed down by ill-health and the desperate anxieties arising from Egypt's defeat, Nasser became a changed man. Gone was much of the self-assurance of bygone years, gone too any pretensions to be the leader of the Arab renaissance. As he confided to me with a wan smile, with no army or air force to defend his own country, he could scarcely aspire to the leadership of any other. Therefore, when the United Nations took up the question of Israel's withdrawal from the conquered Arab territories, he was only too happy for King Hussein to make the running in Washington and New York. In a conversation in Cairo prior to the King's departure for America, Nasser told Hussein not to worry about Sinai which was Egypt's responsibility. 'I got you into this mess,' he said, 'so forget about my losses and go and kiss Lyndon Johnson's hand and ask him to give you back the West Bank.' And though he agreed with the King's argument that they could both achieve more if they worked together, he still made it clear that he wanted Jordan to take the lead in the United Nations. Unlike the Egyptians, Hussein had friends in America whose hearts he could wring with complaints about Israel's annexation of Jerusalem and tales of the thousands of new Palestinian refugees who had fled to Jordan during the fighting and whom the Israelis would not allow to return to the West Bank.

At this point it had not really dawned on Nasser or his fellow Arabs that, with the Americans against them, they would not be able, as in 1956, to mobilise enough pressure in the U.N. to make Israel disgorge her winnings within, at most, a matter of a few months. Nasser was perfectly prepared to revert to the situation as it existed before the 1967 crisis began and even to concede that the whole of Sinai would become a demilitarised zone. But, without some recompense being made to the Palestinians evicted in 1948, he could not accept Eban's statement to the United Nations that Israel would only withdraw in return for a peace settlement. As he saw it, Israel should withdraw without conditions from the newly conquered territories, as she had been obliged to do after the Suez War. Alternatively, if she wanted a peace settlement, she should make amends to the evicted Palestinians. Consequently when the Security Council failed to adopt a resolution submitted by the Yugoslav delegation on Tito's orders, because it demanded Israel's unconditional withdrawal, it came as a bitter blow for Cairo to realise that the United Nations appeared to be supporting Eban's view against the Arabs and therefore encouraging Israel to hold onto her conquests.

The situation clearly called for urgent consideration by the Arab states. Early in July, therefore, the Egyptian Government took up a suggestion of King Hussein's for a summit meeting to be held in Khartoum. Apart from the Syrians who saw the meeting as intended to organise a sell-out to Israel, every Arab state responded to the idea. The Saudis were initially somewhat reluctant to sit at the same table as the Egyptians. But, by dint of a personal visit to Riyadh, Mohammed Mahgoub, now back in office as the Sudan's Prime Minister, managed to persuade Feisal to attend. And on August 31, the assembled Arab leaders duly began their deliberations in Khartoum.

For Nasser this was undoubtedly the most difficult, if not crucial, of all Arab summit meetings. Not only did Syria boycott the conference, but his Iraqi allies also joined with the Algerians and Shukhairy, who represented the PLO, in trying to put Egypt in the dock for having abandoned the struggle and accepting a cease-fire when the Israelis had reached the Canal. The Iraqis also pressed for a boycott on sales of Arab oil to the West and for the withdrawal of Arab deposits, estimated at £4,000 millions, from British banks. Nor were those who favoured a more realistic approach of much help in contesting this hard-line approach. While they refused to cripple themselves by imposing oil sanctions on the West, they nevertheless declined to take the lead in advocating a settlement with Israel for fear of being branded as traitors to the Arab cause. And to make matters still more awkward for Nasser, the agenda also included the delicate question of how the oil-rich Arab states could help to compensate Egypt and Jordan as the two principal victims of the Six Days War for the appalling material losses which they had suffered.

Like so much else, this question was complicated by the still unhealed divisions which the Yemeni conflict had wrought among the Arabs. But, thanks to the skilful and determined diplomacy of Mahgoub, the problem was successfully resolved and in a way which furthermore helped towards a final settlement in Yemen. Iraq, having failed to get her own way about boycotting oil sales to the West, refused to contribute anything to the war damage fund. But, on the prompting of Mahgoub, Saudi Arabia's

Feisal and the Ruler of Kuwait agreed that they should between them pay £105 millions a year to Egypt and Jordan until such time as they could recover their lost lands and revenues. Feisal's only condition, with which Nasser was now very happy to comply, was that Egypt should in return work towards a settlement in Yemen by progressively withdrawing her forces, which Nasser, never more anxious than now to disengage from the area, was only too happy to accept. At first the Libyan representatives, whose King had never been on good terms with his Egyptian neighbour, sought escape by claiming that they had no authority to offer any contribution. But when Mahgoub told them that the conference could wait while they telephoned to Tripoli for instructions, the necessary authority was speedily obtained. The total compensation for Egypt and Jordan was then raised to an annual figure of £135 millions. Egypt, having suffered the greater lossses of the two and having by far the larger population, received £95 millions of this sum which more or less covered the lost revenues from the Canal.

In this respect the conclusions of the Khartoum conference were not only successful but even historic. For the first time in the twenty years since the Palestine problem became an issue of war between the Arab world and the state of Israel, Arab countries outside the immediate area of conflict had accepted a joint responsibility for materially helping their comrades in the battle zone, instead of merely cheering or jeering at them from the sidelines. Also, for the first time ever, Nasser was prepared to make political concessions in return for financial help. Admittedly, he could no longer afford the luxury of keeping some 70,000 troops in Yemen merely to put pressure on the British to get out of Aden. Apart from the financial burden of doing so, he needed these troops to defend Egypt against a possible further Israeli advance on Cairo and the Nile Delta. But more important still, he had begun to see that, perhaps after all, Egypt stood to gain more by allying herself with the 'reactionary' Jordanians and Saudis than with such unbalanced and unpredictable 'progressives' as Syria and Iraq.

Nothing showed this more clearly than the debate in Khartoum on the question of how the Israelis might be induced to withdraw from the territories seized in the Six Days War. Shukhairy had at this point become the target of much criticism from the Palestinian guerrilla groups for having spent too much time posturing with Communist leaders in Moscow and Peking and too little in organising an effective resistance movement. In a desperate effort to rehabilitate himself before his fellow Palestinians, he therefore launched into several bitter tirades against Egypt and Jordan for having betrayed the cause of Arab Palestine. Whatever the cost, he demanded that the struggle should be continued until eventual victory was won. Any Arab who contemplated any compromise with Israel should, he maintained, be dubbed a traitor.

With Iraq and Algeria following Shukhairy's suit and the more moderate Arab leaders holding back, Nasser was obliged to take on the task of pricking this bubble of blustering heroics. He would ordinarily have much preferred to leave it to Feisel to do so. But, apart from Feisal's reluctance to take the lead on this issue, Nasser was deeply wounded by Shukhairy's apparent disregard for the price that Egypt had paid in the war which the PLO leader had done so much to provoke. Casting caution and his existing alliances to the winds, he therefore weighed in against his critics and their absent friends in Damascus with a blistering counter-attack. Reminding the conference of Egypt's and Jordan's losses in terms of men and territory, he made it crystal clear that an Arab counter-offensive could not be mounted within the foreseeable future. The brunt of any such attack would have to be borne by Egypt and, since the Russians had on principle refused to supply her with offensive weapons, Egypt was in no position to undertake the task. The recovery of the Arab territories lost in the recent fighting would therefore have to be accomplished by political pressures exerted on Israel by the U.N. and the great powers. Any talk of the Arabs using more forceful methods was mere bravado or hypocrisy.

Hussein strongly supported these arguments, whereupon Feisal and the rest came out of their shells and endorsed a draft resolution expressing the agreed intention of the conference to work for a settlement by diplomatic action. The relevant passage stated that,

'The Arab Heads of State have agreed to unite their political efforts at the international and diplomatic level to eliminate the effects of the aggression and to ensure the withdrawal of the aggressive Israeli forces from the Arab lands which have been occupied since the aggression on June 5.' Shukhairy, however, objected that this statement on its own amounted to an Arab surrender and, with the support of the Iraqis and Algerians, he insisted on a qualifying phrase being added stating that, 'This will be done within the framework of the main principles by which the Arab states abide, namely no peace with Israel, no recognition of Israel, no negotiations with it, and insistence on the rights of the Palestinian people in their own country.'

For the sake of unanimity Nasser, Hussein and the others accepted this addendum. But they equally made it clear that they would still be free to seek a settlement by diplomatic methods and that, as they understood it, 'no peace or recognition' meant no formal peace treaty or diplomatic recognition of Israel, and that 'no negotiations' did not rule out indirect negotiations through a third party. Thus when, two months later, the U.N. Security Council met to seek a peace formula, the Egyptian and Jordanian representatives dropped their earlier demands for an unconditional Israeli withdrawal. After prolonged discussions behind the scenes in New York, between the parties concerned and the American, Russian and British delegations, a compromise resolution was presented by Britain, known thereafter as Resolution No. 242, which in suitably ambiguous terms proposed that territory acquired by force was inadmissible; that Israel should withdraw to permanent and secure borders; that a 'just settlement' be made for the Palestinian refugees; that the state of belligerency between Israel and the Arabs be terminated; and that freedom of navigation be guaranteed through the international waterways in the area – in other words the Gulf of Akaba and the Suez Canal.

Mahmoud Riad for Egypt, supported by the Jordanians, wanted the resolution to be more precise on the question of frontiers. But the American delegate, Arthur Goldberg, made it clear that he would not endorse any words which limited Israel's right to seek more secure borders than those which existed before the Six Days War. Under cross-examination by King Hussein and Riad, Goldberg however gave an assurance that the Israelis had accepted the draft resolution and that, if the Arabs did so too, President Johnson would guarantee its implementation subject only to minor frontier rectifications and an agreement on a new status for the city of Jerusalem. And since American endorsement was essential to any hope of persuading the Israelis to withdraw from Sinai and the West Bank, Nasser and Hussein agreed, despite vociferous objections from Syria, Iraq and Algeria, to accept the draft as it stood without attempting to secure further precision.

Resolution 242 was therefore adopted by the unanimous vote of the Security Council on November 22 and Gunnar Jarring, the Swedish Ambassador in Moscow, was appointed by U Thant to act as go-between, negotiating separately with Egypt, Jordan and Israel to bring about a mutually acceptable settlement. But any hopes that were raised by the passage of the resolution were not to survive very long. For the two months prior to the Security Council's debate, Egyptian and Israeli forces lining the Suez Canal had been exchanging artillery fire at intermittent intervals and, in October, an Israeli destroyer had been sunk off the northern coast of Sinai. Also there had been several clashes on the Jordanian front, as the Israelis began to dig in on the West Bank, where the building of nahals and other fortified settlements suggested that they were contemplating rather more than a temporary occupation. Then, two months after Resolution 242 was adopted by the Security Council, the Israelis forcibly prevented Egyptian salvage teams from removing some fifteen foreign vessels which had been stranded in the Suez Canal during the June war. And though Jarring persevered in his exchanges with both sides, fighting continued along the whole length of the cease-fire line, but most of all across the Canal. Meanwhile Dayan kept on telling the world that Israel would never give up the strategic areas which she had won. Jewish settlers, he said, would remain permanently on the West Bank and would be protected by Israeli forces from any attempt by the Arabs to recover their lands. Eshkol too, for his part, made it clear that in any peace settlement

Israel would insist on the Jordan river being her 'security border' in perpetuity.

Yet in spite of these adverse indications and heedless of the jeers and insults of Damascus, Baghdad and Algiers, the Egyptians still clung to the hope that somehow Israel would be induced to fulfil her part of the bargain under the U.N. resolution. Riad, on a visit to Western Europe in the summer of 1968, stressed that Egypt accepted the realities of the situation in the Middle East, including the reality of the state of Israel. Egyptian spokesmen never tired of saying that they supported Jarring and wanted his mission to succeed. In the following October, Riad agreed with the U.N. mediator on the principles of a time-table for carrying out the resolution by agreed stages, so that at no point in the process would either party be at a disadvantage. But the Israelis were no more willing to comply with these ideas than they had been to respond to any other proposal or question put to them by Jarring, other than by demanding direct negotiations with the Arabs and insisting on the retention of most of the conquered territory. By the end of the year therefore, even the most sanguine Egyptians had begun to despair of the prospects for Jarring's mission.

Meanwhile, in pursuance of his new political strategy, Nasser had been engaged in some extensive fence-mending with the West. A chance meeting in Russia between Britain's Foreign Secretary and Field Marshal Amer in November 1966 had eventually led to a dialogue about a resumption of relations between Britain and Egypt. In the following October, Harold Beeley was sent to Cairo to discuss the necessary arrangements. Unlike 1961, Beeley now met with the warmest possible reception from everybody from the President downwards; and when, two months later, he returned as Britain's Ambassador for the second time, Nasser and his Ministers went out of their way to treat him as an old and trusted friend.

In part this sudden switch from the dark suspicions and hostility of the past two years was brought about by the efforts which Britain's U.N. representative, Lord Caradon, had played in getting Resolution 242 adopted by the Security Council. But there were other reasons as well. For one thing, Nasser had become not a little worried about the extent of his commitment to Russia in the aftermath of the Six Days War. With no more economic aid from America he was now altogether too dependent on Moscow for food as well as arms. He could therefore no longer strike a balance between West and East and, as Tito had so often warned him would happen, he knew that this would restrict his freedom to steer a neutral course in world affairs. Britain might not be able to make good the loss of American aid but Nasser felt that she could perhaps help to reopen some of those doors in Washington which he had slammed over the past two years.

Yet another reason for seeking a rapprochement with Britain was that it now seemed the British were after all about to withdraw not only their authority but also their military presence from Aden. When Nasser met Beeley in October 1967, during the course of a discussion on Aden, Beeley asked if the President could perhaps use his good offices to reconcile the two rival nationalist groups, FLOSY and NLF, whose mutual antipathy was impeding progress towards Aden's independence. From this suggestion, which he willingly accepted, Nasser assumed that, contrary to his earlier suspicions, Britain now intended, when leaving Aden, to hand over power to a united nationalist front rather than to some puppet regime. Since neither of the two nationalist groups would ever agree to a British military presence remaining after independence, this could only mean that Britain had definitely given up all ideas of retaining a base in the area. From every point of view therefore there seemed to be no objection and considerable advantage in restoring diplomatic relations between Cairo and London.

To Nasser's immense relief these assumptions proved to be correct. On November 29, ten days after the formal announcement that the two countries were to exchange ambassadors, Britain declared that Aden was now independent and that all British troops were being immediately withdrawn. Better still, in the following January, Britain's Prime Minister announced that all British forces would leave the Persian Gulf within the next three years. And when nearly two years after this pronouncement, British and American forces withdrew from Libya following the deposition of King Idris by an army coup d'état, every last vestige of Britain's military presence in the Arab world had been or was about to be removed.

But Egyptian hopes that a resumption of relations with Britain would help to restore the connection with Washington were not to be fulfilled. Nor was this by any means entirely, or even mainly, Cairo's fault. In March 1968, Nasser publicly withdrew the accusation made in the heat of battle that United States forces had helped the Israelis during the Six Days War, which he told America's *Look* magazine had been based on 'suspicion and faulty information'. Also, during the Security Council's debate in the previous autumn, Riad had bent over backwards to secure American support for Egypt's case. But the Johnson administration had from the outset shown little, if any, willingness to put pressure on Israel to pull out of Sinai or the West Bank. When the Russians had originally tried to include in the U.N.'s cease-fire resolution a demand that Israel withdraw to her own territory, the Americans had insisted on a simple cease-fire, contending that territorial issues should be settled later. And though Johnson had given King Hussein his personal assurance that Israel had accepted Resolution 242 and would carry it out in good faith, not only was there no sign of this assurance being fulfilled, but there was equally no indication that the Americans were seriously trying to do anything about it. When Eshkol visited Washington in January 1968 for personal talks at the White House, there was not the smallest suggestion that Johnson had remonstrated with him about Israel's uncompromising attitude. Even when he asked for American jet aircraft to strengthen the Israeli air force, the Americans had not apparently tried to impose any conditions for meeting his request.

Consequently, neither Nasser nor those other Arabs – including the Syrians, Sudanese, Algerians and Iraqis – who had broken with America over the Six Days War, could possibly justify to their people a resumption of relations with Washington, even if Johnson's Government had shown any desire to repair the breach. However, in November 1968, the election of a Republican President in the shape of Richard Nixon visibly raised Nasser's hopes.

When I saw him at that time, he was so relieved to know that he would no longer have to deal with Johnson that he regarded any other American as an improvement. He also felt that Nixon, who had served as Eisenhower's Vice-President and who, as a Republican, would not be so beholden to the Jewish vote, would now take a more impartial line as between Israel and the Arabs. Thus when William Scranton, a personal envoy of the President-elect, shortly afterwards returned from a fact-finding tour of the Middle East, proclaiming that American policy in the area should be more 'even-handed', Nasser's hopes rose higher than ever. And when Dayan, following a private talk with Nixon, asserted that American policy in the Middle East would not change with the new Government, Nasser's inclination was to regard this as a piece of bravado.

But within less than a year Dayan was to be proved all too right. One of Johnson's last acts had been to authorise the delivery of the latest American Phantom fighter-bombers to Israel. Before doing so, he had sent Nasser a message saying that Eshkol had asked for these aircraft on his January visit, but that he hesitated to put such modern and powerful weapons into such an explosive area as the Middle East. If therefore Egypt, together with her Russian arms suppliers, would show willing to pursue a policy of moderation, he would take this into account in deciding whether or not to authorise deliveries of Phantoms to Israel. Nasser had been incensed by this message, coming as it did on top of his acceptance of Resolution 242 and his efforts to cooperate with Jarring in the face of continuing Israeli intransigence. Johnson, he felt, should have addressed himself to Israel not to Egypt and, though he retorted through an American contact of Heikal's that Washington had some gall in asking him to show restraint in the circumstances, he vouchsafed no official reply.

Johnson therefore authorised the shipment of Phantoms for Israel in October 1968, a few weeks before the presidential election. But when Nixon took office in the following January, the Phantoms had not yet left and their delivery was held up pending a decision by the incoming administration. For the next eight months the issue remained in the balance, with the Israelis using every available pressure to force the Nixon Government's hand. Then in September 1969, the first batch of Phantoms was released.

The timing could not have been more unfortunate for Egyptian-American relations. For apart from the inevitable disappointment in Cairo that Nixon had not cancelled his predecessor's decision, the release of the Phantoms happened also to coincide with yet another absolute refusal by the Russians to supply Egypt with any comparable aircraft. Besides, the Nixon administration had meanwhile begun to demonstrate that they were scarcely less reluctant than the previous Government to put pressure on Israel to carry out the Security Council's resolution. In February 1969, when they were invited to join in four-power discussions to find a way round the impasse which Jarring had reached, only the fact that Russia, Britain and France had all agreed to make the attempt induced them to follow suit. Nor, when Eban later attacked the four-power talks as an unfortunate duplication of the peace-making machinery, was there any sign of a rejoinder from Washington. Nixon did, it is true, proclaim before the United Nations General Assembly in September 1969 that 'peace cannot be achieved on the basis of substantial alterations in the map of the Middle East'. But a week later the fatuity of his pronouncement was revealed when Mrs Golda Meir, who had become Israel's Premier on the death of Eshkol in the previous February, declared to an American audience that Israel had been under 'no pressure whatsoever' from Washington to withdraw to her own borders. Nor had Washington responded in any way when King Hussein, speaking in America in the previous April with the full personal authority of Egypt's President as well as his own Government, put forward a peace plan designed to spell out the terms of Resolution 242.

By the autumn of 1969, the Egyptians had begun to despair of the 'even-handed' approach which Scranton had led them to expect from the change of Government in Washington. As Golda Meir had candidly admitted, not even in return for such lethal weapons as Phantom bombers had the Nixon administration deigned to demand that Israel comply with the Security Council's resolution. Desperately therefore Nasser struck out at the American attitude in a public speech on November 6. All Egypt's efforts to carry out Resolution 242, he said, had been stultified by Israel's intractability encouraged by Washington's unqualified support in arms and money. 'The Americans are fighting behind the Israeli forces and supplying the planes which are being used against us,' he declared. Under the circumstances he could see no hope of reaching a settlement by peaceful means and there seemed to be no longer any way out except to use force 'to open our own road to what we want, over a sea of blood and under a horizon of fire'.

Yet, as Nasser equally knew very well, there was no possibility of Egypt liberating Sinai or Gaza by force, at least so long as Russia refused to supply her with offensive weapons. Therefore, the most that Egypt could do, as she had been doing over the past two years, was to engage the enemy in artillery duels and occasional commando raids across the Suez Canal. Indeed even this much activity was becoming expensive and dangerous. For the Israelis had not always confined their own attacks to the Suez front, but on two occasions, in November 1968 and in the following April, had sent commando units by helicopter to attack bridges over the Nile and electricity plants in Upper Egypt. And by the end of 1969, not only had Suez and Port Tewfik been virtually razed to the ground by constant Israeli shelling, but the enemy had demonstrated in no uncertain manner his ability to strike far behind the Egyptian lines without any appreciable opposition.

I spent the evening after the first of these two Israeli raids with Nasser and it would have been hard to find a man more totally frustrated. Unable to make either peace or war with Israel, he could only hope that, by continuing to lean on her occupation armies by artillery bombardments across the Canal, the Egyptians would one day force the enemy to relent and return behind his former frontiers. Meanwhile, he had given orders for the extension of the Egyptian air defence system to cover the whole country. But, as the second of the two raids on Upper Egypt was to show six months later, the country nevertheless remained as vulnerable as ever to Israeli attacks. No less damaging was the assault by an enemy force on an Egyptian island in the Gulf of Suez, which killed twenty-five members of the garrison and destroyed their anti-aircraft guns. More serious still, in January 1970, another Israeli task force captured the island of Shadwan off Egypt's Red Sea coast, which was being used as a tracking station for enemy aircraft, and after killing eighty more Egyptian soldiers, either smashed or removed every piece of the most modern radar equipment.

To make matters worse for Egypt's defence forces, due to losses both in the Six Days War and in subsequent air operations on the Canal front, there was now a serious shortage of trained pilots. So acute was this deficiency that in several air raids on Egyptian artillery positions in the summer of 1969, the Israelis had met with no resistance whatsoever from the Egyptian air force. This was bad enough by itself. But when set against the fact that, from September onwards, Israel could strike at Egypt with American Phantoms which were even more powerful than the Mirages already in their possession, it presented a truly horrifying prospect. Accordingly, within a few weeks of delivering his tirade against the Americans, Nasser set off for Moscow to beg for a shipment of SAM ground-to-air missiles to defend Egypt against enemy air attacks and to ask that, until Egyptian crews could be trained in the use of these highly sophisticated weapons, the Russians should allow their own crews to man them.

The Soviet leaders made no difficulty about supplying the missiles, but they were not at all happy about letting their own men fire them against Israeli aircraft. What, they asked, would the world, and more especially the Americans, say if any of these Russians were killed in the course of doing so? The Soviet Government were currently involved in delicate discussions with Washington about a Middle East settlement and were trying to persuade the United States Government that the best hope was for the four powers to draw up their own ideal solution of the frontier problem and impose it on Israel and the Arabs alike. They therefore did not want to upset any apple carts by some action which the Americans could say was likely to disturb the balance of power in the area. But Nasser was not to be denied. The balance of power, he replied, had already been upset by America's supply of Phantoms to Israel and it was therefore imperative for Egypt to have some answer to these deadly offensive weapons. He was not asking that Russian missile crews should stay on the job indefinitely, but only so long as it took to train Egyptians to take over. Without the men to fire them, no amount of missiles would be of the smallest use if Israel were to start a war of attrition in the air, which she could now do on every city and installation in Egypt.

It took Nasser eight days of argument to induce Brezhnev and Kosygin to meet his demands. And no sooner had he done so than the Israelis, just as he had feared, sent their new Phantoms to raid an industrial suburb of Cairo where seventy people were killed when a bomb destroyed a scrap metal factory. Then again in April 1970, two months later, another Israeli raid destroyed a school in the Delta killing thirty children. Washington deplored the attacks and, albeit somewhat belatedly, called for four-power talks on limiting arms deliveries to both sides. But the only Israeli comment was a statement from Dayan that, if Egyptian schoolchildren had been killed, it was the fault of the Egyptian authorities for exposing them to the risk of being bombed. Then, three weeks later, the Israeli Government adopted the attitude of the injured party by publicly complaining of what they claimed to be 'absolute proof' that Soviet pilots were flying operational missions from air force bases in Egypt under Russian control.

The Israelis were of course confusing missiles with aircraft. Nevertheless there was no disguising the fact that virtually the entire defence system of Egypt was now under Soviet management. That Nasser did not like to be so dependent on one particular power was plain for anyone to see who visited him at the time. But as he explained it to me, he had had no choice in the matter. 'Only Russia helped us after the June war,' he said, 'with everything from wheat to fighter aircraft, while the Americans were busily helping our enemies and the occupiers of our land. What's more, the Russians have asked for nothing in return, except facilities for their warships to use Alexandria. So what should I have done? Should I have waited until the Americans would send me equal quantities of food and weapons? I'd have waited for ever if I had.'

There was indeed nothing he could do, save to accept what aid Russia would give and ask for more whenever he needed it. Yet, although there was no way of asserting his independence of Moscow in this situation, Nasser was nevertheless determined to show the Russians that, however indebted to them he might be, he would not tolerate any Soviet intrigues against his authority. And this he now proceeded to do in his own peculiar way.

Since Amer's death in 1967, Ali Sabry had taken over as the President's principal negotiator with Russia, in which task he succeeded in greatly ingratiating himself with his Soviet contacts. But in the summer of 1969, Nasser heard from his ambassador in Moscow that Sabry had been indulging in loose and disloyal talk on a recent visit to Russia. In particular he had told his contacts that he greatly deplored Nasser's slowness and timidity in adopting socialist policies. To Nasser's way of thinking such talk could only mean that Sabry was involved in some personal intrigue with the Russians. At the very least he was suggesting that they deal with him behind the back of his President. And since one of the reasons for dismissing Mohieddin in 1966 had been the fear that Washington might feel tempted to try this kind of ploy with him, he was not going to let Sabry and the Russians combine in any such devious dealings.

The problem of putting Sabry down presented no great difficulties. Through Sami Sharaf's private intelligence network Nasser knew that, when he returned from visits to foreign parts, Sabry was in the habit of using his official authority to bring large quantities of goods, such as furs and jade, into Egypt without paying a piastre of customs duty. And in July 1969, when Sharaf heard through his grape-vine that Sabry, currently on one of his Moscow missions, had ordered an army truck to meet him on his return, Nasser decided to pounce. The truck with its load of smuggled goods was seized and Sabry was ordered to pay £2000 of customs duty out of his own pocket. Then, after the story of his misdemeanours had been released to the press, he was dismissed from the chairmanship of the ASU. From now on the

President personally took charge of all further negotiations with the Soviet Union; and although Sabry was reinstated a year later, it was only to the comparatively lowly office of presidential adviser on air force matters in which post he could be kept under constant supervision.

Yet, however determined Nasser might be to let the Russians see that intrigue against the regime would not be tolerated, Egypt's ever-increasing dependence on Soviet military aid and advice had become a matter of grave concern to the United States Government. True, Russia was still refusing to supply the Egyptians with offensive weapons. But by the early spring of 1970, Washington was thoroughly alarmed at the possibilities of an escalation of the fighting on the Canal front leading to a confrontation between America and Russia in support of their respective clients. In April, therefore, Nixon sent his Assistant Secretary of State for Middle East affairs, Joseph Sisco, on a tour of the area to discuss with both sides a restoration of the cease-fire which would enable Jarring to try his hand at mediation once again.

In the course of a two hours' interview with Sisco, Nasser made no secret of the fact that he did not trust the Americans, although he freely admitted that they more than any other power held the key to peace. Equally he showed considerable realism in his appraisal of the problems of liberating Sinai by force. And he left Sisco in little doubt that he still hoped that the Americans, even at this late hour, would help to get discussions restarted through Jarring on the basis of the U.N. resolution. Moreover, in a speech delivered on May 1, a week after Sisco had returned to Washington, he combined a severe censure of American policy with a veiled appeal for American help. Relations between the Arab world and the United States, he said, had reached a crucial stage. Any move by the Americans to ensure military superiority for Israel would irreparably damage United States interests in the Middle East for decades to come. 'If the Americans want peace,' he concluded, 'they must order Israel to withdraw from Arab territory.' Or if that were not possible, they should at least refrain from supplying aid to the Israelis as long as they continued to occupy Arab lands.

Taken together with Nasser's statements to Sisco, this speech suggested to the American Secretary of State, William Rogers, that the Egyptians were looking for an American peace initiative and that, despite their distrust of Washington's Middle East policies, they would cooperate with any genuine attempt by the United States to work towards a settlement. Accordingly, on June 25, he put forward a proposal, subsequently to be called the Rogers Plan, for the restoration of the cease-fire between Israel and Egypt for at least ninety days. During this period each Government would appoint representatives to meet with Jarring and discuss how Resolution 242 could be carried out in a way which would provide for an Israeli withdrawal and for recognition by each party of the other's sovereignty and independence.

Nasser knew well enough that, in Egypt's interests, he would have to accept the Rogers Plan. Even though the SAM missiles now being supplied by Russia would help to defend the country against Israeli attacks, there was still no prospect of regaining Sinai by force of arms. The only alternative to the Rogers Plan would therefore be to continue the current war of attrition for an indefinite period with no knowing how long it would take to wear down the Israelis. Besides, it was still in Egypt's interests to maintain a dialogue with Washington. In the previous November, as his exasperated outburst against the Americans had shown, he had begun to despair of the Nixon administration fulfilling its promise of impartiality. But the Rogers initiative had brought fresh hope and there was something to be said for encouraging its author, who had shown in a recent exchange of words with Golda Meir, that he was not afraid to assert that a peaceful settlement could not be made on conqueror's terms.

Nevertheless, there were two snags about the timing of Rogers' proposal which had to be overcome. For one thing, Nasser was now a very ill man. The circulatory problems which had been treated in Russia in 1968 had arisen again. In the previous autumn he had suffered a minor heart attack and his doctors, who had become seriously concerned about his condition, now insisted on his returning to Russia for further treatment and complete rest. For another, the Russian SAM missiles ordered five months earlier had by no means all arrived in Egypt and, before any new stand-still arrangements might be agreed, it was essential that all or most of this vital equipment should be properly installed. Otherwise, if Jarring's negotiations should again reach deadlock, the Israelis would be able to resume their bombing attacks without warning against a virtually defenceless Egypt.

Consequently Nasser hastened to Russia where he succeeded in slightly speeding up deliveries of the missiles before retiring once more to his Crimean sanatorium for a further two weeks of treatment. Thus it was not until July 23, exactly four weeks after Rogers put forward his plan, that Cairo was able to announce Egypt's formal acceptance. And when Israel, albeit reluctantly, had followed suit, the restoration of the cease-fire was set for August 7. But even with this period of grace, the Egyptians were unable to install all the missiles within the time-limit and so were obliged, to the accompaniment of loud protests from the Israelis, to commit a technical breach of the cease-fire by moving the late arrivals onto their appointed sites after the August 7 deadline.

By propounding the Rogers Plan the Americans seemed at long last to have come up with the kind of even-handed policy which Scranton had promised eighteen long months before. And for the first time since the end of 1967, there appeared to be a faint glimmer of hope that Egypt and Jordan might be able to reach a settlement with Israel. That this hope was to be disappointed could hardly be laid at Nasser's door. Nor could he be blamed for the fact that, in the brief span of life that was now left to him, he was obliged to devote more time and energy to repairing the ensuing divisions among the Arab states than to discussing peace terms with Jarring. For no sooner had he declared Egypt's acceptance of the Rogers Plan than the Syrians, the Iraqis and the Palestinian Resistance denounced him and everyone who agreed with him as a traitor to the Arab cause.

Certainly no one could deny that, in the aftermath of the Six Days War, Nasser appeared to have shed much of his former pan-Arab idealism and was primarily, if not entirely, concerned with the needs of Egypt. But this was largely because he knew that, after such a devastating defeat, Egypt had to recoup her own losses before she could again aspire to her allotted role of Arab leadership. Yet, because there were among his fellow rulers those who could not or would not understand this basic truth, he was now to find himself confronted by the vicious hostility of Damascus and Baghdad for having decided to make one more attempt to reach a settlement with Israel. Even worse, he was obliged to intercede in a bloody civil war between the army and the Palestinians in Jordan, which effort was so to exhaust his remaining physical strength as to cost him his own life.

Chapter 22

The Last Summit

Since the 1967 war, and more particularly since the Khartoum summit conference which followed it, Nasser's Arab alliances had been almost completely reversed. The stark realities of political necessity had turned the 'reactionary' enemies of yesterday into the supporters of today and made bitter opponents of such erstwhile 'progressive' allies as Syria and Iraq.

In fact, by 1970, Egypt's only supporters who could qualify for the 'progressive' label were the Sudan and Libya, where in the previous year army regimes had been established by coups d'état led respectively by General Jafar Numeiri and Colonel Muammar Gadaffy. New to politics, these two revolutionary leaders were happy to take their cue from Cairo on most issues of foreign policy. But the other socialist countries, including the newly independent Adenis, calling themselves the Republic of South Yemen, remained implacably hostile to any idea of compromise with Israel. As for Syria, the left-wing Baathists were now no less in the ascendant than in the days of Amin el-Hafiz and, pouring forth all their pent-up venom against Egypt, maintained a constant barrage of accusations that Nasser was selling out the Palestinians and his former allies in a dastardly attempt to recover Egypt's lost territory by a separate deal with Israel. Even Aref lent himself to this chorus of denunciation, if only to avoid being outbid by his opponents of the Iraqi Baath. And when in July 1968, unable to stem the tide any longer, he was swept out of office by the Baathists and replaced as President by General Hassan al-Bakr, Baghdad let fly with a campaign of vituperation against Egyptian policy scarcely less violent than that of the days of Kassem.

Nasser hit back against his critics both on radio and television and in the press. When he met Syria's President Atassi in Libya at the celebrations that followed the withdrawal of the American air base, he told him to his face that Syria's ingratitude to Egypt had proved, if proof were necessary, how little the loyalty of the Baath could be trusted. And in a personal letter to President Bakr, which was released to the press, he suggested that Iraqi energies would be better employed in the Arab cause by fighting the Israelis than by street demonstrations demanding that others should do so. He also protested vehemently when the Iraqi authorities, having executed a number of Arab and Jewish citizens for spying on behalf of Israel, publicly exhibited the corpses of the condemned men on gibbets in a Baghdad square. But, no matter how much Cairo might lambaste the Baathists of Baghdad, there was no more hope of influencing Bakr's regime than there was of persuading the Syrians to change their tune.

However ill at ease he might feel in his marriage of convenience with those Arab rulers whom, prior to 1967, he had dubbed as disloyal reactionaries, Nasser was therefore in no position to reject their proffered friendship. Apart from his desire for a settlement with Israel, ever since the Six Days War ended he had desperately needed to bring his troops home from Yemen, if only to plug some of the holes in Egypt's defences. And he could not finally disengage from this conflict without the cooperation of the Saudis. The Khartoum agreement was to satisfy this requirement and within the next few weeks, he had pulled some 20,000 troops out of Yemen, despite vehement objections from Sallal. Then, when Britain withdrew from Aden at the end of 1967, a further 30,000 men were brought home, leaving only some 20,000 to support the republican cause, together with a guarantee by Cairo to pay for the maintenance of Sallal's army for another six months.

This did not mean that the war in Yemen ended immediately after these Egyptian withdrawals, still less that the republicans had established anything approaching a stable regime of their own. On the contrary, fighting continued, although on a very diminished scale. Sallal was moreover constantly at loggerheads with his supporters and especially with his Premier, Hassan al-Amri. At the end of 1965, Nasser had found it necessary to keep Sallal out of the way in Cairo for some nine months, so as to allow Amri an opportunity to bring some semblance of order to the Sanaa Government. However Amri had then clashed with the Egyptian Command. Whereupon Sallal had returned to Yemen, dismissed his Prime Minister and arrested well over a hundred senior officials and army officers, of whom seven were executed for collaboration with Saudi Arabia. Amri fled to Cairo; but in December 1967, as Egypt withdrew the bulk of her troops, Sallal was obliged to recall him once more to run the Government. Thereafter desultory fighting continued between royalist and republican forces for another twelve months. But towards the end of 1968 the Saudis decided to stop supplying the Imam's army in an attempt to impose a cease-fire. And from that moment on, with the exception of a few brief skirmishes, an effective stand-still existed throughout Yemen until, in May 1970, a final settlement brought the opposing parties together, after more than seven years of civil war, to form a national coalition.

Although he had had little choice in the matter, Nasser had taken a considerable gamble when he pulled nearly three-quarters of his army out of Yemen in advance of any final settlement. But thanks to Saudi cooperation and the timely withdrawal of the British forces from Aden, he had been able to disengage from this luckless venture without further loss of prestige. And with the home front now reinforced in numbers as well as weapons, he felt sufficiently self-confident to call another meeting of Arab heads of state in order to consolidate his new alliances and to expose the hypocrisy of his militant critics. In December 1969, at a conference in Rabat, he bluntly asked those who rejected all ideas of a settlement what precise plans they had for carrying on the war against Israel. If, as they consistently maintained, they were radically opposed to every line of the United Nations resolution, then presumably they had worked out an alternative strategy to evict the Israelis from the territories occupied in 1967, if not altogether from Palestinian soil. Would Algeria for instance provide the main air strike capacity? How many troops would Syria and Iraq commit to the battle? Would they attack only from Syria or did they also plan to use Jordanian territory? What part did they envisage that Egypt should play? Who would put up the money and where would they get the necessary arms to carry the war to the enemy?

All these and many other questions had to be answered, Nasser said. And he had a right to know the answers before being asked to abandon his search for a political settlement. Admittedly Israel had so far proved to be totally intractable. But unless the Arabs had a plan which stood at least a fair chance of gaining them victory in battle, it was sheer folly for them to throw away any chance of reaching a settlement. Needless to say, the militants could only reply that their lack of concrete plans was everybody's fault but their own. On the second day of the conference, therefore, Nasser walked out of the meeting and took himself off to Tripoli for more congenial discussions with the new rulers of Libya and the Sudan.

Apart from exposing the insincerity of Cairo's critics, the Rabat conference had one important by-product, in that it brought Nasser together with Gadaffy and Numeiri and so laid the foundations of a formal alliance between Egypt and the new military regimes in Tripoli and Khartoum. Both of these regimes were led by young officers, whose enthusiasm for revolutionary reforms was hardly matched by their administrative abilities. And since Numeiri and Gadaffy shared an unbounded admiration for their Egyptian elder brother, they had come to lean heavily upon him for guidance and support.

Nasser made no attempt to discourage their doing so. Libya, until very recently so poor that her main export was, ironically enough, esparto-grass for manufacturing other countries' bank notes, was now blessed with a prodigious wealth of new-found oil; and the Sudan, although not nearly so well endowed, had always been of unique importance to Egypt's economic life. Besides, the recent reversal of Nasser's alliances in the Arab world had not been without its embarrassments. Not only was he now aligned with 'reactionary' regimes, but once again he found himself sharing the same platform on the Israeli issue as Bourguiba, which fact the militants had not been slow to exploit in their smear campaign against Cairo. To have the backing of two brand new revolutionary states was, therefore, a thoroughly welcome development. Thus when Nasser met with Numeiri and Gadaffy in Khartoum in May 1970 on the first anniversary of the Sudanese revolution, he readily agreed to form a tripartite alliance designed, in the words of its announcement, to 'fuse the three countries' progressive revolutions in confronting the plots of world imperialism, Zionism and local reactionary forces'.

But if Egypt's associations appeared more respectable in an Arab context by reason of the adherence of these two revolutionary regimes, this did not mean that her position on the world stage was any stronger. In the eyes of the West, Nasser was still the battered victim of his own provocations in the Six Days War who, in the aftermath of his humiliating defeat, had become, however involuntarily, a satellite of Russia and a pawn on Moscow's power-political chess-board. Hence his aspirations to membership, let alone to leadership, of the neutral, non-aligned world had been shattered. Even his old friendships with Tito and Nehru had been dissolved. Nehru was dead but, before he died, he had been deeply disillusioned when Nasser uttered no public protest following China's attacks on Indian territory in the middle sixties, but contented himself with private remonstrances to Chou En-lai. More recently, Tito had been bitterly disappointed by Egypt's failure to join with Yugoslavia in denouncing the Russian invasion of Czechoslovakia in the summer of 1968. No matter how dependent Egypt might be on Russia's charity, he found it incredible that Nasser should have remained mute in face of such brutality.

When Tito visited the High Dam later that same year, Nasser tried to make him understand his silence. He could not, he said, attack the Russians who were his only hope of getting the arms that he needed to defend Egypt. Without their support, his position in the Middle East would be fatally undermined, in which case the only beneficiaries would be the Americans and the Israelis. Surely no friend of Egypt's could wish for such an outcome? Tito inevitably agreed that this was the last thing he wanted. But he equally could not help remembering that not so long ago, when the Russians were stirring up the Communists in Egypt and

Syria, Nasser had not been afraid to attack them publicly as well as privately, even though at that very moment they were doling out huge sums of aid to build the High Dam and to equip the Egyptian army. Consequently he could no longer feel the same respect for Egypt's leader; and with that essential element missing from their association, what had been by far the closest of Nasser's political friendships outside Egypt came abruptly to an end.

The estrangement with Tito came at a particularly bad moment for Nasser. Only a few months earlier, the last of his close associates from the old RCC, Zacharia Mohieddin, had left the Government and, except for Heikal, he now had hardly anyone around him whom he could call a personal friend. The only old comrades from his Free Officer days who were still in office were Anwar Sadat and Hussein Shafei, with whom he had never been very intimate. Even less did he have any close friends among the newer faces around the Cabinet table, some of which he did not even know by sight. As for his new partners from Libya and the Sudan, glad as he was to have their support in the councils of the Arab world, his relationships with both Gadaffy and Numeiri were strictly political and impersonal.

In short, by 1970, Nasser had become an extremely lonely man. And as his health deteriorated, he began increasingly to yearn for the comradeships of bygone years. One or two former associates such as Said Marei were brought back into the Government. And when, in April, he decided to replace Mohammed Faik as Minister of Guidance, so determined was he not to appoint yet another newcomer whom he did not know or want to know that he insisted on Heikal undertaking the impossible task of doubling the Ministry with his editorship of *Al-Ahram*. Three months later, after his doctors had issued yet another serious warning that his physical survival depended on his shedding some of his work-load, he decided to invite Boghdady to come back and relieve him by taking over the premiership. In July, from his Russian clinic, he therefore wrote to ask his old friend to discuss the matter on his return to Cairo.

But Boghdady would not hear of it. He would much prefer,

he told Nasser, to be his friend than his Prime Minister and experience had taught him that he could not be both. Besides, he added with a mischievous dig, if he were thought to be worthy to take over as Premier, why was his telephone still being tapped? Nasser had no reply, except to protest his genuine desire to see his old comrade back in office. And after two further meetings had failed to make Boghdady change his mind, he gave up and, greatly to his doctors' dismay, refused to offer the premiership to anyone else.

Thus, when the Arab world fell apart over the Rogers peace initiative, Nasser was faced with a major crisis without the assistance of his oldest and closest comrades. True, he was not lacking in outside support. The Russians had frowned on what they called the 'unrealistic and adventurist' policies advocated by the militant Arab Governments. They not only applauded Egypt's 'sober and realistic' attitude, but had also sought credit in Washington for having brought this about. Hussein too endorsed the Rogers Plan, although he had been somewhat piqued by Nasser's failure to consult him before announcing his own decision. Nevertheless, within hours of the announcement of Egypt's acceptance, Iraq and Syria flatly rejected the American proposals and the Palestinian Resistance engaged in a series of violent demonstrations in Amman, Beirut and other cities. Nasser was denounced as a traitor and the Rogers Plan as an American conspiracy designed to rob the Palestinians of their just deserts.

Since the Khartoum summit conference the Palestinian Resistance had been largely transformed. Shukhairy had resigned as chairman of the PLO and been replaced by Yasser Arafat, the founder and leader of the Fatah resistance group. With this change in leadership the political emphasis, which Nasser had encouraged as being less dangerous than military activity, was gone and, instead of posturing as a Government-in-exile, the new regime was trying to create a guerrilla army from the refugee camps in Jordan, Syria and Lebanon. Arafat and his associates were no longer prepared to let their future be decided for them by the Arab Governments, the United Nations or the great powers. And they had served notice on all concerned that, having lost all that remained of Palestinian territory in 1967, they were now going to fight their own battles for the liberation of their land. More important still, the PLO had worked out a new policy for a liberated Palestine. They proposed the creation of a non-sectarian state in which the existing Jewish population of Israel and the Palestinian Arabs, including the refugees in neighbouring Arab lands, would have equal rights and obligations as citizens of a united Palestine.

The Palestinian Resistance were therefore by definition opposed to the kind of settlement envisaged in Resolution 242. As they saw it, all their troubles had arisen from the decision of the United Nations in 1947 to partition this tiny country called Palestine – which was no bigger than the principality of Wales or the state of Maryland – and to allow the creation of an exclusively Jewish state in one of the two segments, whence the existing non-Jewish inhabitants had been perforce expelled and the few who managed to remain were treated as second-class citizens. By merely forcing Israel to withdraw to her pre-1967 frontiers, the PLO felt that Resolution 242 would not get to the root of the problem. For this would be to condone the eviction of all those Palestinians who had been driven out to make way for the creation of the Jewish state in 1948. And just as they now accepted that peace could not be made by evicting the Jews who had come to settle in Israel, so they were equally convinced that no settlement would ever endure which sanctioned the permanent expulsion of the Palestinian Arabs from what had been their home for thirteen hundred years.

However, since verbal arguments could never persuade the Israelis to accept the concept of a non-sectarian Palestine, Arafat and his associates had set about organising a resistance movement with the long-term objective of so harassing the enemy as to force him in the end to accept their proffered solution. Indeed, from the moment the cease-fire sounded at the end of the Six Days War, the Fatah group had begun conducting sabotage operations, albeit on a minor scale, within the occupied territories, if only to serve notice on Israel and the Arab states that, for the Palestinians at least, the war was very far from being finished.

Such activities inevitably brought them into collision with the Governments of Jordan and Lebanon where the bulk of the Resistance was now situated. Both the Jordanians and the Lebanese would have been only too happy to settle the issue with Israel on the basis of Resolution 242, and they were desperately afraid that the operations of Fatah and other such groups would make the Israelis all the more determined to hold onto the territories seized in 1967. Scuffles therefore occurred frequently between the guerrillas and the Jordanian and Lebanese armies and, as the guerrillas increased in number, relations with the local authorities became progressively more strained.

Arafat strove desperately to keep the situation under control, conferring regularly with King Hussein. But, though the King might feel that he could no longer deny the PLO the right to organise resistance from Jordan, now that the Palestinians had lost every bit of their own territory, the Jordanian authorities nevertheless deeply resented the guerrillas' presence. Also, while Arafat was nominally the leader of the Resistance, he could not control every group in this highly fragmented set-up. Thus as fast as he and Hussein made agreements to define the scope of PLO activities in Jordan, every arrangement was somehow sabotaged, either by anti-Palestinian factions within the army, or by the more extreme Resistance groups such as George Habbash's Marxist Popular Front (PFLP) who regarded the Jordanian regime as no less an enemy to their cause than the Israelis.

Both sides had some justification for their attitude. The Palestinians complained that Hussein had told the Israelis he would dissolve the Resistance once a compromise settlement had been reached. They also contended that their 'commandos' were being constantly harried by the Jordanian army and police. For his part, Hussein claimed that the Resistance were causing trouble in Amman and other towns in Jordan, where their high-handed behaviour was offending the local population. More serious still, as had been shown by repeated Israeli assaults on irrigation projects in the Yarmuk river valley, their operations on the occupied West Bank were inviting enemy reprisals which could end in the total destruction of Jordan.

Likewise in Lebanon, where the presence of Fatah and the Syrian-based Saiqa Resistance group in the south was stirring the Christian community's long-standing fears of Moslem domination from Syria, the authorities were proving anything but helpful to the Palestinians. Threatened with retaliation for any PLO incursions across the border and afraid of giving the Israelis a pretext to realise their dream of annexing the southern end of the Litani river's fertile valley, the Lebanese Government sent troops to take control of the guerrilla bases on their territory. At Arafat's urgent request, Nasser interceded in Beirut and an agreement was reached whereby PLO operations would be allowed to continue, provided the guerrillas' numbers were reduced. But when the remaining groups intensified their attacks across the frontier, the Israelis hit back with napalm bombs on Lebanese villages alleged to be sheltering the guerrillas. As Beirut complained to the United Nations, feeling ran high between the PLO and the Government, who were under increasing popular pressure to put a stop to all guerrilla activities. By the summer of 1969, with Fatah and Saiqa fighting back to protect their bases, a state of virtual civil war existed in Lebanon. And it was not until November that the Egyptians were able to bring both sides to settle their differences by an agreement, signed in Cairo by Arafat and the Lebanese Chief of Staff, which allowed the PLO to conduct strictly limited activities from certain defined areas in southern Lebanon.

Even the Syrians, for all their much vaunted militancy, displayed a highly ambivalent attitude in their dealings with the Palestinian Resistance. They might support the PLO in rejecting any compromise settlement. But, for fear of enemy reprisals, they adamantly refused to permit any guerrilla activities across Syria's border with Israel. Their practical assistance to the PLO was therefore limited to training guerrillas to operate from Lebanese or Jordanian territory and to providing a clearing station for the obsolete rifles and other small arms supplied to the Resistance by various Communist countries.

Such hypocrisy was not without its effect on the 'progressive' Arabs, most notably the Algerians. By the end of 1969 Boumedienne had become largely converted to Cairo's way of thinking and was no longer to be heard joining in the militant choruses of Damascus and Baghdad. Numeiri too, having sent a contingent of Sudanese troops to stand alongside the Egyptians on the Suez Canal front, was utterly disgusted by the double-talk of the Syrians.

Nasser's reaction was more philosophical, for he had learned not to expect anything but hypocrisy from the Baath. Nevertheless he was extremely worried lest the intemperate utterances of the Syrians and Iraqis might incite the Palestinian Resistance to provoke a major clash with their Jordanian and Lebanese hosts. He therefore spared no effort to keep the peace between the PLO and the authorities in Amman and Beirut. In his dealings with Hussein he showed a particular understanding of Jordan's problems. At the same time, he constantly urged the King to exercise 'the patience of Ayub [Job]' in his handling of the Resistance. Likewise, whenever he saw Arafat, he advised him to turn a deaf ear to the wild words of Damascus and Baghdad and to keep the PLO under the strictest possible discipline. The Palestinians should remember, he said, that Jordan and Lebanon, with their peculiar vulnerability to Israeli attacks, were bound to look askance at anyone who might provoke enemy reprisals. Moreover, the PLO should be careful not to try conclusions with Israel unless they could be certain of getting military as well as financial support from the Arab states.

Although he detested the more extreme Resistance leaders such as Habbash, whose very recent conversion to Marxism he thought to be no more than political opportunism, Nasser had a considerable liking for Arafat. While doubting that he possessed any great political judgement, he admired the courage and determination with which he had tackled the task of leading the Resistance in the field. Also he had much sympathy with the ideals of the PLO, even though he did not agree with their outright rejection of any compromise settlement. Nasser believed too that, provided they did not attempt too much, the Resistance could play a useful role in harassing the Israelis and so bringing pressure on them to take a more flexible line in negotiating with Jarring. Besides, the uncompromising attitude of the Palestinians was not without its uses. For by comparison, Egyptian policy appeared to the outside world to be all the more restrained and realistic, which could only be to Cairo's advantage, especially in the West.

At the same time Nasser realised that the Palestinian Resistance could all too easily get out of control. He personally felt that, instead of recruiting a liberation army at this early stage, Arafat would have been better advised to concentrate on training small bands of highly skilled saboteurs to work in secret behind the Israeli lines. And while from time to time he declared his support for the efforts of the Palestinians to regain their lost lands, he realised only too well that large numbers of armed Palestinians, parading in the streets of Amman and Beirut and calling all compromise a betrayal of their cause, would be more likely to antagonise the host Governments than to impress the Israelis.

Nasser therefore sought to temper the wilder protestations of the PLO by telling Arafat whenever they met that, far from being a betrayal of Palestinian hopes, Resolution 242 could be a stepping-stone towards their eventual fulfilment. Would it not be better, he asked, for the PLO to be able to conduct their resistance against Israel from Ramalla and Hebron rather than from Amman? As for the idea of a war of liberation, Nasser told Arafat, as he had told Shukhairy before him, that it was futile to talk of such things until the Arab states were able to manufacture their own tanks and other offensive weapons. So long as they depended on foreign supplies, any attempt to liberate Palestine by force could be, and almost certainly would be, stopped by those who controlled the Arabs' arms supplies. Finally he warned him against getting involved with the Syrian and Iraqi Baathists, who would only mislead him with false promises.

But even if Arafat had accepted the logic of these arguments, he could not have prevailed on his associates to modify their outright rejection of any compromise settlement. For one thing, any solution based on the recognition of an Israeli state struck at the very roots of their belief in a reconstituted Arab-Jewish Palestine. For another, the PLO were by no means a united organisation. And as time went by with no sign of the Resistance being able to marshal a liberation army, still less of the Arab states mobilising in their support, many PLO members were becoming frustrated. Some had returned to their former civilian occupations, but still more were beginning to drift away into more activist breakaway groups such as the PFLP.

This was not to say that the PLO's resistance efforts had been totally ineffectual. As was shown by the atmosphere in the refugee camps, they had begun to regenerate the Palestinian nation from the grass-roots upwards. They were also organising and educating Palestinians of every age to face the challenge of a long campaign and, when victory should come, to tackle the problems of re-structuring their society for coexistence with the existing Israeli population. In the military sphere, too, the PLO had gained a notable victory when, in March 1968, three hundred guerrillas, equipped only with light automatic weapons and grenades, had beaten off a determined assault by two converging columns of Israeli tanks, with paratroop support, on the Fatah base at Kara-meh in the Jordan valley. By which action they succeeded in denting the legend of Israeli invincibility, as well as inflicting heavy losses on their attackers. Also, despite the enemy's vigilance, several successful sabotage operations had been carried out by various resistance groups in Israel, Gaza and the West Bank.

In some cases the local Arab population suffered heavier casual-ties than the Israelis and, on one particularly regrettable occasion, a bus containing Israeli school-children from one of the frontier settlements was destroyed with a grievous loss of innocent lives. But, in the main, the chosen targets were legitimate enough and the Resistance could fairly claim to have inflicted by no means inconsiderable damage on the enemy. Dayan of course denied such assertions and repeatedly tried to belittle the effect of these operations. But the severity and even brutality with which PLO captives were sometimes treated after capture, together with such collective punishments as demolition of the villages where they had been sheltered, suggested that the Resistance were not as ineffective as the Israeli authorities would have liked to believe.

Nevertheless the Arab love of the spectacular was not to be satisfied by an occasional bomb explosion in Haifa or even an attack on the oil pipeline from Elath. And as the mood of frustration grew with the evident inability of the Resistance to inflict any permanent damage on Israel, so the Palestinian activists began to look for other ways of injuring the enemy and his Western supporters. Taking a leaf out of the Cuban revolutionaries' book, the PFLP turned to the idea of hijacking Israeli and American airliners. In July 1968 an Israeli Boeing on a flight from Rome to Tel Aviv was forced by three armed Palestinians to fly to Algiers, where twelve Israeli passengers were held for two months before being released. Five months later, another El-Al Boeing was fired on as it took off from Athens airport by PFLP guerrillas armed with automatic weapons, who killed one passenger before being arrested by Greek police. Whereupon the Israelis, claiming that the gunmen had come from Lebanon, launched a devastating reprisal raid on Beirut airport with airborne troops, which resulted in thirteen airliners belonging to various Arab states being destroyed or severely damaged on the ground.

However the PFLP were not to be put off by such retaliation. In February 1969, four of their men opened fire on an El-Al airliner at Zurich airport, wounding six crew members and passengers before one of their own number was killed in the ensuing gunfight and the other three arrested by Swiss police. Nor were the PFLP the least deterred by complaints from Arafat that they were giving the Palestinian Resistance a bad name by carrying the war against Israel onto neutral territory. Still less were they impressed when the PLO groups formed a unified military command, which they contemptuously dismissed as mere window-dressing. And although in July 1969 they agreed to affiliate with the PLO, they marked their decision a month later by another hijacking, this time of an American TWA airliner bound for Tel Aviv, which they diverted to Damascus. In September, the El-Al office in Brussels was attacked by PFLP guerrillas and severely damaged by grenades as were other Israeli properties in Bonn and The Hague. Two months after this, a similar attack on the El-Al office in Athens by another extremist Resistance group resulted in fifteen people being injured. Then in January 1970, a second TWA airliner was hijacked flying between Paris and

Rome; and in the following month three Arab guerrillas attacked an airline bus at Munich airport supposedly in an attempt to kill or kidnap Dayan's son who they wrongly believed was on board.

Such continued defiance by the PFLP of the general body of Arab opinion could not be tolerated much longer. Apart from the PLO's need to maintain a coordinated strategy, the Arab Governments were seriously concerned about the possible consequences. Lebanon had suffered a savage and highly costly retaliation when the Israelis attacked Beirut airport and there was no telling where or when the enemy would strike again. In a frantic attempt to spare his own country the Jordanian Prime Minister publicly apologised for the recent incidents and pledged that his Government would in future 'outlaw' anyone who attacked or hijacked an international airliner.

Under pressure from Amman and other Arab capitals, therefore, Arafat announced two weeks after the Munich episode that the PLO would conduct a searching review of the whole question. The result was a declaration, issued in June 1970 in the name of the Palestine National Council, that armed attacks on civilian aircraft were detrimental to the Palestinian cause and were contrary to official policy. But this edict had no more effect on the extremists than Arafat's earlier censures. Far from complying with the PLO's injunction, in the following month the PFLP seized and held a Greek airliner until the Greek Government agreed to release their seven comrades who had been imprisoned for their part in the two Athens incidents.

Meanwhile the PLO were having problems of their own with the Jordanian authorities. Following the failure of the Lebanese Government to stop all guerrilla activities in southern Lebanon, the Jordanian army tried to prevent the carrying of arms by anyone except members of the armed forces. When the PLO declared that they would resist such measures by force, the Government climbed down. But four months after this, fighting broke out between PLO guerrillas and the army in northern Jordan and quickly spread to Amman and other towns, causing casualties estimated at 700, including 200 killed. And it was not until King Hussein agreed three days later to dismiss two high-ranking Generals, notorious for their hatred of the Palestinians, that he and Arafat, helped by a mediating committee drawn from Egypt and other Arab states, were able to bring the fighting to an end.

But despite this latest truce, the situation in Jordan remained as tense as ever and, with the PFLP openly denouncing the King, the army and the Government, it was clearly only a matter of time before the new agreement was broken like all those that had gone before it. Consequently, when Nasser and Hussein decided a month later to accept the Rogers peace initiative, Arafat found himself in a particularly awkward position. He did not want to attack Nasser personally. Yet he seriously believed that Egypt was reverting under a cloak of 'realism' to the policies of the first Arab summit conference which had seemed so timid and negative to every Palestinian at the time. Also he knew that, if he did not protest against Nasser's 'sell-out' in the most vehement terms, the PFLP and other extremist groups would seize the opportunity to outbid him. If only therefore to keep his own end up, he went along with the general Palestinian outcry. Thus, on the morrow of Cairo's acceptance of the Rogers Plan, the streets of Amman and Beirut became the scene of violent demonstrations. Placards depicting Nasser's head on the body of a donkey were paraded by hundreds of guerrillas as they marched on the Egyptian and American embassies to protest the betrayal of their cause. And as the frenzy of the demonstrators rose to fever pitch, Nasser was branded, together with Hussein, as a traitor and an agent of imperialism by mob orators vying with one another for the choicest personal abuse.

Nasser was naturally shocked and deeply offended by the bitterness of this outburst. Although he knew that Arafat had not personally abused him or accused him of treason, he nevertheless held the PLO leaders responsible for what had been said and done. If they could not control the extremists such as Habbash's group, that was their fault and they would have to pay for it. On July 29, therefore, at Nasser's orders, the two PLO radio stations operating from Cairo's transmitters were closed down until further notice.

Arafat, deeply disturbed by this riposte, asked Nasser to see him. But before going to Egypt, he paid a visit to President Bakr to ask if he could count on the Iraqi forces which had remained in northern Jordan after the 1967 war to help in protecting the Resistance in the event of the Jordanian army turning on the guerrillas. By going to Baghdad before Cairo, Arafat could hardly have made a worse tactical error. Not only did the Iraqis fail to lift a finger to save the Palestinians when they were attacked by Hussein's Bedouin regiments two months later; but by first visiting one of Nasser's principal Arab adversaries, he compounded the injury which the recent demonstrations had done to the PLO's relations with Cairo. What is more, when he met Nasser in Alexandria, instead of the customary embrace, he rather coldly shook hands with his host, who remarked somewhat acidly that no doubt Arafat now reserved his embraces exclusively for Hassan al-Bakr.

Not surprisingly the ensuing meeting was extremely frigid. Nasser stubbornly refused to allow the PLO radio stations to be reopened. He also made it clear that if Hussein now rounded on the Resistance they had only themselves to blame. The King had stayed his hand so far, partly because of appeals from Cairo, partly because he did not want to engage in a battle with the PLO which might split his own army with its large Palestinian complement. But, if the Resistance pushed him too far, as some of them seemed determined to do, he would risk everything to put them down. Hussein was extremely well informed from monitorings by his intelligence service of conversations between various PLO leaders which suggested that at least some of them wanted to see him dethroned. The Resistance should be under no illusions that they could withstand the Jordanian army, if the King were driven to extreme measures either by force of circumstances or by pressures from those military commanders who longed to crush the Palestinians once and for all. At whatever cost, therefore, they should avoid further provocations which could only bring disaster upon themselves.

Having administered this salutary lecture to Arafat, Nasser turned his attentions to Hussein. In a message to the King he congratulated him on having shown that 'the patience of Ayub has become the patience of Hussein'. But at the same time he asked him to display even more forbearance in the future. Egypt, he said, would support Jordan in anything, except an attempt to liquidate the Palestinian Resistance. No matter how foolishly or insultingly the PLO had behaved, nothing could justify such action. However, if Hussein could continue to keep his army in check, Nasser said that he would help him to conclude a permanent settlement with the Resistance by which all the PLO groups would have to abide.

But all these efforts were to be in vain. The extremists in the Resistance proved as uncontrollable as their enemies in the Jordanian regime. The army continued to harass the Palestinians. The PFLP stepped up their attacks on anyone professing sympathy for Cairo's policy of compromise. And if only to protect his flank against the extremists, Arafat was obliged to announce that the PLO would not observe the cease-fire with Israel which had been renewed under the Rogers Plan. On the contrary, they would 'escalate their activities' to render it null and void.

In fact, such talk on Arafat's part was largely bluff. For over the past several months, the PLO had been far too concerned to protect themselves against sniping from the Jordanian army to be able to conduct any significant operations in Israeli-held territory. In the current tense atmosphere, it was therefore highly unlikely that they would feel secure enough to step up their activities. But the PFLP, operating as they did far beyond the reach of Hussein's army, had their own ideas about 'escalation' which were anything but bluff. On September 6, they lashed out with a massive hijacking operation designed partly to strike at Israel's American allies and partly to take hostages who would be held against the release of their comrades in prison in Israel, Switzerland and West Germany. A Pan-American airliner was seized over the Mediterranean and diverted to Cairo where, after the passengers and crew had been disembarked, it was blown up by bombs. Two airliners belonging to TWA and Swissair, the former containing American Jews of dual American-Israeli nationality, were forced to land at an abandoned airstrip in Jordan under the PFLP's control. And an El-Al Boeing was hijacked over Western Europe. In this last case the pilot managed to land at London airport, where police promptly arrested the hijacker, Leila Khaled, who had also been responsible for the seizure of the TWA plane bound for Tel Aviv in the previous August. But the PFLP were not to be deflected by this failure and three days later they retaliated for Leila Khaled's arrest by seizing a BOAC airliner en route from the Persian Gulf to London which was also forced to land on their Jordanian air-strip.

With the crew and passengers of all three aircraft held as hostages, the Governments of Britain, Israel, Switzerland and West Germany were informed that their nationals would not be released until the PFLP prisoners held by them, including Leila Khaled, were set free. The PLO promptly disavowed the hi-jackings and the Jordanian, Egyptian and other Arab Govern-ments added their own vigorous condemnations. But neither the PLO nor the Jordanian authorities could do anything in the face of the hijackers' threats to blow up the aircraft with the passengers on board if any attempt were made to rescue the hostages by force. And although about half of the three hundred passengers were immediately released and allowed to go to hotels in Amman, they still could not be sent home for fear of reprisals against those held at the airstrip. After a further three days, the situation was slightly eased when the PFLP, after blowing up the three aircraft, allowed those passengers already released to be repatriated and announced that they were freeing all but forty of their remaining prisoners. But since the four Governments concerned stubbornly refused to submit to what they called plain blackmail on the part of the hijackers, there seemed to be no way of resolving the dead-lock over the release of the remaining hostages.

For four more days the wrangle continued, while Russia, Egypt and other countries tried to reason with the PFLP. Then, on September 16, King Hussein decided to assert his authority at whatever cost to the Palestinians as a whole or to the remaining forty hostages. Martial law was declared and a military Govern-ment was appointed with a mandate to crush the Palestinian Resistance once and for all. And on the following morning

Jordan's Bedouin armoured units and artillery advanced on the refugee camps surrounding Amman to wreak a fearful vengeance on their Palestinian inhabitants. For the next eight days the Jordanian capital became a battleground with the army waging indiscriminate warfare against any area containing Palestinians or their supporters. No allowance was made for the fact that the hijackings had been condemned by all major groups of the PLO, including Fatah, whose members were attacked with no less ferocity than those of the PFLP. For Jordan's army the day of reckoning had come at last.

Nasser was even more alarmed than he was distressed by this explosion. For while he feared for the lives of the Palestinians, he was still more afraid that Israel might use the fighting in Jordan as a pretext to renege on the Rogers Plan and the ninety days' cease-fire. He also knew that the struggle could all too easily involve Jordan's neighbours. The Syrians might march to the aid of the Palestinians, which in its turn might bring in the Israelis. More ominous still, his intelligence reports told him that the Americans had for some time been contemplating a military intervention in Jordan, ostensibly to support Hussein, but in reality to enable them to dictate a settlement between Jordan and Israel and so to isolate Egypt and force her to surrender to Israeli terms.

Certainly, there were contingency plans in Washington to send troops to Jordan if Hussein's throne appeared to be threatened by the Palestinian Resistance who, from being in American official circles merely unpopular, because of their opposition to any compromise settlement, had become anathema since they started hijacking American airliners and holding American citizens to ransom. Moreover, to Nasser's suspicious mind, the orders which had just been issued to the American air force in Turkey to stand by to evacuate American civilians from Jordan might well be a cover for an airborne intervention by United States forces. And the longer the fighting continued in Jordan, the greater the danger became that the Americans would become involved.

Nasser's first thought was to fly to Amman himself to mediate for an immediate cease-fire. But on reflection he decided instead to send an emissary and to summon Hussein to Cairo to meet with him and the other Arab heads of state away from the heat of the battle. Meanwhile he ordered Hafez Ismail, the chief of General Intelligence, to keep him constantly posted about all American military movements in the area and especially those of the Sixth Fleet, currently reported to be cruising off the coasts of Israel and Lebanon with two large aircraft carriers and other warships, including amphibious craft for landing marines.

Among the first arrivals for the emergency summit meeting was President Gadaffy of Libya, who was in a highly excitable mood, vowing that Hussein should be shot for ordering the massacre of the Palestinian Resistance. Having just decided to cancel Libya's payments to Jordan under the Khartoum indemnity arrangements, he wanted the conference to sit in judgement on the Jordanian regime and he was violently opposed to the idea that Hussein should be asked, along with Arafat, to assist in the deliberations. But Nasser was determined to get the King to Cairo, where he would be under much stronger pressure to order a cease-fire than in Jordan where he was surrounded by so much anti-Palestinian prejudice. He therefore bluntly told Gadaffy that, if Hussein could not attend, there would be no conference. Then, in the presence of the Ruler of Kuwait, he telephoned to the King in Amman and, calling him 'Brother Hussein' in tones more sycophantic than censorious, he told him, 'We have the greatest respect for your courage. My brother Sabah Salem, who is sitting here beside me, joins with me in begging you to come here at the earliest possible opportunity.'

Hussein arrived on the next day and the conference got down to its work in an atmosphere which, for all its seriousness, also had its moments of comedy. When Arafat and Hussein appeared in the conference room armed with revolvers and darting ferocious glances at one another, King Feisal suggested to Nasser that, as the first item on their agenda, they should have a disarmament agreement! Gadaffy then declared that the fighting in Jordan showed the Arabs to be so mad that, instead of calling a summit conference, it would have been more appropriate to summon a panel of psychiatrists to examine them all. Whereupon Feisal jokingly

volunteered to be the first examinee. But Nasser quickly intervened to say that the first, and most needy, case would undoubtedly be Gadaffy himself!

Having, with Feisal's help, thus reduced the temperature by
getting his fellow Arabs to laugh at themselves, Nasser then
steered the discussion onto more serious matters. The danger of
an American intervention, he said, was greater than ever. Press
reports from Washington and New York suggested that Nixon
might at any moment send American troops to Jordan. There
were even rumours that a joint American-Israeli intervention was
being planned. On top of this, armoured forces from Syria were
reported to be advancing into northern Jordan to fight for the
Palestinians. And whether or not Damascus was right in saying
that the invaders were in fact Palestinians and not Syrians, the fact
remained that this new development had increased the risk of the
Americans and/or the Israelis getting involved.

Nasser equally made it clear that, if the Americans did intervene in Jordan or Syria, he would not send a single Egyptian
soldier. Besides needing all his available forces to defend the Canal
front, he had learned his lesson in Syria and Yemen, and he
would not be drawn into making the same mistakes again. For
all these reasons, therefore, it was imperative that the conference
should work for an immediate cease-fire without indulging in
recriminations. When the delegation from the newly independent
South Yemen demanded a vote of censure on Hussein, Nasser
retorted that this would be utterly useless. The King would only
put it away in a drawer and ignore it. And when the South
Yemenis pressed their point, he rounded on them saying, 'What
right have you to make such demands? What have you contri-
buted to the battle against the Israeli enemy? Nothing at all. The
Kuwaitis, who agree that there should be no recriminations, have
a contingent at this very moment serving on the Suez Canal front
and have given tens of thousands of pounds to help the Palestinian
Resistance, as well as Egypt and Jordan.' To which Feisal added
with an ironic smile, 'Quite right, Mr President, they and those
who talk like them all want to fight Israel to the last Egyptian
soldier.'

There is an old saying in the Moslem scriptures that those who are about to die often speak and act with exceptional wisdom and vision. Certainly Nasser's chairmanship of this, the last summit meeting over which he was to preside, surpassed any previous performance of its kind. Throughout the long days and nights that the conference remained in session, he astounded all those present by the skill, determination and humour with which he managed to direct the discussions towards the single objective of stopping the fighting in Jordan. Although he felt that the PLO had brought a lot of their suffering on themselves by failing to control their extremists, he nevertheless showed the greatest sympathy for Arafat who, after witnessing the virtual emasculation of the Resistance in Jordan, was in a state bordering on shock throughout most of the proceedings. Yet he equally treated Hussein with the utmost gentleness, refusing to allow his wilder fellows to engage in what he regarded as pointless vituperation against the Jordanian regime. In private discussions with the King, he adopted a somewhat sterner tone, saying that he could not remain neutral unless the Jordanian army agreed without further delay to halt the slaughter. But in the plenary sessions of the conference he showed nothing but understanding for Hussein's problems and for the indignity and enmity with which the PFLP had treated him and his Government.

Nasser was of course deeply shocked that the Jordanian army should have seized upon the behaviour of one small group within the Resistance to wage war upon the entire Palestinian population. But in his determination to induce the King to stop the fighting, he refrained from any public utterance on these enormities. And thanks to his resolute chairmanship, the conference agreed, without any qualifying conditions or condemnations, to send a delegation under the leadership of the Sudan's President Numeiri to negotiate a cease-fire in Amman.

Numeiri could hardly have been given a more difficult task. As he afterwards told me, the Jordanian army wanted a fight to a finish and hotly resented the arrival of his peace mission. He had little difficulty in agreeing with Hussein and Arafat the terms of a cease-fire. But although the King issued immediate directions to his troops to stop fighting, it took another two days to make the truce effective, during which time the Bedouin armoured units continued to vent their spleen upon the refugee camps in total disregard of their orders. When they realised that Numeiri and his colleagues were not going to leave until the fighting had ceased, the army tried to drive them out by shelling the area where they were quartered for their stay. Indeed it was not until Nasser had sent a warning to Amman that, if the army did not stop shooting immediately, he would intervene on the side of the Palestinians that Hussein was able to bring the fighting to an end. The remaining airline hostages were then rescued, the invading forces from Syria retired and, as Numeiri returned to Cairo to report to the summit meeting, Jordan lapsed into an angry and bitter silence amid a scene of devastation described by a correspondent of *Newsweek* magazine as resembling that of Budapest after the Russians had smashed the Hungarian revolt in 1956.

On the following day, Hussein and Arafat signed an agreement in Cairo providing for the establishment of an inter-Arab commission headed by the Tunisian Prime Minister, Bahi Ladgham, to supervise the working of the cease-fire agreement. Whereupon, on September 28, the conference was adjourned and the delegates left for home, seen off at the airport by Nasser in person.

The crisis had been allayed. The price that had been paid was the almost total destruction of the Palestinian Resistance in Jordan. But against this Nasser could claim that, with the cease-fire on the Suez Canal and the Jordan still in operation, the Rogers peace initiative had been preserved intact and that the threat of an American intervention in Jordan, with or without Israeli participation had been avoided. Moreover, as was shown by subsequent reports of the dismay among American diplomats in Amman that the King had not called on Washington for help against the Palestinians, the possibility of the United States intervening in Jordan had not been by any means a mere figment of Nasser's imagination.

But if his efforts over the past eleven days had been instrumental in averting these very real dangers, the strain involved had exhausted the last remnants of Nasser's physical strength. As he left the airport after bidding farewell to the Ruler of Kuwait, h e suffered a major heart attack. And though his doctors fough t for several hours to save him, at six o'clock that same evening he died.

Three days later, on October 1, he was buried amid scenes of such lamentation by the Egyptian people that the funeral cortege had to be abandoned. Men, women and children wept and wailed unashamedly in the streets as thousands upon thousands pressed in upon the procession, straining to get a last view of the coffin which bore their dead leader to his place of burial. His errors and failures were forgotten; only his achievements were remembered by his grieving subjects. Even his enemies in the West were constrained to spare a brief charitable thought for the man whom they had reviled for so long. And the Arab world, to whose emancipation he had dedicated so much of his life, stood stunned by the knowledge that they had lost their foremost champion.

Epilogue

Abdel Nasser was a remarkable man. His contribution to Egypt has guaranteed him a place in history. He gave a sense of dignity and national pride to a people who had known little but humiliation and oppression for two and a half thousand years, and his achievement transformed a nation of backward, down-trodden peasants, ruled by a corrupt and alien tyrant and occupied by a foreign army, into a community of independent citizens with a stake in their own soil. He planted the seeds of a modern industrial society.

In Egypt, with its inexorable rise in population of nearly a million a year, there may never be enough land for the fellahin. But the High Dam and land reclamation have increased the cultivable area by more than a million acres. As a result of the land reforms introduced in 1952 and 1961, about 75 per cent of the agricultural land of Egypt is now owned by those who hitherto were forced to work for alien masters. The industrialisation programme has not been all that was hoped for. Nevertheless, Egypt is today well on the way to becoming an industrial state with factories producing a range of sophisticated products such as refrigerators, television sets and tractors. The value of industrial output was quadrupled between 1952 and 1970. Working conditions, too, were vastly improved; the working day in industry was limited by decree in 1963 to seven hours; and pensions, formerly granted at the whim of the employers, are now guaranteed by a national contributory scheme.

The advantages of education, too, have been spread far more widely since 1952. In the belief that every child has the right to a free education, Nasser's Government quadrupled the school population which today stands at some four million. Illiteracy

477

has dropped from around 80 per cent in 1952 to less than 50 per cent now; and with the expansion of technical as well as university education, Egypt is now producing her own engineers, scientists and technicians. Their success is reflected in the ultra-modern systems of radio and television, which far excel those of any other Arab state in quality and which are equalled in programme time only by the most advanced countries of the world.

For all of these developments a great deal of the credit is due to Nasser himself. Had it not been for his drive in sweeping away the cobwebs of the *ancien régime*, little if any progress would have been possible. But equally Nasser must take the blame for the fact that the social and economic advances made under his leadership were not accompanied by any comparable progress in the political sphere. True, he got rid of the Pashas and the political parties who had battened on the people for so long. But in their place he put a military autocracy which was scarcely more in touch with popular sentiment, especially among the better educated bourgeoisie, and which had neither the experience nor the inclination to control the huge and cumbersome bureaucratic machine that had been for so long a stultifying feature of Egyptian life.

In part this was Nasser's own fault. Conspirator that he was by nature and training, he seldom trusted even his closest colleagues, let alone the people at large, to do what was best for Egypt. For all his humanity and humour, he was never a good judge of men. He often mistook honest criticism for base disloyalty. Just as he suspected that his more successful and popular associates were using their success and popularity for their personal advancement, so he also believed that 'parliamentary democracy' would only encourage the growth of factions dedicated to serving their own interests at the expense of the people as a whole. But it must be remembered that the Egyptian populace had, as was their tradition with leaders from time immemorial, deified Nasser with songs and sayings proclaiming his infallibility. If therefore he responded more as a Pharaoh of old than as a constitutional ruler of the 20th century, they were as much to blame as he was. In the circumstances it is only remarkable that he refused every popular demand that he be elected President for life, insisting on a term of no more than six years at a time.

It was not solely in Egypt that Nasser was the prisoner of his own prestige. After he had thwarted the attempt by Britain and France to destroy him and his revolution in 1956, he became the hero of every Arab nationalist from the Atlantic to the Indian Ocean. He was convinced by the Palestine War in 1948 that only in unity could the Arabs achieve their independence. The Wafd, he believed, had failed to liberate Egypt in the twenties by refusing to join hands with their Arab brothers outside, and he was determined to use his new-found popularity to draw the Arab world under his wing. This was not so much a matter of self-aggrandisement as a fulfilment of a mission to emancipate Egypt and every other Arab state and to create, sustain and direct the dynamic force which the 1952 revolution had let loose.

But if Nasser was acclaimed by the masses outside as well as within Egypt, he consistently failed to understand his fellow Arabs. Identifying himself with their longing for some form of unity, he was misled into thinking that those who waved his banner wanted to live under it. Used to handling his own relatively docile subjects, he failed to see that, with their different backgrounds, even those Arabs who shared his ideological leanings – such as the Syrian Baathists – were bound to resent being dictated to by Cairo. He did not realise until it was too late that his initial success in spreading the message of Arab nationalism had been achieved by example rather than by the use of pressure or conspiracy. And when he sought to exploit these early achievements, he found that he had grossly overrated his capacity to impose Egypt's leadership upon the rest of the Arab world. His intrigues in Syria, Iraq and Jordan, for instance, demonstrated the ineptitude of his intelligence service and his intervention in the Yemeni civil war revealed the inherent weakness of his armies. Hence, whereas throughout most of the fifties he hardly ever put a foot wrong in his Arabian dealings, from the breach with Syria in 1961 and for all the latter half of his reign, his actions and reactions all too often represented a sorry sequence of miscalculation and mishap.

Nasser was frequently able to charm or bludgeon his fellow rulers into endorsing his policies. He was so skilful at manipulating situations that King Hussein once described him as a 'trapeze artist'. For instance, he managed at every Arab summit meeting to marshal the support of a majority for his strategy of militant inactivity vis-à-vis Israel. But because of the compulsions of his role as the Arab's champion, he was driven to overreach himself on every issue from the confrontation with Kassem to the war in Yemen. And when to these compulsions was added the ineradicable suspicion of Western designs upon the Arab world, he was finally impelled to over-react against Israel and so to precipitate the very holocaust which ever since he came to lead Egypt he had tried to avoid.

Paradoxically Nasser managed for all but the last three years of his life to conduct his relationships with foreign powers with a skill and success often lacking in his handling of his Arab associates. Not only did he evict the British army, and the Suez Canal Company, from Egypt; he also contrived to preserve, at least until the middle sixties, a balance in his relations between East and West, buying food from America and getting arms and industrial aid from the Russians. At the same time, he tolerated no interference from the Communists, whom he considered no less an alien threat than the 'imperialists' who conspired to bring about his downfall; and he refused absolutely to accept any political conditions for foreign economic or military assistance. Only in the last few years, when he found himself prostrated in defeat at the hands of the Israelis, did he abandon his neutral posture and concede to Russia a paramount influence in the conduct of Egyptian policy.

Looking back over Nasser's epoch, it is difficult not to conclude that he might have done still more for Egypt's welfare and prosperity if he had not tried to do so much to secure her supremacy in the Arab world. Yet for him to have failed to assert his ascendancy over the nationalist forces which he released would have been to deny the very cause to which he dedicated his life – Arab unity and independence. Besides, even if at the end the Arabs were little more united than they were eighteen years before and had lost still more of their territory to the Israeli enemy, at least they were no longer ruled by alien despots protected by foreign armies.

For all his faults and failures, Nasser helped to give Egypt and the Arabs that sense of dignity which for him was the hall-mark of independent nationhood. As his old adversary, Ben Gurion, was moved to say in the aftermath of the Six Days War, 'I have great respect for Nasser. He is a patriot who wants to do something for Egypt.' This was no less than the truth. For despite every reverse that he and his people suffered in the latter part of his reign, Egypt and the whole Arab world would have been the poorer, in spirit as well as material progress, without the dynamic inspiration of his leadership.

Index